The Bridge Player's
Bedside Companion

THE
BRIDGE
PLAYER'S
BEDSIDE
COMPANION

Albert A. Ostrow

Prentice-Hall, Inc.   Englewood Cliffs, N. J.

PRINTED IN THE UNITED STATES OF AMERICA

08150

FOREWORD

Just about everything that can be said about bridge as a game, as a means of relaxation, as a pleasant and wholesome way of passing the time and as an intriguing, sometimes exasperating, form of mental stimulation has been said in this book. And that's not all.

Since contract is descended from the ancient and honorable game of whist, there is some history. There are accounts too of those incredible early days of contract when a battle between system-mongers could shoulder its way onto the front pages and dominate the stage of public interest.

Because no bridge player can ever be wholly satisfied with a bridge book that doesn't leave him feeling improved, there is plenty of instructive matter. Some of it is given in straight technical description. The greater part of it, however, appears not in the form of textbook precepts but is contained here and there in thought-provoking commentaries, in revelations of how efficient bridge minds operate and even in humorous material.

Incidentally, you will notice that such eminent bridge enthusiasts as Elmer Davis and Somerset Maugham (among others) believe that no amount of study or practice will ever make a real bridge player out of someone not blessed with so-called "card sense." It should be pointed out here that there are many dissenters from this view. In the opinion of these, card sense is a myth which experienced players use to impress novices and indifferent players use to alibi lack of real interest or lack of confidence. The ability to play a superior game of bridge can, as often as not, be explained in terms of such non-mysterious factors as experience, interest, incentive, enthusiasm and concentration. More than one acknowledged bridge expert started out without card sense and many are dubs at other card games.

You'll discover what keeps some people, husbands and wives particularly, from getting along at the bridge table and what helps others to do so. You'll read about commuter-addicts, kibitzers, experts and the sundry types to be found around bridge tables. You'll learn about signals and conventions the bridge laws permit you to use and others it frowns on but can't prevent. You'll be regaled by stories, anecdotes and jokes.

There are classic hands for you to marvel at and enjoy, and problems to mull over at your leisure. There are suggestions for games to fill in with when a fourth isn't available or even a third, as well as variations for four players and a way of handling a fifth.

This is a book for anyone who looks upon bridge as a diversion par excellence. Have fun with it.

ACKNOWLEDGEMENTS

I OWE A SPECIAL DEBT of gratitude to Alfred Sheinwold for his kind help. And I want to express my appreciation to the following individuals for various helpful services: Charles G. Roth, Charley Michaels, Harry J. Roth, George H. Coffin, Alvin Roth, Nat Cohen of the A.C.B.L., Stanley Gladstone, Florence Osborn, Geoffrey Mott-Smith, C.D.P. Hamilton, Jr., and Joseph Stedem.

My thanks go to *Post Mortem* magazine, a bulletin of the New York Chapter of the American Contract Bridge League, and to its editor, Sims Gaynor, as well as to *The Bridge World* and its publisher, A. Moyse, Jr.

My sincere thanks too to my wife, Helen, for her invaluable help in organizing this volume.

TABLE OF CONTENTS

SECTION 1: THE CONTRACT STORY

THE CONTRACT STORY 3

THERE'LL ALWAYS BE A BRIDGE GAME 5
    by William J. Huske

SINCE 1926 8
    by J. Patrick Dunne and Albert A. Ostrow

CULBERTSON'S COUP 21
    by H. Allen Smith

KIBITZER'S FAVORITE HANDS FROM THE
    CULBERTSON-LENZ MATCH 27

THE SIMS-CULBERTSON PRELIMINARIES 34

THE CONTEST 38

SECTION 2: SIX VIEWS ON BRIDGE

PUREST OF PLEASURES: CONTRACT 49
    by Elmer Davis

THE DOCTOR LOOKS AT CONTRACT 57
    by Dr. Harold Hays

HOW I LIKE TO PLAY BRIDGE 60
    by W. Somerset Maugham

ON PLAYING BRIDGE 64
    by Henry C. Link, Ph.D.

SHOULD WE ABOLISH BRIDGE? YESSIR! 66
    by Silas Bent

SHOULD WE ABOLISH BRIDGE? NO-NEVER!. . . . 71
    by Clinton P. Anderson

SECTION 3: THE BRIDGE PLAYING SPECIES

THE BRIDGE ADDICT 79

BRIDGE IS THEIR OPIUM 80
    by Robert L. Heilbroner

HARD LUCK 87
    by Charles H. Goren

BRIDGE SUPERSTITIONS. 89
    by Robert K. Brunner

KIBITZERS DO NOT LIVE LONG 96
    by Lee Hazen

THE GREAT KIBITZERS' STRIKE 103
    by George S. Kaufman

I HATE PARTNERS. 106
    by Sam Fry, Jr.

LIKES AND DISLIKES 112
    by Harry Seymour

BRIDGE BRAWLS 114
    by Frank K. Perkins

COMMUTERS   123

GHOULIES, THE ALL-ACTION GAME FOR TRAIN OR HOME.   125
       by Phillip M. Wertheimer

POST-MORTEMS   129

SECTION 4:   OH MEN, OH WOMEN!

WHO PLAYS BETTER BRIDGE?   133
       by Richard L. Frey

BRIDGE VERSUS THE BRIDE   137
       by Albert H. Morehead

THE FEMALE OF THE SPECIES   142
       by Jane Abbot

ONE SUNDAY AFTERNOON   146
       by A. Moyse, Jr.

THE TIE THAT BINDS   153
       by George W. Beynon

AN AGREEMENT BETWEEN A BRIDGE PLAYING COUPLE .   155
       by Lee Brandt

MARITAL HARMONY AT THE BRIDGE TABLE . . .   158

FUNNY AND NOT SO FUNNY   161

SECTION 5:   LAUGHS AND CHUCKLES

GRAND SLAM GAGS   167
       by Lee Hazen as told to Thomas H. Wolf

Dummy, Dummy! Who's Dummy? 173
    by E. J. Kahn, Jr.

How to Improve Your Bridge Popularity . . . 178

Bluffing at Bridge 179
    by Hart Stilwell

A Hellauva Game 184
    by Robert N. Blum

Murders 188
    by Edwin Victor Westrate

If 190
    by William Talley Elliot

Inventory 192
    by Jeanne S. Marks

Soliloquy 193
    by Maurie C. Bryan

Classic Anecdotes 196

SECTION 6: OF EXPERTS AND TOURNAMENTS

Of Experts and Tournaments 205

The Bridge Expert: Psychic Enigma 211
    by Albert H. Morehead

The Brainiest Card Game (An excerpt) . . . 216
    by Fred Schwed, Jr. and Sam Fry, Jr.

But is it Bridge? 219
    by A. Moyse, Jr.

Tourament Bridge is Tough 228
    by Lee Hazen

How to be an Expert 233
   by S. Tupper Bigelow

The Expert and the Psychic Spade 236

SECTION 7: TWO SHORT STORIES

It Beats the Devil 241
   by Sidney S. Lenz

Four Hearts 246
   by Bruce Gould

SECTION 8: TOWARD BETTER BRIDGE

Where Do You Rank Among Thirty Million
   Bridge Players? 267
      by Albert H. Morehead

How to be a Good Player 273
   by R. R. Richards

How to Remember the Cards 277
   by Albert H. Morehead

Luck and the Law of Averages in Bridge . . . 281
   by Walter Malowan

Instinct! 285
   by Frank K. Perkins

Psychology 289
   by Sam Fry, Jr.

Bluff Bids in Contract Bridge 294
   by Walter Malowan

Do People Like to Play Bridge With You? . . 298
   (a quiz)

SECTION 9: CONVENTIONS—LEGAL AND OTHERWISE

CONVENTIONS — LEGAL AND OTHERWISE 303

  IN LOOKING FOR SLAMS 307

    THE BLACKWOOD CONVENTION 307

    THE GERBER CONVENTION 308

    CUE-BIDDING TO SLAM 309

  THE STAYMAN CONVENTION 309

  PRE-EMPTIVE BIDS, THE FISHBEIN CONVENTION, AND OTHER DEFENSES 311

  OPENING BID OF TWO 312

  OVERCALL IN CLUBS 314

  FIVE-CARD MAJORS 314

  WEAK NOTRUMP 314

  UNUSUAL NOTRUMP OVERCALL 314

  LIGHTNER SLAM DOUBLE 316

  COFFEEHOUSING AND SUCH 316

  THE PROPRIETIES 316

YOU'RE CHEATING! 318
by Jack Goodman and Albert Rice

HOW TO PASS 322
by Ely Lenz

SECTION 10: HANDS—CLASSICS, CURIOS AND DOUBLE-DUMMY

HANDS—CLASSICS, CURIOS AND DOUBLE-DUMMY . . 329

THE MISSISSIPPI HEART HAND 330

THE DUKE OF CUMBERLAND HAND 330

MAKING A SLAM WITH ONLY FOUR TRUMPS . . . 331

TWO CLASSIC PROBLEMS 332

SIX BIDS IN ONE SUIT 333

THE FOUR DEUCES HAND 333

AN "IMPOSSIBLE" CONTRACT 334

BATH COUPS GALORE 335

THE GREAT VIENNA COUP 335

A PROGRESSIVE SQUEEZE AND VIENNA COUP . . . 336

TWO PROBLEMS BY R. GRAY 337

DISCARD ALL FOUR ACES 338

MADE OR DOWN — 1, 2, AND 3 338

THE WHITFIELD SIX 340

30 DOUBLE DUMMY PROBLEMS 341

SOLUTIONS 356

SECTION 11: BRIDGE FOR TWO AND THREE HANDS AND VARIATIONS FOR FOUR

BRIDGE FOR TWO 375

BRIDGE FOR THREE 380

VARIATIONS FOR FOUR HANDS 384

FIVE PLAYER PIVOT 386

INTRODUCTION

ONE USUALLY THINKS of a *bedside companion* in terms of 15 or 30 minutes before you turn out the light. The trouble with Al Ostrow's book is that the entertainment may keep you up all night!

As a contract bridge enthusiast of wide and long experience, Mr. Ostrow has probably read as much of the literature pertaining to the game as any living person. Out of this reading he has selected the very best that has been written on the subject. Here are the stories, articles, cartoons and features which deserve the permanence of book publication.

Himself a player of respected skill, an established writer on bridge as well as various other subjects, he is also a teacher who has helped many of his pupils to become experts. In his popular "leisure time" classes at Brooklyn College he has developed thousands of new players, and all of them have caught from him the approach that makes a player a desirable fourth in any company.

To bridge players the fascination of the game is self evident. They will appreciate the great variety of wisdom and humor in the pages which follow. But there are some people, so I have been told, who do not play bridge. They are to be pitied. Perhaps this book will help them to glimpse the enchantment which, until now, has been missing from their lives.

More power to Al Ostrow and to his book.

ALFRED SHEINWOLD

Section 1

The Contract Story

THE CONTRACT STORY

◇♣♡♠◇♣♡♠◇♣♡♠◇♣♡♠◇♣♡♠◇♣♡♠◇♣♡♠◇♣♡♠◇♣♡♠

IF YOU WANT TO START a controversy among card historians, ask them this question, "How did bridge come into being?" You are likely to get almost as many explanations as there are historians.

One thing is definitely known. Our modern game of contract is a development of whist. This ancestor of bridge was originally played with a forty-eight card deck without the deuces, permitting a play for twelve tricks. It got its name, so it is said, from the early practice of calling for silence before play began — "whist!" The first mention of whist in a book of rules was in Charles Cotton's *Compleat Gamester* of 1680. Some years later the deuces were added to the pack, creating the odd trick, and paving the way for scientific treatment of the game.

From that point on variations gradually crept into the game. The late card authority and historian, R. F. Foster, stated that, "It is interesting to trace how the game of whist was gradually changed until it arrived at its present form of contract by repeated borrowing from other games. In a game called cayenne, the cards were dealt 4-5-4 at a time. The (other) pack was then cut, and the top card turned up to determine the rank of the suits. The dealer had the first say to name a trump suit, or passed the privilege to his partner. In this game we see the first departure from whist to bridge."

The first textbook on bridge was published in 1886 under the title of *Biritch*, or *Russian Whist*. English and American players called it bridge. And thereby hangs another one of those colorful tales in which card history abounds.

According to one story bridge was originally played in Istanbul, Turkey, by the Russian colony. It was brought to England around 1884, and there acquired a new name. Two couples in Leicestershire

3

were wont to visit each other on alternate nights to play the game. The path between the two homes led across a rickety old bridge which wasn't too safe at night. When the game broke up the visiting pair would say with relief, "Well, tomorrow night it's your bridge." And thus the game got to be known as bridge whist, then gradually bridge, with the whist part being dropped.

Another version of the origin of the name is a more prosaic one. In bridge, the dealer had the option of selecting the trump suit or passing — "bridgeing" — the decision to his partner.

Bridge in the form we know it today really began to arrive, however, when a dummy hand was laid face up on the table. And this development too seems to have a story attached to it.

As Foster tells it, three British Civil Service officers were stationed at a lonely hill post in India, with no fourth bridge player within a hundred miles. One of them suggested bidding for the fourth hand which would then be played as a face-up dummy. "The others liked the idea and called the game 'Auction.' It was described in the London *Daily Mail* as a good game for three players, and so it remained for more than a year. Then one of the players at a leading card club asked why it would not be a good game for four players, and so it became in short order."

For further comments on the transitions from whist to auction to contract, here is another card historian, William J. Huske.

THERE'LL ALWAYS
BE A BRIDGE GAME

by WILLIAM J. HUSKE

TENNYSON STATED IN RHYME that "men may come and men may go, but I go on forever." He was quoting the brook, which flowed through still pastures and shady nooks, at other places became tempestuous where the water fell over stones to a pool below. This, in my opinion, is the game of bridge.

My own recollection of bridge goes back much further than most. I played bridge whist, the first of three games which followed each other as the heir of the ancient game of whist. In those Victorian days, there was no bidding. The dealer either named a suit or no trump as the final contract, and before making a lead, the player to his left was supposed to make the formal question: "Partner, may I lead?" and the partner, equally punctilious, was told by the laws of the game that his proper response was, "Pray do."

Time marched on. Someone argued, why not let each side have a chance to determine the final contract, and bidding to decide which pair should play the hand became a part of the game. This was auction bridge.

In my early days, it was impossible to make a game (thirty points being needed) with spades as trumps, as spade tricks were worth only 2 points each, and thus if you took all thirteen tricks you would score

From *The American Contract Bridge League Bulletin*. Reprinted by permission.

14 points below the line; honors and slam bonus were scored above the line.

There were in those dim, drear days only two real game-going contracts with a love score—no trumps or hearts, as you had to make eleven tricks if diamonds were trump and thirteen tricks in clubs would only be worth 28 points. The law-makers solved one question for a while. Spades bid as such were still worth only 2 points a trick, but "Royals" which increased the value of each trick at a spade contract were introduced into the game, with a value of 9 points per trick, placing them thus in the hierarchy of suits above hearts and below the no trump valuation. Players liked the innovation, and this became the accepted valuation, the worthless spade value of 2 points being discarded.

Auction bridge was an improvement on bridge whist. It was a tremendous advance over the ancestor game of whist which, historians say, originated in the servants' quarters of the homes of the English nobility. I have always doubted that origin, but true or false, it soon became the game of the noble and the leisure class in England, and when it made its appearance in the United States, it was and long remained the game of those with money and leisure. In fact, to be a whist player was for many years (certainly in my youthful ones) a ranking somewhat similar to the New York social register. If you played whist you were ipso facto an intellectual.

Contract bridge came along. The die-hards (tories) fought it. Auction, they declared, was the perfect game. Why change it? I admit that for a year or so, I held the same feelings. I argued as many others did that "contract" was the game for experts only. That the "dub" would have no chance at a game where in order to score a game or slam, he had to bid it, but it did not take long to convince the world of card players that this view was mistaken.

Contract was democratic. It appealed to a tremendous number of people without the social background which whist required. It appealed to people of all classes whereas whist, and even auction, had made a much more limited appeal.

Unlike whist, the game made an equal appeal to youth. It has been the young fellows (and young women, too) who have made the great advances in the development of the game. The men who had been great authorities in auction tried to assume as by right the same place in contract. They wrote treatises on the game, but the young fellows went along developing their own theories as to bidding, and also as to play, and soon there developed a new class of experts, who proved at the card table that their theories were superior.

Every once in a while some person says that bridge bidding has reached its ultimate; that no new theories can be found; and that bidding has become standardized. I most emphatically disagree. As one of the "ancients" of bridge I have seen change after change come in bidding methods, and I believe that changes will continue through the centuries. If the game ever became standardized in the manner that some people say it has, then, like whist it would become a dead game. It would be one that would appeal only to those whose arteries had already hardened, and youth would go looking for some other way to find intellectual recreation. It is because, while old in years and ancestry, it is ever young and ever changing, that there'll always be a bridge game, and a game that will cut across social barriers, youth, age, skill and its lack, to give to all an intellectual pastime where all may meet on equal terms and where the expert may easily get a "bottom score" from a "dub."

SINCE 1926

by J. PATRICK DUNNE and ALBERT A. OSTROW

◊ ♣ ♡ ♠ ◊ ♣ ♡ ♠ ◊ ♣ ♡ ♠ ◊ ♣ ♡ ♠ ◊ ♣ ♡ ♠ ◊ ♣ ♡ ♠ ◊ ♣ ♡ ♠ ◊ ♣ ♡ ♠ ◊ ♣ ♡ ♠

LATE IN THE AUTUMN of 1925 a cruise ship docked in Havana Harbor after a voyage from California. The trip had been quite pleasant. There had been lovely sunlit days and balmy evenings. But more important for Harold S. Vanderbilt, who was aboard the pleasure steamer, had been the stimulation of a new and fascinating kind of bridge game.

This game, growing out of the suggestions of a young lady passenger, differed from the then popular auction in that you not only had to win the required number of tricks to receive credit for game or slam but you had to contract for them beforehand in the bidding. More points were scored for tricks, slams, and rubbers; and with a vulnerability innovation penalties for going set were also increased.

The idea of putting a premium on accurate bidding was not new. In *plafond*, for example, which was popular in France, only bid tricks were scored below the line toward game. Trick values were the same as in auction, and bonuses for slams were scored whether they were bid or not. But in the new Vanderbilt-style bridge there were rewards for fulfilling slam bids, and points could be won and lost in large amounts.

Within a few months after the end of the cruise the ocean-born bridge variant, with Vanderbilt its main booster, was monopolizing card tables in social centers from Florida to Maine. As the news of it spread auction

Adapted from selections in *Championship Bridge* by J. Patrick Dunne and Albert A. Ostrow, Whittlesey House, McGraw-Hill Book Company, Inc., New York. Reprinted by permission.

8

devotees interrupted their games to try the contract novelty and were captivated. A scoring schedule devised by Vanderbilt and adopted by the Whist Club of New York was followed in his own circle, but elsewhere it was modified to suit the taste of individual groups. The resulting confusion was so great that it became apparent after a while that if contract, for all its appeal, was to grow or even survive, something would have to be done to put it on a standard basis.

Upon this scene arrived a highly charged personality with a dazzling flair for promotion and organization. His name was Ely Culbertson. He had been making a reputation for himself in club circles as a bridge player and had worked out a system of bidding which he labelled "Approach-forcing." With the aid of a publicity campaign unexcelled in the history of ballyhoo, he proceeded to sell the nation on his system of bidding — and on himself.

The Culbertson System, a fusion of his own ideas and certain principles developed by leading bridge theorists of his day, swept the country. In his propaganda, Culbertson assiduously exploited contract's blue-blood origin and plugged it as a social asset, the smart thing for leisure time, and the king of intellectual partnership games. The fad-receptive public, seeing no reason to challenge the assertions, was willing to be convinced. People who barely knew an ace from a deuce seated themselves at bridge tables and learned the Culbertson count for hand evaluation.

Aroused by Culbertson's success a coalition of bridge writers and teachers — among them Wilbur C. Whitehead, Sidney S. Lenz, Milton C. Work, George Reith, and Winfield Liggett, Jr. — published *The Official Book of the Official System* in the summer of 1931. Certain Culbertson theories were incorporated into the Official System and acknowledgment was duly made. But the essential differences from the Approach-forcing System were the offensive-defensive single table of card evaluation, the no-trump point count — a contribution of Work's — the artificial two-club opening force, and a non-forcing two opener.

Culbertson met the threat with characteristic vigor. He dared the partisans of the Official System to pit it against his own system in a test of 150 rubbers. His chief target was Lenz who, upon the death of Whitehead earlier in that year, had become Culbertson's most serious rival. Lenz was finally taunted into picking up the gage and the result was a bridge extravaganza which broke into front pages all over the world and was billed as the "Card Battle of the Century." It aroused as much interest as a championship heavyweight fight. (See H. Allen Smith's eye-witness account on page 21.)

The standard bearers for the Approach-forcing System were Ely and Josephine Culbertson; and they were spelled by Theodore A. Lightner, Waldemar Von Zedwitz, and a couple of brilliant young comers named Howard Schenken and Michael T. Gottlieb. Lenz, who played throughout the entire match, chose as his partner the young, mercurial Oswald Jacoby. But differences of opinion between the two brought about Jacoby's retirement after the hundred and third rubber, and Commander Winfield Liggett, Jr., came in to finish the match as Lenz's partner.

On January 8, 1932, after a month of play and horseplay before hordes of onlookers who enjoyed the egregious errors as much as the master moves, the Culbertson side came out on top by 8,980 points. The proceedings had been enlivened by a near fist fight between Culbertson and Sir Derrick Wernher, a British kibitzer. The two million or so words written about the match, rivaling the coverage of the celebrated Hall-Mills murder case, sent a new host of curiosity seekers to the bridge tables, many of whom remained as converts. In November of that same year a committee composed of representatives from the United States, England, and France presented bridge players with an International Code.

To consolidate his victory, Culbertson launched and expanded a flock of enterprises. These included the *Bridge World* magazine, the United States Bridge Association, studios and conventions for Culbertson-licensed teachers, and the Bridge Olympics, in which players simultaneously played prepared, sealed hands in a world-wide contest for silver and gold cups. More books, improving on the original theory and keeping pace with the developments in contract, were put in the works. Columns by Ely and Josephine, written under separate by-lines, appeared in hundreds of newspapers. Money also rolled in from movie shorts, radio lessons, lectures, magazine articles, endorsements, patented bridge accessories and cards, and the Culbertson-owned bridge club, Crockford's. A Culbertson intimate estimated his income one year as a half-million dollars.

Ely himself was frank about his methods. In an address before the Sales Executive Club of New York, he had the following, among other things, to say:

"I have formed the greatest advertising and publicity organization in the world. I have sold bridge by appealing to the instincts of sex and fear and by false presentation of my own character and that of my wife. I am not the cocky, smart-aleck, conceited, and ready-to-fight person I have tried to make the world believe. My wife is not the shy, diffident, cool, calculating woman I have tried to make the public believe. It is all a stunt calculated to make the name Culbertson synonymous with contract bridge.

"First we had to build a system. That took six years. Then we had to sell the system. We appealed to women, to their natural inferiority complex. Bridge was an opportunity for them to gain intellectual parity with their husbands. We worked on their fear instincts. We made it almost tantamount to shame not to play contract.

"I have sold bridge through sex — the game brought men and women together. I used the words 'forcing bid' and 'approach bid' because there is a connotation of sex to them."

◇ ♣ ♡ ♠

But while Eastern experts were maneuvering for newspaper space the promotion of contract was receiving impetus from a much less publicized source. In 1927 a group of Middle Western bridge enthusiasts had formed an offshoot of the American Whist League and called it the American Auction Bridge League. The group was led by Henry P. Jaeger and C. W. Aldrich of Cleveland, Chicagoans E. J. ("Ned") Tobin and Robert W. Halpin, and Ralph R. Richards of Detroit. Its declared purpose was to foster the cause of competitive bridge. And to this end it sponsored local and sectional tournaments and annual championships for national titles.

As contract events began to dominate the League's tournament calendar the word "Auction" was quietly and symbolically dropped from the organization's title. A Cleveland tire dealer named William E. McKenney, who had joined the League as a statistician, tinkered with the rubber bridge code to adapt it for tournament play. He also changed the shape of the whist-style duplicate tray, used to retain the original deal, from square to oblong and proposed certain improvements in vulnerability markings. In 1929 McKenney was elected executive secretary of the League, a position he was to hold until the winter of 1948.

By 1932 the League was making impressive progress in promoting tournament play. A classification of "masters" had been set up, entry to which was attained through "master points" won in tournaments. To heighten interest further a number of handsome trophies were put up for competition. The most distinguished of these were the Vanderbilt Cup, symbolic of the National Knockout Team-of-Four championship;

the Cavendish Club Trophy, awarded to the National Open Pair champions; and the Waldemar Von Zedwitz Gold Cup, emblematic of the Masters' Pairs championship.

The League's Summer Nationals, staged at Asbury Park in New Jersey, were growing in attendance and in news value. No small part of the reason was the colorful giant named P. Hal Sims. Sims had evolved a bidding system of his own and with a supporting cast made up of Willard S. Karn, David Burnstine (also to be known as David Bruce), and Oswald Jacoby used it in top-flight competition. The outstanding success of "The Four Horsemen" — an appellation of bridge writer Shepard Barclay — turned the spotlight on their leader and his system.

Sims' ambition was to depose Culbertson as the grand panjandrum of contract. The two had been engaged in a running feud which dated back to a meeting at the Knickerbocker Whist Club. They had met in a number of team-of-four matches over the years with the edge in Culbertson's favor. The latter never missed an opportunity to taunt Sims over his defeat in their brushes. After the 1930 Open Team-of-Four championships Culbertson reported that his partner, Jimmy Carpenter, had never played contract before but had guided himself by the following instructions: never open the bid with more than one; never pass when partner jumps; always jump the bid with a strong hand.

Sims, retired from business and well fixed financially, had a summer estate in Deal, New Jersey, which was a favorite hangout for bridge experts. Waldemar Von Zedwitz had a neighboring summer place. Guests were camped about at all hours of the day and night in both establishments, and there were continuous bridge sessions at the Sims house. One of the many stories that have grown out of those days at Deal is about a visitor who was permanently banished from the Sims premises for a novel form of cheating. It seems this fellow was given to singing hymns in Latin while his partner played as declarer. When the partner showed an uncanny knack in locating missing honors, Sims decided to investigate. An expert in Latin confirmed his suspicions: the singer was spotting honors for the benefit of the player.

The laws of percentage and chance were at Sims' finger tips, and he had a prodigious memory and an incredibly sharp eye. He was known for his ability to spot the most ingeniously marked deck in short order. Playing in a tournament once he called off every card in both opponents' hands. Then he called the director and explained that the same board had been played several days before and had not been reshuffled.

Friends tell of his sportsmanlike warning to challengers at gin rummy: "It wouldn't be an equal contest. Unless you get a perfect shuffle some cards will stay in the same order they came up on the last hand. And I'm the kind of fellow who can't help remembering the exact order in which the cards turned up for the previous three deals."

When Jacoby and Burnstine formed The Four Aces with Howard Schenken and Michael Gottlieb, Sims began to play more of his competitive bridge partnered with his wife. Dorothy Rice Sims, quite as colorful and interesting a personality as Hal, was credited with having introduced the psychic bid into contract.

As she told it, she once picked up a hand containing five spades and five hearts in a duplicate at the Knickerbocker Whist Club. Not knowing which to bid she opened a club, and her partner responded with a heart. It gave them the best score on that board. In writing up her discovery for a magazine she meant to label it "psychological bidding." Her spelling failed her, however, and the word came out "sycic." And deceitful bids have been known as "psychics" or "sikes," since.

Dorothy Sims was the first woman to hold a pilot's license and in her teens tore about on a bicycle with such speed and recklessness that she became known as the "Red Devil," bane of traffic officers. Years later in discussing psychics she told of having been arrested on one occasion for reckless driving. She explained to a sympathetic judge that with modern conditions of traffic it is sometimes safer to be reckless than careful. Psychics, was her point, are just such paradoxes and cannot be considered reckless if they help redress the injustice of a deal. They can also be likened to the stiletto thrust and when combined with the bold simplicity of the street fighter and a perfect knowledge of tactics make for a devastating bridge technique.

Technically, the Simses made an incongruous bridge duo. Hal was a masterful handler of dummy and a deadly accurate analyst on defense. Guided by his complete familiarity with percentages he took no unnecessary chances, and a famous dictum of his was: "Never bid a grand slam unless it is a virtual certainty. Be cautious, conservative, and pessimistic about grand slams — especially in suit contracts, since there is always the danger of a first round ruff because of distribution. A grand slam that goes down one trick represents a sure slam wasted." He used psychics daringly but with logic and when matched against respected opponents resorted to sly mugging to suggest that he was trying to put something over on them.

Dorothy, on the other hand, was passable as declarer and only fairish on defense. She was an inveterate "pusher," with a fine disdain for partials, but she was adept at steering the bidding so that Hal would play the hand. When told she knew nothing of the finer points of the game, she countered that it was like informing Man-of-War that his winning technique was faulty. She responded with equal good nature to her husband's cheerful chiding of her as the "worst bridge player in the world" and simply pointed to her titles won in women's play. She was highly effective with her psychics while that mode of bidding was novel. And she was not averse to fixing her rivals in other ways. The story goes that at one tournament she placed all opposition women's hats on a bed to bring them bad luck.

The success of Sims at Asbury Park and the fact that a couple of youngsters named John Rau and William Barret were doing sensationally with the methods advocated by Hal and Dorothy brought the Sims System of bidding into prominence. Though one authority described it as nothing more than a device to give the stronger player of a partnership a better chance to play as declarer, it aroused great curiosity among the bridge faithful. How, they wanted to know, did it stack up with the much-propagandized Culbertson System?

Late in 1934 Culbertson, who needed a flare-up of publicity in connection with his new version of the Culbertson System, accepted Hal's challenge to a showdown 150-rubber match. It was to be played early the following year and conducted along the lines of the Culbertson-Lenz battle won by the former some three years previously, and Lenz himself would be the guest of honor. Ely and Jo Culbertson would team against Hal and Dorothy Sims in a Mr.-and-Mrs. affair, always a compellingly newsworthy event. (See Culbertson vs. Sims, page 34, for a detailed account of the match and some hands.)

The match which was won by the Culbertsons resulted in another tremendous publicity boost for contract. Hundreds of papers carried stories on the event. There were afternoon and evening broadcasts featuring play-by-play accounts and twice-weekly commentaries by the contestants. Contract was now a big-time sport — and an industry. Thousands were drawing incomes from teaching the game and writing about it; thousands more were capitalizing on the growing demands for the accessories of the playing table.

International competitive contract received a boost through the donation of a trophy by Charles M. Schwab, steel mogul and one-time president of the New York Whist Club. A Culbertson team consisting of Ely, Josephine, Lightner, and Gottlieb bested an English aggregation in

London by 11,000 points in the first competition for possession of the cup. The match was staged at Selfridge's auditorium, and twenty thousand spectators were enabled to kibitz the proceedings through the medium of a giant scoreboard and periscopes. British writers hailed the event and predicted the time when more than fifty nations would compete for the trophy along Davis Cup tennis lines. Matches between nations would be televised on a world-wide network and would take their place as a major sports spectacle.

During these same years, The Four Aces (Jacoby, Schenken, Gottlieb and David Burnstine) were making their weight felt in the world of bids and plays. As a team, in pairs, and individually, they carted off engraved silverware in wholesale lots. Sparking the drive on the trophy cases was Jacoby, the same "Ozzie" Jacoby who had quit the Culbertson-Lenz "Bridge Battle of the Century" after an argument with Lenz.

Jacoby was ten years old when he played his first bridge with his parents and friends. Mathematics was a family interest, and so when young Ozzie was graduated from high school in his native Brooklyn and enrolled at Columbia University he chose that as his major subject. Sheepskin under arm he went over to the Metropolitan Life Insurance Company, was hired, and at the age of twenty-one passed actuarial examinations. This made him the youngest actuary in the history of North American insurance.

At college Jacoby had been active in a number of extra-curricular activities, among them chess, polo, and bridge. With Louis H. Watson, who was to die an untimely death a little more than a decade later, he had played in the Ivy League bridge tournaments staged by clubs from Columbia, Harvard, Princeton, and Yale. A contemporary who remembers him from those days describes him as a tousled, bareheaded undergraduate, who was constantly on the look-out to test his mental and physical muscles.

There is a story that an instructor in physics once placed a problem in ballistics on the blackboard and then gave the class the answer; Jacoby challenged it and got called down for his presumption. Two days later, upon checking over the problem, the instructor was forced to admit that Jacoby's rapid mental solution had been right instead of the one originally given.

Jacoby's first major success in bridge came in 1929 when paired with George Reith; one of the original exponents of one-over-one bidding, he won the Eastern championships for pairs. Caught up by big-time bridge he became a member of The Four Horsemen—his teammates being

Willard S. Karn, David Burnstine, and P. Hal Sims. Brilliant individually and as a foursome, this quartet won the team-of-four championship in the American Bridge League's Summer Nationals.

People who wrote about bridge doings made much of "Ozzie," as they tagged him, and his daring psychics. They wondered why a mind as neatly logical and mathematical as Ozzie's should revel in disruptive, psychological warfare at the bridge table. But they loved the psychics for the copy they made, especially since his partners were nearly as often baffled by them as his opponents. The white glare of publicity that beat down on the Culbertson-Lenz bidding duel made Jacoby's name and spectacular tactics familiar to bridge players everywhere. A "Jacoby" became synonymous with any bid made on practically nothing.

It was sound, yet brilliant bridge, however, that carried Jacoby to a string of famous victories. His special glory was accomplished in the coveted Vanderbilt Cup championship for teams of four — a knockout event. His name went on the squat bowl in 1931, 1934, 1935, 1937 and 1938 and three times he was a finalist in off years.

But while Jacoby and his fellow Aces were winning the victories Culbertson was reaping the shekels. In a bid to divert some of the gold flowing into the Culbertson coffers The Four Aces wrote a book explaining their system of bidding. Harold S. Vanderbilt in a foreword expressed his admiration and listed as the outstanding features of the system the principle of anticipation — bidding so as to prepare for partner's probable response; limiting no-trump responses to hands of suitable distribution; low biddable requirements for suits; and opening bids on a three-card suit in certain hands to enable the partnership to exchange information at low levels.

Mindful of the gorgeous publicity resulting from the Culbertson-Lenz and Culbertson-Sims matches The Aces dared Ely to have it out at the bridge table. The boldest of the challenges offered Culbertson a handicap of 5,000 points in a match of 300 boards and bound The Aces to contribute ten thousand dollars to a milk-fund charity in the event of their defeat. Culbertson would be allowed to set the rules and conditions, "if at all reasonable," and might pick any three teammates.

The challenge added somewhat insultingly, "As to your being in need of rest, you may set your own time for playing the match. Further, you need not wager any money . . . We feel certain that your attitude is prompted by causes other than those stated. First, the fact that we eliminated your team during the quarter-finals in the Grand National Tourney in February may cause you to feel that the proposed match would be an unequal one. Second, that for reasons of your own, you may not dare risk losing ten thousand dollars on the match."

Culbertson refused to be drawn into a showdown contest with The Aces. The Culbertson-conditioned public bought comparatively few copies of The Four Aces' book. And the irrepressible Ely was able to boast that the only person to make real money out of the book was himself. This was the result of collection on a fifteen-hundred-dollar bet he made with Gottlieb that ten thousand copies would not be sold within the year.

Late in 1935 a French team representing itself as the best in Europe played a match against The Four Aces in New York. Somebody had the idea that this could be exploited as a paying spectacle for a paying public. The actual contest took place in a hotel, while in nearby Madison Square Garden men with giant playing cards represented the progress of the play. The venture did not pan out. There simply was no audience for gallery bridge commercially. As still other attempts on this line proved, the majority of the bridge faithful would rather play bridge than watch it.

The development of contract was coming to a point where battles between systems were beginning to lose justification or meaning. There was a growing sentiment among players for simple, standardized conventions that would make the bidding language of a player from Brooklyn or Waukegan intelligible to someone from San Francisco or Albuquerque. The newest editions of the Culbertson books bowed to this mood by incorporating bidding refinements taken over from rival systems.

Contributing toward standardization was the revision of the International Code in 1935 in accordance with ideas popular with the bridge multitudes. Another helpful event was the amalgamation in 1937 of the American Bridge League and the rival Culbertson-inspired United States Bridge Association into a single organization. With the affiliation seven years later of the Pacific Bridge League, the American Contract Bridge League became the only nationally recognized association of bridge players in the country.

The League's master-point plan was drawing more and more players into tournament competition. Players with master points won in club or local duplicates tested themselves in state events and—because of confidence in their ability or just for the heck of it—in regional or national championships. They studied one another's methods and those of the top experts and brought back new ideas and conventions to local bridge circles. The increase in popularity of match-point duplicate in club as well as championship play encouraged the development of special techniques for that form of bridge. Much greater attention, for example, was paid to part-score bidding, which played a more important role in the struggle for match points than it did in rubber bridge.

As an increasing number of players sought the rank of Master, the League expanded the opportunities for becoming a rated expert. Master points were awarded at national and sectional championships to winners, runners-up, and a number of other contestants according to the size of the field. While a few important tournaments were restricted to players holding a certain amount of master points, most others were "open" events in which the amateur with no master points at all might compete in a field containing contestants who had accumulated hundreds of them. Clubs affiliated with the League were authorized to give fractional points in their duplicates.

The competition for master points had the effect of raising the level of bridge play over the country. It also developed an ever-widening circle of experts. New names began to appear in the heads over newspaper stories from the major tournaments and in the boxed hands in bridge columns which demonstrated fine points of bidding or play. The exploits of certain stars became increasingly familiar to the considerable part of the American population that was bridge-conscious.

Now, some three decades after the debut of contract, the game is out of the fad stage. It is still tremendously popular and polls show it to be a firmly entrenched favorite with millions. Sales of bridge cards, bridge books, and bridge paraphernalia confirm this.

Contributing heavily to the continuing high interest in the game, most observers agree, was the introduction of Charles H. Goren's point count for measuring the value of a hand. This gave aces an evaluation of 4, kings 3, queens 2, jacks 1, and also allotted points for distribution factors.

The evaluation of the strength of a hand by points was not new. Various counts had been used in auction bridge and The Four Aces themselves had used a count of 3, 2, 1, and ½. But the public had not been ready for a point count in those years. And besides, Goren's count of 1, 2, 3 and 4 used no fractions and made for simple arithmetic. Its use helped turn dubs into passably accurate bidders.

The man who was responsible for the popularization of the point count had started out as a young Philadelphia lawyer with an interest in bridge. He studied the game at home and in his spare time entered local duplicates. His obvious promise attracted the interest of Milton C. Work, a fellow-Philadelphian, and the latter used him as a technical assistant in the preparation of books, lectures and columns. Work was an Olympian of bridge and his young townsman listened, learned and absorbed.

Goren began to do some bridge teaching of his own. He analyzed winning methods and put his conclusions between book covers. No system plugger, he shrewdly gave his volumes such titles as *Winning Bridge Made Easy* and *Highlights of Winning Bridge*. Goren's pitch was that systems and artificial conventions are caviar to the general run of bridge players, and he emphasized adaptability and natural tactics.

It was not a particularly lucrative period for him. He had turned his back on Blackstone, and his considerable energies were directed toward establishing himself as a bridge somebody. But the upturn in his fortunes came in 1937 when an all-Philadelphia team of Sally Young, Charles Solomon, John Crawford, and himself won the national Open Team-of-Four championship. Goren was the acknowledged spark plug and leader of the group, and publicity stories from the tournament stressed that fact.

He was to go on from there to win every major title in bridge for which he was eligible and stock his bachelor apartment with a dazzling array of cups, plaques, and medals — also bridge tables, ash stands, lighters, and assorted prize loot from lesser tournaments. In the tenth year following his first victory in a national event he accumulated 465 master points — an American Contract Bridge League record.

Today Goren is sitting pretty. He has the prestige of owning more master points than anyone else and is still reaping them in clusters. He is popular with his fellow-experts. His books are racking up juicy royalties here and abroad. The newspaper circulation of his column is greater than Culbertson's ever was.

With Ely Culbertson returning to the bridge wars after a financially debilitating involvement in world-peace plans the bridge generation that remembers the Culbertson-Lenz and Culbertson-Sims duels was hopeful of more of the same. But the big-publicity era of bridge with its page-one war of systems and its wonderful hoopla belongs to the innocent past. The like will probably never be seen again.

After years of deriding point count as an adding machine system ("What will people do when they run out of fingers?"), Culbertson has jumped aboard the bandwagon with a revised point count of his own. It resembles Goren's in its essentials, differing mainly in the evaluation of distribution. The older bridge impresario claims, of course, that his method is simpler, more effective and easier to learn. The younger one pooh-poohs the idea as so much propaganda.

From all indications the battle will remain one of words. Culbertson, it is said, believes that the chief gainer from a card-table contest, win or lose, would be Goren if only from the angle of publicity. Goren's reply to the idea that he and Culbertson get together over a squared table and settle the issue was a disdainful, "No, thank you." He engages only in official competition, he pointed out, under the sponsorship of the American Contract Bridge League. Besides, Culbertson has won only four national championships while he, Goren, has won close to thirty. "No one ranking seven hundredth can challenge me."

Meanwhile, the rank and file bridge player goes on his way enjoying the game despite, or perhaps because of, the innovations and refinements the students of the game are constantly dreaming up for him. The last word on what its future will be is, as always, his.

CULBERTSON'S COUP

by H. ALLEN SMITH

◇ ♣ ♡ ♠ ◇ ♣ ♡ ♠ ◇ ♣ ♡ ♠ ◇ ♣ ♡ ♠ ◇ ♣ ♡ ♠ ◇ ♣ ♡ ♠ ◇ ♣ ♡ ♠ ◇ ♣ ♡ ♠ ◇ ♣ ♡ ♠

IT DOESN'T SEEM like yesterday — it seems like a good twenty-three years ago that we all ganged into the Hotel Chatham for the start of the most spectacular (and goofiest) card game ever played in the history of man.

The Culbertson-Lenz contract bridge grapple began on December 7, 1931, and press association executives agreed that no World Series, up to then, had ever attracted as much national attention.

Weeks of fussing and fuming and name-calling preceded the actual start of the match. Contract bridge, from its quiet beginnings around 1926, had by 1931 become a national rage. It seems likely that the Big Depression was partly responsible. People had no money to spend on other diversions and a deck of cards didn't cost much, so practically everybody played contract.

Into this situation stepped a lean, suave, quick-witted super-irritant named Ely Culbertson. He was then forty years old, son of a Russian mother and an American father and possessed of a manner which some people thought charming but which led others to cast their eyes about in search of blunt instruments. His life in America, up to this time, had been that of an obscure professional card player who haunted the bridge clubs in New York City, sometimes prospering, sometimes broke and in debt. He was certainly one of the ablest card tacticians in the country and his handsome wife, Josephine, was considered to be the best player of her sex.

By 1930 the contract fad was approaching the proportions of a plague, and growing week by week. Culbertson saw the potential, realizing that if he played his cards right he might very well reap both fame and fortune out of the new national obsession. He was not then known as a bridge authority but there were plenty of recognized experts around issuing a confusion of "systems" for playing contract. Culbertson took his time. He spent hours and days and weeks alone with a deck of cards, working out his own bidding system, and when he was satisfied with it, scraped together enough money to start a magazine called *The Bridge World.*

A Sad Lot of Blokes

In the spring of 1930 a British bridge expert published a statement to the effect that American bridge players were a sad lot of blokes. Culbertson promptly issued a sassy challenge. He would bring a team of four to London and play 300 duplicate boards against a British team. The challenge was accepted and now Culbertson had to raise money to get himself and his team to England. Through his magazine he began taking orders for his first book on bridge, not a line of which had been written. He got the money, dictated the text of his book right up to the hour of sailing, and then took off with Mrs. Culbertson and two young men who could play the Culbertson System — Theodore Lightner and Waldemar Von Zedwitz. The arrival of these brash, unknown Americans created a big stir not only in England but on the Continent. The English bridge writers treated them with great condescension and laughed at them in print. Following which the Culbertson team proceeded to clobber the English, winning the match by nearly 5,000 points.

Ely and Jo Culbertson came home famous. Culbertson's *Blue Book* had been published during the play of the match in London and now was selling furiously all over the United States. The name Culbertson was fast becoming almost a synonym for contract bridge and, of course, this didn't set well in certain quarters. As the Culbertson System grew and prospered, the book sales and prestige of the old established masters, such as Milton Work, Whitehead and Lenz, declined.

Culbertson began to needle these older men. He wrote about them and he talked about them on the radio. He charged that they were trying to ruin his reputation through a whispering campaign, calling him a dissolute gigolo and a "suspicious Russian." Eventually he drove them to the wall, and they turned to fight.

A dozen of the old masters joined force in an organization called Bridge Headquarters. Their stated purpose was to "standardize" the game, and they sponsored a method of play which they called the Official System. They went through the motions of inviting Culbertson into the group but he simply threw back his head and cackled at them. It was one against twelve, but Culbertson always loved long odds. He picked out Sidney S. Lenz as the best card player in the group and challenged Lenz to a match of 150 rubbers, Lenz to choose his own partner. Culbertson would bet five thousand dollars against one thousand dollars that he and his wife, playing the Culbertson System, would beat Lenz and his partner, hewing to the Official System.

Sidney Lenz ignored the challenge but Culbertson kept hammering at him, heckling him in the press and on the air. Culbertson's incredible cockiness was paying off — his book sales continued to mount and thousands of bridge teachers were signing up under his banner. The old guard had to put up or shut up, and finally Lenz accepted the challenge.

Between the time when the rules were agreed upon and the match got under way, the nation's press discovered that it had something special on its hands. In the week prior to December 7, twenty-four special cables were laid into the Culbertson apartment in the Hotel Chatham, where the first half of the contest was to be staged. A large press room, complete with rows of typewriters and telegraph keys, was established down the hall from the Culbertson drawing room to make reporters comfortable.

Sidney Lenz was then fifty-eight, an amateur magician, a ping-pong champion, a superb bridge player and a wealthy man. He chose as his partner Oswald Jacoby, a handsome young fellow with dark hair and the build of a fullback, member of the championship bridge team called The Four Horsemen.

On the night the match started there was classic confusion in the various rooms and corridors of the hotel. The place swarmed with reporters and cameramen and society people and celebrities. Chosen to referee the contest was Lieutenant Alfred M. Gruenther, a thirty-two-year-old chemistry instructor at West Point. Everyone was most polite and after two rubbers, Lenz and Jacoby were 1,715 points ahead.

The card table was at one end of the Culbertson drawing room. Across the center of the room stood high folding screens and there were six cracks, each about an inch wide, through which the reporters and favored guests could watch the contest. There was a chair at each crack and the rule said that no reporter or guest could look through a crack more than fifteen minutes at a time, and it was required that everyone walk on tiptoe. Signs ordering "Complete Silence!" hung throughout the apartment and on the door where the two Culbertson children were abed was a sign saying, "Quiet! Little Children Asleep and Dreaming."

"Who's Pickin' Up the Tab?"

A ghostly, unending procession of reporters, columnists and special guests moved in and out of the room. Each New York newspaper assigned at least one reporter to stay with the match to the end. The Associated Press had two men present every evening and the United Press and International News Service had one each. Special writers such as Ring Lardner, Heywood Broun, Damon Runyon, Robert Benchley, Westbrook Pegler, Grantland Rice, Henry McLemore, Eddie Neil and Lucius Beebe dropped in from time to time. Pegler spent one evening ranging through the halls asking the same question: "Who's pickin' up the tab?" Runyon insisted on challenging all the bridge experts to meet a team of Broadway characters in a back room at Lindy's. McLemore came to fulfill a lifetime ambition to become "a crack reporter."

Those of us who were present every night for five weeks might well have become bored with the proceedings if it hadn't been for Culbertson. He needed no press agent. In devising methods of irritating and enraging his opponents, he anticipated the "Gamesmanship" ploys which later appeared in books by Stephen Potter. He was consistently late getting to the card table and this infuriated Sidney Lenz, a man of little patience. Culbertson went into long periods of meditation before bidding or before playing a card, and Lenz soon grew bitter about the entire pro- ceedings. Culbertson would sometimes have a juicy steak served on a corner of the table, eating as he played, and Lenz would complain: "My God, Ely, you're getting grease all over the cards! Why don't you eat at the proper time, like the rest of us?" To which Ely would reply: "My vast public won't let me, Sidney."

At the end of the 27th rubber Lenz was ahead by more than 7,000 points but on December 15 Culbertson took the lead for the first time. He never relinquished it after that and each evening as he arrived (late) at the table he'd smile sweetly at Lenz and in his rich Russian accent he'd say, "Well, Sidney, have you changed your system yet?"

Before long Lenz was accusing the Culbertsons of failure to adhere to the Culbertson System. There were many delaying arguments on this point and Lieutenant Gruenther, a much harassed young man, settled them as best he could. The lieutenant had to travel each afternoon from West Point to New York, supervise the evening's play, start back around one o'clock and be ready for an 8 A.M. class. Mrs. Gruenther did most of the driving while her husband snoozed in the back seat.

Public interest in the contest reached such a pitch that one evening Jack Curley, the wrestling impresario, arrived at the Chatham demanding the right to switch the play to Madison Square Garden. He proposed that the players should occupy a glass cage and the audience follow the play on huge electrical scoreboards. He insisted that a fortune could be made from such an arrangement. "A fortune for you," said Culbertson, "but I'm interested only in making a fortune for myself."

The public got immense satisfaction out of the knowledge that these great stars of the game were frequently guilty of bonehead plays. On December 28 Jacoby quit, after a loud dispute with Lenz. Late in that evening's session Lenz suddenly turned on Jacoby.

"Why do you make such rotten bids?" he demanded.

Jacoby stared at him and didn't answer. Culbertson smiled and said, "Shall we play another rubber?"

"Not with me, you don't!" snapped Jacoby, rising to his feet.

Referee Gruenther intervened, saying that the rules required another rubber. Jacoby sat down again, then turned to Lenz and said: "Sidney, in a hand in the second rubber tonight you made an absolutely stupid defensive play, and then you criticized *me*. I'm resigning right now as your partner."

A New Partner

Lenz looked at him a moment in disbelief. "Well, well, sir; well, sir," he stammered, "all right, sir."

The next evening Lenz had a new partner, a rotund former Navy officer, Commander Winfield Liggett, Jr. Commander Liggett agreed to play as his old friend's partner but told the press that the contest was proving nothing at all about the relative merits of the bidding systems.

On the evening of December 30 came a new sensation. Several of us were sitting around the press room listening to Sir Derrick Wernher, a British-American bridge star, analyze the play. Into the room walked Culbertson. Sir Derrick spoke to him, asking him why he had not responded to a challenge he had issued the previous summer. Culbertson said he hadn't heard of any such challenge. Said Sir Derrick: "You liar. You're a slab-sided piece of beefsteak."

Sir Derrick was standing in a corner, a man of huge physical proportions. Culbertson strode up to him, fists clenched, glared up into his face and said:

"Why, you five hundred-pound piece of English beefsteak, you, I consider you a cheap shark and not worth playing against. I wouldn't dirty my hands at the same table with you."

Sir Derrick responded in kind. Culbertson shrilled that he'd bet five thousand dollars to two thousand dollars that he could pick a team from among the reporters present that would beat any team selected by Sir Derrick. "On second thought," Culbertson snarled, "I'll bet five hundred dollars you haven't got two thousand dollars to bet." Sir Derrick then called Culbertson a liar and Ely advanced on him again, just as Jo Culbertson came into the room and grabbed him. She dragged him away to the playing room but Culbertson refused to start the evening's contest until Sir Derrick had left the hotel. As the Englishman was leaving, Mrs. Culbertson yelled after him, "What a coward you are, Derrick!"

When the Last Card Dropped

The second half of the match was played at the Waldorf-Astoria in quarters provided by Lenz. It all came to an end on the night of January 8, with the Culbertsons victors by 8,980 points. After the last card had dropped, Lenz stood up and shook hands with Mrs. Culbertson. Culbertson walked over to join in the felicitations but Lenz turned his back on him. Lieutenant Gruenther went back to West Point to pursue a career that would eventuate in his becoming Supreme Allied Commander in Europe.

Contract bridge, of course, is not what it was in those frenzied days, but it remains one of the most popular of our indoor sports, and Culbertson still rates as one of the top authorities. Lenz is now eighty-one and Culbertson attended his eightieth birthday party and the two men shook hands. Culbertson, who has been divorced twice in the intervening years, is today giving much of his attention to a system whereby he hopes to bring permanent peace to the world. So far as I know, he doesn't intend to head up the project himself.

KIBITZER'S FAVORITE HANDS FROM THE CULBERTSON-LENZ MATCH

Lenz
♠ 9 6 2
♡ 8 7 5 4 3 2
◇ A J
♣ Q J

Culbertson
♠ A 4
♡ Q
◇ K Q 10 9 7 4
♣ A K 9 4

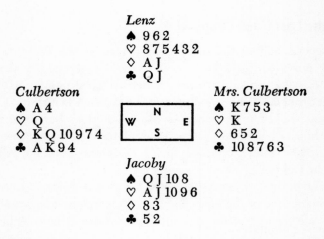

Mrs. Culbertson
♠ K 7 5 3
♡ K
◇ 6 5 2
♣ 10 8 7 6 3

Jacoby
♠ Q J 10 8
♡ A J 10 9 6
◇ 8 3
♣ 5 2

West dealer.
Neither side vulnerable.

The bidding:

WEST	NORTH	EAST	SOUTH
1 ◇	Pass	Pass	1 ♡
2 ◇	3 ♡	Pass	4 ♡
5 ◇	Pass	Pass	Double

Four hearts would have gone down two tricks with ordinary defense. Jacoby won the first lead with the ace of hearts and returned a club.

27

Ely "huddled" for ten minutes whereupon Lenz got up from the table, complaining that his adversary wanted to get his goat.

Culbertson explained that he was trying to ascertain the distribution through the bidding and play to that point. Finally he finessed the ten of diamonds (after previously having lost the king of diamonds to the ace), and went down one.

Jacoby later credited his false card of the jack of spades on the first spade play as the reason Ely went wrong. Culbertson must have figured him for the queen, jack of spades alone and counted his hand as six hearts, two spades, three diamonds and two clubs.

On one hand Lenz picked up the cards absent-mindedly and began to deal when it was Culbertson's turn. The following hand resulted:

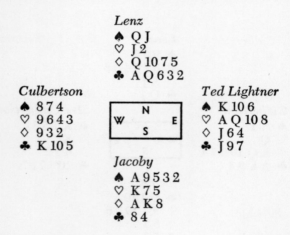

Lenz
♠ Q J
♡ J 2
◇ Q 10 7 5
♣ A Q 6 3 2

Culbertson
♠ 8 7 4
♡ 9 6 4 3
◇ 9 3 2
♣ K 10 5

Ted Lightner
♠ K 10 6
♡ A Q 10 8
◇ J 6 4
♣ J 9 7

Jacoby
♠ A 9 5 3 2
♡ K 7 5
◇ A K 8
♣ 8 4

Neither side vulnerable.

The bidding:

NORTH	EAST	SOUTH	WEST
Pass	1 NT	Double	Pass
2 ♣	Pass *	2 ♠	Pass
Pass	Pass		

*(Lightner was barred from the bidding after the first round.)

When it came Culbertson's first turn to bid he hesitated momentarily. Lenz asked for a review of the bidding. Culbertson volunteered, "I passed, you passed, and Mr. Lightner —"

Lenz interrupted to point out that Culbertson hadn't dealt the cards and in his review had given unauthorized information to his partner. The referees agreed and barred Lightner from the bidding. Lenz then put in a call and his partnership lost a chance to make a good score.

Lightner's semi-psychic could have been beaten several tricks. Or, Lenz and Jacoby had a makeable game.

What was called "one of the most grotesque hands of the entire match" occurred during the 50th rubber.

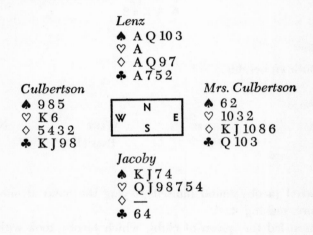

Lenz
♠ A Q 10 3
♡ A
♢ A Q 9 7
♣ A 7 5 2

Culbertson
♠ 9 8 5
♡ K 6
♢ 5 4 3 2
♣ K J 9 8

Mrs. Culbertson
♠ 6 2
♡ 10 3 2
♢ K J 10 8 6
♣ Q 10 3

Jacoby
♠ K J 7 4
♡ Q J 9 8 7 5 4
♢ —
♣ 6 4

South dealer.
Both sides vulnerable.

The bidding:

SOUTH	WEST	NORTH	EAST
1 ♡	Pass	3 NT	Pass
4 ♡	Pass	4 NT	Pass
5 ♡	Pass	6 NT	Pass
Pass	Double	Pass	Pass
7 ♡	Double	All pass	

Seven spades was a lay-down; but the spade suit was never mentioned once by either partner.

◇ ♣ ♡ ♠

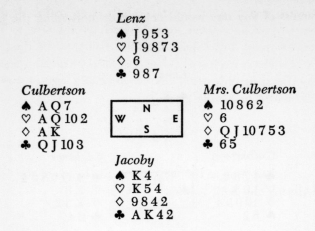

Lenz
♠ J953
♡ J9873
◇ 6
♣ 987

Culbertson
♠ AQ7
♡ AQ102
◇ AK
♣ QJ103

Mrs. Culbertson
♠ 10862
♡ 6
◇ QJ10753
♣ 65

Jacoby
♠ K4
♡ K54
◇ 9842
♣ AK42

East dealer.

North–South vulnerable.

The bidding:

EAST	SOUTH	WEST	NORTH
Pass	1 ♣	Pass (!)	Pass
Pass			

An amazed Jacoby found himself playing the hand at one club and, what's more, making it.

Culbertson led the queen of clubs, which Jacoby took with the king. Declarer led a small diamond and Culbertson returned the jack of clubs. Jacoby won that with the ace, trumped a diamond in the dummy and led a small heart to his king. This was taken by Culbertson's ace.

Ely now fretted and stewed about his next play and finally came up with the queen of hearts and a continuation of the suit. This gave Jacoby two throw-offs of losing diamonds on the long hearts. Culbertson trumped the last heart but was then forced to lead up to declarer's king of spades.

Why didn't Ely bid with his rock-crusher? As he explained it, he was hoping to get in a penalty double if Lenz kept the bidding open. This would bring his side more points against the vulnerable opponents than if it bid game — which, incidentally, was there and makable.

◇ ♣ ♡ ♠

The kibitzers of any day would enjoy post-morteming the bidding on this deal:

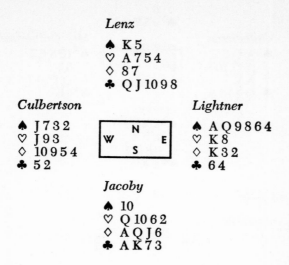

Lenz
♠ K 5
♡ A 7 5 4
◇ 8 7
♣ Q J 10 9 8

Culbertson
♠ J 7 3 2
♡ J 9 3
◇ 10 9 5 4
♣ 5 2

Lightner
♠ A Q 9 8 6 4
♡ K 8
◇ K 3 2
♣ 6 4

Jacoby
♠ 10
♡ Q 10 6 2
◇ A Q J 6
♣ A K 7 3

East dealer.

Both sides vulnerable.

The bidding:

East	South	West	North
1 ♠	Double	Pass	2 ♣
Pass	3 ♣	All pass	

Jacoby was more than a little annoyed at the auction since game at hearts is a snap. He commented later that he would recommend it as an important rule of bidding that take-out doubles of one major should be prepared for the other major. And that, generally, is the style today among good players.

◇ ♣ ♡ ♠

Look at the hand below. Would you believe that North and South can win four overtricks at a contract of two diamonds?

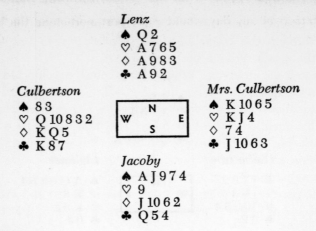

Lenz
♠ Q 2
♡ A 7 6 5
◇ A 9 8 3
♣ A 9 2

Culbertson
♠ 8 3
♡ Q 10 8 3 2
◇ K Q 5
♣ K 8 7

Mrs. Culbertson
♠ K 10 6 5
♡ K J 4
◇ 7 4
♣ J 10 6 3

Jacoby
♠ A J 9 7 4
♡ 9
◇ J 10 6 2
♣ Q 5 4

East dealer.
Both sides vulnerable.

The bidding:

EAST	SOUTH	WEST	NORTH
Pass	Pass	Pass	1 ◇
Pass	1 ♠	Pass	1 NT
Pass	2 ◇	All pass	

The opening lead by Mrs. Culbertson was the three of clubs. Low was played from dummy, the seven by Culbertson and the nine by Lenz.

Now the queen of spades was led and covered by the king and ace. A small diamond was returned and the eight finessed. The ace of diamonds was laid down, leaving Culbertson with the king.

Toward the end of the hand Culbertson used his king of trumps on dummy's fourth spade. Lenz was prepared to ruff that spade in order to drop East's ten. Instead he discarded his deuce of clubs — a loser on a loser. As a result of this play, Mrs. Culbertson's lead of the three of clubs and Culbertson's not splitting his trump honors, Lenz wound up losing only one trick to the king of trumps.

Such boners were headlined by the newspapers. The morning after they were printed in the paper, bridge columnist Robert Neville reported, "The players received challenge after challenge — from San Diego to Bangor, from Miami to Seattle . . . There were so many challenges that Mr. Culbertson was finally moved to declare publicly that the next person who challenged him would have to eat his *Contract Bridge Blue Books*, cover, glue and all."

◇ ♣ ♡ ♠

Jacoby's psychics were the delight of the kibitzers, not only those who watched through the cracks of the spectator's screen but those who followed the match through the news reports.

Commented an observer, "While Mr. Jacoby's psychic bids at times resulted in considerable loss for his side, still, on occasions his penchant for daring maneuvers was rewarded. His adversaries were often unable to divine his intentions. It follows, of course, that Mr. Lenz was equally in the dark, but Mr. Jacoby apparently worked on the principle that the odds were in favor of his tactics since he was fooling two opponents and only one partner."

That one partner, however, got tired of being fooled and his exasperation on the following hand hastened Jacoby's decision to quit the match.

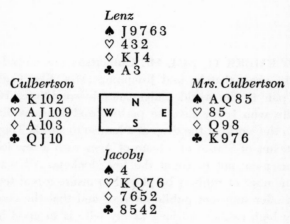

Lenz
♠ J 9 7 6 3
♡ 4 3 2
◇ K J 4
♣ A 3

Culbertson
♠ K 10 2
♡ A J 10 9
◇ A 10 3
♣ Q J 10

Mrs. Culbertson
♠ A Q 8 5
♡ 8 5
◇ Q 9 8
♣ K 9 7 6

Jacoby
♠ 4
♡ K Q 7 6
◇ 7 6 5 2
♣ 8 5 4 2

West dealer.
East–West vulnerable.

The bidding:

West	North	East	South
1 ♡	Pass	1 ♠	1 NT
Double	Pass	Pass	2 ♣
2 NT	Pass	3 NT	All pass

Lenz led the ace of clubs and the hand produced eleven tricks. No lead would have made any difference in this hand.

"What do you mean by bidding on absolutely nothing?" demanded Lenz after the hand was over. "You are just having a lot of fun bidding as you do, and I am always in the dark as to what you actually mean. Give me a break once in a while."

It was the end of a beautiful partnership.

THE SIMS-CULBERTSON PRELIMINARIES

◇♣♡♠◇♣♡♠◇♣♡♠◇♣♡♠◇♣♡♠◇♣♡♠◇♣♡♠◇♣♡♠◇♣♡♠

ON DECEMBER 14, 1934, Mr. Culbertson announced by radio and through the press that he and Josephine (Mrs. Ely) Culbertson would play any pair in the world under suitable conditions. He said:

"My wife who is my favorite partner and I are willing to take on any pair in the world at the drop of a hat, so to speak. They can all come on, be it teams of Simses or a team of Aces with a few jokers, or half a dozen Horsemen, not to count the few donkeys. All we ask is that a sufficient number of rubbers be played to insure a real test of skill, that the match offer sufficient public interest, and that the challengers be of sufficiently high caliber. So long as my wife is in good health and not too busy with the children, I don't believe I will lose a big match; for such a partner as she makes, I have never seen. She is the only player of my acquaintance, among all the experts, who has never cracked. And in any big match it is not the skill, but the morale, that counts. Therefore, far from avoiding any challenges, we are seeking them, and let this be a notice for any bona fide challenge from any logical candidate."

Challenges flooded the Culbertson office and on Christmas Eve, P. Hal Sims of Deal, New Jersey, flung his gauntlet by registered mail.

"For years," read the letter, "you have been subtly instilling into the minds of a more or less unsuspecting public the idea that you and Mrs. Culbertson are the leading pair of the world. After listening to your most recent boastful claims in the press and over the radio it occurred to me that you might be in a frame of mind to accept a challenge from Mrs. Sims and myself.

34

"Contract is really a fascinating game, and I am sure that if you found the time to take it up, you would eventually derive tremendous enjoyment from it."

Replied Culbertson, "Your challenge is accepted with pleasure. All these years I have been itching to lay my bridge hands on you. At last you have emerged from your hiding place to meet your master.

"Though I consider you one of the world's finest card players, even your brilliancy cannot overcome the handicaps of your atrocious system. Let it be a real tough but clean fight to the finish."

◇ ♣ ♡ ♠

Sims moved to the Molly Pitcher Hotel in Red Bank, New Jersey and went into serious training. Mrs. Sims and his trainers made it a real camp. Patterning their methods after those of Max Baer, heavyweight champion of the world, who had trained at the Sims' ocean home the preceding spring, they began a rigorous schedule of road work and shadow boxing.

Gone were the casual, informal days. In their place came early rising (formerly anathema to Hal), road jogging, setting up exercises and controlled dieting. As "sparring partners" the Simses procured Sir Derrick Wernher, A. L. Gotthelf, George Unger, Barbara Collyer and E. M. Goddard.

Curfew rang at 11 P.M. following a couple of hours of shadow bidding after a dry toast dinner.

White turtle-neck sweaters, each bearing a large scarlet letter "S," were ordered for the entire camp, including Duke, the Great Dane.

Culbertson was getting his road work playing one-night stands in the Middle West, Oklahoma, and Texas. For nearly a month he lectured twice a day except when making jumps from one city to another.

In the afternoon he spoke on *Contract Bridge of '35*, and in the evening explained "How I Play It." Culbertson publicity releases pointed out that "with hundreds of questions flung at him, dozens of hands offered for analysis, and the constant reiteration of basic principles and exposition of the latest quirks in bidding, Mr. Culbertson should be 'fit' for the coming contest. He will return to New York primed for the struggle of the systems."

Press agents played up the "grudge" angle between the two men. But the women were pictured as without animosity toward each other.

Physiques were analyzed comparatively as though the contestants were going into an athletic contest instead of a game of cards.

"Happily," said a story from the Culbertson side, "the match will not be decided by weight. When Culbertson enters the battle arena, he will tip the beam at one hundred and twenty-eight pounds. Hal, after strenuous weeks of practice and tournament golf in Florida, still weighs two hundred and seventy-five. Both men are tall, but Sims towers over Culbertson by at least three inches. He is proportionately larger in every way, with a longer arm reach, larger chest measurement and considerably larger head.

"The greater disparity in weights and measurements between the male members of the contending pairs is slightly offset by the diminutive Dorothy Rice Sims, who can claim a featherweight status. Josephine Culbertson is also petite but her height gives her a few additional pounds over Mrs. Sims.

"What value, if any, can be placed upon physical proportions in the forthcoming match cannot be accurately estimated. Strength will be required for such a long grind, and physical condition will play a part, but stature does not necessarily mean stamina."

A legal agreement was drawn up and signed by both Culbertson and Sims, to prevent possible misunderstandings. The contestants were to play 150 rubbers with a time limit of twenty-one days. That called for continuous play, afternoon and evening, every day except Sunday. One day in seven was to be allowed for "relief, recreation and recuperation."

A large side bet was involved. Another money consideration was a five-thousand-dollar forfeit clause to protect each side in case the other quit before the finish. There were many other minor conditions regarding new decks, positions of play, etc.

It was agreed that in the event Dorothy or Josephine was prevented by illness from playing in the number of rubbers specified in the agreement, her partner would have the privilege of choosing a substitute for a period of six subsequent sessions. If at the end of these six sessions, she was still unable to play, the match would be declared forfeited to the other side, provided it led by 8,000 points or more. If it was not leading by 8,000 points, the match would continue with the substitute partner until such time as it would be leading by the specified number of points.

The substitution for Mrs. Culbertson would be a player chosen from the following: Albert H. Morehead, Theodore A. Lightner, and Samuel Fry, Jr. To pinch hit for Mrs. Sims would be Sir Derrick Wernher, B. Jay Becker or John Rau.

Sims nominated Grantland Rice and Waldemar Von Zedwitz for

his corner and Culbertson chose Spotswood Bowers and Walter Beinecke. These men were not only to act as seconds (and thirds) but were to officiate as referees in conjunction with Lieutenant Alfred M. Gruenther.

"For a small fee," said an announcement, "many kibitzers may see in comfort the clash of the colossi, hear them make their bids and watch them play."

THE CONTEST

On MARCH 25 the 150-rubber match got under way. The Sims pair held the lead for the first two days and then lost it for good. At the 50th rubber the Culbertsons led by 3,160 points, at the 100th by 11,210 points and when the ten of spades — the final card — came down in the last hand of the 150th rubber the margin had grown to 16,130 points.

The Sims side held 22 more aces, 50 more kings and 86 more queens than its opponents. But it also had 24 more hands of 4–3–3–3 distribution and Sims complained that he and his wife held few fits.

One of the things the match did seem to settle was whether two married people could weather the storms of 150 rubbers without squabbling. The Culbertsons and Simses exhibited an admirable marital correctness. Sims called his wife, "my sweet," "my angel," "my darling" or just "darling." Culbertson called Mrs. Culbertson "darling" and some-times "Sweetka."

The four contestants sat at the table and talked among themselves just as would any other four bridge players assembled for a casual game at a club or a home. The barbed tongues of the two husbands supplied leading remarks and spicy rejoinders in quantity satisfactory to those who would have been disappointed had the battle been confined to bridge. Culbertson called Sims "Maestro" or "Petronius," and Sims always called Culbertson "Professor." The women called each other "Jo" and "Dorrie."

The terms of endearment with which Sims addressed his wife were delivered through good hands and bad, whether she played well or poorly. But they reached their highest point immediately after the following hand.

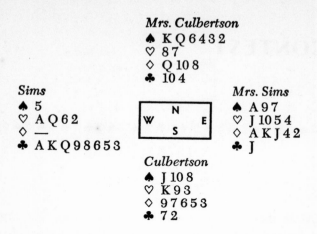

Mrs. Culbertson
♠ K Q 6 4 3 2
♡ 8 7
◇ Q 10 8
♣ 10 4

Sims
♠ 5
♡ A Q 6 2
◇ —
♣ A K Q 9 8 6 5 3

Mrs. Sims
♠ A 9 7
♡ J 10 5 4
◇ A K J 4 2
♣ J

Culbertson
♠ J 10 8
♡ K 9 3
◇ 9 7 6 5 3
♣ 7 2

East dealer.

Neither side vulnerable.

East, Mrs. Sims, psyched an opening bid of one club. Sims jumped to seven clubs and all passed. The contract was made. Sims exclaimed: "My angel!" And then, "My sweet!"

Culbertson was put to the test early when his partner passed out a hand at four diamonds that made six. Culbertson had overcalled Dorothy Sims' opening psychic of a club with two clubs, a bid considered forcing to game. The spectators murmured after the hand was over but Culbertson spoke not a word of reproach.

It was noted, however, that he seemed to be brooding silently about the passed forcing bid through several hands. That is, until his partner carried him to a small slam contract in this deal.

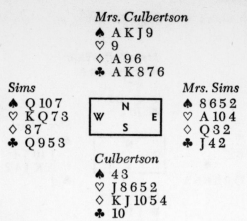

Mrs. Culbertson
♠ A K J 9
♡ 9
◇ A 9 6
♣ A K 8 7 6

Sims
♠ Q 10 7
♡ K Q 7 3
◇ 8 7
♣ Q 9 5 3

Mrs. Sims
♠ 8 6 5 2
♡ A 10 4
◇ Q 3 2
♣ J 4 2

Culbertson
♠ 4 3
♡ J 8 6 5 2
◇ K J 10 5 4
♣ 10

West dealer.
Neither side vulnerable.

The bidding:

WEST	NORTH	EAST	SOUTH
Pass	1 ♣	Pass	1 ♡
Pass	2 ♠	Pass	3 ◇
Pass	4 ◇	Pass	5 ◇
Pass	6 ◇	All pass	

A small club was led and won in dummy. A heart lead set the stage for a cross-ruff.

Culbertson took the club return in dummy, discarding a heart. He ruffed a club in his hand, a heart in dummy, and after cashing the high spades, ruffed a spade.

A heart was ruffed in dummy and a club trumped with the ten of diamonds. The last heart was trumped with the ace in dummy, Dorothy Sims under-ruffing. On the lead of dummy's last spade, Mrs. Sims was forced to ruff and declarer over-ruffed and won the last two tricks.

This was the hand that put the Culbertsons ahead for a lead they were never to relinquish.

◇ ♣ ♡ ♠

The kibitzers got increasingly noisy as the match progressed. But this trouble was as nothing compared with the trouble with feet. During the 110th rubber Culbertson suddenly began shuffling his feet as well as the cards.

"The Simses," he complained, "are getting into my quarter. It's all right for Dorothy's feet to get into my quarter, but not those big feet."

The discussion about feet was still going on when this hand came along!

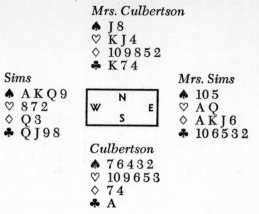

Mrs. Culbertson
♠ J 8
♡ K J 4
♢ 10 9 8 5 2
♣ K 7 4

Sims
♠ A K Q 9
♡ 8 7 2
♢ Q 3
♣ Q J 9 8

Mrs. Sims
♠ 10 5
♡ A Q
♢ A K J 6
♣ 10 6 5 3 2

Culbertson
♠ 7 6 4 3 2
♡ 10 9 6 5 3
♢ 7 4
♣ A

South dealer.
North-South vulnerable.

The bidding:

SOUTH	WEST	NORTH	EAST
Pass	Pass	Pass	1 ♣
Pass	1 ♠	Pass	2 NT
Pass	3 NT	Pass	Pass
Pass			

(How many players today would rebid 2 no trump with the East hand?)

The fourth best heart was led by Culbertson and Dorothy didn't have time enough to establish the club suit. She finessed for the spade jack instead but that failed. Altogether she managed to take two hearts, four diamonds and three spades.

"Could I have made it?" she asked.

"You did make it, my darling," said Sims. "My sweet."

◇ ♣ ♡ ♠

Culbertson was back on the feet business again. He had an usher mark off the quarters with chalk. "If there's anything I don't like it's having other people's feet on top of mine. It's a complex with me."

◇ ♣ ♡ ♠

Two grand slams were bid and made one evening. The first, by the Sims duo, was on the following holdings:

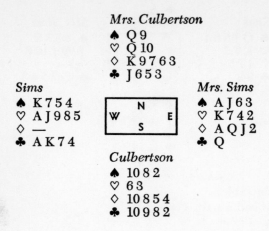

Mrs. Culbertson
♠ Q 9
♡ Q 10
◇ K 9 7 6 3
♣ J 6 5 3

Sims
♠ K 7 5 4
♡ A J 9 8 5
◇ —
♣ A K 7 4

Mrs. Sims
♠ A J 6 3
♡ K 7 4 2
◇ A Q J 2
♣ Q

Culbertson
♠ 10 8 2
♡ 6 3
◇ 10 8 5 4
♣ 10 9 8 2

South dealer.

Both sides vulnerable.

The bidding:

SOUTH	WEST	NORTH	EAST
Pass	1 ♡	Pass	6 ♡
Pass	7 ♡	All pass	

The ten of hearts was led. Sims drew trumps, cashed the queen of clubs and ace of spades and led to the king of spades. He discarded two of dummy's spades on the ace and king of clubs. He ruffed a spade in dummy and now had more than enough tricks for his contract.

Culbertson shook his head and made disapproving noises about the boldness of the bidding. Soon after he got into an argument with Sims about shuffling. Sims, cautioning Dorothy about over-shuffling, explained that "Over three times is the worst way to shuffle. If you shuffle eight times the cards are back the same way they started." Culbertson claimed it was nine times not eight, and the men made a twenty-five-dollar bet that was never put to the test.

The second grand slam was bid by the Culbertsons.

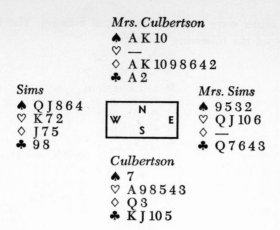

Mrs. Culbertson
♠ A K 10
♡ —
◇ A K 10 9 8 6 4 2
♣ A 2

Sims
♠ Q J 8 6 4
♡ K 7 2
◇ J 7 5
♣ 9 8

Mrs. Sims
♠ 9 5 3 2
♡ Q J 10 6
◇ —
♣ Q 7 6 4 3

Culbertson
♠ 7
♡ A 9 8 5 4 3
◇ Q 3
♣ K J 10 5

East dealer.
Neither side vulnerable.
The Culbertsons had a part score of 60.

The bidding:

EAST	SOUTH	WEST	NORTH
Pass	Pass	Pass	2 ◇
Double	Redouble	2 ♠	3 ♠
Pass	4 ♡	Pass	5 ♣
Double	Redouble	Pass	5 NT
Pass	6 ♣	Pass	6 ◇
Pass	7 ◇	Pass	Pass
Pass			

The hand was a lay-down for thirteen tricks. Culbertson grabbed the radio microphone elatedly and analyzed the bidding for the audience of bridge players listening in on the match.

Mrs. Culbertson's opening two-bid was exactly enough for game but promised a "colossal hand." His redouble unmasked Dorothy's psychic double. His wife's bid of spades indicated the ace or none. Her club bid showed the ace of clubs. When Mrs. Sims doubled that bid he redoubled to place the king of clubs. He couldn't figure out Josephine's five-no-trump call so he "signed off with six clubs" in a loud voice.

"When my wife bid six diamonds I knew she must have nearly a solid suit since I had never assisted them. So I thought maybe my queen of trumps would win an extra trick, and I bid seven diamonds, with fear and trembling, and started to eat my spaghetti, when lo and behold, she makes it."

◇ ♣ ♡ ♠

The most famous deal of the match was the so-called "huddle hand" in which marathon thinking by the Culbertsons precipitated a rhubarb.

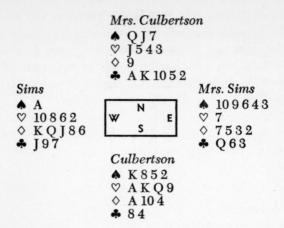

Mrs. Culbertson
♠ Q J 7
♡ J 5 4 3
◇ 9
♣ A K 10 5 2

Sims
♠ A
♡ 10 8 6 2
◇ K Q J 8 6
♣ J 9 7

Mrs. Sims
♠ 10 9 6 4 3
♡ 7
◇ 7 5 3 2
♣ Q 6 3

Culbertson
♠ K 8 5 2
♡ A K Q 9
◇ A 10 4
♣ 8 4

West dealer.
Both sides vulnerable.

The bidding:

West	North	East	South
Pass	Pass	Pass	1 ♡
Pass	2 ♣	Pass	2 ♠
Pass	5 ♡	Pass	Pass
Pass			

Josephine went into a brown study after her partner's rebid of two spades before coming up with her heart jump. She asked the others to forgive her for taking so long and Culbertson quoted Descartes, "Cogit ergo sum."

"Speak English, professor," said Sims.

Sims led the king of diamonds which Culbertson won with the ace. He played the ace and king of trumps and then a spade toward the queen, Sims winning with the ace. The latter returned a diamond which was ruffed in dummy.

Culbertson huddled for five minutes. When Mrs. Sims made a crack about it he complained that his train of thought had been derailed and pondered for five more minutes. Mrs. Sims took a walk and was called back after eight minutes. Culbertson was ready.

"What were you thinking about, professor?" she asked.

"Whether I was going to go down one or two," said Culbertson. Whereupon he led the jack of spades. Sims ruffed and returned another diamond (it wouldn't have mattered what he returned at that point). Declarer was able to set up the club suit with a ruff, draw the last trump and return to the established dummy with the queen of spades. The hand was made.

Sims should have let the jack of spades go, discarding a club on it, and ruffed the queen of spades. This would have given him another trump trick with his ten when Culbertson tried to get out of the dummy. Yet, had Culbertson drawn the first two rounds of trump with the ace and jack, no defense by Sims could have been successful.

Chagrined, Sims squawked vigorously, saying he had been misled by his opponent's remark. But the protest was disallowed by the referees.

After that, the match staggered on to its conclusion in a decrescendo of excitement.

Section 2

Six Views on Bridge

What people see in contract has been the subject of inquiry and discussion ever since the game came into vogue. Presented here are some views and a debate. Naturally, the material is heavily weighted in favor of the game.

Bridge   BY WEBSTER

PUREST OF PLEASURES: CONTRACT

by ELMER DAVIS

◇ ♣ ♡ ♠ ◇ ♣ ♡ ♠ ◇ ♣ ♡ ♠ ◇ ♣ ♡ ♠ ◇ ♣ ♡ ♠ ◇ ♣ ♡ ♠ ◇ ♣ ♡ ♠ ◇ ♣ ♡ ♠

IT WAS SUGGESTED years ago that the average American was behaving very sensibly during the depression in trying to have as good a time as possible, as cheaply as possible, while the men of light and leading were finding a way out. That was during the vogue of miniature golf, a sport which has since fallen almost as low in public esteem as have the men of light and leading. But it is still good sense to have a good time if you can; when a man whose income is going down while his taxes are going up announces that he is tired of work and has determined to devote himself to the pursuit of pleasure, there is nothing much you can say to him but "Try to find it."

The following remarks are an advertisement for the people who find it at what is inaccurately termed the bridge table.

I am an average player (at least I hope so; some of my partners might challenge that claim), and what is said here applies to average players— not to the expert or to the enthusiastic incompetents who are as much of an obstruction to the game as is a hay wagon to boulevard traffic. In our own estimation, we average players are the salt of the earth; for we play the game well enough to have some understanding of it and some pride in it, and still not so well that our love of the pastime can ever be contaminated by any sordid hope of gain.

From *Harper's* Magazine, 1932. Used by permission of the author.

Contract requires no costly equipment; you do not have to go out in the country to play it; you are playing against other people, not against some theoretical standard of perfection, so if you stay in your own class you will suffer no more than an occasional moderate and salutary humiliation. This, I am convinced, is the first and great commandment for those who want to enjoy contract—stay in your own class. It will spare you mental anguish and it will save you money.

To say that you cannot enjoy a bridge game unless there is money on it is about as reasonable as saying that you cannot get interested in a woman unless she has a husband who might shoot you. If you really want the woman you will need no such irrelevant and superogatory stimulation; and if you really like the game you will play it as well as you can, whether there is any money up or not. Contract without a stake can be just as good as if you were playing for a dollar a point. However, there are people who feel otherwise—so many of them that if you refuse to play for money you will be considerably restricted in your opportunities to play at all. But stay in your own class and you will find that—since the law of averages can be counted on to give you a fairly even break in the cards from one year's end to another—your game will just about pay its way.

Contract has further attractions for the reflective. Plato held that smell was the purest of the sensual pleasures because it involved no appeasement of pre-existent pain. The joys of the table derive some of their keenness from the preceding pangs of hunger; but no man ever feels himself starving for agreeable odors. "The pleasures of smell spring up suddenly and present themselves in full force to a man who was not previously conscious of any suffering; and when they have vanished they leave no pain behind." Accordingly they are a hundred percent net profit, and so are the pleasures of contract. The bridge player does not say, "When shall I awake? I will seek it yet again." He may be keenly aware of his lack of love or lack of money, but he does not grow jittery because there is no card game going on. He gives himself over to other preoccupations; and when somebody whispers to him, "Will you make a fourth?" the pleasures of the card table spring up suddenly and present themselves in full force to a man who was not previously conscious of any suffering.

Another merit of the game: as Lord Melbourne might have said, there is no damned nonsense of utility about it. You cannot pretend that it is a form of service; golfers who are too puritanical to admit that they play golf because they like it will discourse at length upon its hygienic, cultural, and social benefits; but dealing the cards is no great exercise, and the bridge table is no place to meet your customers and talk business while you play. (Unless, of course, you enjoy conversational bridge; in which case you had better stop reading this article, and may consider yourself conspued by its author.) There is no good excuse for playing contract except the pleasure you get out of it.

Some attempt has been made to give the game an intellectual snob value; Mr. Culbertson's *Bridge World,* for instance, bursts into the following rhapsody: "If bridge makes strange bedfellows, it is because the pleasures of the intellect are considered superior. Our common meeting ground is the play of intellect in its purest symbolic form." But this is hooey, and a man so shrewd as Culbertson must know it. To him and experts of his class the game does indeed present recondite mathematical-metaphysical beauties for the contemplation of the pure intellect; but these are as far beyond the grasp of the average player as are the high joys of Jeans or Einstein. To play good bridge calls for intellect, but a specialized type of intellect adapted to playing bridge; it is no more a sign of the general brain power flatteringly imputed by the above quotation than is skill at chess. Napoleon was a notably bad chess player; which is a reflection on chess, not a reflection on Napoleon. If bridge brains were good for anything but bridge, you might expect this nation to be ruled by its tournament stars. I cannot recall that any of them has been conspicuously successful at anything but bridge.

Another expert, Mr. Shepard Barclay, is less flattering to his public but more encouraging: "Bridge is not half so hard to learn as some people fear." Maybe not, but it is a good deal harder to learn than some other people realize. The experts, no doubt, would like to have it both ways: to play well is a proof of intellectual power, yet anybody who buys the right book and applies himself to the right system can learn to play well— a new mode of purveying exclusiveness to the masses. It is true that you cannot play good bridge without a bridge education any more than you can practice good law without a legal education; but mere reading of books and attendance at lectures can no more make a first-rate bridge player than it can make an Untermeyer or a Darrow. I believe that anybody of moderate intelligence can by diligent application become a sound bidder; but unless some card sense is born in you, you will never be a really good player, even after twenty-five years of practice. *Crede experto.*

The mere existence of contract, and of its predecessors bridge and auction, is proof of this. They are all variants of whist, and they successively supplanted it in favor because they are easier than whist. Any good whist player will be a good contract player when he has mastered the elements of bidding; but millions of people who pass as good contract players because they bid their hands well and play them well (after the bidding has located most of the key cards) would be quite beyond their depth at whist, where the trump depends on chance and the location of the cards has to be inferred from the play.

As a purely intellectual exercise the play in contract is far inferior to that in whist; you know too much before the first card is led. But the bidding imports an intellectual exercise of quite another order which is almost as good a discipline in applied psychology as poker. If contract has surpassed the vogue of auction, bringing new recruits to the card table and rekindling the enthusiasm of some of us who had begun to find auction something of a bore, it is because it is a better game, with far more action and far more suspense. In auction a good hand is irresistible; in contract it may be only an enticement to disaster unless you bid it right. No doubt the mere change in scoring has impressed some people with the conviction that contract is more of a game. Writing before the present contract scoring had altogether supplanted the auction values, R. F. Foster observed that the stake per point was reduced as the score was increased; "why it would not be just as simple to advance the stakes and keep to the already well-established values is not explained." Here speaks the austere aristocrat; the more practical Barclay provides the explanation. "The higher score appeals to the childish attribute that remains with all adults who are wise enough to avoid growing up completely." However wise such avoidance may be, plenty of adults have managed it with great success; they feel that they are in fast company when they play a game at which you can go down a couple of thousand points on a single hand.

Perhaps contract has certain other advantages peculiarly adapted to these times. Its values, and its interest, are detached, abstracted from reality, from all the heterogeneous and too often unpleasant phenomena of everyday living. I know of no mental exercise which gives so complete an escape from the things you want to escape from. Yet some of its principles have a timely application; in auction you might bid a little and win a great deal, as you could in the empire-building America of the nineteenth century; but in contract you must bid and work for everything you get and risk a disastrous penalty for miscalculation, as entrepreneurs are likely to do in the frontierless and more static America of the future. Vulnerability—the principle that the higher you have risen the more a mistake will cost you—is a concept easily grasped by the American public, which has so often seen the career of a distinguished man ruined by a private peccadillo which would be overlooked in a person of less prominence. (It could be wished that more of our distinguished men might be ruined by their public peccadillos, by their behavior in office.) And finally, in an age of confusion and multiplicity, of an all too visible increase in what the physicists call the random element in the universe, there is a nostalgic charm about a game in which for a little while you devote yourself to a fixed and precise objective.

But all this may be fanciful. The great indubitable reason for the popularity of contract is its merit; more than any other card game it approaches the ideal balance between chance and skill. And the secondary and corollary reason is that more talent has been devoted to exploiting it professionally than was ever before expended on any card game.

But room must be made for the objections of the *advocatus diaboli*. Some of the people who do not like bridge dislike it with a quite inexplicable frenzy. They will tell you that it saps the brain power, if any, of the individual, and disrupts the household by its contentions; it sows discord between wife and husband, between friend and friend; it is nothing less than the terminator of delights and the separator of companions.

Well, most of the complaints about bridge boil down to this, that it is sometimes played by the wrong people. Too much liquor brings out your true nature, whatever that may be; and so does a bad bid, a disastrous take-out, a stupid play by your partner. People who crack under such a strain would crack under whatever strain might be imposed upon them, and I do not see that bridge can be blamed for it. The persons who feel it necessary to conclude each hand with a magisterial correction of their partners (and perhaps their opponents as well) have no place at the bridge table, or anywhere else where they might come into contact with civilized beings; and I do not know that they are more frequently found or more offensively conspicuous at the card table than in some other departments of life.

"Never reproach your partner," says Culbertson, "if there be the slightest thing for which you can reproach yourself." (On the other hand, do not reproach yourself if you think it would give undue encouragement to your partner's baser instincts.) This is not only Christian charity but good sense; the *practical* attitude toward your partner, Culbertson pursues, should be that of a "philosophical, sincere, and sympathetic friend." You share each other's joys, each other's burdens bear; and often for each other flows the sympathizing tear. "Partner, however weak, must feel that you sincerely respect his intelligence and efforts." And if this is odious pretense, if he is so weak that nobody could sincerely respect him — why, that is your fault for not choosing your company. First and foremost, stay in your own class.

You can't always do that when you go out for a social evening and find yourself in an unforeseen bridge game? No; but there is no law requiring a man who can play bridge to play it whenever he is invited. If you play with people you never met before you cannot complain when your partner continually talks over her shoulder to people across the room about her latest round-the-world cruise, meanwhile missing a couple of finesses and overlooking a discard or two. Of course, if you tell the hostess you don't play, and some other guest pipes up with "But you do; I've played with you!" — why, then you are trapped, and may as well resign yourself to whatever fortune fate sends you. But that is no peculiar fault of bridge; it may happen just as well to a man who pretends he doesn't dance because he is alarmed by the weight of his prospective partners. Social life can be made tolerable only by taking a firm stand on such matters; and if indignant hostesses resolve that they will never invite you again, you can always stay at home and read a book.

As for domestic discord, bridge never broke up a home that was not ripe for disruption anyway. If your wife is a very much better player than you, or a very much worse player, you had better not play with her; but you had better not play with anybody else who is very much better or very much worse. Playing against a married couple I knew but slightly, I was shocked by their recriminations; and when I was dummy I suggested to the proprietor of the restaurant where we were playing that maybe the game had better be broken off before shots were fired. "Oh, that don't mean nothing with them two," he assured me. "They love each other like you don't see it any more." Evidently their emotional margin was so wide that they could do without philosophical and sympathetic friendship.

As to the vexed question of bisexual bridge in general, I think that men who say they don't like to play with women are putting the argument on the wrong basis. The point is that you get full value out of a bridge game only when it is a bridge game and nothing else; to play it well requires concentration, and if you are not going to play it well there is no point in playing it at all.

There remains to be answered the weighty criticisms of a couple of psychologists . . . "Bridge may develop brains," said Professor Charles Gray Shaw of New York University, "but the quality of the brains developed is not worth cultivating." Still harsher was Professor Harold Swenson of Chicago: "You couldn't drag a real thinker to the bridge table with a team of horses."

If this means anything except that a couple of professors were picking up crumbs of publicity . . . it means that Professor Swenson's definition of a real thinker is a man who couldn't be dragged to the bridge table by a team of horses. By any other definition he is demonstrably wrong. As for Professor Shaw, he is right this far — that brains specifically developed by bridge are good for nothing much but bridge; but not so much can be said for his further statement that "the habitual bridge player lacks adequate emotional power and must play to stimulate his nerves."

If this, in turn, means that bridge is the refuge of men who do not like or are not pleasing to men, the only answer it calls for is a derisive snort. Confessing that I personally am one who prefers *Götterdämmerung* to *Tristan,* I could cite some of the best bridge players I ever met, of both sexes, who have plenty of emotional power and do not go to the card table when they want their nerves stimulated. Possibly Professor Shaw's intention was more general; in which case his remarks may be true of some bridge players. Some years ago I was in one of the minor European monarchies; and the day I left the capital a local newspaperman said to me, "Can't you stay over till tomorrow? We have a date to go up to the Palace and play bridge with the King." Somewhat flustered, I said that I could not aspire to such an honor. "Oh, it's no particular honor," he told me. "He gets lonesome up there at the Palace; the Dictator won't let him do any work, and he's always glad when somebody will come up to play bridge with him."

Bridge may be a needed stimulus to the nerves of unemployed royalty; but for us ordinary players its stimulation is intellectual, not emotional, even if the intellect it stimulates is of a specialized and unprofitable type. A philosopher, says Aldous Huxley, is a man who dreams of fewer things than there are in heaven and earth; and it is evident that Professor Shaw has never perceived the real attraction of bridge. Choose your company — people who play not much better than you do and not much worse; people who sit down at the bridge table to play bridge, not to talk about irrelevancies — and you will find yourself transported into another world. The agitations and exacerbations of everyday life drop away from you; for a while you dwell in a remote and austere realm of the pure intellect, uncontaminated by any practical applications; and as your game improves you may catch glimpses of some of these mathematical beauties of sequence, distribution, and arrangement such as perhaps the Absolute perceives when it contemplates Itself.

Bridge   BY WEBSTER

THE PSYCHOANALYSIS TREATMENT ——

THE DOCTOR
LOOKS AT CONTRACT

by DR. HAROLD HAYS

THE SERIOUS CONTRACT PLAYER presents a paradox in human nature. During the play, he has to go through a set of mental gymnastics which are far more difficult than learning to make backward somersaults. Ever on the alert to make the most of his play, he is combusting brain power more rapidly than a speed boat uses ethyl gasoline. If he were to indulge in any other mental activity at the same rate of energy and speed, he would be so exhausted that he wouldn't be fit for anything but a rest cure sanitarium. But it is not so with the contract player. No sooner does he finish his game, no sooner is he allowed mental relaxation, than he immediately becomes a normal human being or else, if he is a business or professional man, he emerges from the bridge room with a mind ready to work on his everyday problems, no worse for the wear and tear.

I am not taking into consideration the professional contract player who is at the game morning, noon and night. I marvel at those experts who will play bridge from eight at night until three in the morning, discuss the interesting hands until four, go home and lay the hands on the table until five and readily fall asleep at six. They are human prodigies.

I am more interested in average good players. Some are men; some are women. Some of the men play with their wives; some never do. Some men play with women who might have become their wives if they hadn't

Reprinted by permission of *The Bridge World*, New York. A. Moyse, Jr., publisher.

been in bridge games together as partners. In spite of all the arguments, discussions, vituperations, tearing of hair, weeping and so on, there are few serious after-effects. Except for a few "cats" among the women and a few men with superiority complexes who always blame their partners for every mistake, they forget by the next morning.

Most of the bridge players I know are pretty decent people; every one of them is successful in his chosen field; all of them are normal human beings and react normally to external irritants — except at the bridge table.

From the doctor's point of view, contract bridge is the greatest outlet for excess nervous energy that one has at hand. There are thousands of people who are "bottled up," who are full of nervous explosive material which is in constant turmoil. Many such individuals can let off steam by reading an exciting detective story; others must get rid of this energy in some other way, and contract is the solution.

Few people realize that the sympathetic nervous system is responsible for many of the mental and physical maladjustments in life. This system is not always under voluntary control. Some outlet for excess nervous energy must be supplied. It may happen that this excess nervous energy may be dissipated by some external excitant.

The strain of doing the same thing all the time, day in and day out, leads to dry rot. Most people need an excitant. Often patients ask me where they should go to convalesce from an illness. Shall it be a quiet place or a place where they can indulge in various mental and physical stimulants? My advice depends upon the individual. But in nine cases out of ten, I find that patients recuperate more quickly if they go to a place where their minds can be occupied. Doctors recommend all kinds of games, including contract, to get the patient back to his normal self.

Another point of interest to the doctor is the various complexes which restrain or exalt the person who, on the surface, leads a normal life. The fear complex is inherent in many an individual. Such a type loses his morale if he is criticized by a supposedly better player, if he fails in a finesse or if he is set an unusual number of tricks. A set of fourteen hundred points is a major disaster to him. This fear complex not only exhibits itself in his bridge game but is a definite part of his mental mechanism. As soon as he gets used to bridge disasters he realizes that this fear is ridiculous and, sooner or later, his timidity in other directions leaves him.

These remarks should dissipate once and for all the reflection of the college professor (who probably never played contract) that bridge players are morons and are beneath the rest of humanity in intelligence and common sense. Such critics are like the person who, because he himself doesn't like to drink, condemns the man who goes into a saloon. Not liking liquor, he can't understand why anybody else likes it. My own observation is that there are no more sane people in the world than those who play contract for a pastime and who get a positive mental stimulation out of the game and who, as a rule, sleep soundly after playing. Probably less sleeping medicine is taken by bridge players than by any other class of people — because, for a a few hours at least, their minds have been taken off their everyday cares and worries. I should like to bring this point up for argument to the neurologists, the psychiatrists and the psychoanalysts and hear what they have to say. I venture that, proportionately speaking, they have fewer bridge players among their patients than any other class. Incidentally, I know a number of these brain and nerve specialists who are darn good contract players.

HOW I LIKE TO PLAY BRIDGE

by W. SOMERSET MAUGHAM

◇♣♡♠◇♣♡♠◇♣♡♠◇♣♡♠◇♣♡♠◇♣♡♠◇♣♡♠◇♣♡♠

I AM NOT at all the proper person to write an article on bridge, for I am an indifferent player and my chief asset as a partner is that I never have thought myself anything else. Nor would it ever have occurred to me to embark on such an undertaking if Charles Goren hadn't asked me to write an introduction to a book on bidding that he was about to publish. Everyone knows that Charles Goren is one of the greatest bridge players in the world, and I accepted his suggestion with alacrity. It was a great compliment he paid me, and I felt proud as a lieutenant might feel if he were bidden by his admiral to lead the flagship into battle. But having a practical side to an otherwise idealistic nature, I told him I thought I should let him know at once what my terms were. He paled. They were that he should dine and play bridge with me. He heaved a sigh of relief and accepted. Of course I knew I should lose my money, but I was certain that the fun it would be must make whatever it cost well worth it. I have played only half a dozen times with life masters and it is rash to generalize on such slight experience, but it has seemed to me that they are easier to play with than players of the second or third class, for you know they have a good reason for doing what they do, and when they make a bid, mean what they say. Bridge is a much more difficult game when one has to deal with players who trust their hunches rather than their common sense and allow their wishes to warp their judgment. My story has a happy ending. On that momentous evening I held all the aces and kings and rose from the table the only winner.

From *Good Housekeeping* Magazine, 1944. Reprinted by permission of A. P. Watt & Son, London.

When, then, I came to read Charles Goren's *Standard Book on Bidding* in order to write my introduction, I felt I could never hope to remember all the rules it gave and that to try to do so would only confuse me. But presently it dawned upon me that very few of them, not more than half a dozen perhaps, were obligatory — rules which must be followed as you follow those of any game — and that the rest depended on horse sense, so that if you had that and were prepared to abide by it, you need not clutter up your brain with any great number of precepts. The moral was clear: if you have a cool head, the ability to put two and two together and get the right answer, and if you will tell the exact truth about your hand, you will be a useful partner and a formidable opponent.

But having finished my pieces, I found that I had various things to say about bridge which I had not had occasion to say. I am going to say them now.

The first thing I want to do is to remonstrate with the people who don't play bridge. They are apt to be hoity-toity with those of us who do and tell us they can't understand how presumably intelligent persons can waste their time on such an idle pastime. That is stuff and nonsense. Everyone has a certain amount of leisure and everyone needs distraction, and when you come to inquire of these supercilious folk how they prefer to occupy their leisure and in what they seek their distraction, the chances are that they will say in conversation. The conversationalist needs an audience, and it is true that the bridge table robs him of it. No wonder he is bitter. But the fact is that few people can talk entertainingly for three or four hours at a time. It needs gifts that few of us possess, and even the most brilliant talker grows tedious if he goes on too long; and when, as he is apt to do, he monopolizes the conversation, he is intolerable. I dare say it profits the soul more to read great literature than to play bridge, but not many of us are prepared to spend our leisure in that improving pursuit. When we can't get a game of bridge, we are more likely to take up a detective story. I have read hundreds of them myself, but I cannot put my hand on my heart and say that I am conscious of receiving more spiritual benefit from reading the latest whodunit than from playing half a dozen hard-fought rubbers.

No, let the carping carp, they don't know what they miss. If I had my way, I would have children taught bridge as a matter of course, just as they are taught dancing. In the end it will be more useful to them, for you cannot with seemliness continue to dance when you are bald and pot-bellied; nor, for the matter of that, can you with satisfaction to yourself or pleasure to your partners continue to play tennis or golf when you are past middle age; but you can play bridge as long as you can sit up at a table and tell one card from another. In fact, when all else fails — sport, love, ambition — bridge remains a solace and an entertainment.

But though I think everybody should learn bridge, I do not think everybody should play it. Not lessons, books, or practice will make players of those who have no card sense. These unfortunate creatures must look upon it as a defect of nature, like tone deafness or color blindness, and resign themselves to solitaire, crossword puzzles, or what not.

◇ ♣ ♡ ♠

Bridge is the most entertaining and intelligent card game the wit of man has so far devised, and I deplore the fact that so many people go out of their way to make it a bore. There are the people who, after a hand has been played, will tell you all the thirteen cards they held. Well, you'd seen them played, so you know; but even if you didn't, why should they suppose you care? Then there are the people who during the deal or when you're sorting your cards start to tell you about Aunt Annie's operation or the trouble they're having with decorators in their new apartment. There is no stopping them.

"One heart," you say.

They take no notice.

"My dear, I've had three cooks in the last two weeks and not one of them could boil an egg."

"One heart," you repeat.

"Well, I'll tell you what happened to me," says your partner. "I got a couple. They drove up in their car, looked at the house, and didn't even come in. They just drove away, and I was expecting eight people to lunch on Sunday."

"One heart," you say.

"You know that Betty's got a new beau?" the player on your right puts in.

"Oh, you mean Harry," replies the player on your left. "I've known that for months. She always has liked heels."

Just to get a little attention, you have a mind to say, "Seven no trumps," but of course it might be expensive and your partner wouldn't be sympathetic, so you meekly repeat, "One heart."

But this is nothing compared with the post-mortem. It is the commonest nuisance that besets the game. It is not only boring, but useless, for if you cannot see a mistake when you have made it, no argument will convince you of your error; and if you do see it, the probability is that your vanity will prevent you from acknowledging it; so the critic may just as well hold his peace and deal the next hand. It is a very good rule, when your partner points out a mistake you have made, to agree with him promptly and when on the next hand he lets you down fourteen hundred by grossly overcalling, to tell him cheerfully not to give it another thought. Of such, you will say, is the Kingdom of Heaven, and I heartily agree.

◇ ♣ ♡ ♠

From time to time I have read books on bridge, profiting by them as much as it was in my sinful nature to do, and I have been surprised that they lay no more stress than they do on the advantage it is to you to find out as quickly as you can something of the nature of the persons you are playing with. I had a friend once who held the opinion that you could tell the character of people by the way they played. I think he was generalizing on the single instance of himself. He played a bold, generous, and dashing game, and he liked to think of himself as a dashing, generous, and bold fellow. He was a picture dealer and by the proper exercise of the qualities on which he prided himself succeeded for many years in selling many second-rate old masters to the rich at fantastic prices. Well, I don't know whether there was much truth in this notion, but I'm pretty sure it is a distinct help if you can guess the peculiarities of your partners and opponents with accuracy. There is the diffident player who consistently undercalls, the aggressive player who as consistently overcalls; there is the cautious player who follows the rule when it is obvious that the rule doesn't apply; there is the sly player who thinks you are such a fool he can fox you every time. All these you can size up pretty quickly and deal with according to their idiosyncrasies. But there is one player whom I have never learned how to cope with and that is the player who never stops to consider that you also hold thirteen cards; he will ignore your bids, he will pay no attention to your warnings, come hell or high water he will take command of the hand, and when he has been doubled and gone down several tricks, he'll ascribe it to nothing but bad luck. You are fortunate if he doesn't smile blandly and say, "Well, I think it was worth it, partner." I am still looking for the book that will show me how to deal with him. Shooting is too quick and too painless, and besides, there might not be another fourth available.

As I look now at what I have written, it seems to me that the essentials for playing a good game of bridge are to be truthful, clearheaded, and considerate, prudent but not averse to taking a risk, and not to cry over spilt milk. And incidentally those are perhaps also the essentials for playing the more important game of life.

ON PLAYING BRIDGE

by HENRY C. LINK, *Psychologist*

◇ ♣ ♡ ♠ ◇ ♣ ♡ ♠ ◇ ♣ ♡ ♠ ◇ ♣ ♡ ♠ ◇ ♣ ♡ ♠ ◇ ♣ ♡ ♠ ◇ ♣ ♡ ♠ ◇ ♣ ♡ ♠

PEOPLE have said to me: "No, I don't play bridge. I consider it a waste of time." Others have said: "Yes, I play bridge, but I hate to play with people who take it seriously." Yet I have recommended to hundreds of clients that they learn to play bridge or that they take it more seriously, on the ground that bridge is one of the most fruitful disciplines in acquiring unselfish habits and desirable personality traits.

The person who does not like to play bridge seriously is one who doesn't like to be reproved if he trumps his partner's ace, ignores his partner's discard, fails to return his partner's lead, or forgets what is trumps. As one of four players, three of whom have acquired habits of paying attention to the bidding and one another's playing behavior, the casual player is likely to say such things as: "Oh, is it my turn to bid?" or, "I didn't hear what the bidding was"; or when the bidding is completed, "Now what is trumps?" When he picks up his hand he may say: "Let's have a new deal, this hand is terrible," and during play his thoughtless remarks will reveal the position of cards which will give the opposing pair unearned tricks.

In short, such a person is thoroughly selfish in his disregard for the pleasure of three people. He lacks the habits, and sometimes even the desire, of paying strict attention to the acts and remarks of his co-players. He insults them by saying in effect: Your concentration and pleasure in this game is silly. Why don't you take it lightly as I do? A person who

From *The Return to Religion* by Henry C. Link, The Macmillan Company, New York. Reprinted by permission.

lacks the sensitive habits of tact or considerateness in bridge probably lacks them in other social activities. If he plays bridge at all, he should take it at least as seriously as the people with whom he is likely to play.

Learning bridge involves the acquisition of a whole collection of definite extrovert habits — I have counted fifty-three and there are more — of paying attention to other people and their acts. I have recommended the game particularly to introverts lacking in social charm and effective social techniques. If such a person learns to play a fair game of bridge, it means first of all the concentration of his mind on something outside himself, something that gives many other people considerable pleasure. Being able to play the game gives him a wider opportunity to meet people on a common ground. If his game is acceptable, the fact that he is not a brilliant conversationalist will not be so embarrassing to him. In such favorable circumstances, the acquisition of collateral social graces is made easier. I hold no brief for those who consider bridge a matter of life and death, or for those to whom bridge is an end in itself. But as a discipline in unselfish social habits and as a tonic for an able intellect, it ranks high in the category of worthwhile human activities.

Children should be taught to play bridge at an early age. They may not like it. The process may involve compulsion. A father and mother, asking their two children to sit down to a game with them, may be met by the remark: "I want to listen to the radio." When this issue has been settled, the children may play in a spirit of silliness, and with a deliberate lack of attention or cooperation. Soon they will want to stop. Then it behooves the parents to say: "If you will give the next four hands your complete attention, you may stop. If not, we shall play another four hands."

A year later, one of the children may come home from an evening's visit at a friend's house and say: "What do you think? We played bridge and my partner and I made a grand slam." From being an effort and a bore, bridge has become a pleasure, a step in the building of a more effective personality, an achievement in the techniques of social cooperation — indeed a step in the direction of greater peace and harmony among the nations. Few human activities require such meticulous attention to the rules of good behavior as does bridge.

In 1937 when bridge was still in the fad stage the game could touch off such a debate as the following.

SHOULD WE ABOLISH BRIDGE? YESSIR!

by SILAS BENT

◇♣♡♠◇♣♡♠◇♣♡♠◇♣♡♠◇♣♡♠◇♣♡♠◇♣♡♠◇♣♡♠◇♣♡♠

LET ME CONFESS at the outset that I am a bridge addict. I am virtually illiterate, however, never having read a book about the game, even though a volume on psychic bidding was once presented to me. My acquaintance with trick values, "approach-forcing," the pitfalls of no trump, the conventions and the various "systems" has come by word of mouth or by painful experience at the card table. It may be argued, therefore, that I am not a fair judge.

To offset that argument, let me present on behalf of the sport such merits as I can discern in it. In its industrial aspect there is a good deal to be said for it. Hundreds of thousands of teachers of the craft earn a livelihood, either wholly or in part, but it is impossible to obtain any fair estimate because a large number communicate their cunning to amateurs or backward players as an avocation, "out of hours."

Contract bridge has given an immense impetus to the manufacture of score pads, bridge furniture, trophies, prizes, books.

From *The Rotarian Magazine,* 1937. Reprinted by permission.

Even the beautician has profited. Bridge has made the player, man or woman, finger-conscious as never before, and has multiplied manicures. Where will one see so many scarlet fingernails as at the bridge table? In many correlative ways, contract bridge has improved business. It deserves to rank with air-conditioning as an important and noteworthy industry.

As an industry, then, rather than as a diversion, contract bridge has won its spurs. I recall that Edgar Allan Poe, in *The Murders in the Rue Morgue,* spoke of whist, grandfather of contract, as an encouragement of certain intuitive and deductive processes. "From the manner of gathering up a trick," he wrote of the player, "he judges whether the person taking it can make another in the same suit. He may recognize what is played as a feint by the air with which it is thrown upon the table. A casual or inadvertent word, the variation of face as the play progresses — embarrassment, hesitation, eagerness, trepidation — all afford indications of the true state of affairs." Poe wrote of whist, that is, as though it inculcated some of the virtues of draw poker. I venture to say that Grandchild Bridge does nothing of the sort. Contract bridge players make certain mathematical calculations to determine what hands the other players hold, and they use the psychic bid much as the poker player uses the bluff; and they must be capable of at least as much concentration as the poker player. But as to the analytical processes which Poe described, players are mostly innocent of them.

Draw poker, now, affords a form of moral discipline. The man who turns away from the fair face of a pair of sevens, when a jack pot has been opened, exercises an admirable self-restraint. The man who cannot be bullied into laying down a high hand has the stuff of heroes. But I do not find these character-building tests operative at the contract bridge table. To the contrary, I find a docile obedience to conventions, a lack of that daring and initiative which poker encourages, and a tendency to displays of ill temper, both with partners and opponents, such as never disgraced, so far as I know, any poker game. If there were card "sharks" and cheats at the poker table, we may find them also at the bridge table. And if in the days of the wild and woolly West there were occasional poker killings, we find those today also. Of the two pastimes, poker, which has been much the more berated by the clergy and the Godfearing generally, seems to me much the more meritorious.

Yet poker never became a national institution such as contract bridge is today. One never heard of poker tournaments, and the daily press did not make a practice of devoting a department to the game, giving much more space to it than to the weather and almost as much as to editorials.

Culbertson boasted that he popularized contract bridge and his books by appealing to the sex instinct and to fear. Despite his boasts about his intellectual heft he has never, so far as I can find, tried to advance the game as improving the mind, the faculties of concentration and deduction, or the character. Sex and fear, all of us will agree, are not among the noblest qualities to which to appeal in the promotion of any enterprise, whether of amusement or industry.

Professor Josephine Rathbone of Columbia University has pointed out the unhealthful effects of prolonged and frequent bridge playing. Sitting with the shoulders hunched, tensely and stiffly, with the head seldom moving freely, usually in a smoke-laden atmosphere, for hours at a stretch, obviously is not conducive to the best physical results. Professor Rathbone believes it superinduces, in some cases, organic heart trouble. An acquaintance of mine, who is subject to angina pectoris— not caused, let me hasten to say, by playing cards — was forbidden for a long period by his physician to play contract bridge, and even now is permitted to play only a few rubbers in an evening.

It is true enough that there have been some notable figures in the bridge world who have lived to ripe old age. Some of them are still living, and it must not be supposed that Professor Rathbone meant to consign all the victims of the game to an early grave.

But her strictures seem to me well grounded in the main. The effect of this game on blood pressure and the heart must be obvious, for it is even more exciting than poker, almost as exciting as alcohol when taken as a beverage. Some of my friends have told me that they cannot get to sleep after a hard bout at bridge.

Aside from these deleterious factors, bridge is vulgar because it puts a positive damper on conversation, one of the amenities hard put to it for survival in the United States even without this handicap; and because it is unsportsmanlike. The man who has bid and made a game in a minor suit unblushingly and as a matter of course rubs it in on opponents who had the cards for a game declaration in a major suit. The player who has achieved a slam is so filled with self-aggrandizement that his boasts continue, between hands, for perhaps half an hour. The diversion is vulgar because it kills time which might better be devoted to a good magazine or a good book or good music, and in other ways is inimical to the graces of life.

And it is vindictive, if for no other reason, because such devices as the "squeeze" and the "end-play" are related in their nature to the rack and the thumbscrew. Competition is a form of warfare, which by militarists may be regarded as good sport, but which is manslaughter in one of its cruelest forms; and nowhere is the spirit of devastating competition more fiercely aroused than in contract bridge. Husbands and wives quarrel, families are sundered, because of mistaken bidding or the fall of the cards. The fact that a king is on the wrong side of the board, and that a finesse therefore fails, may precipitate a tempest. The fact that a good card was not employed by the declarer to slough the last of a losing suit may bring ignominy, and even more disastrous results, upon him.

When The Four Aces, by common consent the best bridge players in the United States, excommunicated Michael T. Gottlieb from their sacred company and from their leadership, the three who combined against him adopted much the air of a Nero throwing a gladiator to the lions. These four had been as inseparable as the Musketeers in Dumas' immortal story. They had developed their own bidding system and had published a book together. But the Athos of their group ventured to develop "certain unsound bidding theories," so that Porthos, Aramis, and D'Artagnan combined to depose him; and they did it with the severity of a Soviet casting a Bukharin into outer darkness. Such is the kindliness and good will inspired by bridge.

Contract bridge has introduced to the language a new terminology and a new slang. It has popularized at least one German word, *kibitzer*. The kibitzer illustrates afresh the predilection of the American public for what has been called "spectatoritis," a disease of looking on instead of participating in events.

At most major bridge tournaments the doors are locked against these creatures, each team plays in a separate room amid a sepulchral silence, broken only in low-spoken bids and responses, and the god of chance operates in privacy. But at the Asbury Park convention when seven national titles were to be decided, announcements were broadcast through a loud-speaker, all the players in action assembled in one hall, boisterous conversation was heard on every side, and the kibitzer was in his glory. The occasion monopolized as much public attention as a disastrous concurrent drouth in the Midwest, and more interest than the Presidential campaign then getting into its stride.

Now, it must be admitted that there is a certain sameness about a long-continued drouth, and an iteration in reports from the stricken areas, varied only when new measures of relief are proposed, whereas there are more than six hundred billion possible bridge hands in every deck of cards, affording an almost inconceivable diversity. And it must be admitted that the game of politics is so intricate that the average citizen has much less chance of learning its ins and outs than he has of mastering the one-over-one system of bidding.

One reason we have so many absentees from the polls and so little intensity of interest in campaigns is that the novice, unable to under-stand the complexities of politics, usually lets the bosses take the reins. Yet these are no reasons for arguing that contract bridge is more im-portant to the public than the drouth which touches the pocketbook and should touch the sympathy of every one of us; or that it is better entitled to public interest than politics, which is the lifeblood of a republic.

The truth is that contract bridge, as I see it, has brought a distortion of values and a maladjustment of the national life which needs to be remedied. Our best hope, I think, is that the fad will cure itself, or kill itself.

SHOULD WE ABOLISH BRIDGE?
NO—NEVER!

by CLINTON P. ANDERSON
Past President, Rotary International

◇ ♣ ♡ ♠ ◇ ♣ ♡ ♠ ◇ ♣ ♡ ♠ ◇ ♣ ♡ ♠ ◇ ♣ ♡ ♠ ◇ ♣ ♡ ♠ ◇ ♣ ♡ ♠ ◇ ♣ ♡ ♠

IF THE CARTOONIST conception may be believed, contract bridge is the great American home wrecker. Night after night, we are told, the bridge table is dragged out in a million homes, and husband and wife engage in family warfare.

Cartoon services thrive because the husband gets kicked in the shins when he fails to lead back a suit in which his partner quite obviously was leading from a singleton. Newspaper readers stand up and cheer as the unreconstructed rebel of the bridge arena explains to an unsympathetic spouse why he brought in the contract at one spade when six could be laid down without a finesse.

There are, to be sure, these occasional flashes of lightning and the long, low rolling of thunder, and the rest of it, to quote Kipling, "is just sitting and thinking." Why is the knowledge of such a game seemingly a requisite part of our social equipment?

To begin with, the pairing of husband and wife at a bridge table is food for the cartoonist but is only a sort of footnote to reality. It's there, but the big bold type in which the real story of life is written proclaims that husband and wife would rather play as adversaries than partners. They spend hours working together on the mutual problems that harass

From *The Rotarian Magazine*, 1937. Reprinted by permission.

the home — the children in school, the cook in the kitchen, the budget in the red. When they go out at night, they have lost their interest in cooperative social planning and the collectivist matrimonial state. They seek the solace of the jungle, and if they can't exercise their normal instinct to claw flesh and tear hair in the familiar setting of opponents, they are likely to exhibit it for the edification of the neighbors in the less romantic role of bridge partners.

And for that matter, what keeps bridge alive is not the unquiet evenings at home. It's the quiet rubbers on the 8:13 while headed downtown and a couple more on the 5:15 returning. It's the afternoon battles at the Kentucky Club, as far as the men are concerned, and "just a few friends dropping in this afternoon" as an excuse for the women to get down to cards and spades.

Let it be remembered at the outset that I know nothing of what happens when women gather together for an afternoon of bridge. I have heard repercussions, and at times I have had the questionable pleasure of refereeing arguments as to whether someone did or didn't have an opening three bid; but, in the main, I am entirely agreeable to the idea that women's bridge parties should remain the exclusive property of the fair sex.

On the subject of bridge for men only, I have a completely altered feeling for two reasons: (1) It's an entirely different setting, and (2) It's an entirely different game. As to setting, it is only pertinent to remember that bridge to men represents escape.

Escape! That may sound like a large order. True, in the husband-and-wife pairings mentioned earlier it is frequently slavery, and admission of that fact has been made. However, so unsatisfactory is that form of bridge that it usually brings about its own violent destruction. On the other hand, those husband-and-wife pairs that progress smoothly confirm the claim I have made, because in them the husband has lost his role as the protector and uninvited adviser of a frail and faltering female and has escaped from civilization's bonds into the uncharted jungle where he can run smoothly beside an atavistic maid to plunder and pillage.

But it is in the field of men's games that he truly flees from the business world and its worries and loses himself in the romantic world of kings and queens, combined with the mathematical paradise of thirteen-card suits and fourth-best leads.

As one who has given some study to the advanced theories of the game, I must admit that it is fun to discard some of the technique and play man against man rather than cards against cards. Some of the English bridge clubs protested against the Culbertson four-five no-trump bids since they actually named the aces held and it was deemed to be as unethical to locate all of the aces and one of the kings by the convention as it would have been to lean across the table and say: "Partner, if it will help you in bidding a slam, I wouldn't mind mentioning that you can count on me for the two black aces and the king of hearts."

Bridge as the experts play it tends to create a situation where partners sit down and talk over the key cards of a whopper hand by symbols and signals in a way that now is permitted but does not vary from the old bridge gambler's trick of wearing a five-button vest and pressing his fingers on the right buttons to indicate the presence of aces or the fact that his hand embraced a no-trump distribution.

It can't last. "A great wrong dies in the hour of its greatest triumph." When the declarer of a grand slam knows that it is cold before the dummy is spread, the fun is gone from the game. Suspense is the secret of a good show and it was one of the elements in the sweeping popularity of the game of bridge.

But to return to the thesis of man-against-man. I play in two different games, one an afternoon encounter and the other a once-a-week evening game. Both are one hundred percent masculine, but what a difference there is between them! And I am glad of that, for bridge in its highest or most interesting form is not the inflexible routine of precision bidding. It is a battle between men, and the more difference there is between the men, the more difference between the games they play.

The afternoon game is poker in its finest form. One of the quartet invariably studies his hand with the earnestness of an eminent surgeon engaged in diagnosis, and out of the brown study comes the invariable bid, "One no trump." That means anything from a well-distributed four-and-a-half-honor count to the scantiness of an eight-card escape suit headed by a king-jack-ten. You bid against it or in support of it at your own peril, but it is this very element of risk that makes playing with him a thrill. You sit opposite him to watch him play a doubled contract and see him calmly gather in two extra tricks. A few moments later, as his opponent, you fear to double him and sadly count the tricks as he goes down about four undoubled, when you and your partner had a cinch game.

Another member of the group bangs the bidding to six. What he really likes is to hop. Be surprised if you must, but it is uncanny how many times he lands in the right spot. His mind, an analytic one, just works that way. He'll go down plenty every once in a while, but the next time he comes up with a bid that works and no system in the world would let him make it. Playing with him is like shooting rapids in a canoe — somehow you get through safely but you never are real sure of the strength of the craft.

The evening game, on the contrary, is an exhibit of mechanical estimating and counting. It is rubber play for Howell match points. Having bid five diamonds, you still struggle to make six even though the extra trick is worth only twenty points in the score column.

Play under these circumstances is absorbing even if not exhilarating. The opponents have bid six hearts, which the bidding indicates they can make. You feel that you and your partner can make two spades. Instinctively you stop and calculate whether it is better to go down four doubled at spades rather than let them make a vulnerable small slam in hearts. And when you have fixed them with a bid of six spades from which there is no escape, how you crow as they chalk up a 700 set when they might have made a count of 1,630 points for the vulnerable small slam.

There are players whose mannerisms give them away, who lead from the bottom of a string of cards by just barely skimming the cards along the table, "leading from under," and then lead from the top of a run by slamming the card down on the table, "leading from over."

And there are the poker artists of the bridge table. Take this scene from a California tournament, to see how they operate.

North and South vulnerable. East and West not vulnerable.

North, pass. East, pass. South, one spade.

West, *Two no trump.* An absolutely impossible bid!

If West had really had what his bid said he had, he would have doubled the spade informatively or would have sat back hoping it would get into trouble. But two no trump!

North was so flustered he passed.

East, quickly sensing his partner's poker bid, helped the game along by bidding three no trump.

By this time South, who held a hundred honors in spades and two other sets of ace-kings, was so excited he forgot to rebid his spades for a safe game in his own hand. Instead he doubled and to his amazement West passed.

West, of course, felt that he could trust his partner for another response.

North complacently passed and East redoubled.

South fairly shouted his pass.

West decided the farce had gone far enough and announced his escape suit by bidding four diamonds on a nice nine-card suit.

North, unable to sit tight in the poker game, doubled. The bid was made.

Every once in a while, somebody wonders why men have quit poker for bridge. But not after a hand like that!

The big reason for the onrush of bridge is that the professional gambler hasn't as much chance as he had in the poker era, when he could let the novice win most of the evening and switch in the stacked deck for a single hand. That was enough to leave the novice penniless. That can't be done in bridge. You can take the licking that goes with a pair of grand slams and still emerge winner in an evening's play.

Men like a fair field and they find it in bridge. That's why bridge won't be, can't be, abolished.

◇ ♣ ♡ ♠

One evening I was acting as tournament director. A meek husband called me to his table. Across, as his partner, sat a glowering woman, quite obviously his wife. Wrath was written on her face.

"What must be done if my partner makes an insufficient bid?" asked the meek male. I explained that she must make the bid sufficient and that certain penalties followed.

After a round of the hall, I looked back at the table. No one had made a move. When I returned, the husband looked as if he had bitten into an apple and found half a worm. But his wife was not daunted. Her wrath had increased the color of her face. She was ready to explode. The husband turned appealingly to me.

"What do we do," he begged, "if my partner refuses to make her bid sufficient?"

As I was saying, it's the clash of personalities that makes it a great game!

Section 3

The Bridge Playing Species

THE BRIDGE ADDICT

LET NOBODY THINK that science has been baffled by contract bridge. The other day, a well-known psychiatrist declared that it was inaccurate to call bridge players crazy. "Insanity is relative," he stated, "and there are hundreds of people who are more insane than bridge players. Well, anyhow, at least twenty."

The victim of contract bridge, he continued, is easily identified by these clear symptoms:

1. Almost immediately after lunch the patient loses interest in his surroundings and becomes incapable of performing the simplest routine task. If detained at this stage, he sinks into a stupor from which he can be aroused by the noise of cards sharply riffled.

2. If not detained, the patient rushes off at once to a sort of pest-house, sometimes called a "club," which serves as a quarantine center (somewhat like a leper colony). Most patients show great animation at this stage and appear to be in full possession of their faculties.

3. At the pest-house, the addicts group themselves at small tables and scream hysterically every five or ten minutes. This is less dangerous than it seems.

4. On leaving the pest-house, two hours late for dinner, the patient begins a monologue in a language which closely resembles English. In advanced cases, this persists through the early hours of the patient's sleep.

5. During most of his sleep, the patient seems quite normal — except for an intermittent twitch.

BRIDGE IS THEIR OPIUM

by ROBERT L. HEILBRONER

◇♣♡♠◇♣♡♠◇♣♡♠◇♣♡♠◇♣♡♠◇♣♡♠◇♣♡♠◇♣♡♠◇♣♡♠◇♣♡♠

IN A HOTEL on Park Avenue, in a suite of rooms on Fifty-seventh Street, in an elegant former private house in the East Sixties and in innumerable less posh surroundings up and down Broadway and scattered throughout the city, you will find the retreats of those transfixed New Yorkers for whom life without a game of bridge would be only the bowl without the cherries.

These retreats are the bridge clubs of New York, home and haven to a special world which, like the theatre, sports or underworld, has its heroes, its myths and its traditions. This is the world of bridge, where values begin with the two of clubs, and the Ten Commandments with Thou Shalt Not Rescue Thy Partner's Business Double. It is a world where a man is judged not by his physical prowess or the figures in his bank account, but by the perspicacity of the monosyllabic statements he makes while describing the thirteen cards he holds draped in front of his stomach.

The bridge of the bridge clubs is far removed from the bridge played by an estimated twenty million Americans to pass an occasional evening or to avoid making conversation with the next-door bores. Between just bridge and bridge-club bridge there is the same gulf that divides the fan from the fanatic, and for one who has not felt the Calling, the atmosphere of a bridge club might be a trifle wearing. But for the true bridge addict, the bridge clubs offer everything needed for a heaven on earth:

From *Harper's Bazaar* Magazine, 1951. Reprinted by permission.

for hours on end he can listen with never-ending fascination to the poetry of "Down two," "Okay, we're vul, you're not"; and he can ask such eternal questions as, "Why didn't you lead a club?" and "How should I know he was psyching?"

Bridge as an occupational disease is not limited to New York. Bridge clubs are to be found in almost every community where four people can count up to thirteen. There is a string of Cavendish Clubs in the larger eastern cities, a couple of Mayfairs, three clubs in Miami Beach alone, a flock on the West Coast. But New York is the Athens of the bridge world. From the swanky Regency and the expert's paradise at the Cavendish to the famous duplicates at the Mayfair, and then on down the scale to the so-called "factories" on upper Broadway where the women park their baby carriages outside before going in for a quick rubber, the New York bridge world is bigger, better and balmier than any other.

Aside from the common denominator of bridge, the New York clubs vary in aspect as much as the deuce of diamonds from the ace of spades. The Regency, ensconced in what can be described as a baronial-type mansion in the Sixties, presents an atmosphere of dignified reticence. "This," the atmosphere announces, "is a high-class club. Take off your hat." As a matter of fact it *is* a high-class club and the membership is largely socialite; bridge is an adjunct of the Regency, but not its lifeblood.

The Cavendish, on the other hand, in the catacombs of a Park Avenue hotel has less old velvet and is more leather-and-cork in looks. The athletic equipment — the tables and chairs — is handsome, polished and modern, and the comfortable sofas give the rooms a pleasant air; nevertheless, bridge dominates the air and you feel that the sofas are benches for the players, not places to curl up with a book. In the Mayfair, on Fifty-seventh Street, the world of bridge stands naked and revealed. There is a large room, an expanse of carpet and a small forest of tables. You might well go to the Regency to eat or drink, or to the Cavendish to sit around; when you go to the Mayfair, it is because you are itching to play a game of bridge.

The little bridge clubs present a somewhat more dilapidated vista. Many of them are little more than holes in the wall, up a flight of stairs in not too prepossessing buildings and into a few rooms with a dozen or more tables. And in the Broadway "factories" you will find bridge in the mass: a ballroom filled with tables and women fresh from Fanny Farmer's fudge counter, killing time before the second feature at the Beacon.

Admission to the better clubs is not limited to the experts. It is open to anyone of good character and sufficient loose funds to pay the reasonable club dues. Perhaps a thousand players belong to the Regency, Cavendish and Mayfair Clubs, and another thousand to New York Bridge Whist, the Bridge House, Mrs. Nelson's and a number of other "good bridge" houses; how many thousands frequent the Viennese and Czech *kaffee-klatsch* clubs and the "factories" on the West Side, God only knows.

The looks, the style and the composition of the membership vary, of course, from club to club. You are more apt to find Hattie Carnegie and Bronzini in the two or three top clubs and Ohrbach in the little clubs, but this is no hard and fast rule. And since bridge addicts are not required to wear special costumes and since there are no occupation imprints similar to a golfer's calluses, there is no ready means of telling the bridge maniac from almost anybody else. By and large the better clubs cater to a clientele which is predominantly (but by no means overwhelmingly) male, largely middle-aged but with a substantial sprinkling of both youths and gaffers, and economically substantial. This applies to the regular members; there are also a few bridge bums with little or no visible means of support who are either "sponsored" by wealthy bridge eccentrics or who try, without much success as a rule, to eke out a marginal living by their skill at cards.

Life in most bridge clubs begins in the early afternoon. The first comers, of course, will be the staff and whoever runs the club; they will be followed shortly by the early faithful who will warm up to the day's activities with the same kind of pre-game chatter you would hear in any golf locker. By mid-afternoon the clubs will be in full swing — at the Mayfair, for example, there may be ten games going. And the evening sessions, which begin at about nine and continue until early morning, will usually be even busier than the day's. Weekends are particularly active, for the chance to fling the pasteboards need not be interrupted by such extraneous diversions as the need to make a living.

Average attendance for an average member is a matter of a few hours of play once or twice a week. Thus for the fortunate man or woman who can take bridge or leave it alone, the clubs serve as a convenient means of getting around the business of calling up three other people and arranging who's going to be at whose house. The semi-addict — and by semi-addict I mean someone who still reads the *Tribune* headlines *before* turning to the bridge column — may go as often as four or five times a week, perhaps only for an hour after the office closes or the day's shopping is done or for a few hours' relaxation in the evening.

The real fanatic makes the club his home. There is where he can be reached in any emergency, there is where he does everything but sleep, eat and go to the movies. If he is not playing, the true devotee is kibitzing or off by himself with the glazed expression that means he is playing over a no trump he bungled in the last rubber. For the man to whom bridge and not bread is the staff of life lives in a constant mental state of finesse, squeeze and end-play, much as the billiard addict will play imaginary caroms off the walls of every room he sits in.

But total and complete immersion in the game is not the only reason for joining a bridge club. One member of Cavendish said he joined to get a good obituary notice, and there are a number of members in every club who like to be able to say to their business associates: "Last night Charlie and I had an interesting hand . . ." which leads inevitably to, "Charlie who?" and gives the member the indefinable pleasure of replying, "Who? Oh, Charlie Goren, of course."

As in every world apart from the world, the bridge clubs have their eccentrics. There is a lady at the Mayfair who doesn't like to win tricks because she hates to be on lead, and a gentleman at the Cavendish who doesn't like to be vulnerable because it's too expensive. And there is the man who tore up the singleton king of hearts from his own hand rather than have it caught by the ace.

But the solid core of bridge clubs consist of experts who loom like a shelf of slightly larger-than-life-size Buddhas to give aid and comfort to the ordinary mortals of this card cosmos. Contrary to popular impression, very few of the experts live by bridge alone. The reason is simple: it's too tough. There was a time not so many years ago when the gap between an expert like Sims and an ordinary player was such a chasm that Sims *had* to win over an average number of rubbers. Today that gap has narrowed down to a running jump, largely because of the experts' own teachings which have percolated down through the ranks. In a tournament, of course, the top-rank players will have an edge, but there is only the slimmest of margins in an evening's rubber bridge, and the run of the cards makes even that slim edge highly unreliable. Even in the national duplicate matches the difference between winners and losers is apt to be a matter of relatively few points.

Hence only a handful of experts make their livelihood through play alone, and there are even fewer who can depend on the earnings of their bridge columns or lectures or lessons. The majority must earn their keep with greater or lesser reluctance in some form of pastime that produces money: law, business or what have you.

At the clubs, kibitzing of expert games is fairly common, although most of the members would rather bollix one up by themselves than see it played for all it was worth by Harry Fishbein or Helen Sobel. Sometimes a fairly weak club member will ask an expert to make a fourth (it's a general club rule that anyone can ask anyone to play) and sometimes an expert will oblige.

This does not always work out too successfully, particularly with those players who in the presence of Schenken or Jacoby feel as they might at the Last Judgment. One such player doubled an expert's grand slam bid against him and felt reasonably confident of a set since he held the ace of trumps in his hand. In due course he took his ace, but the expert was so wrapped up in the play of the hand that he abstractedly gathered in this trick along with the rest. At the end of the hand all the tricks were sitting in front of him. At this point, the defender ruefully shook his head and remarked to his partner, "Gee, and I was so *sure* I was going to set that hand." Much the same attitude was evidenced by a mild little lady who meekly passed her expert opponent's six-spade bid even though she held the ace and king of spades in her hand. As she explained afterward, she was afraid that if she doubled, he'd redouble — and make it.

For the uninitiated, going into a bridge club for the first time is like entering a monastery in bereavement. Talk is brief and largely in the nature of post-mortems; concentration is intense. Sonny Moyse — an old *aficionado* and expert — was once in the semi-cataleptic state induced by mentally replaying a no trump, when a vaguely familiar-looking woman walked up to his table and introduced herself to him. "How-do-you-do, Mr. Moyse," she said, putting out her hand. "I believe we've met before." Moyse looked at her as one might regard an interesting fish in the aquarium. "Perhaps you'll remember my name," prompted the lady. "It's Mrs. Moyse."

Bridge players, however, are not all mono-minds. Lieutenant General Gruenther, Chief of Staff, Allied Supreme Headquarters in Europe, was long active in bridge circles and used to run the eastern championships. Jesse Jones has been seen at bridge clubs, as have Harpo Marx, Somerset Maugham, Howard Dietz and a number of other people who seem to function quite satisfactorily away from the tables. Nevertheless, once inside a club, it's cards that count, not brains, beauty or wealth. I have seen an expert nod his head at a businessman who could have bought and sold him ten times over and say, "See that jerk? Can't play a no trump."

Aside from taking the more helpless addicts off the crowded streets and sheltering them from the rain, the bridge clubs serve other functions as well. Most of them contribute to charitable institutions; the Regency is proud of its Red Cross Unit, and the Mayfair and Cavendish have a special affection for the Children's Cancer Ward of the Memorial Hospital and for the War Orphans Scholarship Fund.

Most of the clubs serve drinks and food, all the way from ham-on-rye to the fine restaurant which draws most of the Regency's non-bridging crowd. The clubs also serve as arbiters for the heated discussions that arise in the politest of private games. The Cavendish has been called to adjudicate everything from the finest points of play to the rules for Persian rummy, and now that canasta is breathing hot and heavy on the heels of contract, the clubs are expected to know all the ins and outs of Chilean, Argentinian, Brazilian and Patagonian canasta ground rules.

The clubs also run regular duplicates where the mighty joust for over-tricks. It is perhaps the surest sign of having reached hallowed ground when a bridge player abandons rubber bridge for duplicates, for this is the royal road to the tournaments — the major events of the bridge world. There are five major tournaments each year and an occasional international match. Possibly the most famous national match is the Vanderbilt, but the most unusual tournament event took place at the Winter Nationals at the Bellevue-Stratford in Philadelphia some years ago. One hand held up this match for over a half-hour while rule books were searched in vain for a covering principle. The hand in question went as follows: the opening bidder said, "One diamond." The next bidder, seeing a waiter go by, signaled to him for two cokes. The diamond bidder's partner, who was also thirsty, said to the waiter, "Double that," and the fourth player, who had been studying his cards exploded with, "Redouble!" At this point pandemonium reigned.

When bridge fiends are not playing in tournaments or in clubs or heatedly discussing a hand they played last week, they are apt to be catching up with world affairs by reading *The Bridge World*, a bright and sprightly little magazine devoted to such burning issues as the Point Count System, the Stayman Convention, the Weak Two-Bid and other monuments of controversy. With scholastic thoroughness, this publication mulls over the propriety of a lead of the six of clubs versus the seven of clubs and conducts an interminable correspondence with ten thousand readers in every nation in the world with the exception of Russia. Evidently no one plays bridge in the U. S. S. R.

What it all adds up to — the clubs, the tournaments and, most of all, the people — is probably nothing which will change the shape of our fate much one way or the other. Undoubtedly a case could be made for the function of bridge clubs as an escape from an unbearably complicated world into the relative simplicities of what can happen with fifty-two cards and four people. As one lawyer put it, "Bridge is my opium." But when you consider that fifty-two cards can fall into combinations that are measured in the billions, even this explanation looks a little weak. For the mathematically minded, there are actually 635,013,559,600 possible hands that can come one's way.

I suppose the bridge clubs can be regarded as a pleasant form of lunacy for people who otherwise would be watching birds or collecting edelweiss. The question of whether a man soaked in bridge is more of a total social loss than a man obsessed by some other compulsion — such as devising singing commercials — is a point too philosophical to be unraveled here.

The simple truth seems to be that bridge is one of the most fascinating games ever invented, and for a certain number of susceptible people, its fascination amounts to a total and complete infatuation. Such a love affair may lead to a broken heart, a damaged pocketbook and a rather recluselike existence. But for a man whose pulse quickens as he reaches for that next hand (the one that is going to be The Hand), this is a small price to pay for glory.

HARD LUCK

by CHARLES GOREN

FOR MANY YEARS tournament bridge players, at early morning gatherings, have revelled in the retelling by Harry Fishbein of the story concerning the Unfortunate Responder. It seems this character had been dealt a hand of 7-6 distribution (both minors), and partner, of course, vigorously bid both the other suits. "At the level of seven," he bewailed, "I had to take a preference between two voids, and I guessed the wrong one."

Another bit of master minding is recalled as I browse through some of my archives to find the following hand:

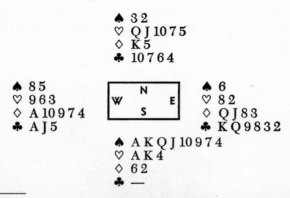

```
                    ♠ 3 2
                    ♡ Q J 10 7 5
                    ◇ K 5
                    ♣ 10 7 6 4

  ♠ 8 5              N            ♠ 6
  ♡ 9 6 3     W            E      ♡ 8 2
  ◇ A 10 9 7 4       S            ◇ Q J 8 3
  ♣ A J 5                         ♣ K Q 9 8 3 2

                    ♠ A K Q J 10 9 7 4
                    ♡ A K 4
                    ◇ 6 2
                    ♣ —
```

From *The American Contract Bridge League Bulletin*. Reprinted by permission.

The bidding:

WEST	NORTH	EAST	SOUTH
Pass	Pass	Pass	7 ♠
Double	Pass	Pass	Pass

Between humor and pathos the boundary line is frequently undiscernible. There was a touch of both in the story that was told me in connection with the above hand. It was at a session where bridge players had assembled to tell of their most unlucky experiences at the card table. (Have you noticed how many bridge players have a tendency to emphasize their hard luck?)

It is a distinct form of hypochondria. An ordinary hypochondriac is one who appears to enjoy bad health. A bridge hypochondriac is one who enjoys bad luck. They appear to take a great pride and to derive immense pleasure from the claim that they are "bad holders." It is strange how easy it is to forget good cards.

The narrator of this episode, a gentleman well in the grasp of Bacchus, submitted this as an example of unmitigated hard luck. His words: "I held the South hand and the bidding came to me after three passes, so of course I bid seven spades (!). This was doubled by my left-hand opponent. He led the ace of diamonds and then the ace of clubs. I was down one. If he had led the ace of clubs first I would have made it."

The humor, of course, lies in the complete confidence with which he contracted for a grand slam with three losers in his hand and the reference, in complete sincerity, to the incident as a case of hard luck.

The pathos of the situation is the fact that the declarer really was the victim of a bad break. If I were on lead, I would have produced the ace of clubs. Surely the declarer must have a void, and since I had only three clubs and five diamonds, there was a better chance that that ace would live. Against me, South would have made his seven spades, and I would have had a hard luck story to tell at the next meeting of the moaner's club.

BRIDGE SUPERSTITIONS

by ROBERT K. BRUNNER

MOST BRIDGE PLAYERS, like gamblers, are extremely superstitious. Some of them admit it, rejoice in it and seem even to be proud of it; others deny it — but not always convincingly. I know an old bridge player who, having lost two consecutive rubbers in the same seat, indignantly exclaimed, "I really don't deserve any better!" and, asked "Why?" replied, "Because I'm not superstitious and didn't change this rotten seat!"

Bridge superstitions are as numerous as the sands of the sea. They start with the choice of seats. Some players refuse to play with their backs against the wall; others can't play *except* under that condition. Most players, having cut the highest card and thus obtained the choice of seats, stay just where they are, especially if the cut card was an ace, since "you must never insult an ace." There are, however, some fateful cards in the deck — the ace of spades, the queen of spades, the ten of clubs, and about forty-nine others — all of which cause many players to quit their old positions in a panic. Ninety percent of bridge players, having lost a rubber, almost automatically change to an opponent's chair, provided they have the choice. If they haven't, then it might, at least, help a little to change seats with partner.

Reprinted by permission of *The Bridge World*, New York. A. Moyse, Jr., publisher.

Next comes the choice of cards. Usually those cards are chosen that "we have cut with." Some players prefer to consult the "oracle" by drawing one more card from the deck: if the red card turns up, they choose the red or pick cards; if it is a black one, the greens or blues are taken. After a winning rubber, and if it is your choice, you must keep not only the same seats but the same cards; after a losing rubber you have to change both.

There is also the matter of a misdeal. This is considered such a calamity by so many players that I sometimes wonder how, in the ensuing new deal, *anybody* can get a good hand!

Even the score pad cannot remain unaffected by superstition. Some players do not allow their names to be put on the top of the ledger, since this would "jinx" them; others, for the same reason, object against the "carrying" of their winning points if the next rubber is to be played in the same setup. In such a situation, the "carrying" process is easier on the score-keeper, but it would patently be unfair, because, as has already been said, it would bring bad luck to the winners of the first rubber.

All these are very silly superstitions, indeed, the observance of which I would never seriously advocate except for the rather diabolical reason that by feigning to be superstitious, and acting accordingly, you get the chance to deprive the opponents of their "good" cards and seats and thereby to drive them mad.

Yet, I must confess that there is one superstition — though only one — to which I myself pay tribute. I have been initiated into the mystery that nobody can win two rubbers in succession with the same partner and against the same opponents with the same cards and in the same seats. Call me what you will — "sissy" included — but in this I firmly believe. Consequently, if I have again cut the same partner in a four-handed game, then, having won the previous rubber, I change (or, having lost it, I keep) the cards I have played with, and I am very angry with myself whenever I fail to do so through having forgotten to put down the color of the deck used before and now being unable to remember it. It is another story if the opponents have the choice, and stick to their losing cards and seats (which they, however, will scarcely do, since they usually subscribe to the opposite creed). Then, at least, it was not *my* fault to have challenged Fate with the same cards and the same partner against the same opponents and in the same seats!

But now let's talk about superstitions involved in the play itself. These are almost invariably linked to the question of whether or not to take a finesse, and which way. The most pointed case is the finesse against the queen, with five cards of the suit missing. In Vienna, where I used to play bridge (in days which now seem so remote that not five, but a thousand, years seem to have passed) there was a proverb in vogue: "Where the nine is, there is also the queen." Accordingly, many players, holding (for instance) five trumps to the king-jack in their own hand, with three to the ace on the table, used to play in the following way: On the first round they led toward dummy's ace, and now the particular card dropped by their left-hand opponent was all-important. If it was any card but the nine, then, after winning with the ace, they finessed against the missing queen; if, however, it was the nine that had been dropped, they continued by cashing the king, thus playing their opponent on the left for queen-nine, alone. Strange as it may sound, the rule worked out in a surprisingly high percentage of cases, as if there really existed a secret affinity between the nine and the queen. (I don't know whether or not this rule is confirmed by experience in the Western Hemisphere.)

Under the same assumption of possessing all the cards of a suit except five with the queen, other players have established the rule that if their eight cards include not only ace, king and jack, but also the ten, so that they can finesse against the queen either way, *they do not finesse at all!* Their explanation is that they "never guess." This rule may be justified psychologically, since nothing irks a bridge player so much as to have taken a two-way finesse the wrong way. Seriously, however, none of these or similar superstitions can be defended as long as they are against the "percentage" which, in the case of the missing queen plus four small cards, definitely calls for the finesse.

But suppose the percentage is 50-50. Then, provided there are two equally reasonable ways of playing and that there is no special indication in favor of either, in my opinion the best thing for a bridge player to do is to make up his mind once and forever, and henceforth *always* to play in the same way. It is again for psychological reasons that I *recommend* the acquisition of certain superstitions for certain situations. Perhaps "predilection" is the better word, but whatever you call it, it will at least give you as good a chance as you can get from any other system. For if you *always* make the same play, then you will never blame yourself for misguessing, as you certainly would if, through changing your tactics from day to day, you ran into a bad streak of guesses, getting yourself "whipsawed" as the experts say.

Let me illustrate this point.

1. Suppose you have in the combined hands seven or eight cards of a

suit including king, queen, ten, and nine, but missing the ace and the jack.

DUMMY

K 10 x x

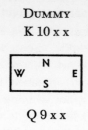

Q 9 x x

How should this suit be played so as to lose only one trick? Obviously, success depends on the way you choose to finesse against the jack, and for this there is neither a rule nor a so-called safety play; nor will the bidding often give you a clue as to the position of a mere jack. In this dilemma I always remember a doctrine which I was taught and which, although only fifty percent effective, is for this very reason good enough for the baffling situation in point. The doctrine is: *Always "place" the two missing honors, ace and jack, in two different hands!* Consequently, if somehow — because of an opening bid, a double, or even a simple overcall — the ace is indicated in one hand, I always play the other hand for the jack. Mere superstition? All right — but a superstition which in fifty percent of the cases will be justified by the results. What more can you ask? By clinging to this rule you will certainly not do worse than by having no rule at all and, like Hitler, relying entirely on "intuition." "Hunches" don't guarantee better results than superstitions when the latter are based on at least "fifty percent premises."

2. You often hold eight cards of a suit, particularly of the trump suit — five or six including ace, queen, ten in your own hand and the rest on the table, thus missing only K-J-x-x-x. For lack of an entry in the dummy, you are forced to play the suit from your own hand. Now, of course, you first cash the ace to see what happens, and if both opponents have followed, and neither of the missing honors has dropped, you are on the spot as to how to continue. At this point only three cards, the king, jack, and small are left in the opponents' hands, and they may be divided in many different ways. If both honors are held by one defender it doesn't make any difference how you play, because you must always lose two tricks. But if the honors are divided, you have the chance to lose only one trick, provided you make the right guess. If the king is blank you have to play a low card; if the jack is blank, you have to lead the queen. This is

obviously a toss-up, one way of playing being as good as the other. But this is precisely why you should have a permanent rule.

Personally, in this and similar occasions, I always play "for the lower honor to be alone," which means that, having first cashed the ace, on the second round I lay down the queen. This, by the way, is also the more spectacular play in that whenever it works, with the queen calling out the king but simultaneously smothering the jack, you will win the applause of your partner and the gallery. It may even be that this is the true reason why I have adopted this particular method, but it is also true that it has produced very satisfactory results for me. Perhaps you prefer the other method of play, but, whatever you do, once having made your choice, *always play the same way.* For reasons already given, it is better to have an established rule — even if based on a half-true and therefore super-stitious assumption — than to have no rule at all.

In this connection I should like to point out that if your suit contains only seven cards instead of eight, but includes the ace, queen, ten, *and nine,* it is compulsory, after you have cashed the ace, to follow up by leading the *queen,* because with four, instead of three cards missing after the first round — K-J-x-x — your only chance to hold your loss to one trick is to smother the unguarded jack. It would not help you a bit to find the *king* blank at this point and to drive it out with the deuce, because you would still have to concede another trick to the jack, which would still be guarded.

3. You have nine cards of a suit, with five or six of them, including king, jack, ten, in one hand, and the rest in the other, thus missing four including the ace and queen:

DUMMY

x x x

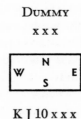

K J 10 x x x

Now, in order to lose only one trick in this suit, you must try to play from the dummy toward your hand. So the first question you have to deal with is whether you are able to do so:

(a) Once
(b) Twice
(c) Not at all

In the first two situations, where you can lead the suit from the table, then, barring special indications which might reveal the position of the ace, and provided, of course, that East follows suit with a low card:

(a) In the first situation the odds favor the play of the king. Most players — even many experts — think that this is just a toss-up, but they are wrong. The outstanding four cards can be divided in sixteen different ways. In ten of these cases, declarer's play after leading from dummy is immaterial—either he *must* lose two tricks whether he plays the king or the jack from his own hand, or (in the case of ace-queen blank on his right) he cannot go astray. In cases where his choice does matter, the king-play gains against Q-x and queen blank on declarer's left and loses only to A-x. The jack-play loses to Q-x and queen blank, and gains only against A-x.

(b) In the second situation, the percentage is definitely in favor of playing the jack.

(c) In the third situation, where you are forced to lead the suit from your own hand, it is imperative to lay down the king, since the only possibility of holding losers to one trick consists of dropping the singleton queen.

But I seem to have lost sight of the theme of this article, which was supposed to be "superstitions in bridge." Let's get back to it.

All the superstitions mentioned so far are connected with the game itself — with your own play and conduct at the bridge table. But there are plenty of superstitions outside this sphere, many of them having their source in the institution of "kibitzing."

Every experienced bridge player knows that a standing or (even worse) perambulating kibitzer spells misfortune for the particular player who draws his attention. But you can have a lot of trouble with stationary kibitzers, too. *Any* kind of hostile kibitzer is sure to become your nemesis; but, on the other hand, a kibitzer who "roots" too strongly for you will jinx you just as quickly and surely.

As for the proper procedure when *you* play the kibitzer's role — if the player you have been kibitzing has lost the rubber and consequently wants you to change your seat, if not to leave the table, etiquette demands that you comply immediately — unless you want to be confronted with an order of expulsion. You are, of course, entitled to burst into enthusiasm about the subtle and inspired play of the kibitzee; but woe unto you if you should rhapsodize over the cards he has held! This would infallibly put the Indian Sign on him and from that moment he couldn't possibly hold another ace or king. As a matter of absolute, sober fact, we know *two* nationally famous masters who have quit games *cold* when kibitzers pointed out what beautiful cards they were holding!

I could go on indefinitely with this list of superstitions but the foregoing should be enough. So I will wind up my enumeration with the sentient observation of a strictly non-superstitious bridge player, who once told me in confidence: "I have no superstitions in bridge, except one: I am convinced that losing rubber after rubber puts a terrible jinx on me."

KIBITZERS DO NOT LIVE LONG

by LEE HAZEN

◇ ♣ ♡ ♠ ◇ ♣ ♡ ♠ ◇ ♣ ♡ ♠ ◇ ♣ ♡ ♠ ◇ ♣ ♡ ♠ ◇ ♣ ♡ ♠ ◇ ♣ ♡ ♠ ◇ ♣ ♡ ♠

UNHONORED and unsung, a famous name will soon observe its twentieth anniversary. No celebration is likely to mark this anniversary. The name is one nobody loves.

The birth date of this unenviable name, so far as the American public is concerned, was February, 1929. The occasion was a play that opened on Broadway — a hit, by the classic definition, for it ran one hundred and twenty performances. Also, it elevated to movie stardom a young actor named Edward G. Robinson. In the title role, Mr. Robinson told various card players what they ought to do and what they should have done. The play was called *The Kibitzer*.

The American language opened its arms wide and took the new word in. "Spectator" and "onlooker" had been drab appellations for the card-table buttinsky; "kibitzer" fitted him to a T. Now nearly everyone knows what a kibitzer is, though most people mispronounce it (KIBitzer is right, not kiBITzer).

Whatever you call him — and it won't be good — the kibitzer is a traditional object of derision, of scorn, of anger, of anything but respect. He is about as popular as the baseball umpire, if not less so. Jokes about him are legion, and he is the butt of them all.

Item. A Chicago court solemnly issued an injunction restraining a particularly obnoxious kibitzer from watching pinochle games.

Item. Four bridge players at the New York Bridge Whist Club, noting

From *Cosmopolitan* Magazine, 1948. Reprinted by permission.

that their kibitzer had dozed off, turned out all the lights and began to bid and slap down their cards loudly, so that the kibitzer, awaking suddenly, cried out in panic, "I've gone blind!"

Item. At the same club, where kibitzers always substitute for players who must temporarily leave the room, an over-kibitzed foursome found occasion to excuse themselves one by one. Finally four kibitzers were left to work on one another while the players, having set up a table in another room, peacefully continued their game — alone.

Item. For seven hours a kibitzer had watched a bridge game in Philadelphia. One player — call him Jones — was losing; the others were winning. As the last rubber began, Jones proposed a side bet, and the kibitzer agreed. The rubber was played; Jones won it and, by virtue of his side bet, recouped his losses and was a bit ahead. So was everyone else. The players all collected. The kibitzer was the only loser.

Obviously, card players consider the kibitzer the lowest form of animal life, and psychologists might tell you there is some reason for this. Here, in very brief, is the long-haired explanation: Man has an instinctive craving for struggle, for war and conquest. When fear deters him from the real struggle, he turns to a mock struggle, a game, where he can enjoy winning but won't be seriously hurt if he loses. Now, the kibitzer lacks even the courage for the mock struggle, and must appease his instinct vicariously by watching others and sharing their triumphs and their defeats. Anyone who has observed gambling games knows that a loser seldom wants to leave, even when all his money is gone. He will stick around for hours to watch the game go on. There are those who insist, though statistics do not support them, that kibitzers do not live long; no doubt the wish is father to the thought.

Being rooted in human psychology, the kibitzer is a universal sect, and as such takes his characteristics from the country and time in which he lives. While "kibitzer" is a fairly new word to us, the Germans have for generations called him *Kiebitz*, whence our name.

This name arose when German card games, played mostly in taverns and coffee houses, were rough-and-tumble affairs marked by loud arguments and much card slapping. The *Kiebitz* or pewit (no cracks about nitwits, please), is a bird noted both for its curiosity and for the way it protects its delicious eggs (it flaps its wings in the face of searchers, thus annoying them greatly).

A German caricaturist popularized the name. He portrayed a sleeping fat man whose mouth was open and down whose big red nose a fly was crawling; caption: *Kibitzer, keep your mouth shut!* This picture proved so successful that it was lithographed for quantity sale to taverns and coffee houses.

The kibitzer first made his appearance in literature in an Italian manuscript of 1250 A.D., but the word for him then was "beggar." The author reported that the spectators at dice games outnumbered the players.

The American kibitzer, to do him justice, is much maligned. Under the influence of the Anglo-Saxon reserve, he is generally quite well behaved. Only when the urge becomes irresistible does he open his mouth. But somehow his good behavior has not added to his popularity.

Rules for kibitzers' deportment have been set down by an expert at the art — Captain Irving Woolfe, a retired businessman and World War I ace, who for some years has attended all the big bridge tournaments to sit, silent and motionless, and watch. "Ike's" rules are: Don't say anything; if asked a question, answer it briefly and without expressing an opinion; never change facial expression; watch the hand of only one player; don't touch a player, or his chair, and don't sit too close. Captain Ike is as much a fixture at bridge tournaments as is One-eyed Connolly at World Series, and he is one of the few kibitzers who have ever appeared as heroes in kibitzer stories. Thus:

A hand had been played, not wisely and not well, and one of the contestants turned to Ike, who was watching closely.

"How do you think he should have played it?" the contestant asked.

"Under an assumed name," replied Ike gently.

But seldom is the kibitzer permitted to talk back, even in the legends. Man apparently has an instinctive aversion to kibitzers, no matter how they act, and no matter how much — or how little — they know about the game. People are embarrassed by an expert kibitzer; his very glance seems critical. They are scornful of the kibitzing tyro. They are worried if they have a kibitzer they don't know, and you can't always judge by appearances.

There is a classic story, told of all games, about the faultless kibitzer who watched with keen interest for six hours and never opened his mouth. At this point a bitter argument arose among the players, and finally they agreed to leave the decision to the kibitzer. He shook his head sadly. "Sorry," he said. "I don't know the game."

◇ ♣ ♡ ♠

Most feared by the expert bridge players is the kibitzer who gasps, asks questions, or whispers to other kibitzers while the play is in progress.

Sometimes no damage is done. At the height of his tournament fame, Ely Culbertson used to be followed about from table to table by a devoted gallery. Their murmurs of approbation provided a pleasing background for the master. On one hand, Ely and his partner somehow managed to land in a slam contract missing the two highest trumps. An opponent led out these two cards, then exclaimed ruefully, "I don't know why I didn't double."

A Culbertson kibitzer piped up disdainfully, "It's a good thing for you that you didn't. Mr. Culbertson redoubles like a flash!"

At other times the kibitzer's remark is a dead giveaway. Today the galleries follow Charles Goren, who has the outstanding tournament record. On an occasion when Goren had made a somewhat unusual lead, a woman spectator gasped and said, "But Mr. Goren——"

"Please, madam," Goren cautioned her pleasantly.

"I'm sorry," she said. Then, turning to her husband, she emitted a stage whisper that was heard all over the room: "I can't understand it. His book says *never* to lead a singleton against no trump."

Among the most coveted trophies for which the bridge stars compete is the Harold S. Vanderbilt Cup. Engraved on this cup are the names of all the great players of bridge; *not* engraved on it is the name of a kibitzer who once won the tournament, practically singlehanded, for Howard Schenken and his teammates.

Schenken, whose name is on the cup five times, was playing a hand at one no trump. The play was completed and scored as down one—50 points for Schenken's opponents. Here the kibitzer spoke up: "Excuse me, Mr. Schenken, but didn't you make that bid?"

Now, Howard Schenken is noted for his politeness to everyone; that is, to almost everyone. There is one natural exception — kibitzers. His answer was sardonic: "When you contract for seven tricks and take only six, you are down one." But the kibitzer was undiscouraged; kibitzers always are. He reviewed the play trick by trick. The review proved that the kibitzer was right. The hand was rescored; instead of losing 50 points, Schenken's side scored 90 points (40 in the trick score; 50 points bonus, always scored in tournaments, for making the contract). This made a net difference of 140 points, and the Schenken team finally won by 130; so if it hadn't been for the kibitzer they would have lost by 10 points.

The sad conclusion to all this is that Howard Schenken still despises kibitzers.

The sport of kibitzer-baiting is popular because no one ever has any sympathy for the victim. Occasionally a rare opportunity arises. For example, there was the celebrated case at the Mayfair Bridge Club, in New York.

A player found himself at a contract of five diamonds, redoubled and vulnerable. He lost the first two tricks, but then spread his hand and claimed the rest, which would give him his contract. His opponents were convinced and would have thrown in their cards — when there was an objection. And who objected? Who but the ubiquitous kibitzer? "He can't make it," proclaimed the kibitzer — "not if . . ." The kibitzer had figured out a complicated line of play that everyone else had overlooked.

A committee was called to sit as a jury upon this crime. In a burst of inspiration, these jurymen saw their duty plain, and they did it. They awarded the declarer 950 points, the score for making five diamonds. They awarded his opponents 400 points, the score for defeating the contract one trick, redoubled and vulnerable. And they fined the kibitzer 1,350 points for being so smart. Everyone applauded. Even the other kibitzers. There is no honor among kibitzers.

If not honor among kibitzers, there is caste. One of our operatives, investigating the habits and habitats of kibitzers, insinuated his way into a club where he found a gallery three-deep around a game. A violent dispute arose; players and gallery partook indiscriminately, until someone was heard to say, "You keep quiet; you're only a tsitser!"

Our operative sought out the proprietor and learned: there are not only kibitzers, but also *dorbitzers* and *tsitsers*. A kibitzer has received permission to watch; he may talk with the players. A dorbitzer has received permission to watch, but only from a kibitzer; he may speak to kibitzers but not to players. A tsitser has asked nobody; he may merely hover in the background and say "Ts! ts! ts!"

The kibitzer's history is not without its flashes of glory. The most famous man ever known to the world of games, Edmond Hoyle, was only a kibitzer, according to his contemporaries. (They didn't use the word "kibitzer," then, of course; Mr. Hoyle died in 1769.) But while Mr. Hoyle only watched, and didn't play, he was the man they went to for advice; he wrote a book on games that was the biggest best seller of his century and has been a best seller ever since; and we still say "according to Hoyle."

◇ ♣ ♡ ♠

Nor have kibitzers always been aimless and gainless. In the honky-tonk gambling houses of the Old West, when men were men and the big game was faro, kibitzing could be a profitable vocation.

In those days, there were hangers-on who sat around the faro game and waited for "sleepers." A sleeper was a bet that someone placed and then forgot about. If the bet won, and nobody else took it, the kibitzer grabbed it. But, of course, he wasn't called a kibitzer then, either. They said he was "cadging sleepers" — a throwback to thirteenth-century Italy, for "cadge" means "beg."

Anyone who wants to go in for kibitzer-baiting can best turn to the most popular American card game, which is, you may learn with surprise, solitaire. There's no better sport than sitting in a railroad car with some intelligent-looking but simple soul beside you, while you play a game of solitaire on your lap, making up the rules as you go along! Your companion will go crazy trying to figure it out.

Nevertheless, *somebody* has to say a good word for the kibitzer. As sole witness for the defense, we call upon Klondike Pete, the old prospector.

"I was all alone and stranded in the North Canadian wilds," says Pete, "and it was midwinter. I was snowed in; my dogs had stampeded; my sled was wrecked; my provisions were low; my fuel was gone; I was out of ammunition; the wolves were howling. There wasn't a human being within fifty miles. Things seemed hopeless.

"But was I worried? Certainly not! I just took out my old pack of cards and began a game of solitaire.

"I hadn't been playing a minute when I felt a finger tapping my shoulder. I looked up. There was a well-fed, fur-clad man standing behind me.

" 'Why,' he asked, 'don't you play that red seven on the black eight?' "

THE GREAT KIBITZERS' STRIKE

by GEORGE S. KAUFMAN

SINCE I WAS A close observer of events leading up to the national strike of bridge kibitzers some years ago, and subsequently a member of the committee that helped to bring about a settlement, I think it is fitting for me to set down the true story of those turbulent days. There has long been a belief that the trouble started when a kibitzer named Lefkowitz — not Sam Lefkowitz, who later demanded that kibitzers be allowed to double any slam contract, but a cousin of his, named Marty — applied a hotfoot to a player during a six-no-trump contract. The Lefkowitz hotfoot case was not without its points of interest, and the depositions taken in the hospital are now preserved in the Library of Congress, but it was not the cause of the kibitzers' strike.

On the night of May 12, 1926, in the old Cavendish Club, on East Sixty-fifth Street, a player named Jymes, or Hymes, or something — the records are unfortunately vague — concealed a queen of spades from a kibitzer, known simply as Commander Smith, during the play of a hand. By holding the spade queen behind the four of diamonds, Jymes completely confused the kibitzer in his calculations, leading him to believe that he would make only three spades instead of four. Since this was during the old game of auction, before contract became popular, not a great deal was thought about it at the moment, and nothing was said. Smith himself stayed in his place for the rest of the evening, but it was noticed when the game broke up that he failed to ask, "What time are you boys playing tomorrow?"

On the following night, Smith didn't show up. It was the first night he had missed in eleven years, but still no one was worried; it was simply assumed that he was dead. This had happened before to kibitzers, and the procedure in such cases was well established. One of the players would deal and say, "Did you notice that Bill Clunk died last night? One spade," and his partner, when it came to his turn, would say, "Yes, I did. Two spades." Or diamonds, or hearts, or whatever it might be. So the players would kitty out three dollars for flowers, and that would be that. (How times have changed! Under today's rules, the death of a kibitzer calls for the cessation of play for a full ten seconds, and the next four hands are automatically doubled.)

But to get back to Smith, when the next day's papers carried no obituary notice, the players began to be worried. That evening, Smith was absent again, and this time one of the players put in a phone call to Smith's house. Smith was home, reading a book! Not a bridge book, either — some sort of novel. The fat was in the fire for fair!

The following night, two more kibitzers were missing, and from then on the thing grew by leaps and bounds. Smith held an indignation meeting at his home on the fourth night, with nearly fifty kibitzers in attendance. Subcommittees were formed and chairmen were appointed in Queens and the Bronx; inside of three weeks there was not a kibitzer on duty in Greater New York. Picketing was started in front of the Knickerbocker Whist Club, and a rock was shied at Oswald Jacoby's head as he was entering the club. Happily, it hit an old lady who was not even a bridge player.

There was, of course, consternation within the clubs. With no kibitzer to say, "You should have played it the other way around" or "Only a fathead would have led the king of diamonds," post-mortem discussions were routine and without color. Without kibitzers, the players became careless and listless; games simply dragged along, sometimes without comment of any sort. The players began to lose weight, had no appetites. In many cases, games were actually cancelled.

Jymes, or Hymes, or whatever his name was, eventually offered public apology to Smith for concealing the spade queen, but by then it was too late. Sympathy strikes were springing up all over the country, a national kibitzers' union was formed, and card players were presented with an ultimatum in the form of a set of rules. Among the stipulations were these:

Recognition of the union as the only bargaining force for kibitzers, and an agreement that no game should be started without at least two kibitzers in attendance.

Cessation of play if a kibitzer was called to the telephone.

The right of the kibitzer to call a revoke if it was confirmed by another kibitzer.

If a kibitzer had to go home before the end of the game, the results were to be telephoned to him as soon as the game was over.

The right of the kibitzer to put his glass of water on the bridge table. And many others.

Negotiations were deadlocked for four months, and in that time there were many outbreaks of violence and sabotage. In a Minneapolis bridge club, the six of clubs exploded in a player's hand, and was found afterward to have been dusted with TNT. In Dallas, a deck of cards was found to have three aces of spades in it, and this crime was traced to a kibitzer who had managed to get a job in a card factory. In New York City, fifteen thousand kibitzers held an indignation meeting in Union Square, and many were beaten by the police when they tried to parade without a permit. In the ensuing riot, three people were trampled to death. In Seattle, a player who went down one on a cold slam claimed that he had been quietly given a needle by a kibitzer who had jostled him on the sidewalk. Ely Culbertson was burned in effigy.

On September 28, President Coolidge appealed to both sides to settle the controversy before there was further property damage or loss of life. Leaders of the two factions assembled in the White House on October 9, and on the night of October 22, at a little after ten o'clock, the formal announcement of peace was made. I do not want to claim too much credit for the settlement, but when the conference had been deadlocked three days over the question of penalties for a kibitzer's foot on a player's chair, it was I who suggested a happy compromise. The foot, I said, should be amputated, not burned off.

I HATE PARTNERS

by SAM FRY, JR.

IT REALLY HAPPENED at a well-known New York City bridge club. The bidding had gone "Pass," "Pass," "Pass," "Pass." As the next hand was being dealt, one of the players mentioned casually, "I almost opened that hand with "Three diamonds." "Hm," his partner answered, equally casually, "if you had, I'd have bid three no-trump." "What do you mean?" rejoined the almost-bid-three-diamond fellow, quite a bit less casually. "You know my three-bids are weak, and you shouldn't disturb them without a rock crusher. Why, we'd probably have been doubled and down three tricks." "Nevertheless," was the stubborn and annoyed reply, "I would have tried for game in no trump. What did you have for your three-diamond bid, anyway?" his partner questioned, briskly.

This went on for quite a few moments. No one picked up his new hand and the argument grew hotter and the vituperation stronger. Finally, the first fellow got up and turned to a kibitzer. "Please finish this rubber for me," he said, as he stalked off. "I can't continue to play with an idiot like that."

I admit I'd never seen one quite like that — a real knockdown, drag-out battle, including the almost unforgivable sin of quitting in the middle of a rubber — over a hand that was never played. But I've seen almost as fantastic performances, in the line of partnership squabbles over bad results, on several other occasions.

There was the time a very good player, whose temperament was ob-

From *Cosmopolitan* Magazine, 1949. Reprinted by permission.

viously not up to his skill, found himself left in a cue bid. He knew he had a sure small or grand slam in spades, and to find out which, was going ahead slowly. The opponents had bid diamonds earlier, so at a certain point in the auction, he showed his void in that suit by calling, "Four diamonds." Exactly what happened to his partner I don't know, but the bidding went "Four diamonds," "Pass," "Pass," "Pass!" Our hero gulped, then wordlessly threw his cards out an adjacent open window, grabbed his coat from a nearby closet, and walked out the door. As an added fillip to this soap opera, let me explain that it was his own house.

I don't exactly recommend this deportment. But I don't recommend leaving partners in cue bids, either. Or passing to their force bids, or their take-out doubles. Or sacrificing against nonvulnerable games to the tune of 1,400 points, or bidding a slam, not on the cards you hold, but just because you "want to make a slam."

So I guess I sound like one of those guys whose war cry is "I Hate Partners." You remember the old and slightly off-color story about the two fellows playing duplicate together. Somewhere near the end of the evening one of them left for the washroom. The other — a real partner-hater — turned to the opponents and said, "For the first time tonight, I know what the blankety-blank's doing."

Let me give you a tip. Usually the fellow who complains most about his partner is a grade-A bridge criminal in his own right. Call it a Freudian defense mechanism, or a guilt complex, or an exploitation of the military theory that the best defense is a good attack — whatever your explanation, you will find that the fellow who is most vehement during the post-mortem has almost invariably been chiefly at fault in the catastrophe that has just been perpetrated in the name of bridge.

The overbidder is undoubtedly the most common type of partner hatee. Those 3,000-point rubbers we hear about, those 1,400-point sets, and those unmade slams are usually his doing. His damage is usually visible on the score pad. An underbidder may miss games and slams, but at least he gets a plus score. Thus, unless the underbidder's partner is particularly astute, he does not come in for much vituperation. The overbidder, on the other hand, strews blood all over and loses money rapidly. When you have an underbidder as your partner, you can, to some extent, make up for his weaknesses by overbidding a bit yourself. With an overbidder as your partner, you are frequently entirely helpless. You can stay out of the auction completely and still find yourself chalking up 1,400 for your lucky opponents.

There is the true story of two Hollywood movie magnates who were partners on a certain hand. One of them opened the bidding with a spade. The fellow on his left overcalled with two diamonds. His partner passed, in an unmistakable tone of voice. The other opponent passed, and the magnet who had opened the bidding rebid with two no trump. His left-hand opponent passed, and his partner passed even more vehemently than before. The other opponent now bid three clubs. Our undaunted hero proceeded to bid three no trump. The opponents, of course, doubled, and the contract was set five tricks vulnerable, or 1,400 points. At the conclusion of the play, the dummy who had contained himself with difficulty up to that point, exploded with the characteristic utterance, "What did you think you were doing, you fool? Didn't you *hear* me keeping quiet?"

The consistent overbidder has a short but concise philosophy: "I Came Here to Bid." He feels that if he just wanted to pass, he could have spent a hundred dollars or so on a round of night clubs, instead of spending an equal or greater amount losing at bridge. He is usually a highly successful businessman who is not only used to making money, but is used to bossing a lot of employees and having his way. He has a kind of non-thinking bravado, a "they-can't-hurt-us" complex. He is exactly like the prize-fight manager who tells his boy to go in and mix it up with an opponent much stronger and much more skillful. The prize-fight manager can't be hurt very much by the blows the fighter receives, and the overbidding bridge player, usually in the high-income-tax brackets, can stand losing those big rubbers better than his poorer partner.

Some overbidders bid a lot solely because they think it is more fun, and they are willing to pay for their losses. They came to bid and that's darn well what they are going to do. Others do it out of sheer stubbornness. The latter feeling is best described by a story a many-time tournament winner told on himself.

This fellow, who happened to be such a brilliant card player and such a keen psychologist that he won championships despite his own stubborn tendencies, was partnered by a weaker player with a like philosophy. Let the champion take over from here:

"I opened the bidding with three spades and this schmo across the table bid four hearts, even though he knew, from my three bid, that I had nothing but a long spade suit. I bid four spades, and then he bid five hearts. Well, I knew I couldn't get anywhere with him, *so to save a couple of rounds of bidding, I bid seven no trump.* Sure, we went down a lot, but what was the use of spending five more minutes getting the same result? He wouldn't have stopped bidding hearts and I wouldn't stop bidding spades, so I thought I'd better get the one sure final bid in first."

Let's take some actual examples of types of overbids that are more or less common. It's easier to tell you what type of overbids to avoid yourself than to tell you how to counteract partner's overbids. There is not too much you can do with a bad overbidding partner. You can play conservatively, but that will just cut down losses a little, and if ever a laydown game is missed, owing to an underbid on your part, your free-bidding partner's scathing remarks will be crushing.

As a starter, our overbidder makes unsound, forcing two-bids as openers. He may have:

♠ 5   ♡ A K J 4 2   ◇ A K 3   ♣ A 10 9 2

and open the bidding with two hearts. This is admittedly a very fine hand, but there are still plenty of potential losers in it. There just can't be a game in this hand if partner is unable to bid over an opening one-heart bid. The overbidder doesn't trust his partner and makes an opening two-heart bid, which forces partner to keep bidding till game is reached, even with an absolute Yarborough. This overbidding chap refuses to think logically at the bridge table.

When his partner opens the bidding, our overbidder never makes any allowances for light opening bids of the type he likes to make himself. For instance, his partner may open the bidding with one spade. The overbidder has:

♠ 9 6   ♡ A J 8 4 2   ◇ K J 2   ♣ Q J 3

He properly responds with two hearts. When his partner makes a minimum rebid of two spades, he bids two no trump. This bid, although slightly on the aggressive side, cannot be severely criticized. His partner now bids three spades, a very weak bid, practically a sign-off. Now the overbidder stubbornly goes to three no trump, blissfully assuming that his partner must have six *solid* spades and an outside ace. Obviously, with such a holding partner would have bid three no trump or four spades, over two no trump. He has made no allowances for the weak hand his partner has tried to show him.

The overbidder loves to jump in no trump. He will open the bidding with one diamond on:

♠ A J 5   ♡ 10 5   ◇ A Q 6 5   ♣ A J 5 4

His partner will respond with one heart, a response that shows no particular strength, other than the minimum necessary to keep the bidding open. The overbidder's rebid is two no trump, based on the theory that he has all suits doubly stopped. How he expects to make eight or nine tricks on the hand (he is doing more than just contracting for eight tricks; he is strongly urging his partner to go to game), unless partner can bid again without being urged, is beyond us. The proper rebid on this hand is one no trump or, if one wants to be a bit more aggressive, two clubs. If the partner can do no more than respond with one heart and pass on the next round, there can't be nine tricks at no trump in the hand.

The overbidder's overcalls are dynamite. They are made without rhyme or reason. He may hold:

♠ K 7 4   ♡ 8 6 2   ◊ 10 7   ♣ A Q 8 3 2

and will pass the hand as dealer. The opponent on his left opens the bidding with one heart, his partner passes, and the other opponent bids one spade. With only about three or four taking tricks in his hand, he now comes in with two clubs. After he is doubled and set Lord-knows-how-many, he usually hasn't the sense to keep quiet. His alibi—get this, they say it all the time — is "Well, partner, I passed originally." Unfortunately, there is nothing in the rule book saying that passing on the first round alters the penalty for being set at doubled contracts.

Overcalls are definitely part of the game of bridge and can and should be made frequently. But safety must be the watchword. We need strength to overcall when vulnerable, more so than when not vulnerable. We need more strength to overcall at the two level than at the one level, and correspondingly, even more strength to overcall with a bid of three. The fine player does not lack courage and makes an intelligent and correct bid even though there is great danger involved. But he does know how to be cautious when the word "Danger" is being sky-written in bright red smoke.

The overbidder is also a sucker for a pre-emptive bid. Good players use opening three-bids and four-bids on weak one-suited hands, on the theory that such a pre-emptive bid takes several rounds of bidding away from the opponents, who probably have the better cards. With these rounds of bidding taken away from them, even master players often have difficulty in finding the correct final contract. But Mr. Overbidder is a wise guy. He knows what these pre-empters are up to, and he won't let them get away with shutting *him* out. The fact that the pre-emptive bidder's partner may have a big hand doesn't enter his mind.

◇ ♣ ♡ ♠

As for the underbidder — well, we've had enough bridge hands for one day. But the greatest underbidder of all time deserves mention before class is dismissed. This is the true story of a sweet little old lady, who was not too bad a player and who was playing in her first tournament with a fairly expert male partner. On a certain hand, early in the session, the F. E. M. P. made an insufficient bid. The tournament director was called for a ruling, and the ruling was quite properly rendered according to the official rules of that time. To wit: the insufficient bidder could bid anything he wished, but the partner, the sweet old lady in this case, was barred from the bidding. The hand passed off without any particularly abnormal result, but as the evening's play progressed it gradually began to dawn on the partner that he was getting no cooperation at all. He was a calm, tactful soul, who usually didn't complain, but after a series of well-nigh incomprehensible passes by the sweet old lady, he gently took her to task. "Why can't you help me?" he asked. "Even if you didn't want to overcall the opponents' bid, you might have raised me after I stepped into the bidding. Then, when I stuck my neck out and bid another time, you could have taken me to game. And you did the same thing on the last board. I can't do it alone."

The old lady seemed hurt. "Why," she said, "rules must be respected. The tournament director told me a while back that I was barred from the bidding. I certainly wasn't going to go against his ruling." All her partner could do was mutter some sarcasm about the Statute of Limitations setting in, and that maybe she would be permitted to do something after seven years had elapsed.

But don't get me wrong. *I love partners.*

LIKES AND DISLIKES

by HARRY SEYMOUR

I like to play with Fishbein Klein, he's very seldom out of line.
I hate to play with Broderick Ott, he just goes sot and sot and sot.

I like to play with Felix Gore, he never overlooks the score.
I hate to play with Braithwaite Marshall, he never knows we have a partial.

I like to play with Maude McPhee, she stays where she's supposed to be.
I hate to play with Tess McBroom, she's always roaming 'round the room.

I like to play with Pete Gapard, he doesn't fight the cards too hard.
While Abercrombie A. Van Blubber distends the neck to save the rubber.

I like to play with Maggie Slick, she doesn't often lose a trick.
Deliver me from Lotta Daze, who overbids then underplays.

I like to play with Luke McElvis, he keeps his mind above his pelvis.
He's a different boy from Oscal Beal who never knows when it's his deal.

I like to play with Homer Keck, he promptly writes an A1 check.
I hate to play with Ignatz Gantz, he leaves his dough in his other pants.

Reprinted by permission of *The Bridge World*, New York. A. Moyse, Jr. publisher.

I like to play with old Joe Cass, he knows exactly when to pass.
It's much less fun with Bull-Neck Bevin, he won't let go this side of heaven.

I like to play with T. Weingartner, who realizes he has a partner.
I hate to play with Jess V. Bubbles, who robs me of my juicy doubles.

I like to play with Osgood Nourse. I'm bad enough but he's much worse.
But when I play with Perc. Van Clupp, it's just a cinch I'll get shown up.

I like to play with Ginsberg Glutz, for he extinguishes his butts.
I hate to play with Stinckham Shay, whose snipes keep smouldering in the tray.

I hate to play with Matt Malone, he's always hopping to the phone.
I like to play with Avery Skeet. He doesn't stop to phone or eat.

I like to play with Snodgrass North, he knows his tactics back and forth.
I hate to play with Wahl Ide Pike, he never tumbles to a psyche.

This might run on and get much thicker, had not your bard run out of licker.

BRIDGE BRAWLS

by FRANK K. PERKINS

◇ ♣ ♡ ♠ ◇ ♣ ♡ ♠ ◇ ♣ ♡ ♠ ◇ ♣ ♡ ♠ ◇ ♣ ♡ ♠ ◇ ♣ ♡ ♠ ◇ ♣ ♡ ♠ ◇ ♣ ♡ ♠ ◇ ♣ ♡ ♠ ◇ ♣ ♡ ♠

W HY IS IT that the bridge table so frequently becomes a regular
battlefield? Is it because the game attracts people who are naturally
quarrelsome, or does the game incite peace-loving players to roar and
argue?

Personally, we believe that it is a little of both. Since contract is a
partnership game, there is bound to be a certain amount of discussion
in regard to bidding and playing methods, and discussion is very apt to
degenerate into unwelcome "instruction" and abuse. There is a fine chance
to give your partner a "bawling out" without the risk of an immediate
punch in the eye; and, no matter how well it may be covered up, we are
afraid that most people have the primitive desire to put others in their
proper place.

We also believe that contract is particularly attractive to people with a
scrappy disposition. The game furnishes mental competition from beginning to end, and we do not think that any player can get very far at
contract without the proper competitive spirit. Years ago the writer
played tournament chess, and we used to say that no one could be a
master player unless he had a "tough disposition and a lot of low cunning."
These qualities may not be exalted in the copy books, but they are very

Reprinted by permission of *The Bridge World*, New York. A. Moyse, Jr. publisher.

effective over the chess board, or at the bridge table. And we have
noticed that many of the best contract players are reformed chess players.

Some who do not agree with us will point out that the leading players
are usually delightful partners, and courteous adversaries. This comes
from long experience in controlling their feelings, rather than from natural
inclination. When you give an expert a bad score in a tournament, he
may compliment you on your play, but he really wants to bend the
duplicate board over your head. And while your partner may not say
anything if you take a 1,400 set, he would like to throw the cards at you.

"A nice quiet game" is the ideal of the management of every bridge
club. There are no loud voices to disturb the fighting at the other tables,
and nobody has his feelings hurt. But we believe that bridge players *like*
to fight; and after a quarrel, the whole crowd will be on hand early for
the next day's play!

Unwarranted Criticism

Here is a deal that led to a bitter argument in a rubber game, but the
incident kept interest alive for several days.

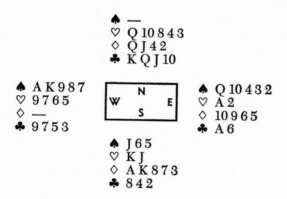

```
                          ♠ —
                          ♡ Q 10 8 4 3
                          ◊ Q J 4 2
                          ♣ K Q J 10
      ♠ A K 9 8 7     ┌──────────┐     ♠ Q 10 4 3 2
      ♡ 9 7 6 5       │    N     │     ♡ A 2
      ◊ —             │ W     E  │     ◊ 10 9 6 5
      ♣ 9 7 5 3       │    S     │     ♣ A 6
                      └──────────┘
                          ♠ J 6 5
                          ♡ K J
                          ◊ A K 8 7 3
                          ♣ 8 4 2
```

South dealer.
Both sides vulnerable.

The bidding:

South	West	North	East
1 ◊	1 ♠	2 ♡	4 ♠
Pass	Pass	5 ◊	Double
Pass	Pass	Pass	

West led the king of spades.

If you look at the deal casually, it seems as though declarer should lose nothing but the two aces; and declarer thought the same thing.

The spade was ruffed in dummy, and the ace of hearts was knocked out on the next trick. Spades were returned and again ruffed in dummy, and then the ace of clubs was forced out. But then another spade forced dummy to ruff with an honor; and East waited patiently, and finally took a trick in trumps to beat the contract.

North let out a bellow like an angry bull, and exposed his partner's stupidity to all who cared to listen. But a kibitzer had noted the deal; and after the rubber ended, the deal was given to *North* with all hands exposed, and the request to "try and make it." North did no better than his partner, and took over three hours to solve the problem double-dummy — aided by the applause of South and the others.

Solution

The hand can be made as follows: On ruffing the first spade, dummy leads a heart which East wins with the ace, and South drops the king. A second spade is led and ruffed in dummy, and the queen of hearts is cashed. The ten-spot of hearts is then led, and East must ruff; for if he discards, South will throw a spade, and the rest is easy. So when East ruffs with the nine of trumps, South over-ruffs. A club lead then knocks out East's ace of clubs, and another spade forces North to use up a trump honor leaving this situation:

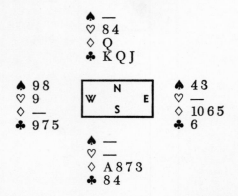

North cashes a club trick, and then leads a low heart. East's best play is to discard a spade, and South ruffs. A trump is then led to dummy's queen, and dummy lays down the last heart which is now good. It makes no difference whether East ruffs or not; he cannot take another trick!

The deal should not take very long with all hands exposed, but the debate still rages as to whether that line of play could possibly be expected without seeing the other hands. And we believe that in the future, North will be more careful about his comments.

Double Fault

The next deal came from tournament play, and resulted in an argument on bidding. As North said, "You could have doubled the five diamonds and collected 800 points by a good defense." And North was so insistent on this point that he lost sight of the fact that South could have secured 800 points anyway by good play. Maybe that was a break for South, for North would have had twice as much material if he had noticed.

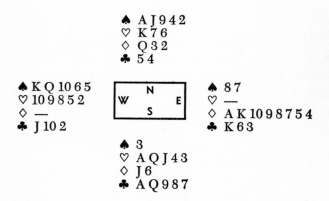

```
              ♠ A J 9 4 2
              ♡ K 7 6
              ◇ Q 3 2
              ♣ 5 4
♠ K Q 10 6 5    ┌─────────┐    ♠ 8 7
♡ 10 9 8 5 2    │    N    │    ♡ —
◇ —             │ W     E │    ◇ A K 10 9 8 7 5 4
♣ J 10 2        │    S    │    ♣ K 6 3
                └─────────┘
              ♠ 3
              ♡ A Q J 4 3
              ◇ J 6
              ♣ A Q 9 8 7
```

South dealer.
Both sides vulnerable.

The bidding:

SOUTH	WEST	NORTH	EAST
1 ♡	Pass	1 ♠	2 ◇
3 ♣	Pass	4 ♡	5 ◇
5 ♡	Double	Pass	Pass
Pass			

West led the king of spades.

Declarer won the opening spade with the ace, and led a club, finessing the queen to hold the trick. The ace of clubs was cashed, and a low club ruffed in dummy. Dummy then made the king of trumps, and declarer learned the bad news about the five trumps in one hand.

But another trump was led, and South ran off his three high trumps, leaving West with the master trump. South then led a good club and West ruffed. So far the play was all right, and South could still make his contract. But when West led the queen of spades, South made the mistake of ruffing, and had to lose two diamonds at the end.

South should have allowed East to hold the trick with the queen of spades, and South could have discarded a diamond that had to be lost anyway. West would then have nothing but another spade to lead, and North would take with the jack and allow South to discard his last diamond. And then South would take the balance. South should suspect that West had no diamonds, else why should he open the adverse suit? But the slip was mercifully overlooked in the face of North's indignation with the bidding.

How to Start a Fight

When a crude steal is perpetrated by the declarer, the defenders are apt to blame each other, and you have the makings of a fine battle. Here is one that we ran across at a recent Duplicate.

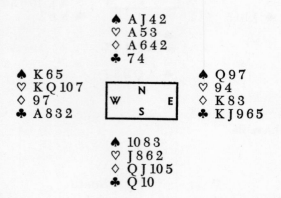

♠ A J 4 2
♡ A 5 3
♢ A 6 4 2
♣ 7 4

♠ K 6 5
♡ K Q 10 7
♢ 9 7
♣ A 8 3 2

♠ Q 9 7
♡ 9 4
♢ K 8 3
♣ K J 9 6 5

♠ 10 8 3
♡ J 8 6 2
♢ Q J 10 5
♣ Q 10

North dealer.
Both sides vulnerable.

The bidding:

NORTH	EAST	SOUTH	WEST
1 ♠	Pass	1 NT	Pass
Pass	Pass		

West led the king of hearts.

When South looked over the mess, he was heartily sorry that he had bid at all. The enemy could run off at least five clubs any time they wished, and it looked like a set of at least two tricks, or 200 points — which was almost bound to be a bad tournament score.

Fearing the immediate club shift, the declarer won the first trick with dummy's ace of hearts, and East dropped the nine of hearts, for reasons best known to himself. South hastily played the six-spot so that the nine of hearts would be sure to look like an encouraging card.

Hornswoggled

The hand still looked bad, and since the clubs could be run off anyway, declarer decided to try to forestall matters. So to the second trick, a low club was led, and the queen played from South; *and it held the trick!* West explained afterward that he was sure that South had the king also, and possibly the ten-spot, and was trying to set a trap for declarer, as well as keep him short of entries into his own hand.

When the queen of clubs held the second trick, South led the jack of diamonds, and it lost to East's king. The four of hearts was returned, and South's eight-spot went to West's ten-spot. Still missing the two of hearts, West cashed the queen, and East discarded a low club.

After some thought, West then led another diamond, and declarer was able to lay down his contract before the defenders repented. Three diamonds, a club, a spade, and two hearts were most satisfactory.

"Yes," growled East, "he took one look at the opposition, and then pulled that phoney."

"Why didn't you lead clubs yourself if you're so smart," snapped West.

And all bridge players can picture what followed without any help from us.

Excuses Needed

The last hand had an amusing aftermath. It came up in the finals of a tournament, and only one player scored the game at four spades. The deal passed unnoticed when played; or, at most, evoked some comment as to overbidding or tough luck. But when the results were posted, there were several players who rather fancy their game, but who had some embarrassing explanation to make to their partners.

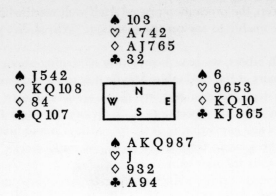

♠ 10 3
♡ A 7 4 2
◇ A J 7 6 5
♣ 3 2

♠ J 5 4 2
♡ K Q 10 8
◇ 8 4
♣ Q 10 7

♠ 6
♡ 9 6 5 3
◇ K Q 10
♣ K J 8 6 5

♠ A K Q 9 8 7
♡ J
◇ 9 3 2
♣ A 9 4

South dealer.
Both sides vulnerable.

The bidding:

SOUTH	WEST	NORTH	EAST
1 ♠	Pass	2 ◇	Pass
3 ♠	Pass	4 ♠	Pass
Pass	Pass		

West led the king of hearts.

The hand is a good example of keeping all possibilities in mind when planning the play. When the dummy goes down, it looks as though declarer can make six solid trump tricks, and three side aces. The tenth trick can probably be made by ruffing a club in dummy. Played on that assumption, the declarer must go down one when the spades refuse to split 3–2, for an unexpected trump trick will be lost.

There is no law that specifies that the trump suit must break 3–2, so one player took the pains to protect himself by a safety play. The first heart was won by dummy's ace, and a low heart led and ruffed by South.

Then the ace and another club were led from the South hand and East had the lead. He came back with a trump to stop dummy's ruffing possibilities, and South won the trick with the ace of trumps. The losing club was led and ruffed with dummy's last trump, and another heart was led from dummy and ruffed in South.

Then the king and queen of trumps were led out, and South discovered that West had a good trump. But the dummy was entered with the ace of diamonds, and the fourth heart led for South to make his last trump by ruffing, and the declarer had collected his ten tricks.

By making it possible to ruff hearts three times, South protected himself as far as possible against a bad split in trumps. And when the jack refused to drop, the precaution proved itself well worthwhile. But several players were unable to answer the question: "Why didn't you make that safety play?"

Along with others, we have been guilty of writing about the beauty of perfect manners at the card table. Maybe it is more civilized and sociable to hide your true feelings. But any game needs action to attain a wide popularity in America. Spectators flock to see a football team that hits hard, or a hockey game that is likely to end in a brawl; and though they may damn the visiting team as "a bunch of rough necks," they will be back in box seats the next time the teams play.

The publicized "bridge fights" of the past have done more than anything else to attract public attention to the game. And one of the reasons why contract has so many followers is that it offers a chance for a battle of wits, with a little quarreling on the side.

Bridge

BY WEBSTER

COMMUTERS

◇ ♣ ♡ ♠ ◇ ♣ ♡ ♠ ◇ ♣ ♡ ♠ ◇ ♣ ♡ ♠ ◇ ♣ ♡ ♠ ◇ ♣ ♡ ♠ ◇ ♣ ♡ ♠ ◇ ♣ ♡ ♠ ◇ ♣ ♡ ♠

Matawan, N. J., Feb. 3 — A Jersey Central commuter train was fired upon near here last night for the second time within a week and state police are combing the area for the sniper whose bullet narrowly missed four bridge players.

◇ ♣ ♡ ♠

NO DOUBT many a commuter-train bridge player who saw that news item let his imagination run a little. Was the person with the gun a vengeful rider who couldn't read his newspaper in peace because of noisy bridge players? Was he a disgruntled kibitzer who couldn't stand the caliber of the bridge he had been observing? Could he be a player who had been drummed out of a game for insisting on playing out one-bids?

Ordinarily, however, commuter-train players like most other bridge players manage to keep homicidal feelings under control. As a matter of fact greater restraint is required of them than of the player operating in more relaxed, unhurried surroundings. Unbelievable bridge blunders are committed while the clicking wheels signal that playing time is growing shorter and shorter.

"The hustle and bustle of a train game, with one to ten 'friendly' kibitzers," reported a veteran commuter-player, "brings on many a blind spot. Take a routine hand the other morning."

123

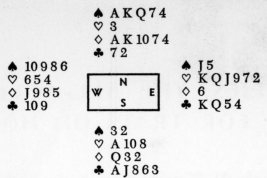

♠ AKQ74
♡ 3
◇ AK1074
♣ 72

♠ 10986   ♠ J5
♡ 654   ♡ KQJ972
◇ J985   ◇ 6
♣ 109   ♣ KQ54

♠ 32
♡ A108
◇ Q32
♣ AJ863

North dealer.
North-South vulnerable.

The bidding:

NORTH	EAST	SOUTH	WEST
1 ♠	2 ♡	3 ♣	Pass
3 ◇	3 ♡	3 NT	Pass
Pass	Pass		

"West led a heart, declarer holding off until the second round. Then he tried out the spades but East showed out on the third round. At this point South regretted not having held off until the third heart trick.

"He shifted to diamonds, leading to the queen in his own hand and then back to the king. Another shock, East showing out. Declarer played another diamond from dummy in disgust and the defense took four hearts and the king of clubs for down one.

"Declarer and seven other kibitzers (count them) didn't see that the hand was cold even after the failure to hold up hearts again and the bad diamond break. All he had to do was lead a club to the ace in his hand and take the proven diamond finesse. He was weeks living down the boner . . . Such is commuter bridge."

Some railroads take official cognizance of the commuter-playing species. The earlier-mentioned Jersey Central, for instance, will fix up a special car for bridge players if you form a club and guarantee a certain number of riders each way. Club members pay the railroad only the regular commutation fare and extra services are paid for out of the club's treasury of dues. The car is marked "private members only." It has built-in bridge tables, air-conditioning and a freezer for refreshments — beer, cokes and so on. A bridge player's dream, on or off wheels.

Since action is the keyword in train bridge, the old game of Ghoulash or Mayonnaise with its cock-eyed distributions has been enjoying a revival. Phillip M. Wertheimer describes his version, known as "Ghoulies," about which he has written a book.

GHOULIES, THE ALL-ACTION GAME FOR TRAIN OR HOME

by PHILLIP M. WERTHEIMER

WHEN THE FAMOUS CARTOONIST Webster was alive, he devoted his Friday space to bridge, and often to the commuter variety. One of his classics that sticks in my memory is the one in which a typical commuter is greeting his wife with a peck on the cheek while waving so long to his bridge-playing crowd. The wife is saying: "Who is that tall man you said goodbye to?" The answer is: "Dunno, been playing with him every morning and night for sixteen years and all I know is his name is Joe."

That more or less typifies the average bridge-playing commuter. The trip is short, the desire for the game long, so amenities are kept to an irreducible minimum and the concentration complete.

On our train and on others I know of, the commuters play Ghoulies and it has quite a hold on the players. If a man finishes his daily stint ahead of time he will drop in on the newsreel theater in the station, visit a nearby bar or browse in a sporting goods store. He will never take an earlier and alien train.

There is a commuter best known as "The Man Who Catches the 8:22." Like many other suburbanites he spends his summer vacations at home. But instead of thumbing his nose at the alarm clock during his vacation he arises at his regular time and makes his regular train to the city. Then he takes the next train home. My reaction to this was, "I wonder why he doesn't hang around for the evening train back. The fellows in that game can't be much good."

How does Ghoulies differ from regular bridge, and why? The latter explains the former. We don't have too much time so we try to crowd as many hands into the forty minutes or so as possible. And we want them as exciting as possible. Consequently we don't shuffle the cards and we deal them in sets. Two sets of five and one of three.

As cards are normally played in suits and only a cut is made to stir them up, we get unusually long suits and many freak distributions. Big hands are the usual, little hands the rarity. You can expect a minimum of six slams in forty minutes.

One of the things this type of distribution does is to increase the optimism of the player. After all, who can resist overbidding on an eight-card suit to the ace, queen, ten, nine? The fact that your left-hand opponent holds the other five does not dawn until too late. Much too late. Sometimes you sit behind the declarer with an axe only to find that the blade turns inward.

One of my favorite hands illustrates that point. In this one, imagine that you are my opponent sitting West. Your partner is a veritable Rock of Gibraltar, a man who prides himself on the fact that "When I bid 'em, I got 'em." He opens, vulnerable, with "four spades." The bidding goes pass (by me); pass (by you); double (a firm business double in Ghoulies).

Nevertheless, noting the delighted gleam in the Rock's eye I take out to "five hearts." Your hand — Spades: none; Hearts: Q 10 8 7 6 5; Diamonds: K Q J; Clubs: Q 10 8 7. You yell "double" and who can blame you?

You lead the king of diamonds. Here is the entire hand.

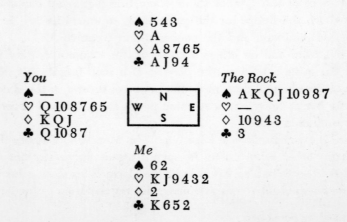

I win the opening lead with the ace of diamonds and test hearts. The seeming bad break is revealed. I play a little diamond and ruff and notice the fall of the jack. Since you didn't lead spades originally I guess that you had none and figure your distribution to be four clubs and three diamonds.

Since this leaves East with one club I lay down the king of clubs. Then I lead a small club and finesse the nine. I play another diamond back, and ruff, bringing down your king.

Another finesse in clubs and then I cash the ace. I have now won eight tricks and you're down to five hearts. I play a spade which you must trump and now you're forced to lead hearts into my king, jack, nine. I win your heart return and play another spade. You are end-played a second time. So you wind up with just two tricks — in trumps and a bad case of frustration. No opening lead, incidentally, will defeat the hand.

When this hand was actually played, West took the cards at the finish, flung them down on the knee board that serves us as a bridge table and screamed, "Blankety-blank-blank, what do you have to have in order to double?"

Yes, Ghoulies is quite a game. Since we try to play as many hands as possible on the train, we rush our bidding. We rush our play and often fail to make the killing lead or find the correct defense. However, we do have an awfully good time and that I believe is still the most important reason there is for playing bridge, the commuter or any other kind.

A Summary of the Rules for Ghoulies

The deal

Only a single deck of cards is used. Cards are shuffled at the beginning of the game only and never again. At the end of a hand, tricks are stacked together, and the deck cut once. Cards are dealt in groups of five, five and three. On an unplayed hand, the deal remains with the same dealer and continues to remain with him until a hand is actually played.

Scoring

Part-score hands are not played unless doubled or unless the part score, if made and added to an existing partial, is enough for game.

If a player bids a part score, he is credited with *one less* than he bid. Thus, if you arrive at a contract of three spades, undoubled, you do not have to play the hand, but get 60 points below the line. However, if on a subsequent hand you bid two diamonds, you must play the hand whether doubled or not. You cannot receive credit for a game-fulfilling partial automatically.

All bids of one receive full credit. Other scoring is as in regular bridge.

Tips

High card evaluation is not so important as distribution.

Don't jump without a fit in partner's suit.

Play hands at no trump whenever possible to avoid a ruff of the opening lead and cross-ruff situations. This applies particularly to slams.

Don't sacrifice to save a part score. The set may be bigger than you expect and besides a big hand may come along on the very next deal.

POST-MORTEMS

MAYBE YOU HAPPENED TO SEE that news item about the deaf-mute bridge players who were hauled into court on a charge of disturbing the peace for a neighbor in the apartment below. The complainant squawked that his ceiling reverberated with the scraping of furniture and frequent thuds as of bodies bouncing off the floor. The spokesman for the defendants explained apologetically that they got so het up going over the hands in the post-mortems that they just couldn't restrain themselves. The judge, a veteran bridge player himself, let them off with a kindly warning to cut down on the sound effects at their next session. But the way he said it you could tell he expected to see them back again.

There are bridge players who maintain they can't enjoy a game without post-mortems. A certain psychiatrist I know says this is perfectly understandable. These people, he says, need a socially acceptable excuse to blow their tops in public. It has something to do with inhibitions and repressions engendered by our brand of civilization. Or something like that. I'd have gotten more of the technical details for you except that this psychiatrist does not like to be quoted for publication — especially for free. He did comment, however, that there's something significant about the way the pattern of jungle behavior is reflected at the bridge table during some post-mortems.

Me, I haven't noticed it myself. I have heard language that would sear the hide off a bull rhinoceros and have had my ancestry raked over by a wisp of a little old lady. Still I've yet to see anyone take a bite out of a partner because of the way a hand was bid or played. But then I suppose I must play with a pretty tame bunch.

There are also bridge players who claim you can learn a lot from post-mortems. Well, you show me a bridge player who'll sit quietly by while his partner and/or opponents are measuring him for a dunce cap and I will show you a regular plaster saint. Because if you criticize the average player he will rare up and rebut at the top of his lung power. That is, if he believes he's right. If he's wrong he'll holler twice as loud. A youth spent in calling hogs is no mean advantage at a bridge post-mortem.

Now and then you hear of a bridge player who actually asks for criticism of his bidding and play. If you can imagine any sane bridge player (the sentence doesn't end here) volunteering to be a clay pigeon for all comers. This means not only his partner, who generally needs no formal invitation to take a running jump down his throat, but also the opponents, the head kibitzer and the nibitzers.* That is certainly stretching one's neck out a long, long way.

Come to think of it I did hear about a gal in a bridge club who learned something from a post-mortem. What she discovered was that while it's in passable taste to call your partner an ignorant crum-bum for taking you out of a business double, it is definitely *de trop* in some circles to throw your cards in his face. She was slapped with a fine for illegal use of the "hands" — as they say in football.

You can't talk about post-mortems without sooner or later getting around to Hairshirt Harry, the gloomy bane of the bridge table. No matter what this character does he's not satisfied.

"I sure loused up this hand," he'll say with a doleful shake of his head. "There was a double Vienna Coup and throw-in there, plain as the nose on your face." Or, "This contract should have been a cake walk. All I had to do was take three double finesses and execute a dummy reversal. It's as plain as the nose on your face." You risk getting a Cyrano complex when you play with this fellow.

Also, he is not above calling you up at some unearthly hour to tell you, "Remember that three-no-trumper I made last night? I told you I thought there was an overtrick in it. Well, I finally figured it out. Listen —." And before you can stop him, or even after you do, he goes over the hand, step by step, and down to the last gruesome detail while you stifle a snore.

I could go on about Harry except that I just recalled a hand that's been bothering me for some time now. If you can spare a minute I'd like to tell you all about it and see if you don't agree with me that my partner acted like a triple-plated knuckle-head. Here was the hand —

Oh, you have to be running on? Some other time then.

---

* A kibitzer, as everyone knows, is a guy who is low enough to walk under a snake's belly. A nibitzer is a kibitzer's kibitzer. That makes him low enough to walk under a snake's belly with a high hat on.

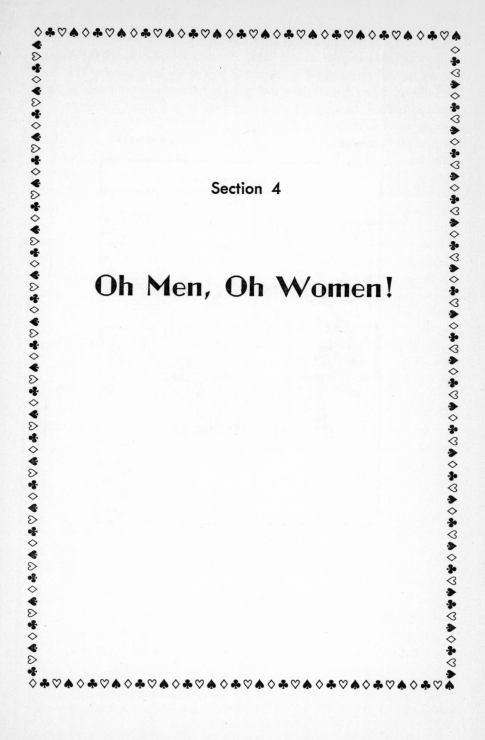

Section 4

Oh Men, Oh Women!

WHO PLAYS BETTER BRIDGE?

by RICHARD L. FREY

WOMEN ARE BETTER BRIDGE PLAYERS than men! That fact can be proved by statistics.

Men are better bridge players than women! That can be proved by reference to the records of the American Contract Bridge League.

How can both these statements be true?

Back in the days when the partnership of Ely and Josephine Culbertson was knocking off the highest bridge honors, you frequently heard it said, "Mrs. Culbertson is a much better player than her husband." Culbertson didn't really believe it, but you couldn't possibly get him to deny it. It would be nice to report that this was gallantry on his part, but it wasn't. Ely, the master publicist, knew he wouldn't get a line of publicity by proclaiming himself the better player. But it was worth a story every time he "modestly" told a reporter that actually Mrs. Culbertson played a better game than he. Privately, however, he lectured his wife about her bridge playing just as vociferously as any other married man.

In the half-world of tournament bridge, there is a rigorous code observed when a high-ranking man has a woman as his partner. This code is known as "the mixed-pair system," mixed pairs being those tournaments limited to entries of one man and one woman. The mixed-pair system goes like this:

1. The lady is never permitted to bid no trump. (There is a myth to the effect that no trump contracts are harder to play than trump contracts.)

From *Cosmopolitan* Magazine, 1949. Reprinted by permission.

2. The lady may not sit down at the table until her male partner has selected his seat. (This, diametrically opposite to all etiquette rules, permits the male, and master member of the partnership, to "sit over" either opponent. He chooses the boldest opponent, which puts him in the best position to double.)

3. The lady's right to listen is unrestricted, but under no conditions may she ever enter an argument.

Nevertheless, if Mr. Culbertson, whom the general public considered the greatest of all players, said that his wife was better than he was, then the conclusion was obvious — women could play better than men. The legend fattened on another fact. While a dozen or more players could and did challenge Culbertson's rating as top man, everyone agreed that Mrs. Culbertson had no serious rival among the women who played tournament bridge.

According to surveys, there are thirty million people in this country who play bridge. If you could pit a team of fifteen million women against the same number of men in a gigantic bridge battle of the sexes, the men would take an unholy shellacking. Become a bit more selective and the tables will be completely turned. Hand-pick a team of twenty men versus twenty women, or a hundred men versus a hundred women, or even the male half of the American Contract Bridge League, with its twenty-five thousand members, against the female half, and the women just won't have a chance of winning.

The fact is that among the top-ranking players — the tournament winners and the big-money winners — men lead by so wide a margin that even the presence of Helen Sobel near the head of the list doesn't give the feminists much of a chance to make an impressive case.

No team composed entirely of women has ever won a national open-team contest; only once has a national open championship fallen to a pair of women. Nevertheless, years ago, out of forty-three top-ranked players, only two were women, and the higher of these, Helen Sobel, was twenty-third. Today, women hold seventeen of the first ninety-four places and Helen has worked her way up near the top of the list.

So women have materially improved their position; the question is, will they ever catch up? There are two decisive factors that control the answer to this question. One factor is physical stamina; the other is a matter of temperament — what might be called the difference between a millinery mind and a military mind. A woman is concerned about her appearance, her family, and a multiplicity of interests that do not permit her to become completely absorbed in bridge to the exclusion of everything else. Perhaps she is subconsciously aware that bridge is not the most important thing in her life. But the top-ranking men are not only unaware of this — it isn't even true of them. While they are playing, at least, it *is* the most important thing in life — almost the *only* thing in life.

To a disciple of Freud, the male expert's utter concentration on his game might be a sign of a weak libido. Once, a lady of superabundant bosom and extreme *décolletage* was playing in a bridge tournament. Against an expert pair, she had frequent occasion to lean far over the table as she extracted a card from the dummy.

"Oooh . . . did you see that?" asked one of her opponents, as they walked away from the table after the game.

"Did I!" was his partner's scornful reply. "How do you suppose I came up with that brilliant defense? Why, you simply couldn't help but see every card in her hand!"

But don't let these observations lead you to agree with the Freudians. The lady experts don't seem to have found the men in the least sexless. In fact, there's hardly a top-ranking player on the distaff side whose profound attachment to bridge was not fostered by a romantic interest in a male expert. Most of these girls already played bridge of sorts; that was how they came to meet the experts. Some of them married their bridge-expert husbands before they themselves acquired any great skill. Some of them acquired the skill without acquiring the husbands. But all of them practically had to become good players in self-defense. If a woman wants to spend a lot of time with a bridge expert, she must either take the game seriously or be bored.

Still, once a woman has set her mind to it, why shouldn't she become as proficient as any man? That's where pure physical stamina comes in.

It would be hard to convince anyone, who hasn't experienced the utter exhaustion of a four-hour tournament session, that bridge requires stamina. The need to concentrate for hour after hour, the realization that every bid and every play may win or cost a victory, imposes an all but intolerable strain.

The best players are young men. As a player approaches fifty, his ability to go through a tough session diminishes. He has not forgotten how to play well; indeed his knowledge may constantly increase. But he can no longer make his mind note, without conscious effort, the difference between a deuce and a trey. After an hour of play, the effort has worn him down. He can't avoid making mistakes.

A woman is as much at a physical disadvantage at the bridge table as she is on the golf course. A man can't outthink her, but he can outdrive her.

Add to woman's physical disadvantage the fact that her proverbial equalizer — charm — bounces harmlessly off the hide of her male opponents, and what does she have left?

Guile? Well, yes. Helen Sobel admits, "I got away with murder when they thought I was a dumb blonde." Her opponents didn't know her then. They do now, but who wouldn't trade scores with her, anyway?

Besides, men can work that ruse as well as women, and in addition they can trade on the fact that, at the bridge table, women are more sex-conscious than men are. Once Wilbur Whitehead, possessed of a vast reputation in the bridge world of the 1920's, had to guess the location of a queen. His opponents were two ladies, all atwitter at their proximity to the great male. Turning to the one at his left, Mr. Whitehead said, "You look like a lady with the queen of spades."

"Oh, Mr. Whitehead," gushed his opponent. "Aren't you wonderful!"

Just once, a bridge-playing lady profited from an exclusively feminine expedient. Having bid a grand slam she couldn't possibly make, she promptly burst into tears. Her male opponents were overcome and threw the contract to her. This may not have been in the best tradition of bridge experts, but it does prove, as I remarked at the beginning, that women are better bridge players than men, and that men are better bridge players than women.

BRIDGE VERSUS THE BRIDE

by ALBERT H. MOREHEAD

ACCORDING TO ROUGH ESTIMATES, seven out of ten bridge games played in the United States are family games, one married couple playing as partners against another. Nor are the estimates all that's rough. A family bridge game can be pretty rough, too. A husband criticizes, a wife waxes supercilious, and suddenly you find yourself right in the middle of an old-fashioned marital spat.

This embarrasses the opponents, even though they're married themselves. No one likes to hear spouses calling each other louses. Considerate couples try to keep their disagreements private, of course, but in a bridge game they just can't manage that. There have to be two other persons present.

From this sad situation arise two questions: 1. Can anything be done about it? 2. And if so, *should* anything be done about it?

There are some who answer "yes" to both questions. They comprise a diversified group, including a few noteworthies like Risë Stevens, the opera star; novelist Ellin (Mrs. Irving) Berlin; cartoonist H. T. Webster. There are others of contrary opinions. These are the bridge-prohibitionists: They would make it illegal for any husband and wife to play bridge as partners. But this they can't do. The character of contract bridge is

From *Cosmopolitan* Magazine, 1949. Reprinted by permission.

rooted in the very structure of our society, for it is an essential means of social entertainment which can't be eliminated. It works like this:

Mrs. Brown, typical suburban housewife, speaks to her husband. "We must," she muses, "we simply *must* have the Joneses over for dinner very soon."

Mr. Brown resists the impulse to reply, "All right, let's have them fried, with catsup on the side." Instead, he merely nods and grunts in a husbandly way.

So the Joneses have dinner with the Browns. The food is consumed and duly praised. What to do next? The movies would entail going out. Listening to the radio is hardly "social." After a while the novelty of television wears off. Reading is out of the question. Conversation, we are told, is a lost art. So the Browns and the Joneses play bridge, papa-mama style, family against family.

Why bridge? Because it's a partnership game. If there are any stakes, pitting husband against wife would make them meaningless. Even when there are no stakes and not any more than one bridge game in ten is played for money — it would still be unwise to put asunder those whom God hath joined together. If you think couples can develop hard feelings as partners, what would be the result of making them antagonists?

Since most married couples can't escape from bridge, it behooves them to understand the underlying causes of marital bridge squabbles, and so to avoid them — or at the very least to learn to take them in stride.

It is not necessarily a bad sign when one spouse is outspoken in criticizing the other; it might be worse if they were cold and formal. Freedom from restraint goes with faith and intimacy. As a bridge expert aptly remarked, "You just don't call a strange jerk a jerk." By squabbling over a bridge hand, couples may even find a relatively harmless outlet for submerged resentments that are far more serious — that damaged fender, say, or whether to invite the mother-in-law. Henry Link, the psychologist, remarked on this in his book, *The Return to Religion*.

◇ ♣ ♡ ♠

When a bullying husband plays bridge with his wife, he may bully her as usual. And don't expect a nagging wife to stop nagging just because she's her husband's bridge partner. But often it works the other way, and bridge offers the marital underdog a welcome chance to assert himself.

"That was an idiotic bid!" rages the husband, but don't look for an early divorce. An occasional opportunity to bawl out his wife as a bridge partner may be his only compensation for knowing her to be the dominant partner in other aspects of their married life. This may keep them happily married, when nothing else would.

At times it's even a compliment when a husband is angered by his wife's bridge mistakes, or a wife by her husband's. Of the most famous married partnerships in bridge, the stormiest were those where husband and wife were quite evenly matched. Ely and Josephine Culbertson, for instance — each expected so much of the other that any slip-up really hurt. (On one occasion Ely, at the end of a tournament, remarked sadly, "We both played perfectly — except Jo.")

Much more serene was the bridge partnership of Hal Sims and his wife Dorothy, in which Hal was acknowledged to be by far the superior player. Not expecting perfection in his wife's game, Hal wasn't disturbed by her occasional slips. Dorothy, by the same token, comported herself with consummate humility. Even when she had done well, she was prepared to think she had done something wrong.

Most often it is the wife, following her usual technique, who pretends that her husband plays better; but when the wife is unmistakably superior, the husband, far from resenting it, is likely to boast about it. "I don't play so well myself," he will say, "but my wife is a whiz!" In one case a top-ranking tournament expert, A. M. Sobel, married a Miss Helen White, who was even better. He practically lost his own desire to compete because he became so interested in rooting for his wife. Mrs. Sobel justified his faith by achieving number-one rank for two consecutive years.

Undeniably, criticism can be dangerous when either member of the married partnership is highly sensitive. Then it is advisable to refrain from either the bridge or the criticism. But some find a better solution in the use of a "code word." Listen in on this bridge game and you'll see how it works.

Husband and wife are struggling against their cards, their opponents, and each other. Things are going generally wrong. Then a hand comes up that costs them a rubber.

He says. She answers. He shouts. She weeps.

"Oh, you're . . . you're . . . " the exasperation in her voice diminishes noticeably; she finishes mildly — "you're a pumpkin!" She pronounces it "punkin," like James Whitcomb Riley and me.

The husband pauses. Dropping his voice some hundreds of decibels, he says, "Yes, I suppose I am. . . . Whose deal is it?"

Peace reigns, but inevitably comes another hand that costs rubber.

She says. He answers. She shrills. He flushes.

"I wish," he says slowly, "I wish, yes, I wish you'd bake another of your wonderful pumpkin pies soon."

His wife grins. "Grin" isn't a glamorous word, but she has a nice way of grinning.

"Darling," she says, "I'll make one for you this very weekend." Again the storm subsides and peace reigns — this time to the end of the game.

You see, they have agreed in advance that the word pumpkin is to be their magic utterance, the incantation that will oil the troubled waters. Whenever spoken, this word will mean, "Hey, wait! This is only a game we're playing; and here we are, we who love each other, getting all het up about it." The charm works; husband and wife both enjoy their bridge games; and they even get subsidiary amusement from finding ways to work the code word into their arguments.

Admittedly, some divorce cases have been based on evidence of bridge incompatibility; and Exhibit A of the group that would bar married-couple partnerships is, of all things, a bridge hand. It's a hand that looked prosaic enough when it was dealt, but turned out to be one of the three most celebrated bridge hands of all time.

It was way back in the autumn of 1929, when contract bridge was young. A prosperous Kansas Citian named John G. Bennett was partnered with his wife against another married pair. He dealt and picked up the South hand.

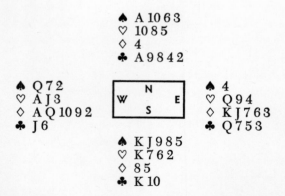

The bridge textbooks would tell Mr. Bennett to pass, but he was a rugged individualist. He bid a spade. West overcalled with two diamonds. Mrs. Bennett raised to four spades, and that was the contract.

West took the ace of diamonds, then led the jack of clubs. After winning this with the king of clubs, Mr. Bennett led the jack of spades as though to finesse and then put up dummy's ace anyway. He lost a trick to the queen of spades, besides the diamond trick and three heart tricks, and wound up going down two.

Mrs. Bennett complained about the finesse. Mr. Bennett answered back. Mrs. Bennett went to her room, got an automatic pistol, and shot him dead.

For the only time in their lives, bridge editors could factually write, "if South had played dummy's three of spades instead of the ace, it would have saved his life."

Oh, well, the jury acquitted Mrs. Bennett. Perhaps they agreed that Mr. Bennett had flubbed the hand, though bridge experts were inclined to think Mrs. Bennett was more at fault when she bid four spades; on her hand, two spades was ample.

A Mrs. Henderson of Detroit also shot and killed her bridge partner (for pulling the wrong card twice in a row), and it wasn't her spouse; in fact, it was another woman. Come to think of it, you don't even have to be a partner. Harry Meacham, of Wilkesboro, North Carolina, got so sick of holding bad hands that he swore he'd kill the next person who dealt him one. On his own next deal he picked up a hand without a face card. He shot himself.

THE FEMALE OF THE SPECIES

by JANE ABBOT

◇ ♣ ♡ ♠ ◇ ♣ ♡ ♠ ◇ ♣ ♡ ♠ ◇ ♣ ♡ ♠ ◇ ♣ ♠ ◇ ♣ ♡ ♠ ◇ ♣ ♡ ♠ ◇ ♣ ♡ ♠ ◇ ♣ ♡ ♠

IF you've ever heard an expert air his views on women—women as bridge players, that is — you may have noticed that his tone holds a world of disdain, not unmixed with disgust. In fact, the general opinion of most experts seems to be that timidity is synonymous with femininity. Women, they say, tend to fawn on and defer to their men partners; at the card table, if nowhere else, they acknowledge male superiority. They lack the dash and daring of the male player, his flair for taking risks, for gambling on a good break. I, however, take exception to this view, for the expert, in voicing his opinion, fails to recognize that woman-in-the-bridge-club and woman-in-the-home are two quite dissimilar cases. There *are* no experts in the home, and it is of the genus femininus in her Thursday-night-at-home game that I speak here.

I side with the psychologists in claiming that women are more emotional than men. They tend to be guided by instinct rather than logic, or to use an old fortune teller's chestnut, their hearts rule their heads. And nowhere—except perhaps in the driver's seat of a car—is this ascendancy of feeling over thought more manifest than at the bridge table.

A woman's course of play may be affected by quite irrelevant and entirely personal emotions—she may strive to outbid an opponent for no better reason than that she envies her her hat—or her husband. Again, if she's just come from a heated argument with her partner, she may deliberately try to play every hand in her own suit rather than his, regardless of which is the wiser course of action, in order to antagonize him

Reprinted by permission of *The Bridge World,* New York. A. Moyse, Jr., publisher.

further and "get some of her own back." A woman likes, too, to be the center of attraction, and enjoys making the "sensational" or "flashy" bid, motivated less by cool reason than by the desire to see what effect it will produce on her audience. This same bid, so eminently satisfying to her, is calculated to drive her male partner to the brink of frenzy.

The other evening Mrs. A. was engaged in a "friendly" game. She had held—vociferously—very poor cards all evening, when she picked up this hand:

♠ A Q 10 8 7   ♡ A K 9 4   ◇ A K Q   ♣ 3

Her opponent, South, dealt and passed, West and North did likewise and looked at her expectantly, ready to throw in their cards. At this point a wild gleam came into Mrs. A.'s eyes and a hot flush of excitement rose in her cheeks. What an opportunity! As she herself later described it, "I simply couldn't resist throwing a bombshell after those three passes. So I *opened* with *six* spades. Wasn't that wonderful?"

Wonderful indeed, considering that the hand held about four losers! At her announcement, her partner's jaw dropped, his eyes began to blink and his hand to tremble, for he knew that while Mrs. A.'s bid might be one of the "flash" variety, there was also the possibility that it was valid. He scratched his head in misery and doubt, and contemplating his hand, which held

♠ K 9 4   ♡ J 8 7 5 4 3   ◇ 6 8   ♣ A 4 2

he decided discretion was the better part of valor, and passed. The spade jack and heart queen succumbing to straight leads, Mrs. A. made a grand slam. The hand over, she could hardly wait to berate her partner for not having shown hearts. He, in turn, had been breathlessly anticipating the moment when he could inform Mrs. A., in colorful language complete with gestures, of just what he thought of opening with such six-bids, but found himself, in some mysterious way, on the defensive instead. His efforts to convince Mrs. A. that if she had opened with a more conservative, but less spectacular (and hence, from her point of view, less gratifying), two-bid, a grand slam might have been reached, were completely fruitless. To all arguments she presented the triumphant and unanswerable query, "Well, it worked, didn't it?" He could, of course, have replied, "Yes, it worked—so well that we contracted for six-odd when we could have reached seven," but he was a gentleman.

Another aspect of the bombshell bid—devised with an eye to the effect

it will produce rather than to any intrinsic merit in the bid itself, and thus calculated to appeal to the prima donna in every woman—is the "trap pass," the catch of which seems, more often than not, to have a reflex action. Mrs. B.'s little foible is to pass when she holds a hand that justifies an opening bid so that she can "come in later and surprise everybody." She does, but "everybody" turns out to be her luckless partner. Take the following performance, for example:

Mrs. B. sat South, dealt, and arranged her cards, thusly:

♠ Q 10 9   ♡ A K Q 10   ◇ A 8 7   ♣ J 10 9

She pondered a minute, and then passed with a beatific smile. (When Mrs. B. holds a bust, her "pass" holds all the anguish and resentment of a child who has just been told it can't have any more ice-cream.) West opened with one spade, North passed, and East bid three spades. Mrs. B., having remained silent almost longer than was mortally possible, sweetly and triumphantly murmured "four hearts." West, the brute, doubled; and Mrs. B.'s partner turned a vivid pistachio, chewed his lip fiercely, and passed. Mrs. B went down four tricks with commendable aplomb. The game over, she was only slightly dashed. "Imagine!" she exclaimed, "going down four whole tricks when I actually had an opening bid all the while." She invested the words "opening bid" with as much awe and reverence as if she had said "Holy Grail." Her partner demanded, somewhat grimly, why, if she had had an opening bid, she hadn't made it, instead of waiting to open her . . . er . . . *rosebud* mouth to say four.

Mrs. B., all injured innocence, said, "But darling, I thought it would be such a nice surprise for you to find, when the bidding got around to me again, that I had over three honor tricks instead of just a measly overcall. After all, just because I passed a three-trick hand originally doesn't mean I wasn't planning to get around to it *sometime*. Why, that's strategy."

Confucius said, "Women and children like having their own way"—or if he didn't he should have. If you have ever, while playing with a woman partner, engaged in the following rather heated sequence of bidding you will know what I mean.

You: One spade.

Your partner, whom we might as well call Eve: Two hearts.

You, holding a void in hearts and a six-card spade suit: Two spades.

Eve: Three hearts.

You: Three spades.

Eve: Four hearts.

You, firmly, and, you think, inexorably: Four spades.

Eve, with maddening blitheness that nevertheless conceals an undercurrent of iron determination: Five hearts.

You realize that nothing short of a gag will ever silence her, and that she will go merrily onward and upward until brought up short, not by any effort of your own, but by the fact that bidding necessarily stops at seven. So you pass.

"*Well,* partner!" says Eve reproachfully, "it's about time you decided to trust my judgment. After all, bridge is a game of trust and cooperation." She smiles forgivingly and passes her hand across the table for your inspection. (Oh, yes! Passing-hands-across-the-table is still very *comme il faut* in social games. If anyone here ever heard of the "Official Law Book," he or she has long since forgotten it, and probably never cared much anyway.) You fan out the passed-across cards with a feeling of foreboding, which is in no wise lessened when you see:

♠ 9 7 3   ♡ A K 10 9 8   ◇ K 10 9   ♣ 8 3

You take another, and more-agonized-than-ever look at your own cards:

♠ A K Q 10 7 6   ♡ —   ◇ Q 3 2   ♣ A J 10 3

The play starts and you quietly leave the table in search of an aspirin. You return to find that hearts have broken 5-3 and that your partner—what a misnomer that is!—is calmly writing a neat 200 above the line—on the opponents' side. It is slightly vexing to realize that if the hand had been played in spades, this scoring procedure would have been reversed to the extent of a satisfying 150 points, *below the line,* and on *your* side.

And now we come to our final chapter on the subject of the woman bridge player. *Is she a good sport?* Several men have told me their opinions on this point, but, in deference to the editor's blue pencil, not to mention the laws against profanity, they will not appear here. Though I am unquestionably guilty of treason to my own sex, I am inclined, albeit reluctantly, to endorse their definitely (and sometimes violently) unflattering views. I have found, for example, that there is quite a difference between the play of a "for fun" game and the play of a "for stakes" game. The gal who, having lost 11,000 points, can pick up her purse and gloves and trip blithely out, after murmuring "Thanks, dear, a lovely afternoon!" is apt to be rather freer in her bidding than the lass who has to open said purse and extract cold cash therefrom.

One point, however, has given me to wonder. Men, obviously, admire "good sports." Why, then, do they so seldom marry them?

ONE SUNDAY AFTERNOON

by A. MOYSE, JR.

"DARLING," I said to my wife, "how would you like to play in the mixed pairs event of the Eastern with me?"

"Oooh — do you mean it?" She all but gurgled. I was touched. She is not a good player (as may appear hereinafter) but what she lacks in skill she abundantly makes up in enthusiasm. Her bridge experience has been somewhat sketchy — "party games" with the girls in her native Cleveland. Her prowess in that field is attested by a set of china duck ashtrays now in our joint service — the prize, I understand, for having the highest score one afternoon . . . at her table.

"Sure I mean it," I said expansively, with the air of a man presenting a mink coat.

"I'll spend the whole day studying," she promised. "Or would it be better if you gave me some pointers just before we start?"

"Well," I said, "considering that it's now twelve-thirty and that we start at two-thirty (this was a Sunday) I doubt that you can do much brushing up."

"Oh, I didn't know it was today!" She looked frightened, but pulled herself together gamely. "Well, we could have an hour's lesson if we skipped breakfast."

"Hey, I'm hungry!" I said.

Reprinted by permission of *The Bridge World*, New York. A. Moyse, Jr. publisher.

"But you surely don't want me to go into an important tournament without a little practice?"

I refrained from stating my opinion on the importance of mixed pair events, and said instead, "Look, angel, I've played bridge for about twelve years; I don't think you could learn a great deal in one hour."

"Oh, all right, but don't get angry if I make mistakes," she said re-signedly, and turned her attention to the Deerfoot sausages. I promised her I wouldn't get angry.

♢ ♣ ♡ ♠

The first hand sent us off to a flying start, my pumpkin pie being the only declarer in the field to roll home a four-spade contract.

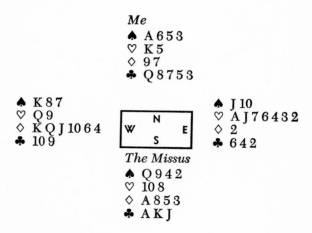

Me
♠ A 6 5 3
♡ K 5
♢ 9 7
♣ Q 8 7 5 3

♠ K 8 7   ♠ J 10
♡ Q 9   ♡ A J 7 6 4 3 2
♢ K Q J 10 6 4   ♢ 2
♣ 10 9   ♣ 6 4 2

The Missus
♠ Q 9 4 2
♡ 10 8
♢ A 8 5 3
♣ A K J

South dealer.
Both sides vulnerable.

The bidding:

SOUTH	WEST	NORTH	EAST
1 ♠	2 ♢	4 ♠	Pass
Pass	Pass		

I was North, and I refuse to apologize for raising to four spades instead of making the proper two-spade bid. I had played with my lady before (although only in social games) and had discovered that when she opened the bidding, there was usually a game if I could supply a couple of queens. My neck-stretcher was very lucky in that it shut out East, with her seven-card heart suit. Of course, we couldn't really make

four spades, hence there was no call for East-West to sacrifice at five
hearts or five diamonds, but we *did* make it, so a sacrifice of 500 points
would have been cheap for them.

West, not being second-sighted, opened the diamond king. Jackie (I
don't *always* call her darling, angel, etc.) scooped up the trick with the
ace, and, without the shadow of indecision, led the trump *queen* through
West. He covered, the ace won, and a trump continuation went to East's
jack. On the club return, my little genius hopped up with the ace, drew
West's last trump, then cashed the king and jack of clubs. For a long and
terrible moment it looked as though she were going to play a low club
from dummy on her jack, but she finally conquered her repugnance
toward using two honors on one trick, and overtook with the club queen.
There was another bad moment when she went into a huddle over what
to discard on my long clubs, but her eventual compromise — one heart
and one diamond — was quite satisfactory inasmuch as she had only
one trump left and would have to concede a heart trick in any event.

"Baby," I said, "that was beautiful — just beautiful!"

She beamed and looked like a rosy cherub. "I had to take a finesse
against the king of spades," she explained.

"And what a finesse!" I agreed enthusiastically.

"It sure was," West put in sourly. "All she missed was the king, jack,
ten, eight and seven. What book did that queen play come out of?"

I gave him a dirty look and said, "We'll take care of our play; you
take care of yours. What's the matter — sore because you didn't make
the right opening lead, a heart?" He almost swallowed his tongue —
imagine anybody leading a heart from his holding instead of a diamond!
But I would have said *anything* to protect my sweetie. Suppose she *had*
played the hand rather strangely — she'd come home with the bacon. Let
the experts play a low spade to the ace and back toward the queen —
and see what happened to them!

"Maybe you shouldn't have covered the queen," East said to West
in a disgusted way. "Then your king would have been a third round
trick, and you could always get in, cash a diamond, and lead through
the king of hearts."

"Oh no!" I said. "Jackie would have passed the second spade lead to
you — wouldn't you, baby?"

"Of course," she said quickly, and her expression was only a shade
puzzled.

◇ ♣ ♡ ♠

The next deal, against the same opponents, was played in a somewhat strained atmosphere:

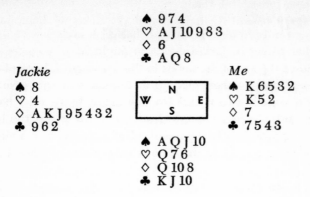

♠ 9 7 4
♡ A J 10 9 8 3
◇ 6
♣ A Q 8

Jackie
♠ 8
♡ 4
◇ A K J 9 5 4 3 2
♣ 9 6 2

Me
♠ K 6 5 3 2
♡ K 5 2
◇ 7
♣ 7 5 4 3

♠ A Q J 10
♡ Q 7 6
◇ Q 10 8
♣ K J 10

North dealer.
North-South vulnerable.

The bidding:

NORTH	EAST	SOUTH	WEST
1 ♡	1 ♠	Double	Pass (!)
2 ♡	Pass	3 NT	Pass
Pass	Pass		

(For the reader's convenience I have changed our positions in order to keep South the declarer.)

Referring to my one spade overcall, I hasten to say that, playing with Jackie, I do not observe all the rules of safety nor do I confine myself to orthodoxy in any respect. South probably thought I was psyching – he was eighty-seven percent correct – hence his prompt penalty double. My angel's refusal to bid her rather fair diamond suit was merely a gesture of perfect obedience and sublime faith. I had warned her, in a general sort of way, against "rescuing"; so, despite her singleton spade and her eight-card suit, she now gave me a smile of perfect confidence – as though to say she knew I'd make any contract I got into – and passed as though it were *she* who held the ace, queen, jack, ten of spades. The rest of the bidding was fairly normal. It is easy, of course, to criticize North for accepting a contract of three no trump but this, it must be remembered, was match-point duplicate, and from North's point of view there might be as many no trumps as hearts in the combined hands. The singleton diamond was a liability, but we had not bid the suit and South figured to have it well controlled. Moreover, at a heart contract, North's three spades might be dangerous in view of the announced spade length in my hand and South's — I might have the ace, if no other honor, and give my partner a ruff.

So much for the bidding. "Your lead, baby," I said.

Now, another player in Jackie's position might have been *tempted*, at least, to lay down the ace of diamonds in the not illogical hope of dashing off eight tricks. Imagine their chagrin at finding that this effort would confine them to exactly two tricks! Not my angel, however! I had bid a spade and by gosh she was going to lead my suit if it was the last card she ever led! Suppose South, vulnerable, *had* doubled a non-vulnerable spade bid and later leaped to three no trump? Who was *he? I* was her husband!

I am almost irresistibly tempted here to digress from bridge and dwell on the moral so magnificently brought out by my wife. If more wives had sublime faith in . . . oh, all right. I'll get back to bridge.

I repeat, Jackie led her singleton spade. I ducked. The declarer won and, though he must have been a bit nervous about the diamond suit, could not avoid taking the heart finesse. My heart king fulfilled his natural function and, merely with the vague hope of collecting one or two diamond tricks, I returned my singleton.

How can I describe the scene that followed? Perhaps I'd better use colors. South was green; North was purple; and Jackie was an adorable pink as, with rippling laughter and twinkling fingers, she played diamonds, diamonds, diamonds.

Down five.

The thick silence that followed was broken by South. Very politely, he said to Jackie, "Pardon me. You had eight diamonds to the ace, king, jack?"

"Let me see, now — yes, that's right," she answered sweetly.

"And a singleton spade?"

"Yes."

"And you not only passed to my double of one spade; you not only kept on passing, but, for your opening lead you selected the spade and didn't even consider a diamond?"

I broke up this catechism. "Who do you think you are — the district attorney?" I said.

"Did I do something wrong?" Jackie said anxiously.

"Wrong!" I shouted. "Why baby, if Gottlieb, who's supposed to know a thing or two about opening leads, had been kibitzing you, first he'd get down on the floor and salaam; then, out of sheer envy, he'd give up the game for life!"

"Which is exactly what I'm going to do," North rasped as she pushed back her chair. The call "All move" rang through the room. "Come on," she barked to South. "The next round will be a cinch — we only have to play against Helen Sobel and Goren."

"They seem angry," Jackie said, as we wandered to our next table.

"Forget it," I said. "They're just a couple of soreheads who can't bear being 'fixed.'"

"Did I fix them?"

"I never saw a neater job," I assured her, and squeezed her hand. A thought struck me. "Listen, baby," I said. "You mustn't expect to keep up the magnificent pace you've set — no one could. Don't be disappointed if something goes wrong."

When she asked, "What could go wrong?" I could only stare at her.

◇ ♣ ♡ ♠

The second round found us against Ozzie Jacoby and a charming partner I didn't know. The first board disgorged this layout:

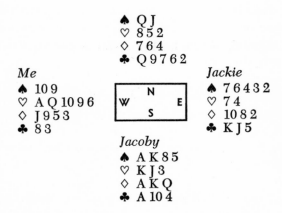

<pre>
                    ♠ Q J
                    ♡ 8 5 2
                    ◇ 7 6 4
                    ♣ Q 9 7 6 2
      Me   Jackie
      ♠ 10 9   ┌───────────┐   ♠ 7 6 4 3 2
      ♡ A Q 10 9 6   │ W   N   E │   ♡ 7 4
      ◇ J 9 5 3   │   S   │   ◇ 10 8 2
      ♣ 8 3   └───────────┘   ♣ K J 5
                    Jacoby
                    ♠ A K 8 5
                    ♡ K J 3
                    ◇ A K Q
                    ♣ A 10 4
</pre>

South dealer.
Both sides vulnerable.

The bidding:

SOUTH	WEST	NORTH	EAST
3 NT	Pass	Pass	Pass

I opened the heart queen. Ozzie won and led a low spade to dummy. I was slightly uneasy over the intent look that Jackie gave my nine of spades but there wasn't much I could do about it. A low club was then led from dummy, Ozzie's obvious intention being to pass the trick to me, the non-danger hand. But a wondrous thing happened: On dummy's club deuce, Jackie popped up with the *king!*

Do I have to explain how this remarkable play sabotaged Mr. Jacoby's thought processes and plans? A mere nine tricks were now insignificant; *thirteen* tricks seemed there for the taking. So, probably with the hope that most of the other North-South teams would also fail to bid the slam, Ozzie took the marked finesse against the club jack.

Ah, if only I had had a camera to record Mr. J's facial expression when baby gobbled up the ten-spot with the jack! It was one of the pleasantest sights in my experience. A sense of awe was beginning to grip me —was Jackie going to produce a scintillating coup on *every* hand? The prompt though silent answer to this question was almost a relief.

Having calmly raked in the fourth trick, angel went into a huddle, and my white-hot enthusiasm cooled at the rate of ten degrees per second. Didn't she have another heart? What *was* she thinking about! Oh, good grief, that horrible nine of spades I had had to play! Could she think . . . she *could!* Back came a spade to my "high signal."

L'Envoi

We finished eighty-third in a field of eighty-eight pairs.

THE TIE THAT BINDS

by GEORGE W. BEYNON

SINCE THE LADY SHOT HER HUSBAND at the bridge table in Kansas City during the roaring twenties, there has grown a legend that man and wife cannot play bridge together. Don't believe it! Probably the gun moll used bridge merely as an excuse to obliterate her partner. Perhaps her husband nightly cached his cash under the pillow, leaving his pants' pocket empty for the pilferer. Who knows?

But this incidental affair should be considered on the percentage basis and the chances of another husband meeting the same fate are approximately 6,728,777 per player per session. Therefore, fear should not be a deterring factor. Nor should that memorable mishap prove the basis of bridge incompatibility.

Nevertheless, many husbands do not play with friend wife and vice versa. The feeling of bridge superiority may keep them apart or the sense of inferiority, depending upon who feels or who senses. It could be both. The little woman is proud of papa expert and sacrifices herself on the altar of poorer partnerships to give him a chance to win with his peer. These are sound and selfless excuses.

But the main reason seems to be the bellicose attitude of both at the table. "Scenes" are abhorrent; cross-table shouting is scandalous. Why do they do it?

There is no need for it. They are not really angry when they argue. Just hurt. The louder the voice, the deeper the wound. Each expects

From *Playtime Magazine*. Reprinted by permission.

perfection in the other. Each has set the other on a high pedestal. When one pulls a boner or misjudges the adverse trumps, crash goes the idol, and turned upward, in full view, are feet of clay and disillusion. Neither are ornamental. Then comes the attack, a defense mechanism, to draw attention away from the fallen while he climbs back to his base and makes like a statue. Not from anger stems the tirade but from deep in the well of sorrow. There is disappointment, also.

The cure? Simple. With more than six billion permutations of cards, nobody can play bridge perfectly. Perfection (if possible) would remove all interest in the game. So why expect perfection in a partner, even your wife? Post her mistakes on the debit side of the bridge ledger to be offset by you on the credit side. Never will there be a big balance either way.

Dr. H. from Terre Haute plays with his wife whenever possible. If a mistake is made by one, the other takes the blame. "My opening bid misled you," "Sorry, I didn't lead a diamond" or "The return of a small club from my hand might have given you a better count." They get real fun out of the game and frequently wind up in the winners' circle.

Mr. B. of New Jersey claims Mrs. B. is his favorite duplicate partner. They have no bickering at the table. Neither gets the chance. At the conclusion of each board he leaves the table, returning only when the next round is called. This gives the wife full opportunity to tell the opponents how pitifully he played the last hand. Later, the hands are discussed in the home — without acrimony.

Mr. and Mrs. S. H. of Detroit use a different technique. Neither is permitted to speak to the other except to pass, bid, double or redouble, during the game. This limits their vocabulary to fifteen words and their tempers to zero.

Husbands *can* play bridge with their wives. And they should. In their life partnership, bridge should not be in small print. In every phase of their daily existence one strives to help the other. The wife even helps her husband spend his money.

Actually, the husband-wife bridge pair has a distinct advantage that almost amounts to cheating. It's not their fault. From close and long proximity they know each other's thoughts. Little things apparent only to partner convey information without intent to be unethical. This ethical and extra advantage sometimes proves the margin needed for victory.

Yes, wives and their husbands can play well together. But will they?

AN AGREEMENT BETWEEN
A BRIDGE-PLAYING COUPLE

by LEE BRANDT

THIS INDENTURE, solemnly entered into the _____ day of
_____, Anno Domini 19__, by and between
_____, party of the first part and _____
_____, her spouse, to her in holy matrimony duly joined,
on the _____ day of _____,
Anno Domini _____, in the City of _____,
State of _____.

WHEREAS, the said parties in furtherance of their avowed purpose
of living their lives together in amity and congenial pursuit have under-
taken to apply themselves to the improvement of their understanding
and playing of the honorable game of bridge and

WHEREAS, it is feared that such application and participation in
bridge playing may be productive of considerable disagreement, acrimony and erosion of the very relationship it is intended to improve, and

WHEREAS, it is agreed in principle:

    1. That it is deemed most desirable to avoid such circumstances
as could create disruptive influences,

    2. That the mathematically infinite combinations of the game
of bridge must inevitably lead to delicate and subtle differences
which defy categoric classification,

3. That it is the inherent right and privilege of all individuals to err in vision, hearing, touch, expression, understanding, interpretation, judgment and opinion,

4. That no one makes deliberate errors,

5. That the occurrence of an error, the loss of a trick or even the loss of a contract is in and of itself a disturbing experience and that a kindly nature would recoil from adding to the resultant discomfiture,

6. That despite all contentions to the contrary one's playing skill is not materially advanced by the constant plethora of "attritional post-mortems," discussion, argument and bickering which accompanies most bridge playing,

7. That it is conceded that excessive "post-mortems" serve more to afford the self-styled authority an opportunity either to parade his superior skill and knowledge or to vent his irritation on the usually unreceptive victim of his tirade,

NOW THEREFORE WITNESSETH, that the parties hereto on the good consideration implicit in the premises do solemnly declare their intention and do hereby agree not to indulge in any of the disruptive acts above described and more specifically listed herewith:

A. To recognize and accept the absence of rigidity in bridge and not to argue the contrary.

B. To recognize and accept human proneness to error and to refrain from any criticism, caustic, sarcastic or otherwise.

C. To recognize and accept differences of understanding, interpretation, judgment and opinion and not to oppose or quarrel over them.

D. To accept the occurrence of errors or defeat with graciousness, poise and equanimity.

E. To recognize the futility of post-morteming ad nauseam and to refrain from indulging therein.

F. To act at all times with restraint, good humor, kindliness and forbearance to the end that participation in the game of bridge will truly add to the pleasure of living for which purpose it was primarily designed.

And finally if the parties hereto find that discords and disagreements incident upon bridge playing affect other areas of their lives together, it is agreed that upon the formal request of either party hereto all bridge playing be thenceforth discontinued without further recrimination.

IN WITNESS WHEREOF, the said parties have hereunto set their hands and seals the day and year first above written.

_____L.S.

_____L.S.

In the presence of

_____

MARITAL HARMONY
AT THE BRIDGE TABLE

◇♣♡♠◇♣♡♠◇♣♡♠◇♣♡♠◇♣♡♠◇♣♡♠◇♣♡♠◇♣♡♠◇♣♡♠◇♣♡♠

TOURNAMENTS FOR MARRIED COUPLES only have not worked out too well generally, and have been dropped in most places in the interest of peaceful bridge. But such a tournament is an important and successful annual event in Chicago where it is run every May.

Perhaps this may be accounted for by the fact that married couples in the Windy City are more forgiving and forbearing than their brothers and sisters elsewhere. Or it may be that they're just stubbornly determined to give public proof annually that husbands and wives can pull together competitively come what may.

What it takes to survive this event with unexploded temper is described by one of the founders of the tournament.

"My wife is a fair player," he reported, "but not particularly competitive, and certainly she cannot be considered strong. In one tournament we managed to finish fifth and might have won except for her aversion to laying down an ace.

"On the very first hand of the afternoon session an expert woman opponent got into a three-no-trump contract with no spade protection except the singleton king in her hand. My wife was on lead three times, but never would try out the wide-open spades in which she held the ace. As a result, declarer was able to wrap up a three-no-trump contract which should have been slaughtered.

"Later in the afternoon we got another rotten result because on defense my wife would not plunk down her ace of hearts, which would have been a logical lead in view of the bidding.

"With cocktails and dinner behind us and not too badly off in the standings we went into the evening session. Came the third hand and we got murdered again because—you guessed it—my darling wife would not lay down an ace, this time of diamonds.

"Up to now I had not spoken a word. But at this point I said, 'Sweetheart, let's go outside for some air.'

"When we got outside we walked up and down silently for a minute or so. Then I turned to her and said fervidly, 'Dear—for the love of Pete, make me this promise. If during any of the remainder of the hands you happen to get the ace of clubs—no matter what the situation is, you'll lay it down on the table on your first defensive lead.'

"She so promised. And sure enough on the second hand after our return she triumphantly banged down the ace of clubs against a small slam, giving me an 'Aren't I a good girl?' look.

"She was, so far as her promise went. The only trouble was that this time her laying down the ace of clubs established a king which could not have been good otherwise. Result: Declarer was able to fulfill a slam which should have been defeated."

There is a husband and wife pair who do fairly well together at tournaments. The secret of their success is that they do not, by agreement, discuss matters between boards. Any reference to bridge must be done in writing.

Out of curiosity an observer got hold of some notes that were passed back and forth. These read:

1. "Play slower."
2. "Don't shake your head at me."
3. "Please pull yourself into one piece from now on and let's roll."
4. "I'll be a good kid."

◇ ♣ ♡ ♠

Freddie Sheinwold who, strangely enough, plays a lot of bridge partnered with his wife gives some tips on how the stronger mate can get along with the weaker one at the table. They are taken from his own experience.

1. Set a quota of allowable errors for a session—so many "catastrophes" and so many "misdemeanors." Set the quota high at first. As your partner makes progress, cut the quota gradually but never too far down. Compliment your partner for staying within the quota.

2. During the game make mental notes on points that come up. Decide which should be discussed now, later on or never. Keep the "now" ones to an absolute minimum.

3. Any comments you feel you have to make should be made in as friendly a tone as possible.

4. Answer questions soothingly and without irritation. Too often bad results come about because the superior player puts pressure on his partner with a bid or defensive play only an expert can be expected to understand. Don't create problems for your partner. But at the same time don't treat him like a half-wit. Imagine the two of you at the dual controls of a car. The major part of the responsibility for staying out of trouble rests on the more experienced and skillful "driver."

5. Don't act like a martyr.

6. And, finally, when tempted to get angry think of the sign in the Western saloon, the one that read, "Don't shoot the piano player. He's doing the best he can."

◇ ♣ ♡ ♠

A woman expert says, "I have seen more wives criticize husbands when the husbands were right than I have seen husbands criticize wives when the wives were right."

To which a male expert added, "Criticism from a wife hurts a husband more than criticism from a husband hurts a woman. There is something inherent in the male that makes him dislike intensely to be criticized by the female. It's the old 'Lord-of-the-species' idea, I suppose."

And together they promulgated this Golden Rule: "For marital amity over the bridge table, do unto your husband or wife as you would do unto any stranger."

FUNNY AND NOT SO FUNNY

◇♣♡♠◇♣♡♠◇♣♡♠◇♣♡♠◇♣♡♠◇♣♡♠◇♣♡♠◇♣♡♠◇♣♡♠

CONTRACT BRIDGE was blamed in a breach of promise suit in England, and the jilted lady was awarded five hundred pounds and costs.

A date had been set for the wedding of Theresa X and Harry Y, and rooms had been booked for the honeymoon. Then Mr. Y played bridge with his fiancée's brother.

The two men disagreed, and the lady sided with her brother saying, "You had no business to argue with my brother. He's always right."

Mr. Y replied, "You ought to be ashamed of yourself interfering in a matter which you know nothing at all about."

Whereupon, claimed Mr. Y, his fiancée promptly released him from his promise. The judge, however, considered that the lady had been shabbily treated and ruled in her favor.

◇♣♡♠

Circuit Judge John A. Matthewman of Honolulu ruled that bridge five nights a week is grounds for divorce. Laura Mc. testified that when her husband, Walter Mc., was not playing he "talked nothing but bridge." The judge granted the divorce on grounds of cruel treatment.

◇♣♡♠

Alwyn W. K. endured indifferent bridge partners for six months after his divorce in Reno by Mrs. Betty K. Recently they were remarried.

"She's the only woman I can depend upon not to trump my aces," explained Mr. K. after the wedding. "She was the best partner I ever had."

The widow of a famous bridge player visited a medium who produced the shade of the expert.

"Darling," asked the widow, "are you happy?"

"I am very happy," answered the spook.

"Happier than you were on earth playing bridge with me?"

"Yes, much, much happier."

"Tell me," said the wife, "what is it like in Heaven?"

"Heaven?" replied the spirit. "Who said anything about being in Heaven?"

◇ ♣ ♡ ♠

First Westerner: "That's right, stranger, I lost my wife in a bridge game."

Second Westerner: "That so? You mean you put her up as a stake?"

First Westerner: "No, stranger. She took me out of a business double, so what could I do but shoot her."

◇ ♣ ♡ ♠

A man who was crazy about bridge was married to a woman who detested the game and objected strenuously to his playing it. The husband made up his mind to get a divorce, but he could find no grounds for it. He didn't want his wife to apply for the divorce because that would mean she would get her hooks on his sizable bank account, investments and property.

His solution? Through a court procedure he got himself declared mentally incompetent and committed to a comfortable rest home. A portion of his income was mailed regularly by the court to his wife.

And he now had time to play bridge and fish to his heart's content.

◇ ♣ ♡ ♠

A man and woman were having a fierce hassle over a hand at a tournament. Suddenly the man got up from the table and stalked away. One of the other players at the table turned to the woman and asked, "Who is that, your husband?"

"Of course," she snapped. "You don't think I'd be living in sin with a man who plays bridge like that, do you?"

◇ ♣ ♡ ♠

She accused him of having forgotten that this day was their wedding anniversary. He admitted it shamefacedly.

She charged him with not noticing the new dress she was wearing for the occasion. He admitted that too and apologized abjectly.

Unhappy, she continued with the catalog of husbandly crimes. He probably didn't even remember where they had gone on their honeymoon. He groped unsuccessfully for a place. Atlantic City? Niagara Falls? California?

No, she interrupted, none of those places. Worst of all, he probably didn't even remember how they had met.

What kind of man did she think he was, he demanded. Of course he remembered. It was at a bridge party. And not only did he remember that but he would tell her the exact hand which made him realize that this was a woman after his own heart. She had six trumps headed by the queen, jack, ten; the ace, small in hearts; the ace, small, small in diamonds; and the king, small in clubs. He had bid one club and she responded —

He broke off suddenly and looked at her in amazement. What in blazes, he wanted to know, was she crying about?

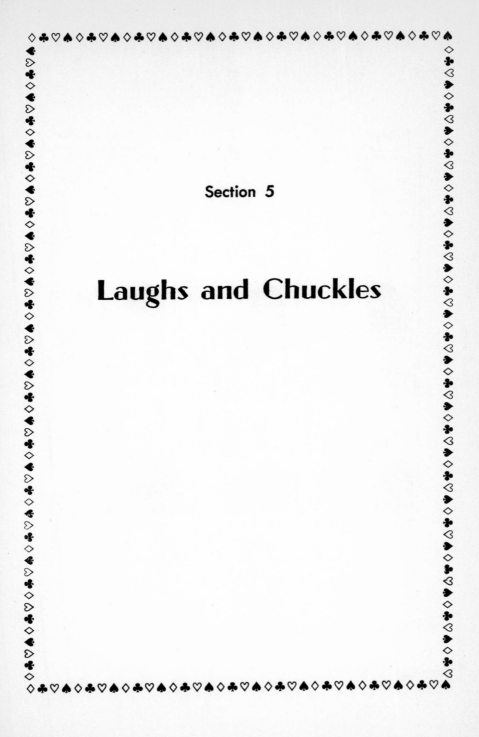

Section 5

Laughs and Chuckles

Bridge   BY WEBSTER

GRAND SLAM GAGS

by LEE HAZEN, *as told to Thomas H. Wolf*

◇ ♣ ♡ ♠ ◇ ♣ ♡ ♠ ◇ ♣ ♡ ♠ ◇ ♣ ♡ ♠ ◇ ♣ ♡ ♠ ◇ ♣ ♡ ♠ ◇ ♣ ♡ ♠ ◇ ♣ ♡ ♠

No matter how serious they may be about bridge, even the experts see some funny things happen. Here a tournament champion passes on some of his livelier stories.

THERE ARE MILLIONS of bridge players in America. Many of these are duffers. But even among the top-ranking few, an ordinary stick of chewing gum may make a world of difference.

A stick of gum actually did win one national tournament. It all came about during the final round of the Men's Pairs Championships in 1934. Most of the players were finished and were standing around the half-dozen games still in play in the center of the huge, smoke-filled Grand Ballroom of New York's Hotel Commodore.

I was in a crowd of perhaps fifty kibitzers who were squeezing around the table at which Ted Lightner and Ely Culbertson were playing the crucial hand against David Burnstine and Oswald Jacoby. Lightner had won the bidding at six spades.

Having played this same hand myself a few minutes before, I knew that success or failure for Jacoby and Burnstine depended entirely on the latter's opening lead. And the tournament score was such that the outcome of this hand would determine the championship.

From *Colliers* Magazine, December 1946. Reprinted by permission.

When the experts play bridge, the cards themselves represent only about fifty percent of any hand's value. The other fifty percent is psychology. In this tight spot, Burnstine made full use of his knowledge of his opponents' weaknesses.

He knew that Messrs. Lightner and Culbertson are among the most nervous players in bridge. Ely, especially, hates to have to wait. When, as in this case, he is going to be dummy, he fidgets and frets until the opening lead is made. Then he flings down his hand, without even bothering to separate the suits, and races away from the table. He can't stand the suspense of watching the hand played.

Realizing that the championship might well depend on his opening lead, Dave Burnstine decided to take his time. Very deliberately he reached into his pocket and pulled out a piece of chewing gum. He carefully unwrapped it, put it slowly into his mouth and gave a tentative chew.

By this time Ted Lightner was actually squirming in his seat. Ely was beside himself with impatience. But still Burnstine couldn't decide what to lead. And, in any event, he couldn't lead until he had disposed of the chewing-gum wrapper. So he threw it down on the table.

Like a flash Culbertson threw down his dummy hand. An instant later he realized his error and hastily scooped up the cards. It was too late. Capitalizing on his unexpected look at the dummy, Burnstine made the lead which set the hand.

Small things often influence the outcome of major tournaments. A bottle of Coke was a big factor in the winning of the National Match-Point Team-of-Four Championship at Atlantic City, New Jersey.

A Finesse or a Prayer?

It happened in a crucial hand on which I had to guess whether to finesse for the king of trumps or to play my ace and hope for the king to fall. There were only three trumps out and I had no way to guess how they were split. The percentage favors a finesse, but percentages are not infallible.

I led a low trump from the dummy, and the player on my right played low — with just the proper air of nonchalance. I paused for a moment to see whether I had overlooked any sign which might give me a key to this move. The opponent on my left, waiting to play, hailed a passing waiter. "Will you get me a Coke, please?" he asked.

Then and there I knew that he had the missing king. No man orders a drink in the middle of a crucial hand unless he is trying to be *too* nonchalant. I played my ace and the king dropped. Our team won the tournament — by one-quarter of a match point.

Hesitation during the play of a hand is perfectly ethical so long as you don't overdo it. On the other hand, hesitation during the bidding is considered extremely bad form. It obviously reveals that the hand in question has some tricky value or that there is a problem in it. This problem can be readily and accurately guessed by an expert partner.

There is a classic bridge story involving Charlie Goren, one of the country's top players. In a local tournament several years ago Goren drew as his partner a somewhat inexpert old lady.

Charlie dealt and bid one club. The opponent on his left overcalled with one spade. The old lady hesitated and finally passed. Goren then bid two clubs, which was promptly overcalled with two spades. This time the old lady paused even longer before passing.

Goren finally got the contract for three clubs. When the old lady's hand went down, it contained little trick value. "My," remarked Goren. "That second hesitation certainly was an overbid."

As chairman of the Committee on Ethics of the American Contract Bridge League, I can vouch for the fact that unethical conduct is practically unheard of at national tournaments. Occasionally, unwittingly, a player gets a glimpse of an opponent's hand. Some players, even good ones, hold their cards in such a fashion as to make it impossible for them not to be seen.

The saying that "a peek is worth two finesses" is the greatest understatement in bridge. But peekers quickly become known and are dealt with then and there by the other players.

I remember one local tournament when I was paired with a most charming lady. After the first couple of hands, it became obvious that one of our opponents was intentionally peeking. After the fourth or fifth deal as his eye started roving toward my partner's hand, she turned to him with her sweetest smile and said, "I wish you wouldn't look at my hand. I'm superstitious."

At another small match I heard an expert turn to the player on his right and remark acidly: "Do you mind if *I* look at my hand first?"

Actually the Committee on Ethics has little work to do. Not so the committees on interpretation of the rules. I remember one incident in which an old lady asked the tournament chairman to rule on a point. She had bid four diamonds over an opponent's four-spade bid. The director explained the routine ruling including the option of making the diamond bid sufficient "with no penalty."

After the hand was over the little old lady sought out the director and complained. "You said I could bid five diamonds 'with no penalty.' Well, I bid it and went down 1,700 points. What do you mean — no penalty?"

Of course, old ladies are not the only goats of the bridge table. But the experts always refer to duffers as "old ladies" — regardless of the sex or age of the offender.

The old ladies get into so many bridge stories because all big tournaments have a few "open tables," where the players of the community are invited to sit in. They don't actually play in the tournament itself, but they often do get to play with the tournament players.

Sometimes the quality of play at the open tables is excellent. But often it is not. I recall a case in which a player was needed to fill out one of the pairs at an open table. The organizer of the tournament spotted an old lady among the spectators and asked her if she played cards.

She nodded, so he took her over to a table where three other ladies were already seated. He introduced her all around and was about to leave when she called him back. "By the way," she said, "which is my partner?"

He Knew Part of the Answer

Once George Kaufman, whose bridge is nearly as good as his dialogue, drew such a partner at an open table. He turned to her and asked: "Do you mind if I inquire when you learned to play?" And before she could answer, he added: "Oh, I know it was today. But I mean, what time today?"

Getting old ladies as opponents used to be the inevitable fate of two real-life experts named Dinkelspiel and Rabinowitz. On one such occasion, Rabinowitz opened the bidding with two spades. One of the old ladies opposing him looked up brightly and asked Dinkelspiel what his partner's two spades meant.

Mr. Rabinowitz left the table (in accordance with the rules) while Mr. Dinkelspiel explained. "Well, madam," Dinkelspiel began, "two spades might mean five to five and a half Culbertson honor tricks. Or it might mean nine spades to the ace-king-queen and an outside ace — which is too strong for a three-bid. Or . . ." And he continued for fully fifteen minutes explaining every possible combination of cards which might justify a Rabinowitz two-bid.

Piling Confusion on Confusion

The poor old lady became increasingly confused as Dinkelspiel added possibility upon possibility. Finally he concluded: "But don't you worry, madam. In this case Mr. Rabinowitz is just bidding a psychic. My hand is far too strong for him to have a legitimate two-bid."

Tournament players who live in the larger cities have a big edge over the experts whose homes are out of town. They have more chance to play against one another between tournaments and to learn the peculiarities and mannerisms of their opponents.

This in turn tends to make the out-of-town players nervous in the big matches. Not an inconsiderable factor in my winning of the World's Individual Masters Tournament in 1941 was just such nervousness on the part of an otherwise excellent player from a small community.

On the hand in question he was under terrific pressure. His partner was Charlie Lochridge, who was tied with me for the match lead. This was one of the few hands where Lochridge and I played directly against each other, so its result would greatly influence the tournament outcome.

Because he was nervous, Mr. X played the hand unnecessarily badly. He went down one in a three-contract where four could easily have been made.

At the end of the hand there was dead silence. Naturally my partner and I didn't want to gloat. And Charlie Lochridge, one of the most considerate players among the masters, held his disappoinment in perfect check.

Into this tense silence, the still-confused Mr. X injected a question. "Could I have done better, partner?" And Mr. Lochridge, completely dead-pan, answered: "Well, sir, I think you could have played it double dummy to go down one more."

Yes, even the experts make boners. At one championship I actually saw a player make seven hearts although he lacked the ace of trumps.

What happened, of course, is that the opposition, playing carelessly because of a sure set, revoked.

On the other hand the old ladies sometimes give the experts their come-uppance. Messrs. Dinkelspiel and Rabinowitz used to delight in telling the following story:

They were playing in a small tournament against the inevitable old ladies. Before the playing started, one of the old girls turned to Dinkelspiel and asked what system he played. "Chinese," replied Dinkelspiel without cracking a smile. That seemed to satisfy the ladies and the bidding began.

"One spade," said the first woman.

"One no trump," said Dinkelspiel.

"Two spades," said the second lady.

"Two no trump," said Rabinowitz.

"Three clubs," said the first woman.

Everyone passed.

When the hand was played, it became evident that Rabinowitz and Dinkelspiel had held a sure small slam in spades — unbid by them because, both having spades, each assumed that the other's no-trump bid was a psychic.

The Post-Mortems Are Absorbing

But whether experts or "old ladies," bridge players get completely wrapped up in the game. At a championship match in Asbury Park, New Jersey, the men's and women's tournaments were held at opposite ends of the gigantic convention hall.

It happened that Howard Schenken, probably America's best player, finished at one table before the next table was ready for him. So he wandered into the middle of the room, where he was promptly button-holed by Helen Bonwit, a top woman player. She wanted his advice on a particularly difficult hand she had just played.

As they talked, they wandered about and eventually sat down to finish the post-mortem. It was fully ten minutes before anyone noticed that the seat Mr. Schenken occupied was right in the middle of the ladies' room.

But you don't have to play bridge to enjoy it.

Until recently I used to play quite frequently at the New York Bridge Whist Club. For many years almost every evening that I played, a charming old gentleman would draw up a chair behind mine.

He was the perfect kibitzer. He never gave an opinion. In fact, he never said a word. I grew to be very fond of him, and after the game we used to discuss everything from politics to morality.

One evening I played a particularly difficult hand and went down. After it was over, the players got into a heated discussion as to how I should have played. The argument got hotter and hotter.

Finally I turned to my kibitzing old gentleman — the first time I had asked his opinion about bridge in the many years he had sat watching. "Don't you think I was right?" I asked.

"Oh, I wouldn't know," he replied quickly. "You see, I don't know how to play the game."

DUMMY, DUMMY!
WHO'S DUMMY?

by E. J. KAHN, JR.

◇♣♡♠◇♣♡♠◇♣♡♠◇♣♡♠◇♣♡♠◇♣♡♠◇♣♡♠◇♣♡♠◇♣♡♠

WITH THE EXCEPTION of my grandfather, all of the bridge players I know often glance at the summaries of bridge hands carried in the newspapers. My grandfather does not care to have his simple, rugged game altered by the gratuitous advice of experts, but other bridge-fanciers take occasional delight in having unfolded for them the mysteries of the Vienna Coup or the triple squeeze. A few weeks ago, while reading the *Sun,* I noticed a report on the progress of the Masters' Individual Bridge Championship, an annual affair as important to bridge fans as the individual shoot at Sea Island, Georgia, is to skeet-shooters. "The final round," said the *Sun,* "produced a few spectacular results, one of the most outstanding being a hand on which most North and South players reached a small slam and made an extra trick." The *Sun* forthwith printed a box score of the hand and the accompanying bidding, as follows:

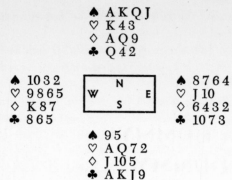

♠ A K Q J
♡ K 4 3
◇ A Q 9
♣ Q 4 2

♠ 10 3 2   ♠ 8 7 6 4
♡ 9 8 6 5   ♡ J 10
◇ K 8 7   ◇ 6 4 3 2
♣ 8 6 5   ♣ 10 7 3

♠ 9 5
♡ A Q 7 2
◇ J 10 5
♣ A K J 9

South dealer.
Neither side vulnerable.

The bidding:

Lebhar	*Glick*	*Fry Jr.-Jacoby*	*Fry*
SOUTH	NORTH	SOUTH	NORTH
1 ♣	1 ♠	1 ♣	Pass
1 NT	6 NT	Double	*Hymes*
7 NT	*Gerst*	*Appleyard*	EAST
Fuchs	EAST	WEST	2 ♠
WEST	Pass	1 ♠	
Pass	Pass	All Pass	
Pass			
All pass			

Any bridge player, even my grandfather, would admit that the results indicated by this chart are spectacular. At first glance, they are also somewhat puzzling. I carried the item around with me for a while, studying it at odd moments, and I finally decided that I could understand it and moreover reconstruct from it the scene at that bridge table. It wasn't an easy job; none of the participants in the game was credited by the *Sun* with saying more than a word or two at a time, and I had to figure out the intervening thoughts and reactions solely from my meager knowledge of the temperament of bridge players. My reconstruction begins just after the cards were dealt. At that point, I figure, the reporter assigned to the tournament, a young man with little or no sense of direction, asked the four men at the table to tell him exactly where they were sitting, to ensure the accuracy of his account. This is what they said, and why they said it:

LEBHAR: South. (*Lebhar is a sound, sensible fellow. He is sitting South and would naturally say so.*)

GLICK: North. (*He doesn't hear the* Sun's *question, as he is telling a kibitzer named Fuchs the title of a play he has recently seen. Actually, Glick is sitting West.*)

FRY, JR.: Jacoby. (*This answer is just silly. It will become clear, as we go on, that Fry, Jr., is a spirited but alarmingly absent-minded fellow. He's sitting North.*)

FRY: North. (*Playing against his son in major competition always makes him nervous. He knows he's sitting East but decides that the other players are having fun with the Sun report and that he'll string along; he doesn't want to seem old-fashioned.*)

After these geographical preliminaries, the men hitch up their chairs and get down to the serious business of bidding:

LEBHAR: One club. (*With three and a half quick tricks, he'd be a fool not to say it.*)

GLICK: One spade. (*He figures that if he tosses in a psychic bid, he might confuse his opponents.*)

FRY, JR.: South. (*Obviously, he's badly rattled.*)

FRY: Pass. (*He can't decide exactly what is going on, so he'll bide his time.*)

LEBHAR: One no trump. (*Although the bidding appears to be screwy, he hopes things will get straightened out. He holds a powerful hand and wants to play it.*)

GLICK: Six no trump. (*Having bluffed originally, he might as well go the whole hog, he thinks. This is the final round of the tournament and the other players are getting on his nerves; he'd like to get the hell out of the joint and into a Turkish bath.*)

FRY, JR.: One club. (*Hopelessly muddled by now, he remembers dimly that Lebhar said "One club" a while back. Fry, Jr., is peculiarly fascinated by everything Lebhar says and often repeats his partner's words, just because he likes the way they sound.*)

FRY: Hymes! (*An ejaculation. Any father might say it under the circumstances.*)

LEBHAR: Seven no trump. (*He's furious.*)

GLICK: Gerst. (*He is evidently asking Gerst, an elderly retainer at the bridge club, to come over and empty an ash tray into which Lebhar has been angrily depositing the shredded remnants of a scoring pad.*)

FRY, JR.: Double. (*Aside from the fact that he is doubling his own partner's bid, this is a perfectly proper remark.*)

FRY: East. (*He has suddenly remembered what he should have said way back at the beginning and is trying to straighten himself out.*)

LEBHAR: Fuchs. (*Mr. Fuchs, the kibitzer, has remained commendably*

*quiet so far. Now Lebhar is requesting him to pay exceptionally careful
attention. Most people, when playing a seven-no-trump contract, doubled,
insist on having an outside witness looking on, so that if they are successful they will have impartial corroboration for the story they plan to tell
their wives.)*

GLICK: East. (*This is an aside, addressed to Fry. Glick is simply
acknowledging Fry's last word and is saying, in effect, "Oh — East. You
mean you should have said that before."*)

FRY, JR.: Appleyard. (*The word "East" started him off on a train of
thought, too. Its destination happens to be an appleyard he was fond of
as a boy. As he says this, he looks in a happy, reminiscent way at his
father.*)

FRY: Two spades. (*There is no rational explanation for this; perhaps
it's a typographical error.*)

LEBHAR: West. (*Close, but not an exact transcription. What Lebhar is
actually saying is "Gerst." The ash trays need emptying again. Besides,
Lebhar wants a drink, quick.*)

GLICK: Pass. (*He feels that the sooner this is over, the better.*)

FRY, JR.: West. (*A statement undoubtedly based on Lebhar's "Gerst,"
which Fry, Jr., misunderstood. Since he has been parroting Lebhar all
along, it is illogical to expect him to stop now. If he had heard Lebhar
say "Gerst," he would have said "Gerst," too.*)

FRY: (*He is speechless by now, and no wonder.*)

LEBHAR: Pass. (*He would be happy if they cut out the kidding and
laid down some cards.*)

GLICK: Pass. (*If only the rest of the boys would follow his example!*)

FRY, JR.: One spade. (*He thinks he is imitating Lebhar again, but is so
confused, what with his father glaring at him and the rest of the boys
drumming angrily on the table, that by mistake he imitates Glick instead.*)

FRY: (*Still speechless.*)

LEBHAR: Pass. (*He's grimly determined to keep a grip on himself, no
matter what.*)

GLICK: (*He has passed twice already, so this time he just nods.*)

FRY, JR.: All pass! (*Being absent-minded, he has failed to notice that
the other players have done little but pass for some time. Fry, Jr., probably thinks he is doing them a favor by issuing this sweeping order to
stop the bidding. They'd have stopped by themselves long ago if it hadn't
been for him.*)

FRY: (*He doesn't say anything; isn't even thinking of bridge.*)

LEBHAR: All pass! (*It took quite a while, but he has finally collapsed*

under the strain and has begun to imitate Junior. It is a tribute to Lebhar's
durability that he held out as long as he did.)

The *Sun's* comment on this extraordinary episode was a masterpiece of subtle criticism. "Score for Fuchs and Gerst on this hand," it said, "was minus 1,520." I do not blame the *Sun* for losing patience with the contestants and attributing the whole mess to a couple of fellows who we know were merely dumping ashes and leaning on shoulders. Perhaps the only man who really relished this singular incident was my grandfather. I showed him the story and his eyes lit up. "Those so-called experts play like a lot of damn fools," he said. "I could have bid the hand better myself."

HOW TO IMPROVE
YOUR BRIDGE POPULARITY

◇ ♣ ♡ ♠ ◇ ♣ ♡ ♠ ◇ ♣ ♡ ♠ ◇ ♣ ♡ ♠ ◇ ♣ ♡ ♠ ◇ ♣ ♡ ♠ ◇ ♣ ♡ ♠ ◇ ♣ ♡ ♠

1. Pick up your cards as dealt. You will be ready to bid ahead of the others.
2. If you get a poor partner, keep score yourself; you must have some advantage.
3. Lead from your own hand or dummy, as convenient.
4. Never hurry. Try several cards on a trick until you are sure which one you prefer.
5. Occasionally ask what is trumps. It will show that you are interested in the game.
6. Trump your partner's ace and cinch the trick.
7. Walk around the table when you are dummy and look at the other hands; tell them what cards are good and how many tricks they can take if they play right.
8. Always ask your partner why he didn't return your lead; this will remind him to lead it next time.
9. Don't try to remember the rules; they are too confusing.
10. Always explain your plays, particularly when set. It shows your card knowledge.
11. Talk about other subjects during the game; it makes for good fellowship.
12. Claim all honors; you might get away with it once in a while.
13. Eat chocolate caramels or other adhesive candy while playing; it keeps the cards from skidding.
14. After the third round, lay your hand on the table and claim the rest of the tricks; you may not have them, but it's much easier to play with all the cards exposed.

178

BLUFFING AT BRIDGE

by HART STILWELL

THE TIME COMES in the life of every bridge player when he gets sick and tired of following suit to the opponents' high cards, and finds that he has, without any visible explanation in logic, indulged in a remarkable bid.

Perhaps he feels that it will change his luck. I knew a player who held stubbornly to this theory. When I was his partner I was always on the lookout for an earth-shaking bid, based on a few tens and eights, after a protracted session of worthless hands. I was seldom disappointed.

"I got sick of following suit," he would explain after we had gone down a few thousand points. "Thought maybe I would change our luck."

Of course when the opponents got through with his bid it was usually too late for a change of luck to do him, or me either, much good. But at any rate, he had broken the monotony of following suit, for it seems that when a man starts getting a run of worthless hands, the distribution is usually 4–3–3–3.

Sometimes I believe his idea is not so bad. I know that every man who plays bridge is likewise tempted on occasions, but few yield to the temptation. There is a modest tingling of pleasure from suddenly calling out "four spades" when you have nothing higher than a jack or queen. You are flinging a challenge into the teeth of fate.

Some of these bids have met disaster. Most of them have. Those I manage to forget in a hurry. No man enjoys remembering the time he went down six, doubled and redoubled, and I say redoubled for a man's partner usually has a nasty habit of redoubling on such occasions.

From *Esquire* Magazine, May 1942. Reprinted by permission.

But when these screwball bids pay off, then I love to linger over them on some quiet afternoon months or even years later, playing the hand over once more, watching the look of astonishment on the faces of the enemy as their aces and kings are ruffed away, and gloating once more over that overtrick which was the crowning insult of all.

I am gloating right now over just such a hand. I had been meekly following suit until it began to lose interest. Any hand I picked up with a king in it began to look big, and I felt a strong desire to bid welling up within me. My partner must have realized this, for he sat there in stony silence when I was doubled, when he had sound reason to redouble if my bid had been based on anything near the values that it indicated. In fact, his thinking was even worse than that, for later he confessed to me that he was contemplating going to a small slam. I still shudder when I think of it.

I sat South, then, and drew this mess of pottage:

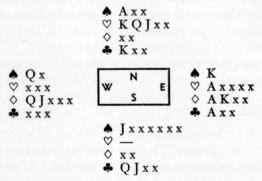

The gentleman on my right, East, dealt and opened one heart. He had been doing it all evening. The only time there was any variation was when he opened one spade instead of one heart. I don't think I had played a hand in fourteen years. When I did get some face cards they were clubs, and I was always outbid. When I finally work out my own system of bridge, there are going to be no clubs in the deck — just a few extra spades and hearts. They are the cards to hold.

So I figured it was time I played a hand. Holding this pile of junk I bid four spades at once, before I had time to reflect on the complete lack of logic in the bid. I realized that even a modest amount of thought on the matter would have resulted in a pass, so I was careful not to indulge in this thought.

This four-spade bid rode all the way back to East, and after a casual glance at his aces and kings, and knowing full well that I was in a humor to make a bid regardless of what I held, he doubled.

When it arrived back at my partner he started studying his hand, and no matter how hard I looked at him he kept right on studying it and wouldn't pass. Finally, when I was on the verge of shouting at him to go ahead and pass, he did pass. I eased back in my chair, figuring I would lose no more than nine hundred or eleven hundred points, since we weren't vulnerable. I figured it was a cinch to take at least four of my spades, and I might even take a club — who knows.

Well, the opening heart lead brought down the dummy, and a shower of delight with it. The spectacle of that dummy, with a heart lead through it, was worth all the bad sets I had suffered in three or four months.

And what followed was worth twice as much.

I put up the king which brought out the ace which was ruffed. I played over to the ace of spades, got rid of my two diamonds on the queen and jack of hearts, which was perfectly safe since the queen was the only outstanding trump and it was high. Then I made the enemy a present of the ace of clubs and the high trump, thus making the doggone bid with an overtrick.

East got up and put on his hat and walked away. I haven't seen him since then, and sometimes I worry about him for as he went out the door he was muttering. "No man objects to losing at bridge, but to sit at the same table with anybody fool enough to bid four spades on that hand and lucky enough to make five . . ."

That was a noble incident in my bridge career.

I recall another flurry into the realm of the fantastic that has given me much to gloat over. We were so far behind that anything might happen. It did.

I dealt and again sat South, since nobody objected. I picked up the stack of junk shown in the South hand below:

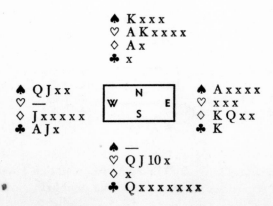

After a casual glance at my hand I opened with three clubs, in spite of the then current rule that to open with three in a minor suit you must have the top honors. West passed and my partner bid three hearts. East passed and I bid six hearts, on the theory that if my partner couldn't make it, he had no business bidding at all.

East opened the ace of spades and began abusing me for foolish bidding as I put down the hearts and clubs and the diamond. It always seems odd to me that people will berate you for making a bid which they expect to set. But when East started looking for spades and couldn't find any, he stopped talking. My partner ruffed the spade ace and led a club. The rest of the tricks were in the bag — at least, we put them in the bag. If there was any way to defeat the contract, East and West never discovered it.

There are plenty of bridge players who might have opened three clubs on the hand. I am not proud of that bid at all. It's the six-heart bid that strikes my fancy. A man might even go back over the hand carefully and justify the six-heart bid. But I hope nobody does it. I love to feel that it was a pure venture into the unknown — and one that paid off nicely.

The interesting part of the hand to me is that six spades could have been made by the opponents.

I even derive a certain fiendish satisfaction from some screwball bids that have been set and set badly. For many is the time when a careful check afterward will reveal that I saved a thousand or so points by such a bid. I never fail to remind the opponents of this, which is another reason why I am extremely popular as a bridge player.

One such hand sticks in my crop, quite pleasantly, at the moment, and I reproduce it here in order to gloat over it a bit more. On this hand I sat North, my partner being a gentleman from South Carolina who flatly refused to occupy that position.

The hand follows:

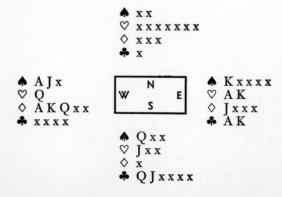

You will note upon careful examination that I held what is known in the profession as a yarborough.

The gentleman on my right, West, dealt and bid one diamond.

Well, I didn't pass. I knew East for a malicious sort of fellow who could think of nothing more satisfying than setting somebody. What particularly delighted him was to hold the high cards in your trump suit and then double. Evidently he held them. At least I didn't.

So I decided to bid just high enough to get doubled. I bid three hearts and East doubled. Thus the bidding ended.

Well, I went down, of course. I lost every trick it was possible to lose, I guess, going down for a penalty of five hundred. But the hand, and particularly my bidding, was an outstanding success. The vulnerable opponents had an ironclad cinch for six spades or seven diamonds, and could have made seven spades by finessing for the queen.

Certainly a small slam would have been bid, except for East's malicious yearning to see me squirm while he took the high trumps.

What irritated the enemy on this hand wasn't so much the points they lost. It was my bidding. They claimed that it was even dishonest and against the rules to bid three hearts holding no honor cards. Perhaps it is. I wouldn't know. But I do know that if that is dishonesty, there are times when it will give a person a certain degree of mild satisfaction.

Incidentally, we won the rubber, which didn't make East and West feel any better.

Now I am not advising you to set out on a course of wild bidding on hands that are doomed, on the face of things, to meet a sudden and disastrous fate. Such bidding would soon take the interest out of bridge, at least for your partner.

I am merely pointing out that there are times when a thing can go just so far and then it not only ceases to be entertaining but it becomes a downright nuisance.

In times like that almost any kind of diversion is likely to enliven the proceedings. When the diversion, in the form of a fantastic bid, pays off — then, brother, you've been through a real experience in bridge. You've got something sweet you can look back on.

A HELLUVA GAME

by ROBERT N. BLUM

◇♣♡♠◇♣♡♠◇♣♡♠◇♣♡♠◇♣♡♠◇♣♡♠◇♣♡♠◇♣♡♠◇♣♡♠

MR. KREMELKOPF was thinking about the payment due on his new car when he absent-mindedly dropped a small trump on his partner's good king of diamonds. He had forgotten that the ace had been played long ago, and there is no question that he did not foresee the immediate consequences to himself.

His partner, a normally quiet, even-dispositioned individual, said nothing. He merely rose from his chair, drew a small automatic pistol from his pocket, and fired once.

The bullet entered Mr. Kremelkopf's head just to the left of center, and he slumped slowly to the floor in a shower of cards. . . .

When consciousness returned to Mr. Kremelkopf, he found himself standing in a luxuriously appointed card room, where several games were in progress.

There was no trace of the bullet's indentation in his head.

"I must surely be dead," Mr. Kremelkopf said to himself, as a recollection of the happenings of a few moments before came back to him. "I wonder where I am?"

He had no chance for further speculation on this point, for at that moment one of the most beautiful young women Mr. Kremelkopf's eyes had ever been fortunate enough to rest on walked over to him, laid her hand gently upon his arm, and identified herself as one of the hostesses.

Reprinted by permission of *The Bridge World*, New York. A. Moyse, Jr. publisher.

"I have a nice game waiting for you," she said. "We've been expecting you for some time."

Mr. Kremelkopf allowed himself to be guided toward a table at which two ladies and a gentleman were seated.

"I just know you're a fine player," his charming companion murmured as they strolled across the room. "I hope you'll give me some pointers about play." Her pressure on his arm increased ever so slightly. "Perhaps you wouldn't mind escorting me to my apartment after your game tonight, and we can have a snack while you explain some of the higher strategies to me," she continued with a smile.

Mr. Kremelkopf, who didn't know a Vienna Coup from a wiener schnitzel, found his heart skipping two complete beats as he managed to stammer his delighted acquiescence.

"That'll be just wonderful," she whispered in his ear, allowing her lips to just graze that delighted organ. "But you'll have to win tonight," she added. "It's a club rule. Hostesses may not accompany losing players from the premises."

Mr. Kremelkopf beamed confidence at his ability to take command with such a magnificent prize at stake.

The strolling couple reached their destination, and introductions were quickly made.

"This is Mr. Kremelkopf," stated the hostess, "a recent arrival. May I present Miss Snood, Colonel Caulk, and Miss Gremlin."

All bowed their greetings, and a quick cut established Mr. Kremelkopf as partner with Colonel Caulk.

Colonel Caulk flipped the cards rapidly around the table. "Our usual stake," he said casually. "Dollar a point . . . and winner escorts the hostess."

The by now thoroughly bemused Mr. Kremelkopf could but murmur his assent as he picked up his hand.

♠ Q 10 7 4   ♡ 9 8   ◇ A Q   ♣ A J 8 7 6

Colonel Caulk cleared his throat with the hearty gruffness which had once stricken terror to the hearts of subalterns in Her Majesty's 212th Palomino Light Hussars, and opened the bidding with one diamond.

After a hearty pass from Miss Snood, Mr. Kremelkopf surveyed his hand with pride and announced: "Two clubs."

The slight shrug of resignation with which Miss Gremlin delivered her pass indicated that L.H.O. had nothing to write home about.

And now Colonel Caulk went into a slight study. He held:

♠ A   ♡ A Q J   ◇ J 9 7 5 3   ♣ K Q 9 4

"Ah ha," thought he. "My partner probably has nothing much in spades, because he didn't mention 'em, but he went up to the two-level, so he's got something. I think the game contract will be three no trump, which I shall play in my usually masterful fashion. So, just to make sure that I don't get a spade lead, I'll stick in a phony. Two spades!" he growled.

Nothing from Miss Snood.

Now Mr. Kremelkopf's eyes returned from their surveillance of his soon-to-be companion of the evening, who was smiling encouragement from the other side of the room, and focused upon his four-card spade holding.

He found his thought processes both lucid and logical. "Never," thought he, "have I been sharper than at this moment. My partner bids a diamond, lacking his ace and queen, yet is strong enough to reverse with his next bid. He must have at least the king and jack of spades four times, if not the ace and king. If this isn't a slam I'll go back to mah-jongg."

He bid: "Four no trump!"

Colonel Caulk's first answer was a gulp. "What is in this maniac's mind?" the Colonel wondered. "What ever gave him the fantastic notion that I wanted to go slamming! And how will I get out of this mess?" But years of training with the Hussars, where chain-of-command and unquestioned obedience to orders were paramount, overruled the Colonel's desire to take the easy way out and pass. For a fleeting moment he remembered Lord Nelson on the bridge of the *Victory*. "England expects . . ." he thought — and manfully Blackwooded: "Five hearts." His voice was firm, his eyes bright, his chin steady. No one could read the black thoughts that filled his mind.

Mr. Kremelkopf paused barely long enough for station identification before firmly closing the contract (he thought) at, "Six spades."

The Colonel's hand instinctively leaped toward where twenty years before it would have grasped the finely inlaid head of his cavalry saber. Then he caught himself, "He got me into this and he'll get himself out!" he told himself. "If he thinks I'm going to play a six-spade contract on a stiff ace, he must start unthinking rapidly! Well, he'll stew in his own juice." And he bid: "Six no trump."

Mr. Kremelkopf nodded approvingly, then his face blanched as he suddenly recalled that his Blackwood query made him the no-trump bidder and that he would play the hand. His eyes met those of the hostess across the room, and he caught the semblance of a very personal wink. So he set his chin and passed.

The Colonel's phony spade bid had impressed itself securely upon what Miss Gremlin laughingly referred to as her mind, and she opened a small heart, away from her king.

The dummy went down, and Mr. Kremelkopf, not without trepidation, played the jack and won the trick on the board. "Now or never," he thought as he drew a small diamond from the dummy, dropped the queen from his hand, and ruefully watched Miss Gremlin take the trick with the king.

Miss Gremlin, unaware that Opportunity always lives up to its reputation, tried to make up for her earlier sin of omission, and knocked out dummy's lone spade ace.

Mr. Kremelkopf scooped up the trick and led a small diamond to his ace, catching two more of the brave lads. "This is it," he told himself, as he went over to the board with a small club to the king, and then held his breath as the jack of diamonds caught the last standouts in that suit, as he ditched a spade. He quickly cashed the two remaining diamonds, discarding his useless spades, returned to his club ace, finessed the heart once more, and took his ace of hearts.

A happy smile wreathed his face as he pulled his queen of clubs and then led the last club toward his only remaining card, the jack of clubs.

"Six no trump cold," he thought happily as he prepared himself to look becomingly modest at the plaudits about to be heaped upon him.

Then came the blow. Miss Snood held up her empty hands. "I'm one card short," she announced.

Mr. Kremelkopf snorted. "So what!" he said, his voice rising some octaves above his usually suave baritone, "the hand is in anyway!"

Miss Gremlin had two bits' worth to add at that point. "Section 50, Laws of Contract Bridge, 1943," she said firmly. "And I quote: 'If during the play period, a hand is found to have too few cards . . . there must be a new deal.' So sorry."

Mr. Kremelkopf, whose face had now taken on a becoming shade of aquamarine, could only surrender. He beckoned to the charming hostess. "I'll win one yet," he said. "Please bring us a new deck . . . this one is a card short."

The hostess shook her blond locks sadly. "I'm sorry," she said, "but all our decks are one card short!"

Mr. Kremelkopf looked stricken. "Why this is Hell," he said.

"Of course," the hostess replied. "Where did you think you were?"

MURDERS

by EDWIN VICTOR WESTRATE

I

He was a guy who talked and talked
  And talked and talked some more,
At chatter he was never balked,
  This non-stop, maddening bore.

On every deal and every play,
On every trick we tossed away,
He had to have his little say,
On what he did one other day,
On hands in which his brilliant sway
Won every coup in every fray.

He left us just one thing to do,
  If we would have release,
So I murdered him last Tuesday,
  And now we play in peace.

II

She was so nice in every way,
  I thought, until with dull
And sickening thud, I heard her say,
  "Let's see—oh, yes—We're vul."

Reprinted by permission of *The Bridge World,* New York. A. Moyse, Jr., publisher.

I didn't mind how long she'd mull
Above her hand a card to cull
And play to end the painful lull,
But then would crash into my skull,
Those words to quickly render null
And void all else, "I see we're vul."

The death decree I had to give,
   There was no other way,
So Wednesday night the deed was done.
   No more "We're vul" she'll say.

III

I should have known right from the jump,
   He'd put me on the skids.
He looked the part—but who could dream
   He'd pass my forcing bids?

In all of contract's playing mass,
I've never met a mind so crass,
I'd bid "Two spades," he'd say, "I pass,"
My jump shifts, too, he'd drop, alas,
My golden tries were so much brass,
While playing with this cheerful ass.

The end, of course, was no surprise,
   Last Thursday was the time
I shot him right between the eyes.
   Who dares to call it crime?

"IF"

by WM. TALLEY ELLIOT
with apologies to Rudyard Kipling, et al.

◇♣♡♠◇♣♡♠◇♣♡♠◇♣♡♠◇♣♡♠◇♣♡♠◇♣♡♠◇♣♡♠

If you can play your hand when all about you
　Are losing theirs and blaming it on you;
If you can trust your partner when he doubts you,
　But make allowance for his doubting too:
If you can wait and not be tired by waiting;
　Or being set too much, don't blame your hand,
Or being baited don't give way to baiting,
　And yet don't look too good, nor talk too bland;

If you can play—and not make play your master;
　If you can win—and not make gain your aim,
If you can meet with Triumph and Disaster
　And treat those two impostors just the same:
If you can bear to hear the bids you've spoken
　Twisted by Fate to make a trap for fools,
Or watch opponents win with each rule broken,
　And deal and play and still abide the rules;

If you can make one heap of all your winnings
　And risk it on a Grand Slam bid and lost,
And smile, and start again at your beginnings
　And never breathe a word about your loss:

Reprinted by permission of *The Bridge World*, New York. A. Moyse, Jr., publisher.

If you can Force your partner and he passes,
   Or deny, and see him still bid high,
And see the score the other side amasses,
   And do not criticize or even sigh;

If you can play with fools and still continue
   To calmly watch your partner wreck his play,
If adverse bids and Overcalls don't irk you,
   If it's always something pleasant that you say:
If you can fill the unforgiven minute
   With sixty seconds worth of fair play done,
Yours is the deck and everything that's in it,
   And—which is more—you'll be a freak, my son!

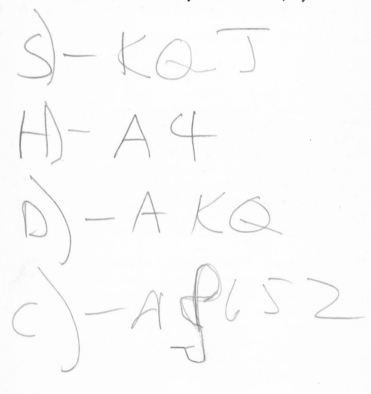

INVENTORY

by JEANNE S. MARKS
with apologies to Dorothy Parker

Four be the things I am wiser to know:
Conservatism, sign-offs, signals, and foe.
Three be the things I am better without:
Optimism, psychics, and the bid-hogging lout.
Four be the things I shall never attain:
Perfection, deception, less loss, and more gain.
Three be the things I shall have 'til I'm dead:
Laughter and hope and a hole in my head.

From *The American Contract Bridge League Bulletin.* Reprinted by permission.

SOLILOQUY

by MAURIE C. BRYAN

To bid or not to bid: that is the question!
Whether 'tis better in the end to suffer
The sets and bottoms of outrageous distribution,
Or to pass against a mess of doubles,
And by passing end them. To win; to place;
No more; and by a pass to end
Redoubles and the thousand natural shocks
A player is heir to, 'tis a consummation
Devoutly to be wished. To place, to win;
To win: perchance I dream: aye, there's the rub;
For in that dream what tops may come,
When we have shuffled off this mortal coil,
Must give us pause. There's the bid
That makes calamity of one night's play.
For who could bear the halfs and zeros, at times
The opponent's scorn, our partner's contumely,
The pangs of sacrifices gone wrong, the kibitzer's pity,
The point count, honor trick,
The chill of bottoms the unworthy takes,
When he himself might quietus make
With a mere pass? Who would conventions use
To squirm and sweat a dazed life,
But that dread of being east-west
That humble seeding from whose bourn

From *The American Contract Bridge League Bulletin*. Reprinted by permission.

No reputation returns, puzzles the mind
And makes us rather hide the cards we have
Than make bids our partner knows not of?
Our systems do make fools of us all,
And thus the simple pass of irresolution
Is sicklied o'er with the pale cast of doubt.
All enterprise of cue bids, take-outs
We now regard as breathless strategy
And skip the chance for action. Soft you now!
Fair partner! Simply, in thy prayers
Be all my bridge sins remember'd.

Bridge

BY WEBSTER

CLASSIC ANECDOTES

A BRIDGE TEACHER took on a mathematics professor as a pupil. When they came to the lesson on the theory and practice of the finesse the teacher went over the whole business very carefully with his student. Together they worked out the odds and probabilities. The professor of mathematics seemed to have grasped the lesson very nicely.

Shortly after this lesson, the teacher got his pupil into a practice game and steered the contract to three no trump, with the latter as declarer. The opening lead drove out declarer's only entry to his hand. Dummy had the A K Q 10 x x of clubs and declarer had three, giving nine clubs altogether. All the professor had to do was run the suit and with three side tricks it would enable him to fulfill his contract. It looked easy.

At the second trick declarer led small from his hand and finessed dummy's ten of clubs while his teacher blinked. The finesse won. Not only that but the hand behind the dummy showed out of the suit. It was the only way all six clubs could be won.

After the delighted declarer had gleefully raked in the nine tricks for the contract, he looked at his teacher for approval. The latter smiled weakly.

"That certainly was an unusual finesse," he said, "even though it was the only way to make the contract. Don't you believe all those percentages we worked out in our lesson when we went over finesses?"

"Oh, I believe them all right," nodded the pupil. "But I was watching the fellow to my left when he played to my club and I saw him pull out the fourth card from the end of his hand."

◇ ♣ ♡ ♠

A number of these stories first appeared in the American Contract Bridge League Bulletin, edited by Alfred Sheinwold, and circulated among some 50,000 members.

The expert was playing a tough hand in a tournament. He led a card from dummy and the innocent-looking miss on his right went into a long huddle before following suit. When declarer led the suit again the miss showed out.

Annoyed, the expert said, "What was all the hesitation about. You had a singleton."

"Yes," said Miss Innocence, dimpling. "But it was tricky, wasn't it?"

◇ ♣ ♡ ♠

It was the tail end of a long evening and the four players were woozy from drink and bridge. A new deck was broken out. The cards were dealt, the bidding went round and round and wound up at seven spades, redoubled.

The opening lead was made and declarer won it. He laid down the ace of trumps, both opponents following.

Suddenly declarer did a double take. There in his hand was another ace of trumps. The backs of the two aces, he saw, were identical so obviously it was a defective deck.

However, this was a grand slam redoubled, so he laid down the second ace of trumps to see what would happen. Opponent to the left dropped the king.

"Darn it," said the owner of the king groggily shaking his head at his equally groggy partner. "That's one card I sure thought I was going to make."

◇ ♣ ♡ ♠

A contestant in a tournament suddenly slumped down in his chair, victim of what seemed like a seizure or fit of some kind. A doctor was hastily summoned. He took the stricken man's pulse and noted that it was steady and firm. Obviously it was no heart attack.

From the victim's white face and clammy hands the doctor surmised that this was a case of shock. A bridge player himself, he picked up the victim's cards and studied them. He then turned to the others at the table.

"Now let me have a review of the bidding," he requested.

◇ ♣ ♡ ♠

The huffy lady got into an argument with one of her opponents at the tournament table. The argument got away from bridge into personalities. Finally, the huffy lady cried out, "Young man, you are very offensive."

"I know it," said the other, "but so are you. The difference is that I'm trying to be, but you can't help it."

◇ ♣ ♡ ♠

The bridge addict dreamed that he was in Hades. He and two other players were looking for a fourth when the Devil happened to pass by.

"How about making a fourth?" invited the bridge addict.

"Glad to," said the Devil and joined the game.

Sizable stakes were agreed upon and on the very first deal the bridge addict dealt himself the following hand:

♠ A K Q J   ♡ A K Q   ◇ A K Q   ♣ A K Q

When he had caught his breath he blurted out, "Seven no trump."

"Double!" said the Devil sitting to his left.

"I redouble!" yelled the bridge addict.

The Devil grinned and made his opening lead. It was a strange-looking, green-colored suit the declarer had never seen before.

"No hippogryphs?" asked the dummy dutifully.

"No hippogryphs," answered the bridge addict dazedly.

And with that the entire green suit was led out against him and he went down thirteen tricks.

◇ ♣ ♡ ♠

A prominent doctor was an enthusiastic but not very good bridge player. One day his friend, a man he occasionally played bridge with, fell sick and the doctor was called in.

The patient was gloomy over his condition, and the doctor made a careful examination. Wishing to reassure him that there was nothing to worry about, he said cheerfully, "You'll be all right. Mark my words, you'll live to play many a rubber of bridge with me as your partner yet."

"Oh Lord," groaned the despondent patient. "I think I'd rather die."

◇ ♣ ♡ ♠

The two little old ladies came to the table of a well-known expert pair at the tournament.

On the first hand, the two little old ladies stopped at a mere contract of one club and were set one.

"Where are you ladies from?" asked one of their opponents with an amused smile.

"Texas," was the reply.

"You mean to say you came all the way from Texas to play a hand at only one club and go down one?"

"If we'd stayed in Texas," was the ever so gentle retort, "we wouldn't have bought the hand for only one club. And if we had, we'd have gone down two."

◇ ♣ ♡ ♠

Two other little old ladies were playing in another tournament against their inevitable foils, the two celebrated masters.

One of the little old ladies opened the bidding with one no trump. The master to her left was looking at a hand containing fourteen points on which he considered bidding. He turned to the opening bidder's partner and asked, "What kind of no trumps do you play?"

"Strong," she answered, "around twenty points."

Whereupon the master hastily passed and so did the opening bidder's partner. Dummy laid down two queens and a jack and the expert silently congratulated himself for not having stuck his neck out.

But the defense started to take trick after trick and eventually accumulated nine of them beating the contract three, undoubled. Game, it developed, was cold in the masters' hands.

The expert with the fourteen-point hand turned to the dummy and said in an aggrieved tone, "Didn't you say you played a strong no trump?"

"I do," answered the little old lady. "But my partner plays a weak no trump, about 12 points."

◇ ♣ ♡ ♠

When the dealer still had made no bid after studying his cards for a long while, one of the opponents muttered something about "getting this duplicate moving."

"What'd you say?" asked the dealer coming out of his reverie momentarily.

"I want to know what you do," said the opponent.

"Oh," responded the other. "I'm in the wholesale grocery business. Why?"

◇ ♣ ♡ ♠

Two life masters playing as partners got into a vehement argument after a certain deal. The dispute waxed hotter and hotter until one of the masters raised a hand and said, "Wait. We'll put it up to our opponents and let them decide who's right."

"That's silly," answered the other. "Anyone can see they don't know the first thing about bridge."

"And anybody can see that we're sloppy too," answered one of the opponents. Whereupon he picked up an ash tray and dumped its contents all over the contemptuous one's head.

◇ ♣ ♡ ♠

Daisy was fit to be tied after she and her husband came home from an evening of bridge with the Browns.

"Why," she wanted to know, "why didn't you pass as we agreed to every time I kicked you under the table?"

"But, darling, I never once felt a kick."

"Oh! That explains why Brown was passing on so many hands."

◇ ♣ ♡ ♠

The bridge dub returned home from a business trip, excited about an event that occurred on the train.

"Imagine, my dear," he told his wife. "One afternoon on the train three men came into the club car looking for someone to make a fourth at bridge. I told them I played and we started a game. It turned out that they were three famous bridge experts coming back from a tournament."

"How fascinating," said his wife. "Did they like the way you played?"

"Oh fine," replied the dub. "Except once when I was dealing I dropped a card accidentally, and one of them laughed and said, 'Why, the so and so can't even deal properly.'"

◇ ♣ ♡ ♠

A young couple had just learned to play bridge and they invited another young couple over for a game. The visitors knew little about bridge, but were eager to learn and the host and hostess tried to teach them as they went along.

Finally they gave up the attempt and suggested another pastime, tossing cards into a hat. The visitors were disappointed but agreed to the suggestion. The evening passed pleasantly enough after that.

That night the host rolled over in bed and woke his wife from a sound slumber.

"You know, darling, I've been thinking—it's a wonderful game."

"Is *that* what you woke me up to tell me in the middle of the night," murmured his wife sleepily, "that bridge is a wonderful game?"

"Oh no, not bridge," replied the husband eagerly. "Tossing the cards into a hat. I never realized it before, but there's actually more skill to it."

"Bridge," said the sage, "is a great comfort in your old age. It also helps you get there faster."

The timid lady was partnered with the club expert during one round of the individual tournament. On the first hand she got him into a sound enough contract but he proceeded to butcher it for down one.

"I'm sorry," said his partner. "It was my fault."

"*Your* fault?" he asked surprised. "There were a dozen right ways to play that contract and I had to pick the one way to get set."

"I know," said the timid lady. "I was trying to use telepathy on you and you took the line of play I concentrated on."

The bridge bug was in an exciting game when word was brought to him that his house was on fire.

He hurriedly finished the hand he was playing and then said, "Sorry, fellows, looks like I'll have to break up the game. Three more rubbers and I quit."

Then there's the shaggy doggie about the horse who entered a bridge tournament. The lookers-on were amazed at the clever way in which he cooperated with his partner to reach a grand slam on the very first hand. He played the hand as declarer, but went down one trick.

"You should have taken the club finesse," his partner pointed out. "With the king on side you couldn't miss making the slam."

"That's ridiculous," said the horse. "Whoever heard of a horse knowing how to finesse?"

Teacher called on six-year-old Johnny Jones, the bridge player's son, to count for the class.

"One, two, three," began Johnny, "four, five, six, seven, eight, nine, ten—uh, jack, queen, king, ace—"

The little old lady was sitting on the porch of a summer hotel. Three people set up a card table nearby. Hopefully, one of them asked her if she would care to make a fourth at bridge.

"Love to," she said and joined them.

The cards were dealt. The dealer bid "one diamond," and now it was the little old lady's turn. Her lips moved as she counted carefully to herself.

"I'll bid six clovers," she announced finally.

They were at a concert. Said she, a bridge addict, "What's that book the conductor keeps looking at?"

"That's the score," answered her escort.

"Oh. Who's vulnerable?"

◊ ♣ ♡ ♠

He hadn't shown up at the club in some time. One night he came down to play duplicate and when he got to the second table a woman member greeted him with, "We've missed you, Cookie."

"Well," he said pleased at the affectionate greeting. "Thanks. You never called me Cookie before."

"I know," she said. "But that's because you've never been a wafer so long before."

◊ ♣ ♡ ♠

A bridge expert received a letter reading:

"Dear Sir—I have been doubled in hearts at love score, and I should like to finesse the queen. However, I don't even own a ten-spot. What do you advise?"

His reply: "You must lead with a diamond if you have one. If you play the knave, her father will make a grand slam with a club, the sexton will play a spade, Gabriel will trumpet, and you will go down with no honors."

Section 6

Of Experts and Tournaments

OF EXPERTS AND TOURNAMENTS

◇♣♡♠◇♣♡♠◇♣♡♠◇♣♡♠◇♣♡♠◇♣♡♠◇♣♡♠◇♣♡♠◇♣♡♠◇♣♡♠

THE WORLD OF MASTERS and their tournaments is a strange one to the uninitiated player, far removed from his bridge experience and understanding. He reads about the accomplishments of the experts in his favorite bridge column or in the newspaper reports of major tournaments and can only shake his head over some of the bids and plays. What accounts for these goings-on, he wonders.

Suppose we examine the expert, his mental processes and his behavior at and away from the bridge table and see what we can find out by way of explanation. First of all, how do you tell an expert? Ordinarily (though this isn't always the final test) by the fact that he owns "master points." The greater the total of these points amassed, the greater his success in formal contests.

Master points are won in club, sectional, regional or national tournaments run under the auspices of the American Contract Bridge League. A player's score in these events depends less on the cards he holds than on how he bids and plays them in comparison with others who will also be bidding and holding those same cards at some time.

Such competitions are run duplicate style. That is, the cards played to a trick are not gathered up by the winner. But each one is placed face down in front of the person who played it. After the deal is over each player's original hand is returned to a "board" which has pockets for the cards. The deal is scored. The board is then played at other tables. And thus, theoretically at least, luck is minimized.

Master points or fractions thereof are awarded to those who score best, second or third best (and in some big events even further down). The number of master points a player has earned in competition decides his standing in a hierarchy of masters.

205

A player who has 1 to 19 master points to his credit is a Junior Master. More than 20 points makes a Master. More than 50 points makes a National Master, provided 5 or more of these points have been won in tournaments of sectional rating or better.

More than 100 points, 10 of them garnered in sectional tournaments or better, gives one the status of a Senior Master. An Advanced Senior Master is a player who has collected more than 200 points, at least 20 of them in regional or national tournaments. The top rating of Life Master goes to any player who has 300 or more points, 30 of which have been earned in specified regional events.

According to the cynical, the climb up the master players' ladder of rankings depends less upon bridge virtuosity than upon other and more ordinary factors. These say that any fairly competent player who is familiar with the techniques of duplicate and has the time, inclination and money to attend numerous events cannot help picking up master points. The law of averages plus perseverance almost guarantee it. They say too that since experts usually play with favorite partners subtle, psychic understandings are established which give such a pair an extra advantage.

All the same, expertness is a definite and recognizable quality, even though it usually takes one good player to really appreciate it in another. Can this quality, or qualities, be analyzed? Well, let's see what the masters themselves say about it.

An expert, in Charles Goren's opinion, is a player who has the ability to do the right thing at the right time. Once an onlooker, after following him through a winning session, commented in surprise, "You know, there wasn't anything you did that I feel I couldn't have done, too."

"Of course," replied Goren with a smile. "That's the main idea in expert bridge—to do it when it has to be done. It's really that simple."

Some claim that experts are born, not made. Others contend that they are made and that their superiority lies mainly in technical knowledge acquired through many hours of play against good competition plus a schooled poise which gives them a psychological advantage.

Waldemar Von Zedwitz, a player of highest class, has described the expert as a pragmatist. "His skill is based on conscious and subconscious knowledge of thousands of hands and psychological situations. Having the backing of experience he knows when to violate theory. He will make all sorts of bids and moves which may be decried in books but are perfectly logical for the situations in which he uses them.

"Take this hand—

♠ K x   ♡ x x x x   ◇ x x x   ♣ J x x x

The bidding goes pass by partner, one diamond by first opponent, pass by you, one heart by second opponent and when the turn comes to your partner he doubles."

What do you do? The book bid to this take-out double, points out Von Zedwitz, is two clubs. Yet any ranking expert, he ventures to predict, will respond with one spade, to avoid going to the level of two and risking a double. Certainly unorthodox, yet characteristic of expert thinking.

A first-class expert is a technical specialist, according to Von Zedwitz. He rejects limitations and thinks of no hand as strictly a double-dummy proposition. He does not rely solely on percentages in making decisions but looks first for other clues that might tip off the way to the most promising line of play. He is not bound over entirely to one particular system but adapts what is useful to his style of play.

As Oswald Jacoby sees it, true expertness is a "combination of soundness and brilliance," sometimes as much as eighty percent brilliance. Flexibility and deception are marks of the real master and most in evidence when he is competing against players he respects.

"No expert tries to play an absolutely sound game against other experts. He must try to push the opponents into making mistakes via such devices as complete psychics, fake cue bids, bidding weak suits to discourage leads, deliberately underbidding to appear to be pushed, overbidding when opponents are likely to sacrifice, suppressing a strong suit and so on."

As for himself, "I am a bridge player first and a bridge authority second. In other words, I throw my system out of the window and make what I know will be the winning bid with the particular partner I am playing with and against the particular opponents I am playing against."

Young William Rosen, a highly ranked expert and member of world championship teams, believes that the expert is not so far removed from supposedly lesser players as most people think.

"The expert often has an edge in a game, beyond his actual skill. Opponents are apt to be awed by his reputation. It's a good idea to remember when playing a so-called expert, or anyone better than you, that no one can make an ace out of a deuce. If the expert gets himself into an unmakable contract, he'll go down the same as anyone else. It is the nervous or unsure player who gives 'presents' to the expert, and permits him to walk away with the big winnings at rubber or tournament victory before the hand is played. I wouldn't say that he will beat a really bridge. The average player can hold his own, if he refuses to concede expert player very often, but he should be able to make him work plenty for his points, and there is always another hand coming up."

Privately, the expert is apt to be amused by the popular picture of the master player as a super bridge being who knows all, sees all and never or hardly ever pulls the wrong card or makes the wrong bid.

"If a dub could see what goes on in some 'expert' games or championship tournaments," said one top-notcher, "it would make him feel a lot better about his own bridge. Personally, I think the best definition of a bridge expert is a man or woman who makes mistakes but fewer of them in the long run than most players. They do slip up — and how."

Shown the above remarks another highly ranked player offered a correction. He admitted that experts have been known to finesse against a king holding twelve cards of the suit or to "pre-empt" with an opening three-bid in fourth position. Masters, he acknowledged, do miscount trumps or lock themselves out of good tricks just like ordinary mortals. But most of their blunders, he insisted, are due to bridge intelligence gone awry.

"They have a logical reason for every move even though it may work out badly. Maybe they do get a little too cute or mysterious at times and look ridiculous because of it. Still, the point is that they're in there thinking constantly. The results are not always happy but you've got to expect some mishaps in tough expert games where the pressure is unremitting."

The expert's penchant for devious, inferential bidding is illustrated in the following deal. The hand involves Alvin Roth, one of the bright stars of the game. And he tells his own story of a personal fiasco, a rare thing in bridge since your average expert has a psychological block when it comes to remembering hands in which he flubbed. Roth held the following hand—

♠ A K J 9 8   ♡ K 10 7 6 4   ◇ 10 7 3   ♣ —

Partner had —

♠ —   ♡ A 9 8 5 3   ◇ A 8 6   ♣ A K 9 7 4

The bidding went:

	Roth	Partner
	1 ♠	2 ♡
	3 ♡	4 ♣
	5 ♣	5 ◇
	6 ♣	Pass

"There we were," reported Roth, "playing at six clubs with five pieces of trumps opposite a void, when we could make seven hearts with a normal trump break. Note my bidding—I was probably too fancy. I had thought that the agreed suit was hearts and that my partner would recognize that I was merely showing the first and second round control in clubs. I had never made a sign-off. I didn't jump to four hearts because of the sparsity of high cards. Now I know better, for it is my policy to keep raising the trump suit, if necessary jumping to show plenty of trumps and good ones, instead of being too devious.

"Why was my bidding so involved? I was looking for seven and I had mistakenly thought that was the best way to bid it. By the way, my partner, a top expert, slipped too. He should have recognized I must be cue-bidding, for he was looking at both the ace and king of clubs. Would I have insisted on raising him twice in clubs with a suit headed at best by a queen?"

The second hand, another horror story, came up at a rubber bridge game. Four internationally famed masters were seated around the table. The expert in (we'll call it) the South position held—

♠ J 10 8   ♥ 10 9 5 4 3   ♦ Q 10 7 3   ♣ 5

His side was vulnerable and opponents were not. *The bidding:*

EAST	SOUTH	WEST	NORTH
3 ♣	Pass	3 ♥	Double
Pass	Pass	3 NT	Double
4 ♣	Pass	Pass	5 ♣
Pass	5 ♦	Pass	6 ♣
Pass	?		

South, trying to find his way through the maze of inferential and obstructive bidding, finally called "six diamonds." This was passed all around.

Now for the complete deal:

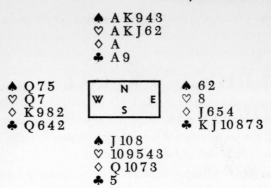

West's calls of three hearts and three no trump were pure mischief-making, with clubs as the intended "out" in case of a double. In any event, South succeeded in taking only seven tricks at a contract of six diamonds, for down five. But a seven-heart or seven-spade contract can be made with the queen of spades onside.

It is a cherished belief among innocents that faced with a certain bidding situation every expert in the same spot would come up with the same call. That this is not so is proven monthly in *Bridge World Magazine* in the columns of the Master Solver's Club. A set of bidding problems are submitted to a number of experts and they are asked to make the bid they believe best. The answers are seldom unanimous. Here is an example:

It is rubber bridge with North and South vulnerable. The bidding has gone:

SOUTH	WEST	NORTH	EAST
1 ♠	Pass	2 ◊	Pass
?			

South holds the following—

♠ A Q 10 7 3   ♡ A J   ◊ A K J   ♣ 5 4 2

What is his bid?

Six experts chose 4 diamonds; four said 3 diamonds; five voted for 3 no trump; three went for 2 no trump; one called three hearts.

◊ ♣ ♡ ♠

The expert can appreciate better than anyone else that there is nothing cut and dried about bridge.

THE BRIDGE EXPERT:
PSYCHIC ENIGMA

by ALBERT H. MOREHEAD

THE TOTAL OF BRIDGE EXPERTS is incredibly small. Probably it is no more than two thousand. Even that figure will quickly be disputed by experts of the highest ranking, who qualify their fellows by the most exacting standards of bidding and play and who find only a hundred or so who measure up. But the true expert is marked not so much by his skill —though that is one of his essential attributes—as by his attitude toward the game.

To the expert, bridge is more than a game, more than a hobby. It is the center of the universe, the beginning and end of all things physical and spiritual in life. The expert plays bridge four to ten hours a day, six or seven days a week. His habitat is the bridge club, where he can appease his gregarious instinct and still be in an atmosphere of bridge. He grows tired of playing, but plays on, just as a man continues to eat even when condemned by chance to a monotonous or unpalatable diet.

The impulse which creates the expert may be the quest of either pre-eminence or livelihood, and is usually a combination of the two. The quest of livelihood is forced upon a sect which devotes so much time to the playing of a game; unless it can coincidentally derive some money from the game it cannot live. But the quest of pre-eminence is, if anything, stronger. The bridge expert must not be lumped for examination with

From *The New York Times Magazine*, 1943. Reprinted by permission of the author.

professional gamblers in such sports as horse racing. The gambler is out for money and exists on hope. The bridge expert likes money, but finds it far less important than ego gratification. The essential food and drink of the bridge expert is victory.

An indigent expert will—and often does—pawn his watch so that he may enter a tournament in which the only possible prize is to have his name engraved on someone else's silver cup. Among the more prosperous experts this need of victory is no less apparent. "Strange," remarked one expert upon leaving a high-stake game, "I have a headache, and yet I'm not very far ahead." Still, it is significant that he was winning.

Sometimes, of course, purely economic reasons are sufficient to keep the expert at the table. Once, in the days before Ely Culbertson became a bridge tycoon, he and Hal Sims played for seventy-two consecutive hours as partners against two inferior players. They fed their opponents whisky to keep them awake; they used browbeating tactics almost to a hypnotic degree to keep the game from breaking up. Sims explained all this by saying, "The Professor (Sims's name for Culbertson) was hooked for more than he could pay." But Sims could have paid; why did he play on?

Psychology has not as yet explained the expert's inordinate appetite for bridge, nor have psychologists offered any adequate explanation of the emergence of the bridge expert. A certain aptitude—"card sense"—is perhaps essential, but it has not been defined by science. In any event, the expert must start with a passion for the game, and, ordinarily, he must start young. Most of the present-day experts took up bridge seriously before they were twenty-five. Almost from the day that the expert-to-be begins to play, bridge almost monopolizes his interest.

The keenness of this interest is beyond description to one who has not "been there himself." To the bridge expert every hand he holds is a thrilling experience. The problems of bidding and play assume an importance and achieve a beauty to which the layman is blind. The expert need not be a mathematician to enjoy the most incredible accuracy in the employment of probabilities; he need not have a good memory to remember every card in every hand he plays.

Even harder to describe is the gulf in playing ability which separates the least of the experts from the best of the non-experts. The ingredients of expert ability are many and complex. Some of them assume a meta-physical aspect, so that the non-expert finds the expert standard incomprehensible and often refuses to believe it exists.

In addition to the indispensable qualities of shrewdness, opportunism and a passion to win, the expert has a degree of awareness amounting at times to clairvoyance. The intonations of bids, the manner of plays, register automatically. The tremendous backlog of thousands of bridge hands, stored up in the expert brain, pass in review almost unconsciously before he rejects one plan and adopts another.

This genius (or call it what you will) gives the expert a margin of advantage which may not show up in a short session of play, but which over the course of time is irresistible. Of one-hundred thousand players who enter championship tournaments, about five-hundred (one-half of one percent) win ninety-nine percent of the championship titles. No one but an expert ever wins the major tournaments, and almost always it is an expert who stands in the top four or five dozen.

◇ ♣ ♡ ♠

Considering the expert's passion for victory, and in many cases his need to win money when the game is played for stakes, it is remarkable that the bridge expert has escaped the stigma of dishonesty which attaches to professional players of other games. But the public accepts bridge as a game of skill, in which the better player can win without cheating, and the bridge expert has done his bit to earn his relatively good reputation. Bridge experts do not cheat. In the life of contract bridge, only two experts have even been suspected of cheating.

This good reputation depends, however, upon the contract bridge code, which makes a sharp distinction between felonies and misdemeanors.

There are only two bridge felonies. One is manipulation of the cards —marking them, stacking the deck or crooked dealing in general. The other is collusion—having signals, or purposely losing so as to divide one's partner's losses with the other players in the game. For commission of these felonies the penalty is ostracism, and it is automatically and unremittingly applied.

The bridge misdemeanors include peeking, the use of mannerisms or remarks to inform partner and mislead the opponents, and such bad manners as intentionally breaking the bridge laws. For committing a misdemeanor the penalty depends upon the offender's position on the bridge ladder. A player's ethical standards, in expert company, are distinctly secondary to his ranking as a player.

If a mediocre player should transgress the bridge proprieties, he would soon be asked to play elsewhere. If a great player transgresses, the matter is overlooked or forgotten. Two leading experts, themselves most scrupulous, once detected an opponent in an intentional revoke. This is an offense so grave that the laws term it "dishonorable conduct." But the offender was a brilliant player, and within a year each of his victims had played as his partner in some game or tournament.

◇ ♣ ♡ ♠

Peeking, too, may be an open joke, though only four of five of the experts may be classed as offenders in this respect. There is nevertheless recorded an exchange of conversation between two famous players at a national tournament.

"Look out," remarked the first, "or you'll fall off your chair." The implication was that the other was leaning far to the side, the better to look into his opponent's hand.

"I'm only trying to balance you," replied the other with mock plaintiveness. And here the accusation was thrown back in the teeth of the original speaker.

Apologists for expert ethics invariably argue that the code of bridge sportsmanship is far better observed in an expert than in a non-expert game. Superficially this is quite true. The code is little known in the casual game, and breaches are frequent; but they do no damage because the other players are not keen enough to take advantage of them. The spirit of the code is known to all experts, however, and all do it lip service. About half of the experts scrupulously observe it. The other half circumvent the code whenever they can do so without risking proof of unethical intent.

Joint ownership of peculiar qualifications necessarily engenders among the experts the strongest sort of group consciousness. Each expert acutely requires the companionship of other experts, so they must congregate. Yet, perhaps because of their passion for pre-eminence, the experts are mutually so jealous that they feel toward one another a form of hatred, constant or recurring.

The group consciousness of the experts is clearly evidenced in their attitude toward bridge-playing non-experts. The expert's rudeness is proverbial. He seldom troubles to disguise his boredom when regaled with the bridge experiences of a non-expert, though he likes to discuss bridge hands with his peers. A greeting from a fellow expert he will invariably hear; a greeting from a non-expert he is as likely as not to ignore.

◇ ♣ ♡ ♠

Among all the bridge-playing groups the experts are the only one in which men and women are not about equally represented. Among the experts men outnumber women by ten to one.

The experts themselves explain it by saying, "Women just don't have the killer instinct." That is, the ability to press an advantage when the opponent is hurt, to take a victim's last dime and feel no qualm.

There have, indeed, been a few "miraculous manifestations" — women who could talk the same language and play on even terms with the best men. But from the day of Mrs. Culbertson, who was the first of these miracles, to the present reign of Mrs. Sobel, there have always been a few men whom the women could not quite match. The women stars have not been quite ruthless enough to employ the extremely predatory tactics; they have been fundamentally too honest to match the best men in deception. These two qualities, hardness and trickiness, are prime ingredients of the expert.

THE BRAINIEST CARD GAME

by FRED SCHWED, JR. and SAM FRY, JR.
An Excerpt

◇ ♣ ♡ ♠ ◇ ♣ ♡ ♠ ◇ ♣ ♡ ♠ ◇ ♣ ♡ ♠ ◇ ♣ ♡ ♠ ◇ ♣ ♡ ♠ ◇ ♣ ♡ ♠ ◇ ♣ ♡ ♠ ◇ ♣ ♡ ♠

W HAT CONSTITUTES a really fine bridge player, one who, over the whole year, is always ahead? If you have known few crack players you might guess that the game at that level takes great intelligence, a phenomenal memory and some mathematical genius. This is far off the mark. Many brilliant players are brilliant in their daily occupations; some are not. Many are wise and urbane. And yet sometimes. . . .

The following true story illustrates the vagaries of remarkable bridge brains. Many years ago Eddie Hymes, the late Louis Watson, and Sam Fry (one of the collaborators on this article) journeyed together to Chicago to play in a national tournament. They were fast friends as well as bridge masters. They found the hotel had only a double and a single room available. They matched for the single and Fry won it. Next morning Hymes told Fry that Louis had snored through the entire night, without missing a note. "How can I play tournament bridge without sleep?" he asked. "It's only fair that *you* room with him tonight." Fry, his sportsmanship appealed to, agreed; and Watson, sportsmanlike, snored just as loudly for Sam as he had for Eddie. Thus they alternated for the worst part of a week.

When Hymes got home his wife asked how everything had gone. He began to splutter about the sleeping arrangements. Mrs. Hymes, who has never won a single master point in her life, asked, "Why didn't you put Louis in the single room?"

From *Holiday* Magazine, October, 1954. Reprinted by permission.

Memory, contrary to general belief, has little to do with winning play. An experienced player does forget once in a while what cards have been played, but not often enough to make him a losing player. The heady word "mathematics" does not apply much either. Adding and subtracting up to thirteen is simply grade-school arithmetic.

Success at bridge seems to involve two things — card skill and temperament. High skill is a sort of intuition as to the best of several roads to take. It is not entirely rational, as most printed matter on the subject insists. A great player has all the stock stratagems and maneuvers at his finger tips. But a great many "merely good" players have that equipment too. Bridge isn't quite so complicated a mystery as it is often made out to be. Although 635,000,000,000 different hands are possible, there are only some dozens of different basic situations, all of which can be mastered by experience or book study or both.

The chief secret weapon of the masters is the ability to "see," to a surprising extent, all four hands instead of the conventional two to which most of us mortals are limited. They do not do this by peeking. They do it by a species of exhaustive research, much of which takes place in the subconscious, and all in a matter of seconds. The opposing bidding is assessed and analyzed, the early defense is scrutinized. *Why did East do what he did?* is an elementary question. *What did he hold in last Thursday night's game on similar bidding?* goes a bit further. Also the master player is not above observing that West is squirming as though his underwear didn't fit, or that East looks complacent. He may even make some deduction from the fact that the kibitzer's eyes are popping. This is not quite cricket, but they are not playing cricket.

After the maestro has started putting the jigsaw puzzle together, he usually knows fairly well — say by trick four or five — how the opposing cards are divided. If the early evidence doesn't permit him to be certain, he'll try a daring strategy. He will *assume* that the missing cards *are* located the way they *have to be* if the contract is to be made. For example, if the ten tricks necessary to make four spades can be won only if East has the queen, ten, and another club, and West has three or fewer hearts to the king, the good player will mentally "put" those cards where they belong and plan his play accordingly. On those occasions when the cards turn out to be "where they had to be," some of the kibitzers will salute the declarer as a dizzying genius and others will wonder if he hasn't a roving eye.

Many consider that temperament is at least as much a factor as skill, just as it is in many other forms of keen competition, including the one

called living. The temperamental virtues of bridge are composure, courage, self-control, and getting your partners to like you, even though some
of them be creeps. The vices are terror, temper, greed, fatigue, boredom,
hang-over, stage fright, and getting your partners to dislike you. More
vices than virtues, as usual. Yet another vice is losing. Most players after
several disastrous hours find the fine edge of their judgment dulled, but
the great player continues to play the same thoughtful game. He knows
there will be another game next week. The hysterical losing player bids
each hand dealt after eleven-thirty as though it were to be his last on
earth.

S — KQJ

H — A4

D — AKQ

C — AJ652

BUT IS IT BRIDGE?

by A. MOYSE, JR.

◇♣♡♠◇♣♡♠◇♣♡♠◇♣♡♠◇♣♡♠◇♣♡♠◇♣♡♠◇♣♡♠

THE MONDAY NIGHT team-of-four contest continues to flourish despite the slurs cast on it by the wives of its members. Stung, no doubt, by our candid assertion that they are persona non grata at these grim affairs, they have childishly retaliated by dubbing the proceedings "The Monday Night Male Sewing Circle."

Considering the brand of bridge we are all exhibiting, I'm afraid the girls have got something! Confidentially, we are odoriferous. Each and every one of us — eight players who somehow or other have acquired reputations as experts — have made the most monumental errors of judgment and technique — inexplicable, inexcusable bulls costing thousands of points. It is this very fact that has led me to report some of the hands. Presumably, if eight players of supposed expert ranking can stub their individual and collective toes so masochistically, many less "expert" can profit from their gruesome example.

The star hand of our last session was this little headache:

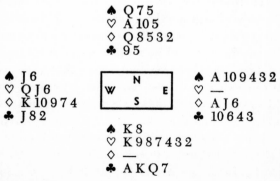

```
                    ♠ Q 7 5
                    ♡ A 10 5
                    ♢ Q 8 5 3 2
                    ♣ 9 5
  ♠ J 6                              ♠ A 10 9 4 3 2
  ♡ Q J 6           N                ♡ —
  ♢ K 10 9 7 4   W     E             ♢ A J 6
  ♣ J 8 2           S                ♣ 10 6 4 3
                    ♠ K 8
                    ♡ K 9 8 7 4 3 2
                    ♢ —
                    ♣ A K Q 7
```

East dealer.
North-South vulnerable.

In the room where I disgraced the West position, the bidding went:

EAST	SOUTH	WEST	NORTH
1 ♠	Double	Pass	2 ◇
Pass	2 ♡	Pass	2 NT
Pass	4 ♡	Double(!)	Pass
Pass	Redouble	(final bid)	

It is probably redundant to point out that my double was not notably successful. South made an extra trick with the greatest of ease, and the 1,380 points he chalked up did nothing to improve my partner's disposition.

I put up as vigorous a self-defense as possible under the sorry circumstances, pointing out that East, for all his opening bid, had taken only one trick, and further moaning that we had had an ace and a king put to sleep due to declarer's diamond void, but I can't say that I convinced even myself.

As a matter of fact, my overwhelming penchant for close doubles proved my individual downfall in this session — as you will see by reading further. It is difficult to rationalize poor bids or doubles after the fact; I can only say that at the time I felt that my sure heart trick, my shortness in partner's spade suit, and the hope that declarer might be counting on a diamond fit, seduced me into believing that a double might pan out. How wrong I was!

Yet, without the slightest attempt to alibi this double, and purely as a philosophic discussion of a *typical* situation, I am inclined to think that East should have gone to four spades after the redouble. His opening bid had been justified, but the 2½ honor tricks on which it was based were certainly not well placed for defense of a four-heart contract. The plus value in the heart void was anything but a plus *defensively*.

Moreover, the opponents were vulnerable and we were not; with East's six-card spade suit there should be no holocaust for a four-spade rescue. As against that, however, I realize only too well that if we really had been able to defeat the contract, I never would have forgiven East for taking me out of the double and redouble. A perplexing situation.

Our team's loss on this board was not substantially reduced by our dear partners, who, of course, held the North–South cards in the other room. They collected the huge amount of 200 points! The bidding there was one spade by East, *two hearts* by the bold, brash South player — pass, pass, pass!

◇ ♣ ♡ ♠

Perhaps my best bet is to complete the story of my own ignominy and thereby clear the decks for more enjoyable mud-slinging — at my team-mates and opponents. Here was the second deal in which my "killer's instinct" overruled my judgment.

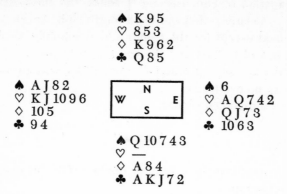

```
              ♠ K 9 5
              ♡ 8 5 3
              ◊ K 9 6 2
              ♣ Q 8 5
♠ A J 8 2                      ♠ 6
♡ K J 10 9 6      N            ♡ A Q 7 4 2
◊ 10 5        W       E        ◊ Q J 7 3
♣ 9 4             S            ♣ 10 6 3
              ♠ Q 10 7 4 3
              ♡ —
              ◊ A 8 4
              ♣ A K J 7 2
```

South dealer.
Both sides vulnerable.

The bidding:

SOUTH	WEST	NORTH	EAST
1 ♠	Pass	2 ♠	Pass
4 ♠	Double(!)	Pass	Pass
Redouble	Pass	Pass	Pass

Again I was Wet — no, I mean West — oh, let it go the way it was! This time I can't even *try* to justify the double. Despite the fact that declarer was held to his contract, this double, in my opinion, was infinitely worse than the previous one. For one thing, East had never opened his mouth, hence I had no earthly right to expect an ace-queen and a queen-jack in his hand; for another, while the double in the first hand had no bearing on the play, this time I handed declarer a blueprint of the trump situation. This latter fact was made painfully apparent to me when I heard that at the other table, where the bidding had been identical except for the double, the contract went down three tricks merely because declarer made the natural play of a low spade to the king and a spade return, and as a consequence lost all control of the hand.

At my table the ridiculous double took the declarer by the hand and led him like a little child! I opened the heart jack. When East played the ace and declarer ruffed, my feelings were a bit scrambled — I was de-lighted to have found East with high hearts but a bit depressed over their

being put to sleep. South led a low spade, I ducked, and the nine-spot
held.

Now declarer calmly went about his business, cashing two top clubs
and the ace-king of diamonds, then, ignoring my trumps, resumed the
pleasant occupation of club cashing. I ruffed the third round and led
another heart. Declarer ruffed and led a fourth club. At this point I could
tear up my hand except for the trump ace. Eventually, declarer had to
concede a diamond to East and the trump ace to me.

"Your doubles are getting sounder," my partner said admiringly. "This
time there were no overtricks."

I maintained a dignified silence.

And now to complete the trilogy of doubles. On this one, however, I
refuse to take the rap.

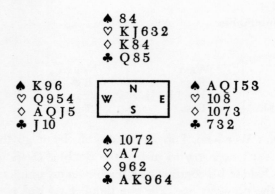

West dealer.
Both sides vulnerable.

The bidding:

West	North	East	South
Pass	Pass	Pass	1 ♣
Pass	1 ♡	Pass	2 ♣
Double	Pass	Pass	Pass

I opened the club jack and thereby prevented any spade ruffing in
dummy, but this was small solace in view of the extra trick that once
more was slapped right into my face. Indeed, if declarer had had the
nerve to take the heart finesse he would have come out with two extra

tricks, and then, I suppose, I would have been maimed instead of merely cursed.

As noted, however, I refuse to plead guilty in this case. In my opinion, East unquestionably should have bid two spades after I doubled, this despite the fact that in a purely technical sense it was a penalty double. I had passed originally, hence it was almost inconceivable that I could have six tricks in my hand against a club contract. It should not have been too difficult for East to read my true intention — to offer a contest in the part-score range. East himself had three clubs, which was some evidence against great length in my hand, and this evidence was strengthened by the fact that North had unhesitatingly accepted the double of two clubs. The fact that I had not doubled at my first opportunity was not important in view of my original pass; East might have guessed that I had begun to think well of my hand *only* because the opponents' bidding had been unimpressive. Two spades would have been ice-cold and it is doubtful that North or South would have persisted to three clubs after having been doubled at two.

The double in this case cost only 240 points — the expense was decreasing all the time. Perhaps if I'd kept on doubling I eventually would have defeated a contract!

And now, thank heaven, having purged my soul, I can really go to work on my confrères. As I claimed later, I had only been a doubling fool, whereas they ran the gamut.

After the following deal, I called "time out" for an indispensable Bromo Seltzer (*no advt.*).

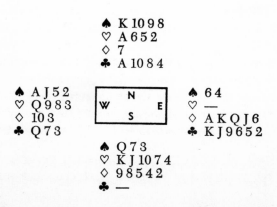

Perhaps it was because I managed to get out of that accursed West seat after the halfway change that I was only an innocent bystander in this affair. Now I was North, and the bidding in our room went:

NORTH	EAST	SOUTH	WEST
1 ♣	1 ◇	Pass	1 ♠
Pass	2 ♣	2 ♡	Pass
3 ♡	4 ♣	4 ♡	Double
Redouble	Pass	Pass	Pass

"Aha!" I said viciously, after West opened the diamond ten and I lovingly placed my cards on the table, "this time the redouble is on the other foot! Partner, this will be just a cakewalk."

I don't know whether it was a conspiracy to prove every statement I made wrong, or whether my dear partner had had one glass of soda pop too many, but the hand did not work out just as I expected. East permitted the diamond ten to hold and West shifted to the club queen. The ace was put up and declarer made his first lousy play when he discarded a spade instead of a diamond. A club was then led and ruffed and the spade seven was returned toward dummy. West hopped up with the ace and shifted back to diamonds, ruffing down the dummy.

Declarer now put on an exhibition of pure butchery. He ruffed another club with the heart seven, then, "to guard against a possible singleton heart queen in the East hand," laid down the heart king! East, brutal player, refused to play the heart queen; in fact he refused to play any heart at all.

Declarer next cashed the spade queen and ruffed a diamond. West hastily and gratefully discarded the spade five. Now declarer could discard on the spade king, but he was very near his finish. At this point dummy was down to the blank spade ten, the heart ace and the club ten. Declarer still had the jack-ten of hearts and a diamond; West was reduced to the queen, nine, eight of trumps. Obviously, the trump ace was the only trick declarer could take. If he led the spade ten and passed it, West would ruff and return the heart nine; if declarer ruffed the spade ten or club ten, West would overruff and return a trump. Down one!

I was not exactly pleased to see the opponents gravely enter 400 points in their own column instead of the 980 points that should have gone in ours, but it was some compensation to be able to speak freely, and not in self-defense.

Rarely have I seen a declarer go to so much trouble to lose a redoubled contract. The hand could have been made in any number of ways; so many, indeed, that perhaps my dear partner deserved congratulation instead of abuse for having found one of the few methods that could lose four tricks.

The main reason for his atrocious play had been his failure to picture East's hand from his bidding. After the club queen showed up from West, it was inconceivable that East could have bid three and four clubs on a mere five-card suit. He was marked for at least six clubs and of course for at least five diamonds. He could not have held a singleton spade and a singleton heart because in that case he would have overtaken the opening diamond lead and returned the spade for a ruff.

Thus, from every point of view, including the four-heart double, West was marked with all four missing hearts and declarer's play of the heart king was absurd. Strangely enough, however, even that play would not have been fatal if declarer had so maneuvered as to win three spade tricks before West could discard a spade.

There was an amusing corollary on this hand in the other room. Our partners, of course, held the East-West cards. The contract they reached was no work of art (five clubs would have been ice-cold for East-West), but it had the advantage of causing a row between North and South. The bidding there was:

NORTH	EAST	SOUTH	WEST
1 ♣	Double	1 ♡	Double
Pass	2 ♢	Pass	2 NT
Pass	3 ♣	Pass	3 NT
Pass	Pass	Pass	

North, overimpressed by West's prompt double of South's heart bid, refused to open the heart suit, choosing instead the unmentioned spade suit and leading the deuce. A very remarkable choice, I think. No matter how weak South's heart bid had been, North had four to the ace, and it was scarcely to be expected that any other suit was as good in the combined North-South hands. The opening, however, would not have been fatal except for South's subsequent method of discarding.

The spade queen was won by the ace and a low club was led toward dummy. North, of course, ducked and the king held. South, forced to discard, selected the heart four. Naturally, he was influenced by North's failure to open the suit and by the further fact that West had doubled one heart, but such decided discouragement of a heart lead was not in order. The proper discard for South was a spade. With that play he would announce to North that he was keeping at least one spade for communication purposes (since he would not dream of voiding himself in the suit opened by partner).

Now, when another club was led to the queen, South, by discarding the heart seven, emphasized that he did not want any heart return. North, on lead with the club ace, concluded that successful defense was hopeless unless by a miracle the spade jack were to drop, hence laid down the spade king. The contract still could have been defeated by a shift to a low heart, giving the defenders three heart tricks, but, for reasons known only to himself, North continued with the ten of spades and the jig was up.

The only question is whether South at my table or North and South at the other table showed greater genius in discovering how to lose points and infuriate partners.

◇ ♣ ♡ ♠

As indicated heretofore, I had the unique distinction this session of not making a single statement or prophesy that stood up under the march of events. After the following hand, a slight coating of foam might have been discerned on the lips of my partner and self.

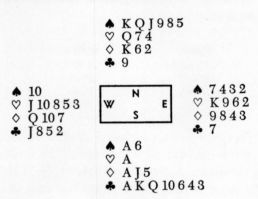

East dealer.
Neither side vulnerable.

East dealt and passed, and South, my partner, went into a three-minute huddle, finally emerging with a bid that one does not hear very often, namely, six no trump. Why, I can't say. Even assuming that the club suit was solid, he still had three losers and therefore I don't know why a two-club bid, or, if he wanted to be fancy, a four-no-trump bid would not have been more logical. As it was, when I heard six no trump, I challenged the opponents to waive the laws and permit me to bid fifteen or sixteen no trump, with a commensurate bonus for success or penalty for failure. I thought their refusal rather stuffy, and had to be content with a timid seven-no-trump call.

All I can say is that this was not our night! Down one again! The clubs did not break and, struggle as he might, South could never take more than six spade tricks, one heart, two diamonds, and three clubs. No squeeze was possible against the adverse lay of cards. After the opening lead of the heart jack, ducked in dummy, East held grimly to his heart king and West, discarding after declarer, could not be embarrassed by the run of spades.

This was perhaps the most infuriating deal of all, because in the other room our misbegotten partners managed to psych the opponents out of the grand slam contract that couldn't be made. There the bidding proceeded:

EAST	SOUTH	WEST	NORTH
1 ♠(!)	2 ♠	Pass	4 ♠
Pass	6 NT	Pass	Pass
Pass			

When I said the grand slam couldn't be made I was referring, of course, to seven no trump or seven clubs. Seven spades was there for the taking, but in the light of the bidding in both rooms, a no-trump contract was almost inevitable. So, while we in our room were going down 50 points (the cowardly opponents did not double!), our partners were losing 990 points to a contract that represented pure, unadulterated pusillanimity. At the end of the match, when the opponents were crowing over their 5,000 point victory, the best we could do was sneer at a team that had settled for a small slam on the cards held by North-South in this deal.

TOURNAMENT BRIDGE IS TOUGH

by LEE HAZEN

IF CARDS HOLD the slightest fascination for you, can you imagine anything more delightful than to be seated opposite your favorite partner, with congenial companions at your left and right, a cool drink by your elbow, cigarettes at hand, and even a lovely vista on which to rest your eyes when the cards seem a bit baffling? You have nothing to do but be at ease, sip your drink, make bids, and play your cards as your judgment directs. Not a single penny is at stake, so you all play without worry or care.

This pretty little picture, when applied to tournament bridge, is just about as false and misleading as anything could be; for no one works harder, is under greater mental strain, is more tense and excited, than a contestant at a national tournament. I know, for I have played in many of them.

Several times a year the tournament players of the United States, literally hundreds of them, gather in pairs and foursomes to play against other pairs and other foursomes. Nothing but a title is at stake; yet that title is as dear to every bridge player as the Davis Cup is to the tennis player or the World Series to a ballplayer, and it is competed for just as keenly. There are events for men and women, mixed foursomes, and men foursomes. For the elite of the bridge world — those who can qualify by reason of points earned by former victories — there are the master events for master players.

From *Good Housekeeping* Magazine, 1948. Reprinted by permission.

From twenty-eight to forty hands, depending on the particular event, are played each session, and sessions are held afternoons and evenings. Not more than five or six hands are played each hour. So you can see that the playing time is long, and as each event is played over two or more days, what sleep the player gets during tournament week usually occurs only after he's completely exhausted. Lack of sleep is wearing on the nerves; but consider, in addition, the feats of memory the tournament player is required to perform; he remembers every bid made, every card played, and counts out the various distributions of the cards in each of the players' hands as they are played; and like a part memorized by an actor, they are not easy to forget. They stay with you. And you alter them to figure out what might have happened "if." I find myself often in the position of my fellow-lawyers, of whom it has been said that they make three summations to a jury: the first is the one they prepare; the second is the one actually delivered; and the third is the one they think of after the trial is over.

Not many years ago, bridge tournaments were conducted by the firm hand and commanding voice of a young West Pointer. He was teaching mathematics at the Academy, and his wife drove him to and from the tournaments. They had a specially built car, with a bed for him to sleep on, so he wouldn't be too groggy when he returned to his classes. I am referring to Alfred M. Gruenther, who also found time during his brilliant military career to write a book on duplicate bridge.

In 1942 General Gruenther was a member of one of the most famous bridge foursomes in history. He and three other players had completed their preparations for a project in which they were interested. While the project was under way, they decided to engage in a few rubbers of bridge. Gruenther's partner was General Dwight D. Eisenhower, and their opponents were General Mark Clark and Captain Harry Butcher, Eisenhower's aide. The project was the invasion of North Africa, and the game was played on board the flagship of Admiral Cunningham of the Royal Navy, in the Mediterranean.

It seems that generals are as affected by their bridge conquests as ordinary players are, and like the latter are not above bragging about pleasant results. In one hand, General Clark reached a bid of four clubs, which was doubled by General Gruenther. General Clark made his contract with an overtrick. So pleased was he that he became far less modest about this bridge victory than he subsequently was about his military one. He talked about his bridge triumph all over Africa, Sicily, and Italy. Eventually it became known back in the States. The story came to the attention of General Eisenhower, who is proud of *his* bridge, and *he* wrote home. He made sure it was known that it was not he who had doubled, but the "expert" General Gruenther.

Bridge tournaments happily have their lighter moments. I recall one in which Charles Goren, who has doubtless won more championships than any other player, was my partner. He knows all there is to know about the game, and his dry humor never deserts him. We had arrived at contract of three no trump, through some razzle-dazzle bidding, although neither of us held a stopper in the club suit. Our opponent led the club ten from a sequence of ace, king, queen, jack, ten, nine, and eight and took the first seven tricks, setting us three tricks. Charlie looked steadily at his opponent and, in the tone of the bridge master he is, said to him witheringly, "Don't you know that you should lead your fourth highest card of a suit against a no-trump contract?"

I have often been asked if luck plays much of a part in winning a major tournament. My answer lies in my favorite anecdote. A long-distance call came to me from an important client as I was about to pick up a hand from the duplicate board. I did not want to keep my client waiting, nor could I hold up the play of some fifty other couples, so I looked around for someone to play my hand while I was gone. Everyone seemed to be busy elsewhere; that is to say, everyone but my brother Ben. Ben had been kibitzing at my table, and although he is a swell guy, a former Brown University football player, and well thought of in the live-poultry business, he is certainly no bridge player. All I could do was hope that nothing too terrible would happen. I picked up the cards, and without looking at them, thrust them into Ben's hand and rushed to the phone, pausing just long enough to tell him not to open his mouth and to be sure to follow suit. My bridge is on the conservative side.

When I returned to the table, my partner was smiling broadly. My opponents looked as though they had been robbed of their train fare home. The story was short and sweet. Ben had taken me literally and passed a hand on which everyone else in the room had bid either a grand or small slam, but, because of an extraordinary 1,000-to-1 lay of the adverse cards, had failed to make either of them. We received a top score on this board!

Who are these people who come from all over the country to play for bridge championships; who, for a week, will do nothing but eat, drink, and sleep bridge, and for whom there is no subject for conversation except bids, leads, and plays?

A few — yes, I mean a few — are professionals. They teach bridge, write columns for newspapers, and generally look to the game as a means of livelihood. Make no mistake about it, the professional is engaged in hard labor far exceeding the forty- or even fifty-hour week — and he is not paid for overtime or holiday work. But the great majority of tournament players are business or professional people, who have to make a special effort to arrange their schedules so they can play. For most of them, the tournament, with its rigorous week's labor, is, oddly enough, either a vacation or added to a business trip. Quite a few Hollywood people exchange klieg lights for bridge lamps for a week of tournament play, and I know a conductor of a famous orchestra who arranges his concert schedules so that they do not conflict with a major bridge tournament. A United States district judge attends tournaments frequently. Then, invariably, there is the best bridge player of XYZ County or State, *the* bridge authority in his home community. He comes to compete, modestly disclaiming any idea of winning, but secretly sure he is just as good as the better-known players. In a few cases he is.

Bridge partnerships are arranged without distinctions of any kind. You can see an industrialist playing with his clerk and not at all immune from a bawling-out. Socialites play with the *hoi polloi*. I have seen a general with a sergeant as his partner, and the speech of neither was inhibited by his rank. Nor is sex regarded as conferring any special privilege. When a woman and a man play as a team, they do so on equal terms, and are treated and treat each other accordingly. There is a classic story about the fiery-tempered Fred Kaplan. A pretty girl was his partner in a tournament. He had given her specific instructions never to support his bid with fewer than four trumps. On one hand she raised his bid with only three, but these three were the ace, king, and queen. Quite properly she concluded that possession of the three highest cards was equivalent to holding four of lesser worth. She had not reckoned with Fred. When she put her cards down, he glared at her and said, "I'll give you just thirty seconds to produce another trump!"

◇ ♣ ♡ ♠

What makes already successful people submit to a week of painstaking drudgery and hard work? The tournament holds no financial inducement, either present or future, nor does the fame achieved in winning carry beyond the next tournament. Every mistake a player makes is recorded and shown mathematically in his score. A week of good play can be overcome by a single error. A Masters Team-of-Four competition was won by only 40 points, yet until the last 14 boards were played, the winners were 2,500 points behind. Obviously, many errors occurred during the play to the finish. I don't profess to know the answer. Every year I solemnly swear, "No more. I've had enough. Never again will I beat my brains out. Nobody and nothing on earth can persuade me to play in another one of these things." But every year I go back. I guess I must like it.

HOW TO BE AN EXPERT

by S. TUPPER BIGELOW

To GET A REPUTATION as an expert bridge player is not as difficult as it sounds. Possibly there are many dubs who would much rather get such a reputation than win a million dollars at bridge. These would be the ones who for years have suffered in silence the abuse and vilification of partners for whom, in other spheres of activity, they probably have the greatest contempt. They would be the ones who have on many occasions recognized pained expressions come over the features of other players as they realize they have cut the dubs as partners. Such dubs as these, needless to say, have been aching to do something about it. And now they can.

First, forget all about manners. Manners have no place in the equipment of one who would be known as a bridge expert. Grimacing and scowling at partner's bids, lead and plays is also extremely effective for this purpose.

Second, play your cards slowly. This will give other players the idea that you are concocting some amazing strategy that will make five trumps to the king-jack in your left-hand opponent's hand look like something the cat brought in.

Third, invariably post-mortem. Discussing a hand after it is played is sure to prove of incalculable benefit to the other players, and you are bound to impress them with your vast fund of knowledge of the game.

Reprinted by permission of *The Bridge World*, New York. A. Moyse, Jr., publisher.

So much for the general rules. Particularly, the dub will find the following rules extremely useful:

1. After each hand is played, point out to your partner the mistakes he made. If he didn't make any, allege that if he had played differently, you would have made one more trick. The cards will be all mussed up, and nobody can prove it.

2. When the opponents go down one on a contract, smile patronizingly and say: "Too bad. Of course, the contract could have been made by a triple squeeze. I could see that coming up on the second trick." No one will argue with you, as practically all triple squeezes that ever happened are invented by people who write books on bridge.

3. When you gum up a hand and someone notices it, explain that one of your opponents had you in the Cavendish Coup position, and congratulate your opponent on his play. (There is no such thing as the Cavendish Coup, but you will still get your opponent to agree that that was what happened.)

4. When you make a hay-wire lead, and are asked about it, say it is the new Culbertson psychic lead, and profess disgust at its not immediately being recognized as such.

5. When you make a finesse and it fails, and perhaps is not necessary in the first instance, explain that by mathematical laws, it has been established that that particular finesse works 87 times out of 104.

6. Refer to all other bridge players you know as "lousy," "terrible," "quite indifferent," "very loose bidders," "execrable players," "too conservative," "too daring," etc., etc. This will make people believe you are better than they are.

7. Talk with disdain of recognized authorities. Explain that they are duplicate players, and while some of their rules may be all right for duplicate, most of them would be suicidal in rubber play.

8. If you go down anywhere up to 700 due entirely to your own bidding and play, congratulate your partner on the nice save you made; if you do down more than that, get out of the mess the best way you can; we've tried it and failed. (The method generally used by the author is to blame his partner for overbidding, if he bid; or if not, to explain that if the hearts had broken, we'd have made an overtrick. Neither of these methods has ever been invariably successful.)

9. If you bid three or four spades when only two is necessary for game, explain it away as a slam invitation, and reprimand your partner for not having assisted you.

10. If, before the hand is finished, you have spoken harshly to your

partner for not having bid game and in the play it turns out you do not make game, explain that had he bid game you would have played it differently to make it.

11. If, at the conclusion of a hand, it appears obvious that you should have taken a certain finesse, and your partner asks you why you didn't take it, say: "Finessing only works half the time, and sometimes loses to a singleton king or queen. By not taking a finesse, I beat the Law of Average, because now and again I will catch the singleton kings and queens." At first glance, this looks fairly logical, and your partner will be kept so busy figuring it out that in no time at all, you will be able to say to him: "Come on, partner, wake up; it's your bid."

12. Under no circumstances ever apologize for anything or admit being at fault. Blame everything on your partner. He probably did something wrong, anyway.

THE EXPERT AND
THE PSYCHIC SPADE

by C. L. W.

"The time has come," the Expert said,
  "To speak of many things:
Of suits and sluffs and singletons
  And Jacks and Queens and Kings,
And why the distribution's hot
  And whether slams have wings.

"One time I trumped," the Expert said,
  "My partner's diamond ace.
Dark anger glittered in his eye
  And red suffused his face
As irate incredulity
  To just plain ire gave place.

"Declarer'd bid, upon my right,
  A spade of psychic brand
Which suited me most perfectly
  In fact I thought it grand!
That diamond ace I butchered on
  The eighth trick of the hand.

Reprinted by permission of *The Bridge World*, New York. A. Moyse, Jr., publisher.

"My partner won my spade return
  And led his diamond king.
I ruffed it with the five of spades
  As slick as anything
Because I held no other suit —
  A most peculiar thing.

"That ruddy face," the Expert said,
  "Did now deep crimson burn.
A snort of fury burst upon
  The trump I did return;
But when I killed his ace of clubs
  I really felt concern!

"His eyes went cold, completely glazed
  With homicidal hate,
And sweat made ice upon his brow
  His dander was so great.
Strange noises blurped within him
  Quite inarticulate.

"I threw my lone remaining trump
  Face up for him to see
In pitiful endeavor just
  To save his sanity,
But hatred screened from out his eyes
  The sight of aught but me.

"My bare white throat," the Expert said,
  "That paranoiac eyed!
As venom driveled from his lips
  I sought some place to hide;
But Providence was merciful,
  He bit himself, and died!"

Section 7

Two Short Stories

IT BEATS THE DEVIL

by SIDNEY S. LENZ

◇♣♡♠◇♣♡♠◇♣♡♠◇♣♡♠◇♣♡♠◇♣♡♠◇♣♡♠◇♣♡♠◇♣♡♠

FOR MORE THAN FIVE YEARS Burke Wilson had experienced every kind of bad luck that could be imagined. He had worked his way through college, studied law and passed the bar examination with very little to spare. The few cases he tried did not help his prestige. He still had to win his first suit, perhaps because his personality was not the sort that made a good impression at the start.

It had been a sore disappointment to lose his case today. Discouraged, despondent, and broke, he was retiring for the night when there was a tap on the door.

A dark, good-looking man entered.

"Mr. Wilson," he said, extending his hand, "you saw me in court today. Would you take it as an affront if I ventured to point out why you lost your case?"

Burke was too depressed for resentment.

"Go to it," he replied. "The breaks have been against me so long that I have no pride left."

"That's just it," answered the visitor. "Your spirit has been broken by your continued bad luck. I have specialized in luck, both good and bad. Unless I can put you one hundred percent right, there is no obligation."

"Well, well!" Burke said. "So you are a psychoanalyst. I'm sorry, old man, but I couldn't raise a hundred dollars to save my soul."

The visitor smiled gently.

"It is not a question of money," he said, "and — why do you want to save your soul?"

"What's the big idea? Are you trying to work a Faust on me?" asked Burke.

From *Liberty* Magazine. Reprinted by permission of the author.

"Possibly," answered the visitor. "Are you willing to take a chance?"

Burke was bewildered. However, dreaming or awake, he would see it through.

"Let's have your proposition," he said.

"It's like this," replied the strange guest. "I am prepared to guarantee you every happiness this world can give you for a period of — shall we say twenty years? After that time you belong to me."

"Seems fair enough," Burke answered facetiously. "I believe it is customary in these matters to give a fellow a chance to escape when his time is up. How about it?"

"Most assuredly," replied his accommodating guest. "I'll give you any fifty-fifty chance for an out."

"Fine," Burke answered. "I'll sign on the dotted line."

"Right," said his guest. "I have an agreement here. I'll just add the escape clause. Have you a pen handy?"

"Back of the chair," said Burke, "you will find a couple of fountain pens in my coat. The one with the jade band has ink in it."

The visitor took a paper from his pocket, added a few lines, and passed the paper and pen to Burke. The legal phraseology was perfect. Burke signed. His visitor took the paper, bowed, and — was gone.

When Burke awakened the next morning he remembered every detail of his dream.

As he put on his coat, he noticed that one of his pens was missing. He must have left it in the office, although he was almost certain he had put it in his pocket.

"Say, Burke," said Bill King at luncheon that day, "you look a bit fagged. I'm driving to the races this afternoon. How about coming along?"

Burke and Bill had been together at college. They had a pleasant drive, and at the races Bill placed a few bets without much success. There was a big stake race that day with an odds-on favorite that looked to be unbeatable. As Bill got up to place a bet on the favorite, a man who looked somewhat familiar to Burke handed him an envelope and said:

"Wilson, will you do me a favor and place this bet for me? I've been called away suddenly. See you later."

In the envelope was a hundred-dollar note and a card on which was written: "Devil's Imp — to win."

"Your friend is daffy," laughed Bill. "He has picked the rankest outsider."

Burke took the ticket at a hundred to one, and Devil's Imp won by six lengths.

With ten thousand dollars belonging to a man whose name he could not even remember, Burke was in a quandary. A personal in the newspaper did no good and he wondered uneasily whether his dream had anything to do with it.

King was very much impressed to find that Wilson had friends who could pick hundred-to-one shots as a matter of course, and was instrumental in getting him the most important client of his career. With new offices, new clothes, and a general appearance of affluence, his success was phenomenal. From a mediocre lawyer he changed into a silver-tongued orator.

The most wonderful girl in the world jumped at his offer of marriage. There were times when he pondered over his extraordinary change of luck and wondered if it had any bearing on the curious dream.

Wilson had changed very little in the past twenty years. He had a fine home, a loving wife, and a clever and pretty daughter who won cups at golf, tennis, and bridge.

Today in court he had won a decision in a difficult case. As he was about to leave the courtroom, a dark pleasant gentleman approached him.

"Remember me, Mr. Wilson? It is some years since we last met. My name is — Cifer."

It suddenly flashed on Wilson that this was the man of the race-track episode.

"Seems to me I am in your debt," Wilson answered.

"Would ten o'clock this evening be a good time to settle our business?"

"Sure thing," said Wilson. "See you at my home."

Seated in the library, awaiting his guest, Wilson's thoughts persisted in reverting not only to the day at the track but to the night before the day. Of course it was idiotic to associate the two events, but —

"Mr. Cifer," the butler announced.

"You are looking better today than you did twenty years ago," Mr. Cifer said, "I trust you have been prosperous and happy."

"Yes, I have," said Wilson simply. "And here is my check to cover my indebtedness to you."

"Your indebtedness? Isn't there something more?"

Wilson winced. He had tried to fool himself, but it was no use. Incredible as it seemed, the compact he had entered into had not been a dream but a reality. There was no escape.

"Mr. Cifer," he said, "will you . . ."

"Of course," replied Cifer. "All or nothing. Shall we toss a coin or cut the cards?"

Wilson remembered his joking remark about a final chance. Well, he would take it, although he knew it was hopeless against such an adversary. He took a deck of cards from a case and placed it before his guest.

"Let's cut," he said.

At that moment the door swung open and a vision of loveliness burst into the room.

"Father!" she cried. "I —" Then, as Mr. Cifer arose, she continued, "I didn't know you were engaged."

"It's all right, Lucy. . . . Mr. Cifer, this is my daughter."

Lucy glanced at the check and the deck of cards.

"Have you men been gambling?" she inquired severely.

"Oh, no," answered Cifer. "We were about to decide a — er — business matter by cutting the cards."

"What a poor way to decide anything," Lucy pouted. "I have been playing bridge and we had a fuss about the play of a hand. I was playing with Bruce. You know, father, he gets worse every day. Do you play contract, Mr. Cifer, or am I boring you?"

"Not at all," replied Cifer, "I invented the game."

"Really," said Lucy. "You must be older than you appear to be."

"I am," answered Cifer.

Lucy brought to light a deck of cards she had been holding behind her back. "May I show you the deal?" she asked.

"Certainly," said Cifer.

Lucy held the deck with her fingers separating the four hands. She spread the cards on the table in this order:

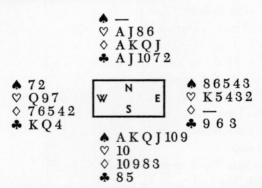

```
                      ♠ —
                      ♡ A J 8 6
                      ◇ A K Q J
                      ♣ A J 10 7 2

      ♠ 7 2            ┌─────────┐      ♠ 8 6 5 4 3
      ♡ Q 9 7          │    N    │      ♡ K 5 4 3 2
      ◇ 7 6 5 4 2   W  │         │  E   ◇ —
      ♣ K Q 4          │    S    │      ♣ 9 6 3
                       └─────────┘
                      ♠ A K Q J 10 9
                      ♡ 10
                      ◇ 10 9 8 3
                      ♣ 8 5
```

"I sat North and opened with a club. East bid a heart and Bruce bid two spades. With my wonderful hand and Bruce's jump bid, I was bound to bid for a slam; but there was no stopping my partner until he had bid for a grand slam in spades, which East doubled and Bruce redoubled. Because of the double West led the queen of her partner's heart suit, and there, with his declaration made to order for him, Bruce let them defeat him! Wasn't it awful?" she asked Cifer confidently.

He looked the hands over carefully before he answered.

"Miss Lucy, I am afraid your partner was not culpable this time. He had no way of getting rid of the losing club. It was simply an unfortunate distribution."

"If I had been playing the hand," Lucy said, "I would have made it without question."

"Not against good play," said Cifer.

"You wouldn't dare bet me?" Lucy asked pertly.

"I might," replied Cifer cautiously.

"All right," said Lucy. "I'll assume father's side of your — 'business matter.' "

"If you should lose," said Cifer, "you stand by his agreement?"

"Certainly," agreed Lucy.

"I've got you. Would you mind signing this card?" Cifer handed Lucy a fountain pen and a visiting card. Lucy signed and sat down to play the South hand.

"It is understood that after the first lead I play the East and West hands as I wish," said Cifer.

"Of course," said Lucy sweetly. "And I play the North and South hands the way Bruce should have played them."

Lucy took the queen of hearts with the ace and then led the jack. The king covered and Lucy trumped.

Lucy played her five spades and discarded from the dummy one club and the four top diamonds. Cifer followed twice on the spades, then discarded a club and a diamond, but on the last spade he hesitated.

"Now do be careful," cautioned Lucy in honeyed tones, "because if you give up a diamond, my four diamonds will be good and you will be sunk on the eleventh trick. If you discard a heart, the dummy will have two good hearts, and a club discard will be ruinous. So far, Mr. Cifer, you have done very well, but where do you go from here?"

"Hell!"

Whether Mr. Cifer was merely replying to Lucy's question or had lost his temper, will never be known. He rushed out the door without another word.

Lucy picked up the card she had signed.

"What an odd name — L. U. Cifer," she read. "Such a nice man, but what a bad temper and so profane. Look, father. He forgot his fountain pen."

As Wilson placed the pen in his pocket, he noticed the jade band on the end.

FOUR HEARTS

by Bruce Gould

"Double," said Richard Fenway.

He led a small singleton club to his wife. It was their only chance. A quick flicker of chagrin clouded Corinne's lovely blue eyes, smoldered there. As Joe Beecham topped her jack, she bit her naturally scarlet lip, pointedly avoided his eyes. May Dillworthy, dummy, hazarded another opinion about the way the bicentennial celebration was being run. It had been overdone, she said. May was a schoolteacher. Politely, Corinne agreed. Joe, pursing his lips, said, "Ye-e-es," but pointed out that, after all, George Washington was the Father of His Country; Joe being one of your on-the-other-hand men.

With a flourish of triumph, Corinne took a trick with an ace; but she led Richard back a spade. Too bad. There went their one chance of setting Joe, by making Richard's single trump good. Corinne, absorbed in her own plans, had ignored the significance of his club lead. Blandly, Richard played his highest spade, a nine. Joe, with a chortle, took it with dummy's ten. Joe loved getting his tricks cheap, even if it meant he had to discard higher cards later. Corinne's astonishingly histrionic face, which, in bidding, was unintentionally as useful to her partner as two quick tricks, registered an abrupt crescendo of exasperation. The sympathetic May tried to look distressed at Corinne, happily at Joe, and partially succeeded; no little accomplishment, Richard thought. A harassed what-could-you-expect expression settled on Corinne's face. Richard wondered

From *The Saturday Evening Post*, 1932. Reprinted by permission.

whether it wouldn't be a happier world if husbands were permitted to carry spare aces up their sleeves for use in just these domestic emergencies.

Steadily Joe raked in the glittering cards, methodically boxed his book of six tricks. Their gold edges gleamed against the high polish of the marquetry table which had come down to Corinne from her grandmother. He studied his cards as though the rest weren't his on a lay-down; cautiously piled up two more tricks out in front; threw down the rest of his hand; his honest face beamed triumph.

"An ace — the rest trumps," said Joe.

"Both usually win," said Corinne, with that elaborate sweetness of one who has lost a game she expected to save.

"Five diamonds, doubled," said May affirmatively, giving Joe the smile women reserve for conquering heroes, successful husbands and the men they hope to marry.

"Vulnerable," said Joe.

"Game and rubber," said Richard. "You played that cannily, Joe."

Joe gently ran his hand around his incipiently bald head, caressed it narcissistically, took his honors with becoming modesty.

"It was the distribution," he said, looking around hopefully for someone to contradict him. May obliged.

"I was afraid, after I raised you," said May, "we were going to be set." Smiled.

Joe smiled back. Richard genially added up the score. May looked happy. Corinne pushed back her chair, asked, with the air of a prestidigitator miraculously about to produce pigeons from billiard balls:

"Would anyone like a sandwich and one of Richard's drinks?"

"Lovely," said May.

"If you're sure it wouldn't be too much bother," said Joe conservatively.

"Not at all, Joe." Over her shoulder she called back, "Richard, would you like to help me, please?"

Richard would have preferred not to enter the kitchen, with Corinne in her present mood of angry frustration. Their losing at bridge had only intensified the pronounced strain between them, following their argument at dinner. Annoying that maids must be out every Thursday. But, he reflected philosophically, in the present topsy-turvy state of society where men have relinquished the high hand, women must be treated more or less like human beings. And so, husbands, even though misunderstood, must be polite. He rose amiably, therefore, wondering how Daniel felt on entering the lions' den.

"Women need a man's directing hand even in the kitchen," he excused himself airily. "I tell her when the water is boiling."

"Why, Corinne's a marvelous cook!" May was easily shocked, and had never learned the easy uses of hyperbole.

"An expert like you should know, May." It seemed to Richard that Joe's always simmering interest in May visibly increased. "I always wondered why you didn't teach domestic science, as long as you insist upon teaching at all."

"Cook for girls!" exclaimed May. "When I cook ——"

"It does seem perverted," admitted Richard quickly.

May laughed. "There's no kick in cooking, unless you know some man is hungry." She sighed. "I wish I could make a chocolate soufflé like Corinne's. It melts in your mouth."

"You will, when you have someone to cook it for," Richard assured her at the doorway, leaving Joe to savor the soufflé in his active gustatory imagination.

"Close the door, darling," called out Corinne liltingly. To Richard, her cheer sounded ominous. As he entered the kitchen, she quickly closed that door, too, and looked at him with the angry surprise of a normally loving wife who has just seen her husband, before her not particularly unbelieving eyes, metamorphose into a snake in the grass.

"Now!" she plunged in, with the bridge player's disdain of polite beating about the bush. "Will you please tell me, Richard ——"

"Why I doubled?"

"Yes, darling." It was no more than a polite form of teeth grinding at a person one sometimes, strangely enough, loved.

He didn't care to tell her that if she'd led him back clubs the score might have been different. Unlike most bridge players, Richard didn't enjoy discussing why he lost, much less quarreling about it. For, despite all appearances to the contrary, Richard held the attitude that bridge was a civilized game. The mere fact that it made atavistic cave men and screaming fish wives of its most ardent devotees, he declined to admit as damning evidence against his quaint, other-worldly theory. Besides, he knew that if he spoke of his singleton club, it would only make Corinne, if anything, feel worse about losing.

"I'd really like to know," she was insisting impatiently.

"Oh, I just thought we'd set them," he proffered vaguely.

"On those diamonds, I suppose."

"No, darling, I ——"

"You're irresponsible!" she cried wildly, apparently still thinking of his, to her, mysterious bidding.

"Nothing ventured, nothing gained," he retorted. "Any expert ——"

"Who's talking about experts?" — witheringly. She stamped her foot angrily, because he wouldn't quarrel and have it over with.

"—— will tell you it's better to overbid than underbid," concluded Richard equably.

"You're irresponsible." Overcome by the kind of exasperated hysteria which, he had noticed, bridge often brings down upon the female addict, she positively hissed it, looking very lovely, very live, very young, though very annoyed in her light green chiffon. Her eyes darted fire, and her tiny red tongue flamed with what Richard had long ago designated as bridge rage.

"Joe and May'll hear you, honey," he warned soothingly.

"Why do you think I closed the doors? And don't honey me, please. You're irresponsible, I tell you!" Her voice rose an anguished octave or two higher: "In bridge. In everything! If you could have seen the shocked look Joe gave you when you doubled on that last hand ——"

"Why didn't he redouble then?"

"Joe is wisely conservative." She rushed on: "Just like the shocked look he gave when you began talking truck expansion — at this of all times."

"Joe Beecham," he said, "is a fine fellow, an upstanding citizen of Langhorne County, and a credit to the community of Bragden, but" — he paused to give his remark the full significance it deserved — "he's an economic barnacle."

"Well, he gets there, just the same," triumphed his wife.

"In his barnacle way," admitted Richard, picking up a knife and beginning to spread mayonnaise lightly over the buttered surface of thinly sliced bread.

"Barnacle! Barnacle! What's a barnacle?"

"A barnacle," said Richard, reminiscently poising his buttery knife with the pedagogical punctilio of old Professor Wormser, "is any of the numerous marine crustaceans of the order Cirripedia, which, though free swimming in the larval state, are permanently fixed in the adult state and protected by a calcified shell. They have usually six pairs of biramous feathery appendages which are modified limbs. These are protruded and drawn back with a grasping motion, serving to catch the food that floats within reach."

Corinne had been looking at him for some time with lethal intensity. While lovely and intelligent in all necessary feminine ways, Corinne was, after all, only a college graduate. She resented conversation beyond her depth.

"In a word," he ended solemnly, "Joe."

Her appreciation of his rather extraordinary scientific flight was frigid, to say the least. He added conciliatingly:

"A barnacle is also an instrument of torture — supposedly outmoded."

Corinne, like Queen Victoria not amused, looked daggers until he felt like the human target of a knife-throwing act. He pointed mutely at the unmade sandwiches and waited for the hostess to triumph over the dagger thrower. It worked. Deftly she inserted thin slivers of chicken and shredded lettuce leaves between the neatly sliced bread, while Richard squeezed half a lime into tall glasses and thought that Corinne, though lovelier than ever, was harder to please these trying times, particularly on the subject of business enterprise; of the desirability of initiative in these days of industrial doldrums; of Joe the barnacle. If only she wouldn't worry about the possibility of his coming a cropper. A man could take a skinned nose occasionally. But Corinne was too proud of him to want even to run the risk of seeing him humiliated. That accounted for her sharp annoyance when he seemed to lay himself open to criticism for over-enthusiasm.

Glumly he measured out the needed ingredients, found ice, soda, melancholily added sugar to taste, noticed in passing that he had spotted the tip of his vest with a drop of mayonnaise, and in trying to remove it picked up a buttery knife, which hardly helped the situation on his vest. Silently, with the saddened eyes of a woman whose cross is almost more than she can bear, Corinne handed him a clean knife, turned her back.

Moodily he returned to the mixing of drinks and wondered why there was such an opposition at this time to young men with initiative. Everyone urged Richard to sit tight in his secure actuarial position, jubilant that he had a job.

That was all right, of course. He intended to do that. But he felt that he was capable of doing more. He wanted to branch out on his own. His one effort so far had been a disaster.

He had acquired a wooded, hilly acreage in the direction toward which the best residential section was growing. But a smart pair of politicians had spoiled his well-laid plans and gypped the town by selling the adjoining acreage for an aviation field. It was such a bad choice for an airport that Richard, who had tried to consider every possibility, had not even thought of that ruinous eventuality. The result was, his shoestring development was frazzled and his latest project was being assailed as visionary and likely to meet a similar setback.

It wasn't fair; what was more important, it wasn't sensible. But the more vague Corinne and Joe's doubts, the less able to voice concrete objections they were, the more certain they seemed to become that it was best merely to sit tight, venture nothing, wait for someone else to start the ball rolling. Joe was agreeing with Corinne, Richard supposed, because he had always been as violently in love with her as a man with biramous appendages can be. Had Corinne permitted herself to drift — quite casually, of course — within Joe's grasping distance, she would no doubt have been drawn to Joe's slightly calcified bosom long before Richard had even laid eyes on her. But Corinne, as Richard had instantly perceived the moment he first saw her across the dance floor and his heart stood still, was a woman who danced and beckoned one on like a will-o'-the-wisp. It had taken all Richard's rash willingness to plunge through swamp, bramble and thicket — and damn the thorns and quicksand — to win her. She still possessed that same wild loveliness of a marsh-fire for him. Not time nor familiarity had dulled the radiance of her blond glamour. And her gray-green eyes, as she now electrically crackled indignantly over his high crimes and misdemeanors in bridge and business, lost none of their allure because he had so often looked into them, nor because he didn't at all agree with her present indictment. But it did depress him.

He watched Corinne skillfully guillotine the crust of her sandwiches with a thin French blade rather like that instrument to which M. Guillotin gave his name, and it worried him slightly. Richard thought she added an unnecessary viciousness to her strokes. It made him uneasy, as though his neck were somehow in jeopardy. Himself ready to risk his future on the uncertain project of his transportation company, he could get nothing but opposition and accusations of recklessness from Corinne, and heavy aphorisms of caution from Joe, just as Bradley Forman had treated his explanations in the bank this afternoon with a prolonged silence which might have meant anything.

Joe's opinion must be sought, of course, because once he had seen the Fenway ship of matrimony safely launched, he had attached himself automatically to it — as chief barnacle. Richard had grown, except on such occasions as this, almost fond of Joe in a weary way. And to a woman he represented stability, solid achievement, calm judgment, the rock of Gibraltar, Richard supposed. He couldn't help thinking gloomily that Corinne might occasionally look at Joe and speculate on how pleasant it would be to nestle under the protective shell of one permanently fixed in the adult state. A harassed woman might even overlook the biramous feathery appendages. Certainly, May Dillworthy was showing every willingness to float within reach. Indeed, between Corinne and May this evening — Corinne treating Joe like a bridge Solomon and May hearkening to his voice as if it issued from an authentic burning bush — Joe was in a state of masculine glow which could only be described as incandescence. Anyone less resistant to electric impulses than Joe would have flamed up hours ago.

"We'll play one more rubber," Corinne was saying, "and I hope, Richard, you'll play it as well as you really can. They're terrifically ahead." She was bending attentively over a plate of sandwiches. "And I think I wouldn't say anything more to Joe about this truck business. After all, if he is sensible enough to have invested his money wisely, it isn't very friendly to try to talk him into taking a flyer with you."

With the precision of long practice he kissed her just where any woman, be she maid, wife or widow, likes to be unexpectedly kissed, neither on the ear nor on the shoulder blade. Before she could remember that she was furiously angry with him, her hand rose automatically to press his head closer, even as she protectively sputtered camouflaged concentration on more prosaic matters.

"You'll knock that plate off the table" — flustered — "dear."

Obligingly, with a blind hand, he shoved the plate farther away and no further word was spoken, until she gasped:

"Richard! You mustn't!" — twisted from his grasp, skillfully armed herself with two plates of sandwiches which she used to fend off his advances, and fled. But at the door she stopped to smile and remark: "That's no way to answer the argument of a lady."

"You're my wife," he corrected her, but she refused to admit the distinction.

Defeated, he picked up his trayful of clinking drinks and followed a suddenly serene and coolly gracious hostess, no longer an agreeably surprised nymph, into the living room.

He saw Joe's eye light up as Corinne appeared, but whether it was the sight of her dancing loveliness and the still flaming color in her cheeks, or the promise of ambrosial food for which she was famed, Richard could not guess. May's eyes, too, were noticing Joe.

"What lovely-looking sandwiches," said May. That, apparently, was May's guess — or hope.

"These are chicken — these, tongue and pickle," said Corinne.

"On rye!" added Joe, his eye glistening.

Plied by May and Corinne, Joe ate sandwiches with a gusto little less than apocryphal. His naturally high color rose like a barometer of apoplexy. Fearing disaster, Richard suggested starting the final rubber, but Joe, without seeming to know what he was doing, kept eating even as he ruminated over his bidding.

The first hand proved a dud, no one, apparently, having sufficient strength to open with a bid. But on the next deal, May bid a club, was jumped by Joe, bid game and made it easily.

"We're vulnerable now," warned Joe, the corners of his mouth drooping significantly.

"I know," said May, suddenly solemn too.

Corinne dealt, bid a spade.

Joe looked over his cards like an owl telling fortunes. "Two hearts," he said, bit his lip slowly, looked anxiously at May, then Corinne, finally at Richard.

Richard consulted his cards carefully. He held a singleton ace of hearts, spade support, and two outside tricks. He thought it might be a good idea to cut off May, in case she should try to encourage Joe.

"Three spades," he said.

"By," said May, after a moment's thought, with a worried look at Joe.

"Four spades," spoke up Corinne promptly.

"By," said Joe; said Richard; said May.

Joe led a club.

"Do you think that's strength enough for jump bid, Richard?" asked Corinne as he laid down his cards. He said nothing as she proceeded to make game with comparative ease.

"You played that very well, Corinne," said Richard.

"I was somewhat confused by your jump bid."

"That was to confuse May, not you," apologized Richard.

"I could have raised Joe's hearts," confessed May.

"We were vulnerable," said Joe.

"Oh, well, we made it," laughed Corinne forgivingly.

"Now we're both vulnerable," said Joe, relieved, and helped himself to his sixtieth sandwich before he dealt.

The timely arrival of Bradley Forman, their neighbor and vice president of the Bragden National Bank, saved Joe from sudden death by spontaneous combustion, Richard believed.

"I was driving just out of town, thinking things over, Dick, when that truck of yours passed me," said Mr. Forman, slipping off his generously fur-collared overcoat. "Looked as though it was carrying a full load. Bowling right along too."

"We've carried capacity on every trip," said Richard briefly. He'd told old Forman all that this afternoon, and much good it had done him.

"I didn't know Richard had been talking to you about his ideas," he heard Corinne saying, like a man's good wife to an important neighbor.

"Neither did I," said Joe, seeming a little hurt, for Joe had been the first one to whom Richard had mentioned the project.

Joe would like to turn it over in his mind for the next four or five years, Richard told himself bitterly, and then decide it was too risky.

"Oh, yes. Of course, in these days ——" Richard could hear nothing further from the kitchen. And though he hurried, by the time he returned with the cool, dark drink, the subject was changed, and Bradley Forman had definitely saved Joe's life by appropriating most of the remaining sandwiches, keeping the plate firmly at his elbow.

Richard hadn't expected Forman to drop in this evening. Certainly he had seemed far from enthusiastic about financing the expansion of the infant transportation company during their long talk this afternoon in his temple of finance, where Richard had begun to feel very silly and over-optimistic. Bankers, merely by their stage set-up, managed to put one at a mental disadvantage. With all their elaborate hocus-pocus of pillared edifice, vaulted quiet, hushed opulence to disguise an essentially simple transaction, they seemed like inviolate priests of commerce whose opinions one should somehow not question, despite the depression which had exposed their Achilles' heel. They — at least Mr. Forman — managed to convey the impression that their votaries should willingly lay down their eight percent and a bonus on the altars of superterrestrial finance, knock their obedient heads silently on the marbled floors and retire obsequiously, ecstatic over having been merely allowed to worship.

Though he knew old Bradley Forman well as a warm friend of his father, Richard had found himself this afternoon outlining his scheme badly, failing to detail salient facts, falling back at last on the bald record of success with his trial truck over a six months' period. He had managed to point out the difference between the straight-line truck haul from Bragden to Chicago of sixty miles, compared with the two-sided railway haul of one hundred and five, besides one transfer at the junction of the spur with the main line of the C. N. & W. But, on the whole, Richard felt he had presented his survey badly, and had left the banker's presence in a sadly dispirited mood. That probably accounted for his being sharp with Corinne at dinner.

But in this merely neighborly atmosphere, Bradley Forman appeared less formidable, particularly as he seemed to be enjoying his drink. It had been friendly of the older man to drop in to explain, at least, that he had noticed his truck, which, handsomely red and snorting with power, traveled twice a day between the Midwest metropolis and the rising young industrial town. The nucleus of a future fleet of express and freight carriers, Richard hoped, if only he could get backing before someone else thought of the same scheme. Not everyone seemed to be aware how fast Bragden was growing, probably because most of its industries were still small; nor how dependent it was on Chicago for a continuous stream of supplies.

"Would you and Richard like to go into the study for a little talk?" Corinne suggested tentatively.

Richard hoped so, looked up at Bradley Forman's experience-lined face.

"Wouldn't think of it, my dear — wouldn't think of it," old Forman replied brusquely. "Not when people are playing bridge. Think too highly of the game."

Richard remembered, then, that he had been among the first in Bragden to embrace contract, and still used to go to Chicago, at times, to play at the Tracy Club there.

"Your father," Bradley Forman was saying, peering at Richard keenly, "played a very smart hand of bridge. He had card sense."

"It isn't hereditary, is it?" asked Corinne, managing to convey a deadly insult to Richard while seeming merely to direct a polite inquiry to her guest.

"There was only one Canfield" — succinctly.

"The game?" asked May.

Forman turned politely. "You like solitaire?" he asked, ignoring her gaff.

"No" — with seemingly unnecessary vehemence — "who wants to sit around with herself and play cards?"

"It's friendly," said Joe, coming suddenly into the conversation, "when a man's lonely."

"Don't you think rummy's a better game?" asked May hopefully.

"But it takes two to play that," argued Joe.

"Can't one always get a partner?" urged May, shooting the works.

"One doesn't always want one," said Forman, a bachelor these fifty-three years, pleasantly. "There are times when a game of solitaire ——"

Heroically, Corinne rushed into the breach. May seemed crushed.

"Don't you really think, Mr. Forman, that contract is the best game of all?"

"As a matter of fact, Mrs. Fenway, I do."

"Better than poker?" Joe was astonished.

"Poker is a man's game," said May contemptuously, recovering miraculously.

"I know, but ——" expostulated Joe; rose, much upset, and was not calmed until he had wandered around the table and snatched two sandwiches from under their new guardian's watchful eye.

"Poker, considered as a game, is really quite inferior to contract," said Bradley Forman. May smiled triumphantly. He continued: "The most that can be said for poker is that it offers men — those who need it" — he smiled — "sanctuary from the home when domesticity becomes too appalling, permits them such male pleasures as bad air, shirt sleeves, chewed cigars, the occasionally wholesome dissipation of being out at all hours — in short, a complete release from the cramping fussiness of the too-feminine home, which ——" He broke off abruptly, as though suddenly fearful of having been carried away by his subject, smiled benignly. "I trust nothing I have said will be considered in any way derogatory to ——"

"Not at all," said Corinne inclusively, thereby managing to be both polite and deny her denial in the same breath.

"Oh, no," echoed May icily, righteous indignation battling for possession of her politely agreeing face.

"Personally, I've always liked poker," said Joe doggedly. May looked at him with the glitter of reform in her eye. "For small stakes, of course," he added hastily.

"Poker, if you will permit me, Mr. Beecham," said Mr. Forman earnestly, "should never be played for small stakes. It is solely a gambler's game. If one is to play it at all, one should play beyond one's means."

"That's why I never play it," said Richard. "That, and one other reason." He smiled at Corinne.

"Very sensible of you, Dick. Bridge is the better game, and contract best of all. Though most people play for a small stake ——"

"Never more than a twentieth," said May virtuously.

"—— it is no less exciting to play for nothing at all. The game demands sound judgment, an accurate appraisal of your opponent's psychology, the knowledge of when to bid and when to penalize overconfidence, and a steady campaigning, once the bid is made, until the hand is played out. It furnishes, indeed, a fine working index of character, much sounder, as a basis for judgment of personality, than poker, in my opinion. Contract has yet to provide us with such expressions as 'playing close to the chest' and 'poker-face,' but it obviously will, because it is a game that calls for both skill and psychology, and approaches much nearer to the problems of everyday life than poker."

"You really think one can tell the character of a person by the manner in which he plays contract?" asked Corinne, significantly calling Richard's attention to her query.

"I'm reasonably sure of it," said Bradley Forman — "reasonably sure of it."

"So am I," agreed Corinne triumphantly. "Richard, however, doesn't share my opinion, I'm afraid." She tossed her head.

Bradley Forman said nothing, after looking first at Richard, then at Corinne.

"We're quite a bit ahead," put in Joe. "Of course ——"

"The score," interposed Forman, "is incidental — only a temporary guide. After all, no one can contend against a run of bad cards. It isn't so much the score as how the cards are played. Now finish your rubber, and don't let me bother you any more."

"Wouldn't you like to take my hand?" asked Richard hospitably.

"Not at all, Dick — not at all," Forman protested vigorously. "I wouldn't think of breaking up a foursome. Go right ahead. I'll kibitz."

"At least I'll make it easier for you," said Richard, taking his empty glass and disappearing into the kitchen.

Corinne appeared after him, so quickly the swinging door nearly decapitated her as she stuck her head into the kitchen.

"For heaven's sake, Richard, do try to be cautious," she hissed. "As long as Mr. Forman attaches such importance to the game, try to make him think you at least know what you are doing." She ducked back.

He returned to find that Joe, swallowing the last sandwich, was already flipping out the bright cards from the blue-backed deck.

"You've taken our deck, Joe. You know what that means."

"I'm not superstitious," asserted May. Joe silently got up and walked around his chair. "All right," agreed May, and followed suit.

"That ought to take the curse off," admitted Richard.

Joe sorted his hand methodically. His eye brightened. "Diamond," he said.

Richard studied his hand. It hardly looked promising. Seven spades, jack high. Six hearts, ten high.

♠ J 10 8 7 6 4 3   ♡ 10 8 7 5 4 2

It was odd enough. If it happened to fit in with Corinne's hand, however, something might be done with it.

"One spade," said Richard.

"Two clubs," said May quickly.

"By," said Corinne, after a cursory glance at her cards.

Richard knew Corinne disliked passing. She didn't enjoy losing to anyone, much less to Joe and May, even when the cards were manifestly stacked against her. Therefore, she must possess simply nothing on which to base a personal bid.

"Two diamonds," said Joe humbly. Apparently, Joe, though strong in his own suit, had nothing with which to help May in clubs.

Once more Richard looked at his strange hand. He had nothing in the two suits his opponents were bidding. He wondered how strong Joe and May really were. If they were only too strong, he might turn that very strength into their weakness. He meditated an attack pleasurably. But he would have to wait for more information.

"Pass," he said.

"Three clubs," said May tentatively.

Corinne passed.

"Three no trump," said Joe, with sober excitement. Doubtless he should have said six, but Joe was Joe, and a game was game to him. Apparently he had a sizable suit in diamonds, was protected in spades, but had little else.

Richard looked again at his hand — thoughtfully. Joe's bid would give them game and rubber. There was no doubt Joe could make game — probably more. Still, his own hand was unusual, full of strange promise. His excitement quickened. By overbidding Joe, he might possibly scare him from going higher. Save game, at least; possibly do something for himself. Seven spades, jack high. Six hearts to the ten. Richard loved to take a chance, when it seemed reasonably justified. No one had mentioned hearts — they might be his adversaries' weak point. He ignored Corinne's caution; he forgot that Mr. Forman was looking over his shoulder, doubtless expecting him to show due conservatism. Nothing ventured, nothing gained.

"Four hearts," he said authoritatively, as though he had just begun to fight. Behind him, Bradley Forman leaned forward quickly, then slipped back, sipped his drink.

"By," said May after a pause. Apparently her hearts weren't high enough to jump back to Joe's no trump.

"Pass," said Corinne quietly.

Would Joe continue no trump over his heart bid? He might go on to five diamonds, of course. But he'd received no raise in that suit from partner, and Joe was Joe. For a long time Joe gazed hopefully into his hand. The creases of worry rolled across his brow like waves over a reef.

"Double," he said at last. It was evident he didn't want to relinquish playing, but feared to go on in the face of Richard's strong heart bid

unless May could guarantee to stop hearts. Richard had found their one
weakness, apparently.

At his four-heart bid, the what-could-you-expect expression had leaped
back into Corinne's face. She had passed quickly. To be doubled when
vulnerable meant one could be set badly. Her eyes had pointed that out
to him. Richard, alert, considered every possibility now. Four high hearts
were out against him. Ace, king, queen, jack. Corinne must have one,
possibly two. Chances were she had the ace. For if either May or Joe had
hearts stopped, they would have continued on in no trump, since it must
be fairly obvious to them by now that his was a two-suiter hand.

If Corinne had the ace, perhaps he could make the other honors fall in
one trick, or, at most, lose but one round. Corinne must be short in
spades, of course; she hadn't raised him. But she might have a high one.
It was a long chance, the sort he loved to take. Might as well be hanged
for a wolf as a lamb.

"Redouble," he said calmly.

"By," said May bitterly.

"Pass," said Corinne frigidly. Richard could see her adding up in her
imagination how much she feared he would go down. Double and redouble. It could be plenty.

"By," said Joe with heavy reluctance.

Behind him, Bradley Forman moved his chair a little closer, looked
carefully into his hand, rose, went round to Joe.

"Do you mind?" he asked, peering eagerly over Joe's shoulder. After
a minute inspection, he went on to Corinne, who held her hand ready to
lay down.

In a glance he was able to take in her cards, apparently. He moved on
to May, puzzling over what to lead. When she finally threw down the king
of clubs, Mr. Forman moved back to his chair and studied Richard's
hand once more.

Corinne, without a word, laid down her hand —

♠ A 9   ♡ A 9 6   ♢ 10 4 3 2   ♣ 10 8 3 2

was what it was. She had the ace of hearts.

Corinne rose hastily, as if she could no longer contain herself. "Richard,
let me see your hand!"

He motioned her back to her chair imperatively, and hastily turned
the face of his cards downward.

"Sit down and cross your fingers," he ordered.

But she was not to be denied. "I can't wait!"

Quickly, she came round behind his right shoulder. Well, she might better get the jolt at once. He held the cards up, looked at her. A glance was all she required. She turned away, her face stony.

He would have preferred not to let Corinne see that he was bidding four hearts with only six to the ten. If she had thought him irresponsible before, she undoubtedly now thought him mad. It might turn out that he was. After all, a man shouldn't be expected to explain too thoroughly his psychic hunches, even in bridge. Every man has to cross the Rubicon sometime. He shot a quick glance at Corinne again. She was visibly biting her lip, and, to him, it was apparent she was trying to keep back tears of annoyance as she stared past him at Bradley Forman. Well, he wouldn't look at Mr. Forman. He would just play out his hand for all it was worth.

May's king of clubs lay in the center of the table. Richard picked up the two of clubs from dummy. Joe dropped on the five, and so confident was he of taking the trick, he was about to sweep it in when he saw that Richard had dropped a red heart, the deuce, on May's black club.

"Having no clubs, partner?" Corinne murmured automatically.

"Having no clubs," Richard replied, raking in his trick, and leading the four of hearts from his hand.

May threw out the jack, seeing the ace in front of her in dummy. Richard played the ace, Joe the trey. Only two hearts — the king and queen — were now out against Richard. One should be in either hand, according to the bidding. He should catch them both with the next heart lead.

He led out the nine. Joe played the king. So far so good. He dropped on the five. May apologetically threw down the queen. Joe frowned as he raked in his trick.

That was dandy. Now, no more hearts were out against him. Joe hopefully led diamonds this time — the queen. Richard played the seven of hearts on it, trumping.

"Having no diamonds?" murmured Corinne, still weakly.

"Having no diamonds, partner," said Richard formally.

May discarded a six, Richard played a two from dummy.

This time Richard led a trey to his ace of spades in dummy. May threw in a five. Joe contributed a deuce. If the distribution were again equal, one more round would clear that suit and establish his spades. Otherwise, he could trump in dummy.

He led the nine from dummy. Joe took the trick with his king, Richard added the four, May once more dropping a queen with a wry grimace.

Joe frowned again. Richard could hear Bradley Forman leaning forward in his chair, for the springs creaked in the quiet room.

"Sound," he said.

Richard could appreciate Joe's difficulties now. Both his diamonds and May's clubs were being trumped. Yet that was all Joe had to lead. He led the king of diamonds. Richard trumped with the eight, raked in the trick.

His five spades were now established from the jack down. He still held one trump and one in his partner's hand — the six of hearts. The remaining six tricks were his on a lay-down, but just for fun he played them out, one after another, while May and Joe sorrowfully scattered aces and queens in clubs and diamonds on his low spades and hearts.

"Five hearts made, four hearts bid," he announced as modestly as possible, considering his feeling of elation. He looked at Corinne expectantly.

"Doubled," said May gloomily.

"And redoubled," added Joe, in an awed voice.

"Vulnerable," said Richard, as if it were no matter.

"That makes game and rubber," said Corinne, unbelieving still, looking about from face to face.

Joe was figuring up the score, none too happily.

"How does that leave the rubbers for the evening?" asked Richard. Joe bent to his task.

Bradley Forman, who had finished his drink, rose.

"My boy, anyone who can bid a hand like that, and play it as you did, deserves to win." He looked reprovingly at Joe, who had finished his figuring. "You might have made five diamonds or no trump, yourself. At least you could have made game and rubber."

"We were vulnerable," said Joe meekly. "I was afraid, since May didn't raise me, that Corinne was quietly sitting there with all the rest of the diamonds. I didn't want to risk that."

"I was afraid of Richard's hearts," said May bitterly.

"And I figured," added Joe, "he had both our suits stopped, and his coming in when the bidding was all going our way upset me a little, I guess."

May nodded.

"Of course when he bid spades and then four hearts, I naturally counted on him for high cards in those suits, at least. So what was I going to do?"

"Well," said Bradley Forman, "it's always easy to see the disadvantages against bidding. Let's see, you had king, deuce of spades; king, trey of hearts; ace, king, queen, eight, seven, five of diamonds; and jack, six, five of clubs; and Miss Dillworthy had queen, five of spades; queen, jack of hearts; jack, nine, six of diamonds; and ace, king, queen, nine, seven, four of clubs. There was an easy game for you in that layout."

"Yes, I guess there was," admitted Joe.

"It's seeing the advantages and then making the most of them that wins rubbers," said Bradley Forman severely.

"What's the total score?" asked May sadly.

"They're two hundred points ahead for the evening," said Joe.

"That's a nickel apiece, Corinne," said Richard gayly. "I'll buy you an ice-cream cone." She only nodded her head, looking strangely at her husband.

Bradley Forman was putting on his fur-collared overcoat, ready to go.

"Dick, that was fine playing. Very impressive. Anyone who can handle his strength and come through the way you did —— Well, anyway, drop in about 3:30 tomorrow, and we'll have another talk. Come in by the side door. I'll be expecting you. . . . Good-bye, Mrs. Fenway. . . . Good night, Miss Dillworthy. . . . You missed an easy game and rubber there, Mr. Beecham. Chances like that don't come too often, you know."

He departed quickly. A minute later they heard his car drive away.

"It's not losing the money I mind," said Joe, laying two nickels melancholily down on the table. "It's feeling like such a fool."

"Well," said Corinne briskly, almost with an edge of criticism in her voice, "nothing ventured, nothing gained, you know, Joe."

Joe looked at her earnestly. Something seemed to die in his face.

"I guess you're right, Corinne," he muttered, winding a scarf round his neck against the night air.

"I don't know, Joe," said May quickly. "In the long run, I still think good conservatism pays."

Joe looked up at her gratefully. "Can I drive you home, May?"

"It's quite a bit out of your way, isn't it, Joe?"

"Not at all" — gallantly — "not at all. And" — Joe seemed suddenly determined — "we'll stop down at Scarpia's for a banana split."

"I'd love it," said May, hurrying into her coat and jamming on her hat any which way.

Just before they were leaving, Joe turned to Richard, worry corrugating his brow, but decision shining in his face.

"Dick," he said, "about that trucking idea of yours. Bradley Forman seemed interested. He's a smart man. I think I'll just go along with you on that proposition too. Say, for about twenty-five percent."

"Good boy," said Richard. "Let you know tomorrow afternoon."

The door closed on Joe and May. Richard turned laughingly to Corinne.

"Well, the old barnacle's coming along with the ship, now that he sees it's launched."

"Joe may be a barnacle," said Corinne, significantly looking out the window where May was fairly leaping into Joe's sedan standing under the electric light, "but he's going to launch a ship of his own tonight, unless I miss my guess."

"I can see it," said Richard, "sliding down the ways of a banana split."

Corinne nodded, laughed. Then her brow clouded.

"I know you made it and all that, Richard darling, but honestly, whatever possessed you to bid four on that crazy hand?"

Richard looked into the lovely gray-green eyes of Corinne.

"I knew all along you had a high heart," he said.

Section 8

Toward Better Bridge

Bridge

BY WEBSTER

THE KIND OF MAN WHO BLOCKS HIMSELF IN DUMMY

WHERE DO YOU RANK AMONG THIRTY MILLION BRIDGE PLAYERS?

by ALBERT H. MOREHEAD

◇ ♣ ♡ ♠ ◇ ♣ ♡ ♠ ◇ ♣ ♠ ◇ ♣ ♡ ♠ ◇ ♣ ♡ ♠ ◇ ♣ ♡ ♠ ◇ ♣ ♡ ♠ ◇ ♣ ♡ ♠ ◇ ♣ ♡ ♠

IF YOU PLAY BRIDGE and think you're a good player, it's ten to one you're wrong. But if you think you're a bad player, it's a thousand to one you're wrong.

Polls have indicated that thirty-five million Americans play bridge, but you can write off five million immediately. They're faking. They just think bridge has more snob appeal than, say, rummy, or one of the games they actually play. Still, that leaves some thirty million persons who do play something they call bridge.

But how they play! Twenty million of them can't count trumps, or even keep score without referring to the scoring tablet after every hand. So let's put it this way:

If you play contract bridge three or four times a year, no matter how badly you think you play, you're an average player. You've got to be — because the law of averages is overwhelmingly on your side.

If you know you shouldn't make the first bid without two or three aces and kings in your hand, you're slightly better than average.

If you know you should lead the king, not the ace, when your best suit is headed by ace-king, you're an advanced player.

And if you know any more than that, you're practically an expert.

From *Cosmopolitan* Magazine, 1950. Reprinted by permission.

Not quite a real expert; theirs is an exclusive and highly self-critical company. Let's listen in on two experts as they discuss a third, who has a considerable reputation.

"I admit," admits the first, "that Joe is a dangerous opponent and a good partner. But he's such a lousy dummy player!"

"Yes," agrees the second. "There must be a hundred people who play the dummy better than he can."

One hundred, out of thirty million! Joe was being damned by what the vast majority would consider far from faint praise.

You've met a sample of about twenty million if you've ever been desperate to make up a game in a resort hotel on a rainy day, or in a ship's lounge on a cruise. Perhaps you approached the most likely-looking prospect and said:

"Will you make a fourth at bridge?"

"W-e-ll," replied your prospective fourth (and right away you started wishing you'd asked someone else). "I don't play very often, but if you want me to . . ."

If this ever happened to you, you'd remember — and wish you could forget — just how badly he (or she) played. But according to the statistics, he was a bridge player, one of the thirty million.

The next nine million up the ladder may not play well, but they play more often. They use bridge as a social vehicle. The ladies meet among themselves one or two afternoons a week and exchange the latest gossip, or recipes, or comments on the newest fashions, the while they manage to get in a couple of rubbers. Their husbands often join them in the evenings.

These are the social players. They play bridge not so much for its own sake as because it fits the occasion. Many of them feel that as long as they are going to play, they may as well play acceptably; so they buy books (but seldom read more than a few pages), they take lessons (but rarely remember what they have learned), they listen to their partners' advice (but don't pay too much attention to it).

Now we've reached the top million. Ninety-nine percent of this million may not be genuine experts, but they are highly advanced players who treat bridge as a hobby. They are intolerant of poorer players and humble in the presence of the experts. They follow systems and adopt new ideas almost as rapidly as the experts promulgate them. They like to read about bridge, like to play it, and find it engrossing — but not the only engrossing thing in the world. Any of these advanced players finds his family, his business, and even a war, somewhat more important than a bridge game.

To the genuine expert, nothing is more important than bridge. His only habit is bridge, and his habitat is the "bridge club."

Here, then, you have the strata of the thirty million; and here, too, is the answer to a puzzle that has bothered a generation of advertising men. Time and again they've tried to find a radio show that would appeal to the suppositious "mass audience" of bridge players, and time and again they've failed. Why? Bless them, because there isn't any mass audience of bridge players. With thirty million bridge players divided into a thousand different groups, you can't give them bridge lessons; whatever you say, half of them will be bored because it's too simple (they already know it), and the other half will be bored because it's over their heads (they aren't ready for it yet).

The big exception was Goodman Ace, whose "Easy Aces" program started as a bridge show and was a big success — because he cheerfully kidded bridge and all classes of bridge players, and didn't assume they knew something they probably didn't.

Have you decided which segment of the thirty million you belong to? It isn't especially important for you to know. As long as you enjoy playing bridge, what else matters? But you're probably curious, so here's a test for you. Look at your hand in each case and decide which of the four bids you'll make; perhaps you'll find that as a bridge player you're one in a million!

Where Do You Rank in Thirty Million?

Select your answer to each of the following questions; then rate yourself by the schedule given at the end. You'll learn whether you're one in ten thousand . . . one in a million . . . or just one in thirty million.

1. You hold:

♠ —
♡ Q J 8 6 3
◇ A 7 2
♣ K Q J 10 5

No one is vulnerable. Your partner deals and bids *one heart*. The opponent at your right bids *one spade*. Do you bid:

        (a) Four hearts?
        (b) Three clubs?
        (c) Three diamonds?
        (d) Two spades?

2. You hold:

♠ Q J 10 9 6 5 4 2
♡ 3 2
◇ A 4
♣ 6

Neither side is vulnerable. You dealt. Do you bid:

        (a) Pass?
        (b) One spade?
        (c) Three spades?
        (d) Four spades?

3. You hold:

      ♠ A Q 6 3
      ♡ 8 6
      ◇ A K 7 5
      ♣ J 5 4

Your opponents are vulnerable, you are not. The opponent at your right dealt, bid *one spade.* Do you bid:

        (a) Pass?
        (b) Double?
        (c) Two diamonds?
        (d) One no trump?

4. You hold:

      ♠ Q 10 6 5 2
      ♡ A K Q 7 4
      ◇ 6 3
      ♣ 5

You are vulnerable, your opponents are not. You dealt. Do you bid:

        (a) Pass?
        (b) One heart?
        (c) One spade?
        (d) Two hearts?

5. You hold:

      ♠ Q 8 7 6 3 2
      ♡ K Q
      ◇ 8 7
      ♣ 8 4 3

Both sides are vulnerable. Your partner deals and bids *one heart.* The opponent at your right *passes.* Do you bid:

        (a) One spade?
        (b) Pass?
        (c) One no trump?
        (d) Two hearts?

6. You hold:

$$\spadesuit\ 2$$
$$\heartsuit\ K\,7\,4\,3$$
$$\diamondsuit\ J\,5\,3$$
$$\clubsuit\ A\,K\,9\,5\,4$$

Both sides are vulnerable. Your partner deals and bids *one spade*. The opponent at your right bids *two diamonds*. Do you bid:

> (a) Two hearts?
> (b) Three clubs?
> (c) Double?
> (d) Pass?

Answers

1. Give yourself:

> 5 points for three diamonds (c)
> 3 points for three clubs (b)
> 2 points for two spades (d)
> 0 points for four hearts (a)

Your hand will probably make six hearts if the opponents do not open a diamond; the cue bid in spades discourages the very lead that gives you the best chance to make the slam.

2. Give yourself:

> 5 points for four spades (d)
> 2 points for three spades (c)
> 1 point for pass (a)
> 0 points for one spade (b)

Unless spades are trumps, your hand will take only one trick. If your partner cannot help you, the opponents will probably make a slam. Four spades is better than three; you would bid four spades if forced to, and in such a case you should bid the limit the first time.

3. Give yourself:

> 5 points for pass (a)
> 3 points for one no trump (d)
> 1 point for double (b)
> 0 points for two diamonds (c)

Your best chance for profit, unless your partner is strong enough to take *independent* action, is to hope the opponents will not get too high. Any bid you may make is dangerous, because if an opponent can double you are likely to go down three or four.

4. Give yourself:

> 5 points for one spade (c)
> 2 points for one heart (b)
> 1 point for pass (a)
> 0 points for two hearts (d)

The higher-ranking five-card suit should be mentioned first, regardless of greater honor strength in the lower-ranking suit. With two five-card major suits, and better than two sure tricks, you should not pass.

5. Give yourself:

> 5 points for one spade (a)
> 2 points for one no trump (c)
> 1 point for pass (b)
> 0 points for two hearts (d)

When a long suit can be shown at the one level it is always preferable to a one-no-trump response. Partner's suit should not be raised with fewer than three trumps.

6. Give yourself:

> 5 points for double (c)
> 2 points for two hearts (a)
> 1 point for three clubs (b)
> 1 point for pass (d)

When you have such a good hand, but can't support your partner's suit, it's odds-on that you couldn't make your bid — and they can't make theirs! Double and you'll score points; bid and you'll lose them.

Now count up your score. The maximum number of points you can have is thirty — one for each million of bridge players. *Every point you scored means a million bridge players who don't play as well as you do!* And if your score is 10 or lower, you're just one of the thirty million, but don't worry about it. Thirty million Americans can't be wrong — even if they can't all be good players.

HOW TO BE A GOOD PLAYER

by R. R. RICHARDS

◇ ♣ ♡ ♠ ◇ ♣ ♡ ♠ ◇ ♣ ♡ ♠ ◇ ♣ ♡ ♠ ◇ ♣ ♡ ♠ ◇ ♣ ♡ ♠ ◇ ♣ ♡ ♠ ◇ ♣ ♡ ♠

W E CANNOT ALL BECOME first-class players, but everyone who is keen on bridge can make himself a good player if he cares to take sufficient pains. The only people who are hopeless are those who are so self-complacent and conceited that they fondly imagine they know everything about the game, and those who are too lazy to try to learn more.

To the former I would say that no matter how well you play, do not imagine you have come to the end. Bridge is such a wonderful game that there is no finality about it. The finest player on earth has something left to learn. And it is the mark of your real progress if, after long years of play, you become more and more humble because you realize the wonderful possibilities of the game.

First, then, you must be convinced that you have something to learn. It is the want of appreciation of this truth that accounts for such a general prevalence of bad play. People fancy they can become good players by mere practice, which is a great mistake. They only move on in one eternal blundering round. I know players who go on year after year and never improve. On the contrary, some of them get worse. The reason is that they cannot, or will not, take the trouble to have lessons, read books or articles on the game. They never get down to bedrock or realize the fundamental principles of bridge as distinct from Bumblepuppy. They follow suit correctly, make their aces and kings and think there is nothing more to it. They are like people who imagine that they know all about

Reprinted by permission of *The Bridge World*, New York. A. Moyse, Jr., publisher.

modern scientific astronomy by watching for a few weeks the apparent motion of the planets.

Bridge is worth a little trouble and study. The better you play, the more you will enjoy the game. If you find yourself a perpetual loser, you don't get much fun out of it. And, although it is quite possible that you might find yourself a loser over a reasonable period, through bad cards and bad partners, if you continue to lose over an extended period it is a sure sign that there is something wrong with your play or bidding.

The best methods of improving your game are:

1. Take instruction from a good teacher.

2. Play when possible with players better than yourself.

3. Watch good players. This is a cheaper method than No. 2, and still more effective. Study their bidding and play. It is quite a fascinating pastime, and you can pick up a great deal of useful information.

4. Solve problems and read bridge articles. In many of the daily newspapers and periodicals, problems appear which throw valuable light on bidding and on play. A study of these will be helpful and will rectify faults and mistakes in your bidding and play.

5. Practice at home. You can do this with your wife or even by yourself. Deal four complete hands and look at each hand in turn, and decide what you would bid if you had not seen the other cards. Look at your own first, leaving the others face downward. Decide what you would bid. Then look at the hand opposite you, which would be your partner's, and make up your mind what he ought to do. Then examine the other hands and work out what they should bid. Having arrived at the proper declaration, play out the hands, not as if they were double-dummy but as if you had not seen your opponents' cards.

This exercise is particularly useful for those who are addicted to overbidding, and practice with it will often correct distorted vision. Deal yourself a no-trump hand over the average with, say, two aces, a king, two queens and a knave. Then deal out the other three hands at random, and see how it works out in play. If things come out too favorably, and you find your partner with all the good cards, transpose the hands. You can easily construct for yourself a number of exercises on similar lines — playing a trump suit, supporting partner's bid, "taking-out" your partner and so on.

6. Cultivate your card memory. Do card calisthenics. Deal out four or six cards to each hand, look at them and memorize them. Then turn them face downward and see if you remember them accurately. After a little practice extend the operation with more and more cards. After, say, half

an hour a day, in three or four weeks' time you will find that without any superhuman effort on your part your card memory has improved miraculously. Within a limited period, varying according to your quickness and natural memory, you will be able to remember the distribution of the whole pack. You may think this a rather boring exercise, but, as a matter of fact, it is quite amusing and an excellent indoor pastime. You can take your friends on at it, and you have no idea how it will improve your game.

7. Study the human element. The successful bridge player must be something of a psychologist. He must play men as well as cards. The acute observer who is quick to note the follies, foibles, idiosyncrasies and weaknesses of his partners and opponents has an immense advantage over the player who is guided merely by rule of thumb. I know certain old-fashioned players who object very strongly to this idea. "I play the game," they say, "exactly the same under all circumstances."

The auction has introduced an entirely novel factor. Try as experts may to bring the bidding within the limits of mechanical formulae, there always remains the human element. The bold and agile speculator who judges his men has the advantage over the mere theorist all the time.

8. Don't judge by results. A mark of the good player is that he does not judge by results. It is very galling when you have made a perfectly legitimate bid and gone down, owing to some freakish distribution of the cards, to see your partner shake his head and remark, "A bit rash, wasn't it?" or something of the kind. A good player will usually distinguish between the reckless and silly bid and a justifiable risk. His comment, if he makes one at all, will be, "Bad luck. Your bid was absolutely sound, but you found the cards massed against you in one hand."

Again and again have I heard good bids execrated because they did not happen to come off, and vice versa. I have heard shockingly bad bids applauded because, through a fluke, they have proved successful. It takes a good player to appreciate a good player. Just as at billiards, or at golf, or any other game you like to mention, the expert can tell in a few minutes whether the player knows what he is about, so at bridge the good player is soon recognized by a kindred spirit. He may win or lose. His bids may come off or fail. But that does not make the least bit of difference. It is not by his success or failure that he will be judged, but by his methods of play.

9. Don't be in a hurry; don't "press." The good player is never in a hurry. By that I do not mean that he is a slow player. Far from it. But he has not that feverish, hectic quality, which we all know, of playing

every rubber as if it were his last. He is content to go slowly and let time tell. He does not rush at it or snatch at it. He waits and bides his opportunity. But he never misses a chance. These are a few of the "human" attributes. They are really more difficult to acquire than any amount of bridge lore. What is called "card sense" or intuition may, of course, be a natural gift. But it can be gained by practice just as card memory can be acquired. Cleverness alone, inborn or learned, does not make the good bridge player. When you come down to rock bottom, it is character that tells all the time.

10. Get a good reputation. Be reliable. To have a good bridge reputation is an invaluable asset, and it is worth while taking pains to get it. It makes all the difference between winning and losing rubbers. It is astonishing how quickly a club player acquires a reputation which either makes or mars him. He is soon summed up as "sound," or "unreliable," "erratic," "dangerous," "nervy," "panicky" or "hopeless." Everybody who takes the trouble can win a reputation as a reliable player and partner. And this quality is more to be coveted than brilliance. The dashing, fireworksy person, who now and then does wonderful things, is often a sore trial and source of perplexity to his partner. Be reliable. It is not always easy. It involves a good deal of self-restraint, self-denial and grit. It means standing by and strictly adhering to principles. By this I do not mean that there can be no elasticity with a reliable player's game. But it rules out wild and fantastic bids that so often prolong rubbers and result in heavy penalties.

HOW TO REMEMBER THE CARDS

*If You Can't Remember, You Just Can't
Win*

by ALBERT H. MOREHEAD

THE GREAT ACTOR shook his shaggy locks, known to a generation
of theatergoers. Beetling his bushy eyebrows, as he had when portraying
the Duke of Wellington or Cardinal Richelieu, he directed the famous
Arliss glare at — the dummy! George Arliss was playing three no trump;
he had eight tricks tucked away, and he simply didn't know where the
ninth was coming from.

Reposing in dummy, along with the lead, was an innocent-looking
three of diamonds. To Mr. Arliss' opponents it was dangerous looking,
too. All the other diamonds were gone; the three was a "thirteener." If led,
it would win the game and rubber. But Mr. Arliss obviously didn't know
this. He had forgotten. So he led a club and was down one, and his
relieved opponents went out on the next deal.

Now, George Arliss could recite sixty-odd dramas, including some two
dozen of Shakespeare's, without missing an if, an and, or a but. In his
struggling younger years, he sometimes had to learn a new part in the
afternoon and go on with it that night. He could recall ten thousand
performances — the dates, places, and other players in the cast. But he just
couldn't remember how many diamonds had been played!

In contrast, tune in on two bridge addicts who might have trouble with
the line, "Madame, the carriage awaits without." Not long ago, at a

From *Cosmopolitan* Magazine, 1949. Reprinted by permission.

party where some of the guests were bridge experts and some were not, the conversation turned to Winfield Liggett, a noted but eccentric player of bygone days. One of the experts, naturally enough, got to reminiscing. "I remember the last time I played with Lig," quoth he. "It was back in 1932. There was a hand where I held five spades to the ace-king-jack, three hearts to the queen, the king and one club . . ." and he rattled them off, complete with bidding and play, while the non-expert guests stared at him, aghast.

The expert wasn't being a show-off. Like most of his kind, he takes his card memory so much for granted that he is vaguely surprised when other people call it phenomenal. There was a case at a national bridge tournament when Geoffrey Mott-Smith picked up a bridge hand and promptly summoned the tournament director. "I played this hand two weeks ago," he announced. To prove it, he named every other player's hand, card for card, pip for pip. Hands played in tournaments are kept intact in duplicate boards, and someone had forgotten to reshuffle this one. The other players found nothing unusual in Mott-Smith's perform-ance; such occurrences are quite frequent.

At the same tournament, a little amphitheater was built around one of the tables. As a thrill for the spectators, Oswald Jacoby and William E. McKenney staged a stunt there. Each glanced once at his hand, gave it to a spectator, and then called his plays "blindfold" without again looking at his cards.

But these are not difficult feats of memory. They are not based on tricky systems for remembering, nor are they isolated instances of freak mnemonic powers. It may not be possible for everyone to learn to do it, but there's no problem in telling how it's done.

Most bridge players want to know. They consider their faulty memories among their worst bridge-table defects. Ask the average player what he most wants to learn. First, he will answer facetiously, "How to hold aces and kings"; but then he will say, more seriously, "I want to learn how to remember the cards."

Plenty of people have paid good money to find out how. It began just over two hundred years ago, in 1744, when Hoyle (of "according to Hoyle" fame) published a system of card memory. Though it consisted of only three pages, Mr. Hoyle charged a guinea for it. While you may say that an English guinea was only five dollars, its purchasing power in those days was closer to forty. The Hoyle System comprised a way of arranging your cards: Put any best card to the left of your trumps, any second-best card to the right of your trumps, the suit your partner leads in the middle of your trumps, and so on. A lot of people paid Mr. Hoyle his guinea, but very few used his system — the general opinion being that it was harder to remember the system than to remember the cards.

Many mechanical devices have been put on the market to assist the faltering memory. A patented bridge table was built with a row of buttons, representing the fifty-two cards, in front of each player. Every time a card was played, you pushed down the appropriate button; the buttons that remained unpushed told you the cards that hadn't been played. Another gadget was similar to one used in the gambling game of faro, where a "casekeeper" is employed to keep track of the unplayed cards. And very recently a firm has marketed, under the name "Bridge-eze," a set of extra cards that you add to your hand and arrange so as to aid your memory.

But, alas, all these devices are illegal. This fact was established some years ago when Mrs. James Lemon, of Washington, created a test case in a national tournament. She was playing a grand slam. She saw a chance to make it by a complicated squeeze play — if she didn't lose track of the cards. So she took a pad and pencil and began to jot down the cards as they fell. The committee in charge ruled that she couldn't do it.

Besides, the average player doesn't want to go to so much trouble. He wants to remember but, if it's going to be an unconscionable chore, he'd rather forget. Nor is he concerned with remembering all the spots so he can execute a complicated squeeze play. He will be satisfied if, without too much mental torture, he can recall how many trumps are out . . . if anyone else has another heart. So he asks, "Is there some secret formula the experts know and I don't?"

There's no short cut, but there is a way. You can follow the same system the experts use; oddly enough, the system makes it fairly easy. It won't cost you forty dollars, or even a guinea.

The expert economizes on mental energy. He does not try to remember individual cards that have gone before. He merely keeps himself aware of what is left — always in relation to the cards he still holds in his hand.

Thus: He picks up the ten, eight, and three of spades. At first he pays no attention; his chance of winning a trick with the ten is too remote. But the first trick includes the jack, queen, and ace of spades. Now he does note that the king is the only spade that will beat his ten-spot. He notes also that if the nine is led, covered by his ten, and won by the king, his eight-spot will be high. This system of remembering is obviously less effort, and, at the same time, it keeps the players thinking ahead instead of thinking back. He always knows whether his eight-spot is high, or what must happen to make it high.

When the expert says he "counts," the word doesn't mean what it usually does. The first step comes when you pick up your hand; you fix in mind its pattern — that is, the number of cards you have in each suit. You consciously repeat to yourself, "I have five hearts, four diamonds, three spades, and one club — five, four, three, one." You need this information as a guide in bidding; you remember it in play. When the dummy goes down, you count its pattern the same way.

Since bridge is a follow-suit game, the expert counts in terms of tricks — not eight spades, but two spade tricks — and keeps track of breaks in this pattern when someone discards or someone trumps. A failure to follow suit stands out because it is different.

Suppose you have lost track of the diamonds. But you do remember that you held four diamonds originally, and now you have only one. You don't recall anyone's trumping a diamond; you don't remember discarding one; ergo, diamonds must have been played three times, and the one you have left is probably good. By such thinking, George Arliss might have led that three of diamonds and won the rubber.

The seemingly phenomenal memory of the serious bridge player does stem partly from another cause — his keen interest in the game.

Bob Feller, or any other big-league baseball pitcher, after working a game in which he threw the ball anywhere from 125 to 150 times, can tell you in consecutive order every pitch he made, why he selected it, and precisely where the ball went. For that matter, your twelve-year-old-son can probably tell you Joe DiMaggio's batting average and how many home runs Babe Ruth hit. It means so much to him, he remembers it. It is the same with a bridge expert and cards.

Next time you play bridge, try the experts' way of remembering. Concentrate first on the suit pattern of your hand. "Promote" your cards as higher ones fall. Look twice at any trick where someone fails to follow suit, and trust to visual memory to recall that trick if you have to. By burdening your mind with less, you will actually remember more.

One thing more: Don't try to memorize the cards, but don't fail to notice them. Milton Work, leading bridge authority of his era, once put this principle very succinctly. Said Mr. Work, "You can't remember a card you didn't see."

LUCK AND THE
LAW OF AVERAGES IN BRIDGE

by WALTER MALOWAN

BRIDGE PLAYERS are by no means a united lot. They are divided by systems, differences in ability, preferences as to stakes and various minor inclinations. One bone of contention is the question whether there is any such thing as luck or whether the law of averages distributes "the breaks" fairly evenly. If Ibsen's dogma that the majority is always wrong has a *raison d'être,* then there is no luck in bridge, as most players are firm believers in luck.

A Test Case

For my part I give full credence to the law of averages, and the only adequate test in bridge history that can be applied supports me. I have in mind the famous Culbertson-Lenz match. Here are the statistics of the match:

	Culbertson	Lenz
Rubbers won	77	73
Small slams made	29	27
Aces	1,745	1,771
Kings	1,775	1,741
Honors — Culbertson honor trick table	3,649½	3,648
Honors — "Official" no-trump count	18,091	17,898

From *The Literary Digest* Magazine. Reprinted by permission of the author.

The law of averages functioned almost perfectly in this comparatively small number of rubbers, as is attested by the distribution of aces and kings. Over a period of a year it can scarcely fail to work at least as well.

A player whose game has suffered because of a belief that he was born under an unlucky star should take heart after studying these figures. Such a player does not need a change of luck but a change of opponents. Probably he is outclassed in the skill he ordinarily displays and should find easier opposition until his game has improved.

It is one of the most common occurrences at the bridge table to hear a player bemoan his hard luck after losing a rubber, when he might have won it through even average skill. A few days ago I was a disinterested kibitzer when a hand, shown in the diagram, was dealt, both sides being vulnerable.

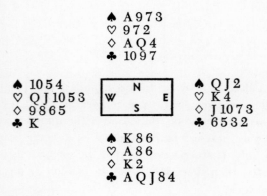

```
                    ♠ A 9 7 3
                    ♡ 9 7 2
                    ◇ A Q 4
                    ♣ 10 9 7

     ♠ 10 5 4          N            ♠ Q J 2
     ♡ Q J 10 5 3   W     E         ♡ K 4
     ◇ 9 8 6 5         S            ◇ J 10 7 3
     ♣ K                            ♣ 6 5 3 2

                    ♠ K 8 6
                    ♡ A 8 6
                    ◇ K 2
                    ♣ A Q J 8 4
```

The Play

The North-South players contracted for three no trump and West led the queen of hearts. East overtook with the king in order to unblock and returned the four of hearts. South held off the ace until the third round, then entered the dummy with a diamond and led the ten of clubs, which was allowed to run. West made his blank king and took two more heart tricks setting the contract 100 points. In one way it was bad luck that West's only club should be the king, but South could have protected himself. Naturally, he had to set up the club suit to make the needed nine tricks, but even if East made the king of clubs it would have been of no importance, as he had no hearts left. The declarer, for that reason, should not have tried the club finesse, as there was the possibility of West having the king alone, and West was the one to be prevented from taking another trick. South should have played the ace of clubs, and if the king was held by East, he should have been more than welcome to that trick.

Became Anxious

After having missed the chance of winning the rubber and being patted on the back by his partner, South became over-anxious to make up for it and was set 500 points on the next hand.

The subsequent deal favored the opponents, who held: West — Spades: K J 10 7; Hearts: 6 4 3; Diamonds: K Q 7; Clubs: A K 9. East — Spades: A Q 9 4 2; Hearts: A Q 7; Diamonds: A J; Clubs: 8 7 3.

They reached a small slam contract in spades, South leading the queen of clubs. The dummy won with the ace and the declarer played two rounds of trumps, on which the adversaries followed. A losing club was discarded on dummy's third diamond, and then the nine of clubs was led, East discarding the seven of hearts instead of trumping, as the lead had marked South with the jack and ten of clubs. South was forced to take the trick, and irrespective of what he led, the small slam contract was assured. Incidentally South held the king of hearts, and had East tried the heart finesse instead of the strip and end play, he would have been defeated. These two hands taken from one rubber demonstrate the difference between skilful and wooden play, and luck has nothing to do with the fact that South loses steadily to East, month after month.

When players of about equal strength meet regularly, one or the other, at times, will have a lucky streak, when every finesse works, trumps always "break" and the vital cards are in the partner's hand. But such luck is short-lived, and a good knowledge of the game is much more solid ground on which to build.

Good players, when pursued by bad luck, for a few weeks, should take their misfortunes stoically and know that better times are ahead. During the worst streak of bad luck I have ever experienced at the card table, two vulnerable grand slams were bid against me through misunderstandings of the opponents. The first one ranks as a classic.

Turn in Fortune

The dealer bid a heart, I passed and third hand bid two clubs. The dealer, in the meantime, had forgotten that he had opened the bidding, and believing that his partner had made an original forcing two-bid, immediately went to seven hearts, which contract, thanks to four successful finesses, was made. A few days later the player to my left bid spades, the partner responded with three clubs and finally by slow degrees reached six spades. The original spade bidder responded with six no trump, because he held only four spades. He intended the bid as a "sign-off," yet it was understood as an encouragement, drawing a grand slam bid in spades from the partner. I held king, jack, nine in spades in front of the declarer and, of course, was annihilated. The contract could not have been made had either of my two spade honors been in my partner's hand. After two weeks of misery a sudden turn in my fortunes took place, and in addition to other lucky breaks I made two grand slams in one afternoon.

Superstitions

Most players are irrationally superstitious and try to give luck a helping hand with all kinds of idiosyncrasies. This does not exclude the players who do not believe in luck. Very few players, when having the choice, would fail to take the seats in which the previous rubber has been won. They also prefer to deal with the deck with which they have cut for partners, provided their card has been high. Two of our greatest players become utterly furious when any one touches their chairs with his foot. Once, on the eve of a national tournament, I stayed at the house of one of the favorites, and upon entering my room threw my hat on the bed. This, it seems, augurs the worst possible luck, and almost ended a beautiful friendship. Some excellent and otherwise normal players believe that certain other players are their hoodoos, either as partners or opponents. Results naturally will bear them out — not because their contention is correct, but because their superstitions cause their play to be influenced. For an expert pair to lose to two average players, after a few weeks of continued play, is as preposterous as for a chess champion to be defeated two games in succession by a fair amateur. The law of averages, inexorably governing the luck in deals, just won't permit it.

INSTINCT!

by Frank K. Perkins

Last SUMMER, Harry Fishbein, winner of the Masters' Pairs, rushed over to Lawrence Weiss, of Boston, in great excitement.

"I'm instinctive! I'm instinctive!" he cried.

"What do you mean?" growled Larry who had troubles of his own.

"LOOK! You hold the spade king four times, the queen and two little hearts, the jack and two rags in diamonds, and the king three times of clubs. Your partner opens one heart. What do you do?"

"I pass of course," said Larry, who began to smell a rat.

Poor Harry looked crestfallen. "Guess you must be instinctive too," he muttered as he slunk away.

Card instinct is a much abused term. It is the pride of the expert, but the downfall of the fellow who bellows "three no trump" at every opportunity — then goes down on a hand that ought to produce an extra trick.

There is no question that success at the bridge table depends a great deal on the ability to size up competitive situations. Often, they are outside any book or system, and experts claim they depend on card instinct. We doubt this, and go so far as to deny any inherent card instinct. We believe the so-called instinct is the result of tremendous card table experience, backed up by a sound knowledge of technique. Furthermore, you will notice that the fellow who depends on "card sense" alone is almost always a losing player. We prefer to take our chances with a

Reprinted by permission of *The Bridge World*, New York. A. Moyse, Jr., publisher.

partner who is willing and able to count to thirteen. The hell with instinct! Let the other fellow have it if he will promise to rely on it alone.

Instinctive players have a great yen for no-trump contracts, so here are a couple of deals where declarer played too much "by ear."

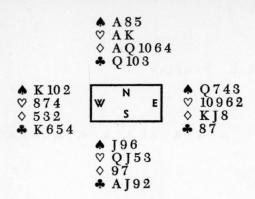

North dealer.
North–South vulnerable.

The bidding:

North	East	South	West
1 ◊	Pass	1 NT	Pass
2 NT	Pass	3 NT	Pass
Pass	Pass		

West led the two of diamonds.

Being an instinctive player, South was delighted that West had opened the long diamond suit; and declarer had visions of winning every finesse in a blaze of glory.

So declarer played a low diamond from dummy, and East won with the jack. But East knifed declarer by shifting to a low spade. Declarer was now alarmed, and allowed the ten and the king of spades to win the next two tricks. If West now led a third spade, declarer would be all right!

But after making his second spade, West led another diamond, and declarer again finessed, which was as good as anything at this stage. East won the trick with the king, and then came back with a club, and declarer was ruined. If he put up his ace of clubs, he would eliminate his heart entry. So that finesse was tried too, and the king of clubs beat the hand.

A player who felt less gifted might have taken the trouble to grab the game and rubber which was possible against any defense and any distribution after the first lead.

Dummy's ace should have taken the first diamond, and the ace-king of hearts should be cashed. Then the queen of clubs should be led and allowed to run, and declarer would be sure of four hearts, three clubs and the two side aces. South was helpless against the actual defense after the first mistake.

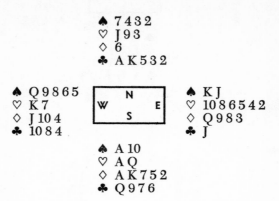

```
              ♠ 7432
              ♡ J93
              ◇ 6
              ♣ AK532
♠ Q9865      N         ♠ KJ
♡ K7      W     E      ♡ 1086542
◇ J104       S         ◇ Q983
♣ 1084                 ♣ J
              ♠ A10
              ♡ AQ
              ◇ AK752
              ♣ Q976
```

South dealer.
Both sides vulnerable.

The bidding:

South	West	North	East
1 ◇	Pass	2 ♣	Pass
3 NT	Pass	Pass	Pass

West led the six of spades.

Declarer ducked the first spade when East played the king, but the ace captured the second round.

A quick glance assured declarer that he could run home with nine tricks, so he cashed the queen, the king and the ace of clubs. Then he suddenly saw that South's six of clubs was higher than any club left in dummy, and that it would block the suit. The heart finesse now seemed necessary, and the hand went down one when West showed up with the king of hearts and ran off the spades.

After the queen and king of clubs showed the club split, dummy should have led a losing spade on which South could get rid of his troublesome six of clubs. Let the enemy make the remaining spades, for that would take only four tricks for the defense. After that declarer could regain the lead and spread his hand for the balance.

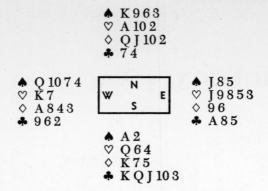

```
                    ♠ K 9 6 3
                    ♡ A 10 2
                    ♢ Q J 10 2
                    ♣ 7 4

  ♠ Q 10 7 4         N          ♠ J 8 5
  ♡ K 7         W         E     ♡ J 9 8 5 3
  ♢ A 8 4 3          S          ♢ 9 6
  ♣ 9 6 2                       ♣ A 8 5

                    ♠ A 2
                    ♡ Q 6 4
                    ♢ K 7 5
                    ♣ K Q J 10 3
```

South dealer.
Both sides vulnerable.

The bidding:

SOUTH	WEST	NORTH	EAST
1 ♣	Pass	1 ♢	Pass
1 NT	Pass	2 NT	Pass
3 NT	Pass	Pass	Pass

West led the four of spades.

South knew instinctively that the hand that opens the auction is usually the stronger, and that it is dummy in such cases that is likely to need entries.

So declarer held off the first spade and won the second round. The king of clubs was allowed to hold the next trick, and then another club was taken by East. East led a third spade, knocking out dummy's king.

Dummy played the queen of diamonds, but was allowed to hold the trick. Then the two of diamonds was covered by South's king and taken by West's ace. The last spade was cashed, and West got out of his hand with the eight of diamonds. South had no entry for his clubs, so dummy was stuck with the lead and a heart trick beat the contract.

The next time you draw a partner who is "instinctive," run for the nearest exit!

PSYCHOLOGY

by SAM FRY, JR.

◇♣♡♠◇♣♡♠◇♣♡♠◇♣♡♠◇♣♡♠◇♣♡♠◇♣♡♠◇♣♡♠◇♣♡♠

PSYCHOLOGY IN THE BIDDING of contract bridge hands consists chiefly in playing up to the strength and weakness of your partner and against the strengths and weaknesses of your opponents.

For example, it is very often quite difficult to decide on certain close hands whether the final game contract should be three no trump or four of a major. The following was the holding of an expert player, playing with an astute, fine partner. He held:

♠ A 6   ♡ K Q J 9 7 4   ◇ Q 3   ♣ A K 10

He naturally opened the bidding with one heart. Over his partner's one-no-trump response he continued with the practically forcing rebid of three hearts and his partner then bid three no trump.

It is really pretty much of a guess with a holding of this kind whether to let the final contract stand at three no trump or to proceed with four hearts. In such a case the only thing you have to go by is your previous experience with your partner.

A great many players will almost automatically make an immediate response of three no trump with a weak hand over the three-heart bid, regardless of the fact that they hold a suit or suits unguarded and even with good support in the heart suit. They bid three no trump to show they have no additional values, even though they might guess that four

Reprinted by permission of *The Bridge World,* New York. A. Moyse, Jr., publisher.

hearts would probably be a better final contract with a partner good enough to bid one and three of that suit. With such players as your partner, for safety's sake, you have to go back to four hearts.

With certain other expert partners — in fact, I could name three off-hand — I am convinced that the correct procedure is to pass to three no trump because these players will lean toward supporting your major if they can possibly do so. Thus when they bid three no trump you know their heart support is at best negative.

◇ ♣ ♡ ♠

Playing your opponents is of great importance. There are some people who are known to see red when the bidding is opened in front of them with a pre-emptive call of three or four. Their hair will stand up on end, they will fret and fume at your audacity in trying to shut them out, and with the slightest excuse they will overcall your pre-emptive bid, regardless of vulnerability. When you sit at the right of a player of this type, you can "fix" him by judiciously inserting very strong pre-emptive bids every now and then, despite the fact that usually pre-empts are made on weak, defenseless hands. You can bid three spades on a strong all-around hand and if your calculations have been correct, this opponent will very promptly overcall with four of another suit which either you or your partner will double and severely penalize.

Another psychological bid which has been known to work with excellent effect, but which can be used only very rarely, is to pass your partner's opening one-bid with considerable strength in your hand. The time for this is when the next player is of the aggressive type who will automatically reopen the bidding on the theory that his partner, rather than you, must have the balance of power. If you pick the correct spot, another big penalty score can very well accrue to your side.

◇ ♣ ♡ ♠

The artful bidder must be able to adapt himself to his partners. When playing with an expert partner, a player who is faced with a choice of responding to his partner's opening one-bid with one of another suit or two no trump will usually choose the former call. By approaching slowly with suit responses, every bit of available ground is thoroughly explored, and the best final contract can thus be ascertained.

With weak partners you cannot afford to probe. One reason is that the weak partner may let the bidding die prematurely because he does not recognize strong bids unless they skip a level or two. Another reason is that with such a partner you want to make every effort to get in the no-trump call first. Since the mostly likely final declaration is three no trump you want to be the eventual declarer, but if you bid one of a suit your inexpert partner might gaily leap into no trump himself. It will avail you little to get to a contract of four of a major which is makable rather than three no trump which can be beaten, if in the play your partner throws two tricks and goes down at the major, whereas you in all probability can pick up a trick and fulfill a three-no-trump contract.

◇ ♣ ♡ ♠

But a word of warning should be inserted at this point. You must not go too far with this bidding idea, no matter how weak your partner. It is bad strategy to play the hand yourself at a contract which is in the wrong suit by a matter of about three tricks, when you could have let your partner play the hand in the correct suit, where even though he plays it badly, he still will have enough leeway to permit him to fulfill his contract.

In addition, in bidding with weak partners, when faced with a difficult hand you very often cannot make the really fine bid — the bid which with an expert would give the greatest amount of information and allow the greatest possible choice of final declarations. Such a bid is very often beyond the mental scope of your partner, and if you give a weak partner too much of a guess he will almost surely make the wrong decision. In such instances, you have to be content not to try for a maximum result. Instead your watchword should be safety.

Likewise, don't deliberately take heavy penalties to save the rubber when playing with a neophyte. After all, even though you do save the rubber, you will still be at a disadvantage on the next hand. So it is best to give up a little more easily.

◇ ♣ ♡ ♠

In the play of contract bridge hands when playing against strong opposition, the expert will almost invariably take the correct percentage play. By the correct percentage play, I mean that play which will work out successfully against the greatest number of possible combinations of the outstanding cards. When playing against weak opposition, however, a good player quite frequently rejects the play which mathematics tells him is the correct one in favor of another line of play which, although the percentages do not favor it as much, puts a weak opponent completely "on the spot." In other words, although he has lost a little in disregarding the laws of chance, he will gain that back and a little more by having human fallibility working for him.

◇ ♣ ♡ ♠

The art of false-carding is entirely psychological in nature. Every bridge player knows that by dropping unnecessarily high cards in following to a trick, or by winning a trick with an equally unnecessarily high card, one can quite frequently mislead the opponents as to one's holding and induce them to misplay. However, no general rule can be made as to when to false-card and when not to.

Take the classic example of when you have the queen-jack alone in a suit behind the declarer who is marked with the ace-king-ten and several small cards. He lays down the ace and you have to follow. Obviously, it is immaterial which one you drop, as the cards are equals.

Against the absolute beginner, you undoubtedly choose the queen. He will naturally assume that, since you drop the queen, you cannot have any lower card, such as the jack, and he will consequently finesse the suit on the next round and lose a trick to your jack.

Against a player who is just getting on to the tricks of the trade, however, you have to adopt the opposite procedure. He, knowing you are a good player, will at this stage of his bridge development assume that with such a combination of cards as the queen-jack alone, you, the master, will of course drop the queen to fool him. It is now up to you to doublecross him by dropping the jack.

Against a top-flight player, however, neither card will help you particularly. The best thing for you to do, if you want to fool this advanced type of enemy at least half of the time, is to alternate. Probably on Mondays, Wednesdays, Fridays and all legal holidays, you should drop the queen; and on Tuesdays, Thursdays, Saturdays, Sundays, Lincoln's Birthday, and Valentine's Day, you should drop the jack. At least then your opponent, if he doesn't know your schedule, will not have anything to go by and he will have to guess himself.

◇ ♣ ♡ ♠

Of course, this is only one of hundreds of possible false-cards. Generally, you have to study your opponent, decide upon his mental level

— just how keen he is and just how hard he is trying to outguess you — and then remember previous experiences with him in similar situations.

And even if you do all this, if your opponent is your equal, you will have reverted to the old head or tail guessing game. You place your coin, head face up on the table, and he guesses it. Now when he is going to guess again, you probably reason something like this: The logical thing for me to do is alternate and put tail. Therefore, I will make it a head and fool him — but he expects me to try to fool him. Maybe I had better try tail after all. But maybe he expects me to expect him to expect me to expect him to expect me to — ! You can go on far into the night with this sort of thing, and very often you may get two guesses ahead of your opponent and consequently lose to him.

One more point may be mentioned in this very incomplete discussion of psychology in bridge. In playing the defense with a weak partner, you have to make his plays as easy as possible for him.

When you are partnered with an expert and you are not absolutely certain as to what he should continue, you should give him nothing but negative signals and let him decide for himself. With a bad partner it is best to try to make all the decisions yourself, even though you cannot see your partner's hand and even though you may not be in as good a position to tell the correct play as he is. The chances are that your guess will be better than his, and you should tell him what to do by dropping a high-card signal, or better still by overtaking his card and making the correct lead yourself.

BLUFF BIDS IN CONTRACT BRIDGE

Time and again, despite repeated failures, "psychics" are called, yet the object is attained about as frequently as a triple play in baseball is effected without aid.

by WALTER MALOWAN

◇ ♣ ♡ ♠ ◇ ♣ ♡ ♠ ◇ ♣ ♡ ♠ ◇ ♣ ♡ ♠ ◇ ♣ ♡ ♠ ◇ ♣ ♡ ♠ ◇ ♣ ♡ ♠ ◇ ♣ ♡ ♠ ◇ ♣ ♡ ♠

PSYCHIC BIDS (bluff bids) in contract bridge are about as rare as unassisted triple plays in baseball or holes-in-one in golf. Small wonder that "psychics" are tried so much despite many failures.

Years ago, times were more propitious for psychic bidders, as effective counter-measures had not been found; also because the element of surprise helped the adventurer. Now the average player is on the look-out for psychic bids, and usually succeeds in thwarting them.

There are many who claim the credit for having originated the "psychic," but Dorothy Sims, well-known bridge player and sculptress, has the strongest claim. Whether or not the psychic bid actually was an origination is open to question. My own opinion is that it merely is an adaptation, for there is no essential difference between a so-called psychic bid in bridge and a bluff bet in poker — and the latter probably is as old as poker itself. Strictly speaking, psychics were not unknown even in

From *The Literary Digest Magazine*. Reprinted by permission.

the heyday of auction bridge, when the following trap-bid was used frequently:

The opening bidder would rush into a one no trump, and after two passes the fourth hand would bid two hearts on a hand something like this:

♠ 7 4 2   ♡ A 3   ◇ 4 2   ♣ A K Q 9 7 4

It was probable that one of the opponents then would go to two no trump, and, after the lead of a heart, the nice club suit would be run off.

Classes of Psychic Bids

Psychic bids which are employed in contract bridge and which have occasional chance of success may be divided into the following groups:

1. The opening bid on a trickless or almost trickless hand. This bid is made on the principle that attack is the best defense, but it is rather dangerous for first or second hand, as the partner may easily be more deceived than the opponents. A third-hand bid is now always looked upon with suspicion, and the partner is supposed to watch his step until the third-hand bidder has shown some definite signs of strength. Against fairly strong opposition this bid will work only as a lead-director. For instance, when third hand holds — Spades: 9 4 2; Hearts: K Q J 9 3; Diamonds: 7 4; Clubs: 10 9 2; a heart bid may succeed in preventing a no-trump contract, which might possibly be the best bet for the opposing side.

2. Bid of a suit, when holding one or two small cards in it or a void. This bluff bid should be used as an overcall only, and preferably when the partner has opened the bidding.

3. Psychic no-trump bids. The opponents' suit bid is overcalled with a no trump without any sign of a stopper, or other defensive strength, but holding one good suit to which to turn in case of a double. This bid is made for the purpose of buying the contract cheaply, possibly without being doubled. In some cases the fake no-trump bid, if taken at its face value, will prevent a slam bid.

4. Psychic three-no-trump bids. These are used only after the partner has passed, preferably when the opponents have a partial score. If North, your partner, has made no bid, and East bids a no trump, with sixty on the score, you may safely assume that West will bid a suit, as this is the safest way to make game. If you hold Spades: 10 9; Hearts: 8 7; Diamonds: J; Clubs: Q J 10 7 6 5 3 2; your best bid, paradoxical as

it may sound, is three no trump. If you do not take a single trick you will lose 450 points, while the opponents apparently can score a grand slam. If you are doubled, you turn to your club suit. Even if your dummy is trickless, you lose only 700 points, and experience the "grand and glorious" feeling of having prevented a slam bid, and at a bargain price.

5. The psychic informatory double. This is the one psychic which may safely be used even by vulnerable players. Let us assume that you are looking at six solid spades (or preferably more) and nothing else, and are faced by an opponent's suit bid. Instead of bidding your spades, you double for a take-out. This bluff may or may not win, but is worth trying.

6. The psychic two-bid. This kind of smoke-screen is virtually valueless, as it has no satisfactory continuation in the bidding. The last time I saw it tried, a few months ago, the dealer started with two clubs and his partner responded with two spades. As the entire honor-strength of the dealer consisted of a queen and a jack, he passed, for he was in danger of being taken to a slam. As an opening two-bid is a forcing bid in almost any system, and, in others, guarantees at least one rebid, the pass over the two-spade bid gave away the entire show and exposed the bluff immediately.

7. Psychic bids made on strong hands. To give an example, let us take this hand:

♠ K J 7   ♡ A K Q 10 7 4   ◊ 7 3   ♣ A Q

South, the fortunate holder of this pleasing array, starts the hostilities with one heart, and his partner obliges with a one-spade bid. The best continuation for South is a forcing bid of three diamonds. This apparently fatuous bid has a dual purpose. If North can go to four diamonds, a slam in hearts or spades should be ventured. But even if he should respond with three hearts or three spades, South might risk a five bid, inviting the partner to bid a slam. It is probable that the three-diamond call would prevent an opening lead of that suit and a slam would be made.

Addicts to psychic bids always should have a fairly safe suit to fall back on when caught in their own trap. Furthermore, vulnerable psychics, with the exception of the informatory double, are not advisable, as vulnerable sets are very expensive even though undoubled. The most important consideration is not to be too venturesome when playing with "mechanical" partners, otherwise a tragicomedy may result — as happened with the following hand.

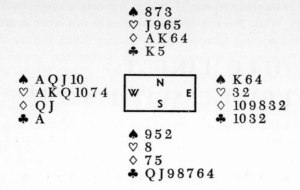

♠ 873
♡ J965
◇ A K 6 4
♣ K 5

♠ A Q J 10   ♠ K 6 4
♡ A K Q 10 7 4   ♡ 3 2
◇ Q J   ◇ 10 9 8 3 2
♣ A   ♣ 10 3 2

♠ 9 5 2
♡ 8
◇ 7 5
♣ Q J 9 8 7 6 4

North dealer.
Neither side vulnerable.

The bidding:

NORTH	EAST	SOUTH	WEST
1 ◇	Pass	1 ♡	Double
2 ♡	Pass	3 ♣	4 ♡
Double	Pass	Pass	Redouble
Pass	Pass	5 ♣	Double
5 ♡	Pass	6 ♣	Double
Pass	Pass	Pass	

Failure of Psychic Bid

The bidding of this hand demonstrates that South was theoretically right when he made his psychic heart bid, as the East-West players actually had an easy game in that suit; South's tactics might have succeeded had not West's heart suit been very strong. In practice, however, South lacked good judgment, as he selected a time for his psychic bid when he was not only faced by an able opponent, but was handicapped by a partner who could see no farther than his own hand, and was quite unable to solve even the most obvious bidding problem. At one stage of the auction, South might have allowed West to play the hand at four hearts redoubled, but declined to do so. How North, under such conditions, could imagine that South preferred to be the declarer at five hearts, rather than five clubs, defies explanation.

DO PEOPLE LIKE TO
PLAY BRIDGE WITH YOU?

◇♣♡♠◇♠♣♡♠◇♣♡♠◇♣♡♠◇♣♡♠◇♣♡♠◇♣♡♠◇♣♡♠◇♣♡♠

PUT A CHECK alongside each question if your answer is "no." Then look on page 299, and see your result.

1. Do you ever say plaintively when your turn to play comes, "What do I do now?"

2. When asked what system of bidding you use, do you say, "Oh, I don't believe in systems. I just use horse sense."

3. Does your partner usually have to resort to threatening looks and slamming down his hand on the table to get you to recognize a sign-off bid?

4. Is your idea of saving a rubber handing your opponents anywhere from 700 points on up?

5. Is your answer to every helpful tip a helpless "But that isn't what you said before"?

6. Do you ever, ever say, "Who dealt this mess?"

7. Are you forced to explain several times an evening, "I didn't know we had a partial, partner"?

8. Do you overcall a spade or a heart bid with "two diamonds," vulnerable, holding five diamonds to the ace-king and an outside king, "because I wanted to show my partner something"?

9. Do you frequently maneuver the bidding so that you get to be declarer regardless of the fact that the hand would probably play more safely at your partner's declared suit or no trump?

10. When pointing out your partner's error do you point and point and point?

11. Do you slavishly follow such rules as "Never lead away from a king"?

12. Do you insist that partner always return your lead regardless of the circumstances?

13. Do you hastily play a card from dummy and your own hand to the first trick before formulating a plan for the hand?

14. Do you greet partner's well-meant advice with "Aah, what do you know"?

15. Do you believe that there's little room for improvement in your game?

16. Do 100 honors make you stubborn about playing the hand?

17. Do you consider defense as something you want to get over with quickly so that you can get on to the next hand?

18. When your partner is pondering an intelligent lead do you snap impatiently, "Come on, lead anything. What difference does it make?"

19. You have just gone down two tricks, redoubled, vulnerable, on a hand a beginner could have rolled with ease. Would such an occurrence throw you for the rest of the evening?

20. Do you frequently ask for a review of the bidding and after getting it say, "Now how did that go again?"

21. Do you close every losing evening with the remark, "I just couldn't hold a card tonight"?

22. Do you expect congratulations every time you fulfill a contract?

23. Do you switch your cards around after you've played a singleton?

24. Does every other partner get more consideration than your spouse?

25. Do you, umpteen times an evening, look at the others when the fresh pack is at your left and waiting to be dealt by you and say, "Well, let's get going. Who deals?"

Scoring for Quiz on Page 298

Count each check mark as 4 points.

Under 32: No wonder people don't smile when they cut you as partner.

32 to 48: Passable, but nothing to shout about.

52 to 68: For you they'll crack a slight smile.

72 to 86: They're not likely to forget your phone number when there's a bridge game brewing.

90 to 100: You're sure you're not kidding, now?

Section 9

Conventions—
Legal and Otherwise

Bridge

BY WEBSTER

THE UNDERSTANDING

CONVENTIONS—
LEGAL AND OTHERWISE

◇♣♡♠◇♣♡♠◇♣♡♠◇♣♡♠◇♣♡♠◇♣♡♠◇♣♡♠◇♣♡♠◇♣♡♠

"**O**NE OF THE GREAT CONSPIRACIES of modern times," said Alfred Sheinwold, "is the pretense that contract bridge can be played and that anybody ever actually does so. The fact is, of course, that no more than five people ever played the game; and four of them are known to be incurable liars.

"The physical impossibility of contract bridge can easily be demonstrated by mathematics:

"First, consider the difficulty of Basic English, which seeks merely to reduce the 400,000 words of the English language to a few hundred words. This is a reduction of only about 1,000 to 1, yet the wise money is betting that it cannot be done.

"Now, consider the fact that the bridge player sets out to describe each of the 635,013,559,600 different hands with only the following fifteen words:

1. One	9. Hearts
2. Two	10. Diamonds
3. Three	11. Clubs
4. Four	12. No trump
5. Five	13. Pass
6. Six	14. Double
7. Seven	15. Redouble
8. Spades	

"This is a reduction of more than 40,000,000,000 to 1!

303

"It doesn't take a mathematician to realize that if the wise money is willing to bet against a reduction of 1,000 to 1, then a reduction of more than 40,000,000,000 to 1 is too absurd even to talk about."

George S. Kaufman expressed the belief that much of the bidding difficulty encountered by the average player could be done away with by seating partners differently. Instead of facing each other they should be allowed to sit side by side on a small bench. This would enable them to look at each other's hand and do away with the need for systems and conventions. He considered it superior to an alternate method, the use of transparent cards, which was unfair because it made things difficult for the near-sighted.

Both gentlemen, of course, were having a little fun. Still, being limited in what you can reveal about one particular hand out of hundreds of billions to the use of just fifteen words (minus gestures and facial expressions) does complicate things. Hence systems and conventions which are designed to impart special meanings to certain bids or sequences of bids and thus facilitate an exchange of information between partners.

Says Charles G. Roth: "If partners could see each other's hands they could arrive at accurate contracts. If they could also see the opponents' hands, they would become bidding perfectionists. They would know when to compete, sacrifice or double and when to retire gracefully from the auction.

"The evolution of bidding technique has sought to produce improved methods by the use of which partners may exchange information and more accurately determine the valuation of their combined hands. The route has been from hit or miss, to honor tricks, to point count for no trumps and, finally, to overall point count.

"Conventions employ artificial bids with specialized meanings. The artificial bid is usually an asking bid. Some conventions are too complicated to have general appeal for the multitude. A convention of this type never attains great popularity. Other conventions may be found wanting for one reason or another. A few combine simplicity with efficiency. These stand the test of time. Eventually this type of convention becomes part of the equipment of all experienced players.

"It is improper and unethical for partners to have private understandings. To give a bid a meaning which differs from the normal connotation is equivalent to adopting a private convention. When partners use known and published conventions they should, of course, announce the convention to their opponents. When they use conventions which have not had wide publicity, or when their opponents confess to unfamiliarity, they should offer a detailed explanation whenever the convention bids come into use."

From time to time tournament directors will report the use of the One-Under-One System. This is generally employed by a couple of college boys. After they play several rounds, causing havoc and devastation among players who misunderstand their bids, the cry of "Director" swells to a chorus. Investigation then reveals that the bright lads have devised what they consider an "original system." In this method a bid of one club really means one no trump, one diamond means one club, one heart means one diamond and so on.

Numerous systems and conventions have been proposed and used since contract became popular. A partial list would include the Vanderbilt Club, Barton Club, Pochabo System, Losing Trick Count, Sims System, Reeveu, Carson-Roberts Step Ladder System, Joshua Crane "Common Sense System," Simple System, The Direct System, The Four Aces System, The Winslow, The Chronological Order System, The Bulldog System, Power Control System, The Eighteen System, Picture Echo Calling, The Acol System, and the Roth Stone System.

Though various bidding systems keep clamoring for attention, the great majority of today's players favor One-Over-One bidding with variations to suit individual taste. Basically, what One-Over-One means is this: If partner has not previously passed or does not respond with one no trump or a raise of the opening bidder's suit, the latter is required to bid again every time the responder shows a new suit. Another exception to this obligation could occur because of the condition of score.

The contract enthusiast doesn't mind experimenting with and perhaps eventually adopting individual bidding gimmicks to go with One-Over-One. Especially those that will permit him to "see" into his partner's hand better or cause his opponents difficulty. Even the player who starts off not taking the game "too seriously" is apt to pick up conventions in sheer self-defense.

According to Mr. Roth, "The casual player prefers a hit or miss approach, with each player using native intelligence and card sense. He resents conventions and bids which, while clearly understood by opponents, may lead him or his partner to incorrect inferences.

"As experience grows, he notes the superior results achieved by opponents with the aid of conventions. Even though he may continue to protest and to voice contempt and resentment, he gradually adopts conventional play and bids. He will play a high card when he desires partner to continue leading a suit. He will use the defensive echo to show partner he can ruff the third round of a suit. He will double an opposing three-no-trump contract when he desires partner to lead the first suit bid by dummy.

"He will bid a Blackwood four no trump expecting partner to show aces even though he and partner have not agreed to use Blackwood. If this type of player took the pains to study and understand all conventions in common use, he would profit (by) openly adopting some or all of them. He would materially improve the equipment which he brings to the game."

How far players should be permitted to go in the use of artificial bids is a question that has been agitating tournament circles for some time now. Those who would let the chips fall where they may counsel an all-out permissiveness in the use of conventions. They call the objectors to artificial bids, "self-satisfied persons, who no longer want to make progress themselves nor permit others to improve on current bidding."

Bidding, they point out, is a code and there should be no restrictions on the meanings assigned to bids. Bridge should be a game of deception as well as skill. Allow players to use the approved vocabulary of fifteen code words as they see fit and let the devil take the hindmost. Why penalize the forward-looking and the innovators just to make things easy for those too stupid or too lazy to keep up with new developments?

"The last word has not been said on contract bidding," commented P. Hal Sims in his day. "I hope it will never be. If the time comes when the game ceases to grow, contract will no longer hold our interest."

There is another side to the argument, of course. Its main points were summed up in a letter to *The Bulletin of the American Contract Bridge League*.

Said the writer: "Conventions will eventually kill bridge as a recreation. Over-emphasis of the playing conventions caused the downfall of whist. Over-emphasis of bidding conventions will do the same to contract bridge."

Artificial bids "are . . . attempts to take away, by confusion, the legal values dealt to players by the fall of the cards.

"In every deal each player is dealt certain values. It is his right to have a fair shake to use or misuse those values to his benefit. The greed to win by the use of unusual bids and responses tries to take away the values and their benefits from those who rightfully hold them. This is a misguided attempt at strategy . . . (It) does not lend itself to the pleasant social realities at the bridge table. . ."

Which side is right? The argument is far from settled. Meanwhile, here are outlines of today's better known conventions.

In Looking for Slams

The Blackwood Convention

In this convention a bid of 4 no trump is understood to be artificial and asks partner to name the *number* of aces he holds. Asker is not required to hold any aces himself.

With no aces, the response is 5 clubs.

With one ace, the response is 5 diamonds.

With two aces, the response is 5 hearts.

With three aces, the response is 5 spades.

With four aces, the response is 5 clubs. (The same, note, as the response for no aces. The earlier bidding should make clear what a 5-club response means — no aces or all.)

After aces have been shown, a bid of 5 no trump by the original convention-user asks for the number of kings partner holds. The stair-step method is then used as in ace-showing.

With no kings, the response is 6 clubs.

With one king, the response is 6 diamonds.

With two kings, the response is 6 hearts.

With three kings, the response is 6 spades.

With four kings, the response is 6 no trump.

Kings are not asked for unless all aces are accounted for, and there is interest in a grand slam.

If the partnership uses Blackwood, it is best to agree that a 4-no-trump bid *always* asks for aces when either partner has previously named a potential trump suit, even though some players contend that 4 no trump immediately following a no-trump bid is *not* Blackwood. (For ace-checking at no trump, see The Gerber Convention, page 308.)

It is generally understood that the 4-no-trumper is captain and decides what the final contract shall be. A recognized exception: Responder believes there is a chance for slam because of the possession of a void in addition to one or more aces.

Voids are shown by some players as follows: With one ace and a void, the bid is 6 clubs; with two aces and a void, 6 diamonds; and so on.

If the 4 no trump is overcalled by an opponent in an attempt to sacrifice or disrupt exchange of information, many players proceed as follows: The cheapest call over the interference bid shows no aces, the next step one ace, and so on.

Danger: If clubs are to be the trump suit, the 4-no-trumper should hold at least two aces. If diamonds, he should hold at least one ace.

Experts don't use Blackwood with a doubleton in an unbid suit. Otherwise the bidder may find himself in a slam willy-nilly.

If a player cue-bids in an opponent's suit, and then uses Blackwood he is asking how many aces partner holds *outside* of the cue-bid suit.

If he wishes to play the hand at a final declaration of 5 no trump, the 4-no-trumper acts as follows: Over his partner's response to 4 no trump he bids a previously unnamed suit. Partner must now bid 5 no trump which will be passed.

The Gerber Convention

In this convention, a variation of Blackwood, any bid of 4 clubs is understood to be artificial and asks partner to name the *number* of aces he holds. Asker is not required to hold any aces himself. The convention is at its most effective when the contract is eventually going to be played at no trump. But some players use it with all suits since aces and kings can be shown at a lower level than in Blackwood.

With no ace, the response is 4 diamonds.

With one ace, the response is 4 hearts.

With two aces, the response is 4 spades.

With three aces, the response is 4 no trump.

With four aces, the response is 5 clubs.

After aces have been shown the original 4-club bidder makes his *cheapest rebid* to ask for kings. For example: 4 clubs — 4 hearts (showing one ace). A bid of 4 spades would now ask for the number of kings, even though spades was the agreed trump suit.

These are shown stair-step fashion in the same way that aces were. For example: over 4 spades, a response of 4 no trump would indicate no kings; 5 clubs, one king; 5 diamonds, two kings; and so on.

Many players, however, use the agreed trump suit to sign off with. For example: the agreed trump suit is spades. The convention bidding goes 4 clubs — 4 hearts. A bid of 4 spades by the asker would mean: "I'd like to stop here, partner. If you proceed it's on your own responsibility." A bid of 4 no trump, the next step up after the sign-off, would ask for kings.

If the eventual contract is to be in no trump, asker uses 4 no trump as a sign-off after aces have been shown. Five clubs is used to fish for kings.

Cue-Bidding to Slam

Where specific information is desired about specific aces and kings rather than the number of these held by partner, experts use neither the Blackwood nor Gerber. When a suit has definitely and strongly been agreed upon as trumps (usually after a jump by one partner) a bid of a new suit is understood to show the ace or a void in that suit and slam ambitions.

Partner then names an ace or void, if he has same, and if he is interested in going along toward a slam. Otherwise he returns to the agreed-upon suit.

A raise of a cue bid shows the king of that suit.

A repeat of a cue bid, or a new cue bid (after a previous one has been made by that player), requests partner also to cue-bid, if possible, regardless of his strength.

The Stayman Convention

This is a response in clubs by the partner of an opening no-trump bidder. Its primary aim is to find out whether the partnership holds eight or more cards in spades or hearts between them. Except where distribution is flat, contracts played in majors are considered to be superior to the ones played at no trump.

A 2-club response to an *opening 1-no-trump* bid is artificial. It does not promise clubs or show an interest in that suit. It is made on 8 or more points. Some players make it with 7 points and a fair five-card major suit, or 7 points and two four-card majors headed by picture cards. Some players do not set any minimum requirement for the 2-club bid.

The 2-club response asks opener for further information about his hand. If opener holds four or more cards in a major suit headed by the queen or better (some make this jack or better) he names that suit. Thus, 1 no trump — 2 clubs (Stayman).

If opener *does not have a suitable major* he rebids 2 diamonds or 2 no trump. The first is artificial, does not necessarily promise diamonds and shows a minimum no trump of 16 points. The second indicates 17 or more points.

If no-trump opener has two biddable majors he may follow one of three styles (as agreed between partners):

a) Name spades first and then hearts on the next round.

b) Name hearts first and then spades.

c) Bid 3 clubs which is artificial and means, "You pick the major, partner. I have both." Some use this bid to indicate a maximum no trump as well as both majors.

Stayman Bidder's Rebids

Having heard from his partner, the 2-club bidder now rebids:

(If there is no major fit) Two no trump or 3 no trump depending upon his estimate of the combined point count.

(If there is a major fit) Four hearts or 4 spades if he sees 26 or more points in the combined hands.

If he has a five-card or longer major, he names it. Thus, 1 no trump — 2 clubs (Stayman) — 2 diamonds (minimum no trump; no major) — 2 spades (five-card or longer spade suit). No-trumper must always bid again over such a response — either another no trump with only two of partner's suit, or a raise of partner's suit, with three cards or more. (But some players consider such a rebid non-forcing.)

No-Trump Bidder's Second Rebids

If the Stayman bidder rebids short of game he is asking the no-trumper to make the final decision. The no-trumper goes to game or passes depending upon whether he has a minimum or a maximum no trump.

Responses to One No Trump Other Than 2 Clubs

In the Stayman Convention a response of 2 diamonds, 2 hearts or 2 spades over 1 no trump asks the opener to pass — unless he has a maximum no trump and a fit with partner's suit.

A jump response to four of a major shows that the responding hand sees a play for game on a very long suit and distributional values mainly.

A jump to three of a suit shows a game-going hand, containing 10 points or more, and an unbalanced hand.

A raise to 2 no trump or jump to 3 no trump shows balanced distribution and the requisite number of points.

On slam-possible hands, the 2-club (Stayman) response is made and appropriate action taken after the no-trumper rebids to show what kind of hand he holds.

Pre-emptive Bids, The Fishbein Convention and Other Defenses

The Pre-emptive

One kind of pre-emptive or shut-out bid is an opening bid at the level of three, four or five. It is intended to rob opponents of the opportunity to exchange information at the lower levels of bidding. It hopes to shut out a game or slam.

A pre-emptive bid is made on suits of at least six cards in length (preferably seven). The suits should have no more than two probable losing tricks. (Yet some experts do pre-empt on weaker suits.) Over-all the hand should not be good for an opening bid. (Though with partner already having passed, 4 hearts or 4 spades may be bid on hands that are not likely to produce slam with partner's passed values.)

Pre-emptives are sacrificial in nature. Vulnerable, the hand is expected to go down no more than two tricks; non-vulnerable, no more than three tricks. Partner cannot be counted on for any help.

Pre-emptive bids are not recommended on a long minor suit when the player also holds a fair to good four-card side suit in a major.

Another kind of pre-emptive bid is an overcall that jumps more than one level of bidding. Thus, 1 diamond — 3 hearts; or 1 heart — 4 diamonds. It is made on the same type of hand as an opening pre-emptive and is intended also for interference.

Some players also consider *any* jump overcall as pre-emptive. Thus, 1 heart — 2 spades (overcall) is played as pre-emptive. With a strong major overcall they will make a take-out double.

A third kind of pre-emptive is a jump in a minor of more than one level of bidding in response to partner's opening bid. Thus, 1 club — pass — 4 clubs. Again the purpose is to make trouble for opponents with nothing much more than length of suit.

Responding to Opening Pre-emptives

No response is made unless partner has *more* than enough high-card tricks to take up the deficiency announced by the pre-emptive.

The Fishbein Convention

This is a defensive device against opening bids of three or four. The bids of the Fishbein Convention are used by the opponent immediately to the right of the opening bidder.

If he wants his partner to show his best suit he overcalls the pre-emptive with the next higher suit. Thus, 3 diamonds (pre-emptive) – 3 hearts (overcall). The 3-heart overcall may or may not show hearts. But it is basically a take-out double and asks partner to bid.

If he overcalls in no trump he wants to play the hand there and partner is expected to pass. Thus, 3 hearts (pre-emptive) – 3 no trump (overcall). The overcaller thinks he has a chance for nine tricks.

If he doubles the pre-emptive he means it is for penalties and partner is asked to pass.

If he makes any other overcall it should be treated naturally. Thus, 3 diamonds (pre-emptive) – 3 spades (overcall). Overcaller wishes to play the hand in spades. 3 hearts (pre-emptive) – 4 diamonds (overcall). Overcaller wishes to play the hand in diamonds.

Other Defenses Against Pre-emptives

Some players reserve the double over an opening pre-emptive bid for penalties. For take-out they use the cheapest overcall in clubs. Any other bid is natural. Thus, 3 diamonds (pre-empt) – 4 clubs (overcall). The overcall asks partner to take out in his best suit.

Three diamonds (pre-empt) – 3 hearts (overcall). The heart overcall has its natural meaning.

Many experts use the "optional double." This double over an opening pre-empt suggests primarily that partner respond with a suit only if his hand is unbalanced in distribution.

Opening Bid of Two

The Strong Two-Bid

As most players use it, an opening bid of two in a suit describes a hand with a long suit, or two five-card suits, and so strong in playing values that it can practically produce game on its own.

Such a bid *must be kept open* until at least game is reached or one partner doubles an opponent's overcall.

Responses: Two methods are used generally in responding to a strong two-bid: ace-showing and natural responses.

In ace-showing, a suit of any length is bid provided it contains an ace. If responder holds two aces, it may be agreed that he shall *jump* in the suit of higher rank first and then show the lower-ranking ace on a later round. Or, it may be agreed that he shall jump to 3 no trump.

With no aces, responder calls 2 no trump.

Others play that with three kings, or king-queen and king, responder jumps to 3 no trump over the opening two-bid. (In this case, two aces are shown by a suit jump as described above.)

Some players treat a king of partner's suit as though it were an ace. Thus, 2 hearts (opening) — 3 hearts (response). The heart response shows either the ace or king of hearts.

In natural responses, the over-all strength of the hand is shown first, not aces.

As a general guide: If partner would respond in a suit to a one-bid, he does so over a two-bid. If he would raise a one-bid to two, he can raise a two-bid to three. If he would pass or bid 1 no trump in response to a one-bid, he responds with 2 no trump to a two-bid.

Aces and voids are then sought for and shown in later rounds.

The 2-Club Force

In this convention the only strong opening two-bid is 2 clubs. Other two-bids in a suit are considered mildly pre-emptive. (See below.)

The 2-club bid is artificial and does not necessarily promise a club suit. (The real suit may be diamonds, hearts or spades.)

With a weak hand, responder bids 2 diamonds, which is artificial. A weak hand is one that does not have at least an ace and a king; or three kings; or a king-queen and a king; or a five-card suit containing five points in high cards.

After the opening bid and response, all subsequent bidding is normal. Opening bidder's rebid names his real suit. Responder, if he has first bid 2 diamonds, shows his real suit, raises partner, or rebids 2 no trump as a continued sign of weakness.

Some experts play that a 2-club is not forcing to game in this sequence: 2 clubs — 2 diamonds — 2 no trump.

Opener, having rebid 2 no trump over a weak 2-diamond response, is supposed to be showing a hand which cannot insist on game. Partner may, with a worthless hand, pass it.

The Weak Two-Bid

This bid — an opening call of 2 diamonds, 2 hearts or 2 spades — is mildly pre-emptive in nature. It shows at least a respectable six-card suit and a hand of from 7 to 10 points in high cards. Experts do not usually make such a bid on a hand containing a singleton in a minor or where there are too many cards in the majors.

If partner responds to the opening two-bid with a raise in partner's suit, the opener may pass if he wishes to.

If partner responds with a new suit or 2 no trump, opener must bid again. Either of these responses are taken to mean partner of opener sees a chance for game.

In general the defense against two-bids is similar to that against higher pre-emptives.

Overcall in Clubs

Many of today's players bid 1 club on a short suit. Consequently a convention has sprung up in which overcalling opponent's 1-club opener with 2 clubs shows a good, long club suit and a fair but not strong hand.

Five-Card Majors

In a convention followed by some players an opening bid of 1 heart or 1 spade as dealer or second hand shows at least five cards in that suit. With only four cards a minor suit must be opened.

Weak No Trump

Some players open a non-vulnerable 1 no trump on 10 to 12, 12 to 14, or 13 to 15 points, depending upon the range agreed upon with partner. Vulnerable no-trump hands are opened on the usual range of points.

Unusual No Trump Overcall

In this convention, an overcall in no trump of opponents' major suit bids at the level of two or higher shows strength in the minors. It asks partner to name his best minor. Thus,

NORTH	EAST	SOUTH	WEST
1 ♡	Pass	2 ♡	2 NT

West's 2 no trump asks partner to bid clubs or diamonds.

Bridge

THE LADY WHO HUMS WHEN SHE GETS A GOOD HAND

Lightner Slam Double

A double of a slam in this convention asks partner to make an unusual or unnatural lead.

Coffee-Housing and Such

Coffee-housing, according to one definition, "is an action not specifically prohibited by the rules, but calculated either to convey information to partner or to create the wrong impression in the mind of an opponent." The term is supposedly derived from the conduct of players in the card games held in coffee-houses of the lower East Side in New York City.

A coffee-housing act may be deliberate or unconscious. Here is an example of the not so innocent kind:

North: "One heart."
South: "One spade."
North: "Two hearts."
South: "Three diamonds."
North: (loudly) *"Three* hearts."
South: "Four diamonds."
North (*banging his cards down on the table*): "I bid the fourth and final heart."

George S. Kaufman once found it necessary to ask for a review of the bidding, "including all the inflections." And Groucho Marx, trying to protect himself in a game that was rife with coffee-housing, advised his partner, "If you like my lead don't bother to signal with a high card, just smile and nod your head."

Most players would deny being guilty of coffee-housing tactics. But how many of them would stick to their disavowal after taking a good look at "The Proprieties" section of *The Laws of Contract Bridge,* which are listed below? Or, after reading the articles that follow?

The Proprieties

Section 3

A player should refrain from —
(a) Varying the formulae used in calling. The recommended calling

formulae are: "Pass" (avoid "I pass" or "no bid"); "1 heart" (avoid "I bid"); "1 no trump" (avoid "without" or "without a trump"); "double" (avoid stating the number of tricks or the denomination doubled); "6 spades" (avoid "little slam").

(b) Calling with special emphasis, inflection or intonation.

(c) Passing or doubling with exceptional haste or reluctance.

(d) Making a call with undue delay which may result in conveying improper information to partner.

(e) Indicating in any way approval or disapproval of partner's call or play.

(f) Giving by word, manner or gesture an indication of the nature of the hand held.

(g) Making a remark or gesture or asking a question from which an inference may be drawn.

(h) Giving unauthorized information as to an incident of the auction or play.

(i) Volunteering information which should be given only in response to a question.

(j) Requesting, except for his own benefit, a review of calls or a placing of cards played to a trick.

(k) An unnecessary hesitation, remark or mannerism which may deceive the opponents.

(l) Attracting attention to the score, except when necessary to do so for his own information.

(m) Calling attention to the number of tricks needed to complete or defeat the contract or to the fact that it has already been fulfilled or defeated.

(n) Playing a card with special emphasis.

(o) Playing with undue delay when the play does not need consideration.

(p) Preparing to gather a trick before all four hands have played to it.

(q) Detaching a card from his hand before it is his turn to lead or play.

(r) Failing to keep the tricks in correct order and distinct from one another, or allowing some to be placed on the opposite side of the table.

(s) Watching the place in a player's hand from which he draws a card, and drawing any inference therefrom.

(t) Making gratuitous comments during the play as to the auction, the adequacy of the contract or the nature of the hand.

YOU'RE CHEATING!

by JACK GOODMAN and ALBERT RICE

*You may not know it, but it's ten to one
that you play thistletree bridge.*

WE ALL KNOW HER. Let's call her Mrs. Thistletree, because that isn't her name. She's very virtuous. She's a bulwark of the D. A. R., and a pillar of the neighborhood charities. Once every year she informs the graduating class of the local high school that honesty is the best policy.

Yet every single time Mrs. Thistletree sits down for a session of contract bridge, she does things which, if attempted in a faro joint of the old West, would have resulted in her speedy departure from town — on a rail.

Mrs. Thistletree employs three weapons at a bridge table — tones, gestures, and expressions. When using all three at once, she conveys more information to her co-worker across the table than experts do by a series of the most brilliant bids imaginable.

She calls a spade a spade — but she has a lot of ways of doing it. In any one of the major systems of contract, a bid of one spade means that the declarer possesses from two and one-half to five quick tricks. The Thistletree System does away with all that vagueness. If her partner has played with her long enough, she can tell within a half-trick what cards Mrs. Thistletree holds.

Suppose Mrs. Thistletree sits bolt upright in her chair, leans forward eagerly, and says buoyantly, *"I bid one spade, partner!"* That means a four-and-one-half-trick hand, not *quite* enough for a two-bid. Conversely,

From *Delineator* Magazine. Reprinted by permission.

when she coughs deprecatingly and murmurs, "One spade," in a small, hushed voice, as if she'd just learned of the death of a dear one, it is clear that she has opened the bidding with a minimum holding.

These are conventions that you won't find in any bridge book — but Mrs. Thistletree's system is the one which is really played more widely than Culbertson's or Sims'. To list all her methods would require several books. Here we have time for only a few of the most efficient, any one of which — when used judiciously, and at the right moment — is guaranteed to swing the tide of conflict in favor of the user.

There is, for example, *The Soul-in-Torment Pass.* This is employed only when firm handling of the partner is imperative. Mrs. Thistletree's partner, let's say, has gone on a bidding spree and has ignored the dour frowns and irritable passes which greeted each declaration. At last the partner bids five hearts and the opponent on the right says five spades. Mrs. Thistletree's relief that the five hearts has been overcalled is tempered by a gnawing fear that her doltish co-worker will bid once more. Now comes *The Soul-in-Torment Pass,* uttered with a frenzied twitch of the shoulder muscles and a tortured little laugh.

This indicates even to the most obtuse partner: "I know that you have gone completely mad and will probably keep bidding on and on, but don't expect anything from me. If you don't pass *now,* you belong in an asylum!"

The Amazed Query is another powerful weapon. Opponent on the right bids one diamond. Mrs. Thistletree finds herself with six diamonds headed by the ace-queen and an outside ace. In a voice in which incredulity, geniality, and high spirits are nicely blended, she says to the opponent, "You bid one *diamond?*"

This is far more effective than the most emphatic double. Although addressed to the opponent, it is actually directed to the partner and conveys the glad tidings: "But that's *my* bid. If you have any sort of holding, partner, this is going to be too, too wonderful!"

The Happy Nod, although often employed in the bidding, is an even more powerful weapon on the defense. Suppose the partner lays down an ace and Mrs. Thistletree is unable to signal that she has the king-queen because she has no other card higher than a four in the suit. This emergency is easily met. She now places the four-spot on the table with a sharp click, smiles a slow, sweet smile, and raises and lowers her head graciously.

If, however, she doesn't want that suit returned and is forced to play a *high* card, you can expect *The Pursed Lip,* a grim gesture which says very plainly: "If you persist in this blind folly, we will be ruined. Pay no attention to this discard."

A less forceful, but just as efficient, way of handling the same situation is *The Dejected Discard*. This involves flicking the high card disinterestedly on the table, trying to slip it under the others so it won't be visible. Then, when partner asks. "What did you discard?" she answers dully, "Who? Me? I don't remember."

The Part Score Wigwag is another emergency measure. Mrs. Thistletree and partner have, let's say, ninety points toward game. Partner opens the bidding with one of a suit and Mrs. Thistletree has everything in her hand but the four aces in the other deck and wants to try out slam possibilities. She also wants to make certain that her partner will realize that the subsequent bid is based on knowledge of the score. So she leans forward and closely scrutinizes the score pad, making sure that she catches her partner's eye. If she is unable to do this, she will then say firmly and with emphasis on every syllable, "Let's see — we have ninety on frame? One spade puts us out. I bid two spades!"

Another convention which calls for fast thinking is *The Determined Double*. The opponents flounder beyond their depth and are doubled by Mrs. Thistletree. Glancing in a satisfied way across the table, she sees to her horror that her partner is debating another bid. Stern measures being necessary to avoid this, Mrs. Thistletree doesn't wait for that bid, but says, hastily and significantly, "It is my lead, I believe." This means, of course: "Partner, if you bid again and let these suckers out of my double, I'll never talk to you as long as I live."

As a matter of fact, Mrs. Thistletree's doubles are invariably airtight. Although the printed rules mention only two types, she has about twenty. No partner of hers is ever in doubt as to whether her double is business or informative. Sometimes her doubles are informative even when the bidding has reached the six-level. A curled lip, a snort, a shrug, a raised eyebrow, a sharp whistle — each of these helps convey to the partner just what Mrs. Thistletree expects to do to the enemy.

There is no situation with which her system cannot cope. Are you her partner, worried whether or not she has made a psychic bid? Have no fear — she'll remove all doubt from your mind by a gesture peculiarly her own, a slow weaving of the torso back and forth, accompanied by a roguish smile and a tongue in cheek. Are you playing the hand, with Mrs. Thistletree as the dummy, and are you worried about which way to take a finesse? Just notice which of the opponents' hands she peers into lengthily. That'll be the one that contains the missing honor.

Even when these more subtle methods can't be used, Mrs. Thistletree can always fall back on the more obvious ones: *The Simple Groan, The Dismayed Outcry, The Gnashed Teeth.* But don't be too critical of her. It is just possible that you yourself use a few of her little tricks — unconsciously, of course. There are few bridge players who don't. That's why the Thistletree System has caught on so widely, and why her methods will be used universally until someone invents a robot player, a thing of steel and solder, soulless and emotionless.

And when that day arrives, the robot, deprived of the many advantages of the Thistletree System, will almost certainly play a mediocre game.

HOW TO PASS

by ELY LENZ

◇ ♣ ♡ ♠ ◇ ♣ ♡ ♠ ◇ ♣ ♡ ♠ ◇ ♣ ♡ ♠ ◇ ♣ ♡ ♠ ◇ ♣ ♡ ♠ ◇ ♣ ♡ ♠ ◇ ♣ ♡ ♠ ◇ ♣ ♡ ♠

An anonymous benefactor sets forth the rules and regulations for the use of this bridge tool.

IT IS A MIRACLE to me that, in all the literature of bridge, there is not a single chapter on *How to Pass*. It is true that passing is mentioned. "In such a case, pass" is frequently quoted, and "Pass, instead of doubling" is another phrase we meet, but there is absolutely nothing on *how* one should pass.

Such neglect is absurd. It is like saying, "On falling into a lake, swim," without any instruction on how to keep above water. Imagine a textbook on surgery that told the eager student that trepanning was necessary and let it go at that, without any illustrations or advice on how to do it! Yet passing is as necessary to a bridge player as trepanning is to a surgeon — more, in fact, for trepanning is seldom indicated, yet every hand of bridge necessitates three passes before it can be played.

I do not speak of tournament bridge, for that is not a game at all, but a miniature battle played with cards and dirty looks instead of guns and bayonets. I refer to the family or bridge-club game — the friendly game, as my wife sarcastically calls it.

Let us first look at the pass with intent to pass, or *The Pass Direct*. You are West, and South has dealt. You pick up your cards and arrange them. They are — Spades: J 8 5 2; Hearts: 9 4; Diamonds: 10 7 5; Clubs: Q 9 6 3. South passes. The question arises: How should you pass?

From *The Rotarian* Magazine, 1942. Reprinted by permission.

Don't just say, "By," or, "I pass." Look at your cards hard. Moan with anguish. Screw up your face into a grimace of utter despair. Then say, firmly, "PASS!"

This leaves your partner with a clear understanding that this is not a trap pass, nor a reluctant pass, but an out-and-out no-bidding-values pass. Suppose he was planning to bid on three honors. This will tell him, in one simple word, that he cannot count on you for anything but grief.

If, in spite of your warning, he insists on bidding, just leave your hand in a bundle before you and mutter, "Pass," at every opportunity. Even if it isn't your turn, interject a "Pass" into the bidding now and then. Thus you convey in no uncertain manner the information that you have an absolute bust.

The next hand, you are still West, you deal and pick up — Spades: A K 10 4; Hearts: 9 7 3 2; Diamonds: 10 4 3; Clubs: J 7. Almost a biddable hand, but not quite. But how to get the information across to your partner? Merely passing won't do it. And The Pass Direct will mislead him. So here we adopt the technique of *The Informative Pass*. Look over your hand carefully. Then look directly at your partner and say, "How many spades will it take to give us a game?" Of course, as you already know, he will answer, "Four," so you look regretfully at your hand and say, "Then I pass."

By this maneuver your partner knows you have strength in spades and practically nothing else. It isn't enough strength for a three-spade declaration, so it must be one-and-a-half or two honor tricks in spades only. With this information he is much better equipped to make his first bid. If he says, "One heart," you can go to two, which shows him that your spade pass meant control of the suit and something in his suit as well. If he says, "One club," use *The Business Pass*.

In The Business Pass, pick up the bidding directly after South speaks, and snap, "Pass," as if you meant it. This conveys to your partner that you have no club support and that you gave him all you had on that first spade pass.

Another form of the Informative Pass comes up on the third hand. You look at your hand and find — Spades: A Q 4; Hearts: Q 9 8 6; Diamonds: K 2; Clubs: K J 10 5. North bids one diamond, your partner passes in such a way you cannot tell if he means it or is stalling, South bids one heart, and it is up to you. Instead of bidding on this round, you can pass the burden to your partner together with much information if you hesitate a moment, and then say brightly, "Have we anything on game?" This immediately tells your partner that you have a fairish sort of hand, and if he has anything at all, he should bid it, and thus give you a chance to carry it on, but that if he has nothing, it might be best for you both to shut up.

Closely allied to The Informative Pass is *The Lead-Directing Pass.* Let us suppose you hold ace-king-queen of spades, but haven't had a chance to show them, because the level is too high by the time it reaches you. Turn an astonished face to your right and demand, "Did you say *three spades?*" in a shocked and incredulous tone. Of course, he will correct you, and you can then laugh lightly and remark, "I didn't *think* you did — I pass." Naturally, your partner, who, it seems, will have first lead, will promptly lead spades, unless he is an absolute ass.

The Trap Pass is a tricky thing, but can be made to pay great dividends, if not overworked. Let us suppose your opponents are bidding spades. You haven't much of anything, but you do have five spades to the nine-spot. When your right-hand opponent says, "Three spades," you sigh lugubriously, and say, "I could have guessed *that* — pass," and the trap is set. Both your opponents look for the bulk of the spades in your partner's hand. What a cheerful surprise they get when you ruff aces!

The Warning Pass comes in handy when your partner has a tendency to overbid. Suppose you have a part score of 60, and a fair-to-middling hand, but certainly no slam in prospect. Your partner bids two clubs, and you fear he may carry it on indefinitely. Instead of a mere "Pass," it may be well to remind him of the part score. You can do this by saying, brightly, "Well, that's all we need to go game, isn't it, partner?" Thus you imply that unless your left hand opponent pushes the limit up, you are willing to let well enough alone. Maybe you *can* make four clubs, but why take unnecessary risks?

Another form of The Warning Pass is when you cannot make a game bid and your opponents evidently cannot either. The bid comes to you from them at three diamonds. Laugh lightly and remark, "They won't get fat on that, partner — I'm going to let them have it." This establishes the fact that they haven't a game and your support for his hearts is none too hot, so don't go on!

The Diversion Pass comes in handy when the opposition is headed for a game in a suit in which you have a void or a singleton. It must not be confused with The Lead-Directing Pass. The latter is where you name the suit you want led, which is NOT the one they mention. The Diversion Pass is similar, but you name the suit they DO name. Thus, your right-hand opponent says, "Three hearts." You look at him incredulously and say, "Did you say *three hearts?*" Then laugh happily and quickly say, "I pass!" This immediately convinces your left-hand opponent that you hold all the missing hearts, and he chokes the four-bid he was about to make — maybe even shifts to diamonds, in which you hold five to the king, queen.

Going back to first-round passing, do not overlook the use of *The Query Pass*. This is where you have a pretty good hand, but prefer to have your partner declare his preference in suits first. So you pass — but not without asking for information. Look at your cards carefully, shake your head doubtfully, mutter to yourself — but clearly enough for your partner to hear — "I wonder" — and then pass, slowly, regretfully. This clearly indicates that you want his cooperation, and are prepared to help him in almost any suit. This pass may lead to a slam.

Do not overlook the use of inflection of the simple word "Pass." A straightforward, crisp pronouncement means that you do pass, without mental reservation or secret evasion whatever. But a slower "Pass" implies that you could, if you would, make an opening bid. A drawling pass after an opponent's bid is almost as good as a double, and much less expensive should he make any overtricks.

So you see, the pass is a weapon in your armory of bridge. A careful study of the art of passing is worth at least one quick trick. I have seen hands that, by ordinary rules, would not permit a game bid not only get to game, but make it. And I have seen cold slams (or, at least chilly) defeated by the proper use of The Lead-Directing Pass.

Current bridge experts have overlooked the well-worn maxim that the best defense is an offensive. They have relegated the pass to a defensive maneuver entirely. I hope that these few directions will convince you that, properly used, the pass is not only a good defense, but that it can be offensive, too.

Very.

Section 10

Hands—Classics, Curios and Double-Dummy

Bridge   BY WEBSTER

HANDS—CLASSICS,
CURIOS AND DOUBLE-DUMMY

◇ ♣ ♡ ♠ ◇ ♣ ♡ ♠ ◇ ♣ ♡ ♠ ◇ ♣ ♡ ♠ ◇ ♣ ♡ ♠ ◇ ♣ ♡ ♠ ◇ ♣ ♡ ♠ ◇ ♣ ♡ ♠ ◇ ♣ ♡ ♠

Bridge columnists and bridge editors can testify to the never-ending interest in classic and freak hands. Requests are received often to reprint deals which have become a part of the lore of the game. A few hands — such as the Duke of Cumberland Hand and the Mississippi Heart Hand, for instance — are carry-overs from bridge's ancestor, whist. But their fascination does not lessen with the years, and, if anything, seems to grow for successive generations of bridge players. Some of the best of these hands are presented in this section.

As for the double-dummy problems, these should be looked on primarily as mental-teasers or relaxers. The bridge poser is a cousin to the crossword puzzle, detective story and similar intellectual exercises — a challenge and therefore fun to work out. They provide a refreshing shift of mental activity.

The most beautiful and intriguing plays in bridge rarely come up at the card table — or, at least — are seldom recognized, even by the experts. But double-dummy problems are replete with wonderfully improbable situations. Cards can be manipulated and tricky plays made to your heart's content. Squeezes, end-plays and throw-ins are a commonplace and there is a tremendous satisfaction in spotting and executing them.

The objection has been raised that double-dummy problems are not instructive for practical play, that they teach nothing about counting out a hand, safety plays, deception and so on. Still there are many who believe with R. Gray that "situations giving scope for double-dummy problem tactics arise far more often than is supposed. When the average player says he has never met any, it merely means he has missed them. Again, when the expert says that a study of double-dummy problems is of little value he assumes that everybody has the same close familiarity with elementary problem strategy that he has himself, being an expert."

If you are inexperienced at double-dummy problems it is suggested that you try them with the cards laid out face up on the table. As you make your plays turn the cards face down in each hand, duplicate style. Don't mix them in tricks. In this way you are helped not only by seeing the actual cards but you will have the original hands. At any time you wish to go back over the play you just turn cards face up to restore a previous situation.

The Mississippi Heart Hand

Any number of fanciful tales have been woven around the Mississippi Heart Hand. The most common one has it that the hand was a favorite bait of card sharpers who worked the Mississippi steamboats. They would inveigle a victim into a game of whist, let him win a few hands and then rig this beauty.

In whist a card is turned up to determine the trump suit and on this hand a heart would be faced, not exactly by chance. Unlimited doubles and redoubles would be permitted in the manner of poker raises and Mr. Easy Mark naturally would bet his bottom dollar that he could take all thirteen tricks with this rock-crusher.

Seems as though that should be easily accomplished. But wait, look at the entire deal on page 356.

The Duke of Cumberland Hand

This is another classic deal that has intrigued whist, auction bridge and now contract players. According to the most persistent legend the hand was originally held and played at whist by the Duke of Cumberland, notorious son of George III. His Grace, so it's said, was dealt something like the following by a larceny-bent opponent:

♠ A K Q J   ♡ A K Q   ◇ A K Q   ♣ K J 9

Clubs were trumps on this deal and the crooked opponent offered to bet that he could take all the tricks with clubs as trumps. The Duke, for good and ample reason, doubted that it could be done. He backed his opinion, it is reported, to the tune of some twenty thousand pounds and some kibitzers to whom he showed the hand got in sizable side wagers of their own.

The Duke and his supporters, of course, got clipped. And if you want to see how this was accomplished turn to page 356. Like almost every good story, by the way, this one is probably apocryphal since this type of hand was known and recorded as a whist problem some twenty years or so before the Duke made his entry into the world. On the other hand, maybe the sharper who had read or heard about the hand figured it was a good one to spring on the royal mark.

Making a Slam with Only Four Trumps

The bridge books tell you that playing a contract with fewer than seven pieces of trumps in the combined hands is generally a losing proposition. And so it is. But how would you like to play a *slam* with only four trumps?

It was done, so it's been claimed, on the following hand. North and South wound up in a fantastic contract of six clubs through a misunderstood cue bid, or perhaps two cue bids. What's even more interesting is that the hand can have a happy ending.

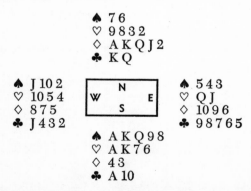

```
                    ♠ 7 6
                    ♡ 9 8 3 2
                    ◇ A K Q J 2
                    ♣ K Q

   ♠ J 10 2          N           ♠ 5 4 3
   ♡ 10 5 4      W       E        ♡ Q J
   ◇ 8 7 5          S            ◇ 10 9 6
   ♣ J 4 3 2                     ♣ 9 8 7 6 5

                    ♠ A K Q 9 8
                    ♡ A K 7 6
                    ◇ 4 3
                    ♣ A 10
```

Opening lead: Jack of spades.

Solution is on page 356.

Two Classic Problems

Classic Problem No. 1

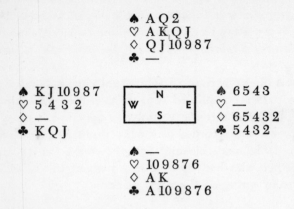

♠ A Q 2
♡ A K Q J
◇ Q J 10 9 8 7
♣ —

♠ K J 10 9 8 7
♡ 5 4 3 2
◇ —
♣ K Q J

♠ 6 5 4 3
♡ —
◇ 6 5 4 3 2
♣ 5 4 3 2

♠ —
♡ 10 9 8 7 6
◇ A K
♣ A 10 9 8 7 6

Contract: 7 hearts by South.
Opening lead: King of clubs.
Solution is on page 357.

Classic Problem No. 2

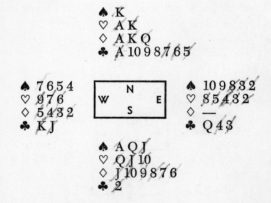

♠ K
♡ A K
◇ A K Q
♣ A 10 9 8 7 6 5

♠ 7 6 5 4
♡ 9 7 6
◇ 5 4 3 2
♣ K J

♠ 10 9 8 3 2
♡ 8 5 4 3 2
◇ —
♣ Q 4 3

♠ A Q J
♡ Q J 10
◇ J 10 9 8 7 6
♣ 2

Contract: 7 no trump by South.
Opening lead: seven of spades.
Solution is on page 357.

Six Bids in One Suit

Ever hear of six consecutive bids being made in the same suit in the same deal, and all of them logical ones? Here is one the experts talk about. North dealer. East-West vulnerable.

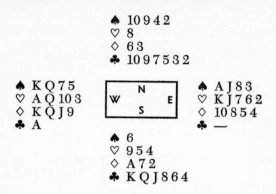

♠ 10 9 4 2
♡ 8
♢ 6 3
♣ 10 9 7 5 3 2

♠ K Q 7 5
♡ A Q 10 3
♢ K Q J 9
♣ A

♠ A J 8 3
♡ K J 7 6 2
♢ 10 8 5 4
♣ —

♠ 6
♡ 9 5 4
♢ A 7 2
♣ K Q J 8 6 4

The bidding:

NORTH	EAST	SOUTH	WEST
Pass	Pass	1 ♣	2 ♣
3 ♣	4 ♣	5 ♣	6 ♣
Pass	6 ♡	All pass	

West's overcall in the same suit as opponent shows a powerful hand with club control.

North's bid is for the purpose of interference on distributional values.

East's club call is a cue bid and seeks further information.

South's rebid is also for interference and is sacrificial in nature.

West's six-club bid asks partner to choose the suit for the slam.

The contract is cold.

The Four Deuces Hand

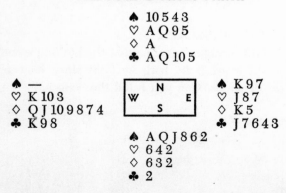

♠ 10 5 4 3
♡ A Q 9 5
♢ A
♣ A Q 10 5

♠ —
♡ K 10 3
♢ Q J 10 9 8 7 4
♣ K 9 8

♠ K 9 7
♡ J 8 7
♢ K 5
♣ J 7 6 4 3

♠ A Q J 8 6 2
♡ 6 4 2
♢ 6 3 2
♣ 2

This hand was said to have been played at a contract of seven spades by South against a lead of the queen of diamonds by West. Not only was the contract fulfilled but it was done so with *the four deuces being led to the last four tricks.*

Can you figure out how this was accomplished?

See solution on page 357.

An "Impossible" Contract

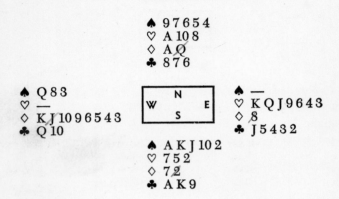

```
                    ♠ 9 7 6 5 4
                    ♡ A 10 8
                    ◇ A Q
                    ♣ 8 7 6
   ♠ Q 8 3          ┌──────────┐         ♠ —
   ♡ —              │    N     │         ♡ K Q J 9 6 4 3
   ◇ K J 10 9 6 5 4 │ W     E  │         ◇ 8
   ♣ Q 10           │    S     │         ♣ J 5 4 3 2
                    └──────────┘
                    ♠ A K J 10 2
                    ♡ 7 5 2
                    ◇ 7 2
                    ♣ A K 9
```

South dealer.

North–South vulnerable.

The bidding:

SOUTH	WEST	NORTH	EAST
1 ♠	4 ◇	4 ♠	5 ♡
5 ♠	All pass		

Opening lead: Jack of diamonds.

To give point to this problem, assume that the bidding went as shown. West would open a heart if he had one, but since he can't, he lays down his jack of diamonds. Can you fulfill the contract?

Solution is on page 358.

Bath Coups Galore

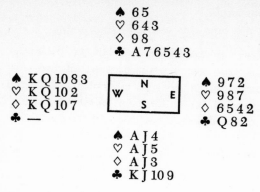

```
              ♠ 65
              ♡ 643
              ◇ 98
              ♣ A76543
♠ KQ1083      ┌─────────┐   ♠ 972
♡ KQ102       │   N     │   ♡ 987
◇ KQ107       │ W     E │   ◇ 6542
♣ —           │   S     │   ♣ Q82
              └─────────┘
              ♠ AJ4
              ♡ AJ5
              ◇ AJ3
              ♣ KJ109
```

Contract: 3 no trump by South, doubled by West.
Opening lead: King of spades.
The problem here is created by the club spots. But can you find a way to bring home nine tricks anyway?

Solution is on page 358.

The Great Vienna Coup

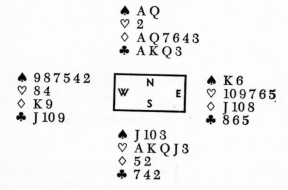

```
              ♠ AQ
              ♡ 2
              ◇ AQ7643
              ♣ AKQ3
♠ 987542      ┌─────────┐   ♠ K6
♡ 84          │   N     │   ♡ 109765
◇ K9          │ W     E │   ◇ J108
♣ J109        │   S     │   ♣ 865
              └─────────┘
              ♠ J103
              ♡ AKQJ3
              ◇ 52
              ♣ 742
```

Contract: 7 no trump by South.
Opening lead: Jack of clubs.
If you're an expert you'll probably eat this problem up. If not, you're bound to have an interesting and instructive time with it. The Vienna part of the name? Listen to James Clay who originally reported this poser in connection with whist:

"I may permit myself to present to my readers one of the most beautiful problems I have ever seen. It occurred a few months back in actual play in Vienna, and at double-dummy. Its story runs thus: The most celebrated player in Vienna had to play hands North and South. As soon as the cards were exposed, he exclaimed: 'Why I shall make all thirteen tricks.' This appeared impossible to the bystanders. . . . Large bets were made against the accomplishment of the feat, which was, however, performed; and it became evident that if hands North and South are rightly played, hands East and West are utterly helpless, and in spite of three guarded suits, must lose all thirteen tricks."

Solution is on page 358.

A Progressive Squeeze and Vienna Coup

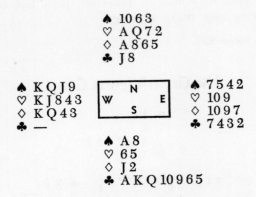

```
                    ♠ 10 6 3
                    ♡ A Q 7 2
                    ◇ A 8 6 5
                    ♣ J 8
    ♠ K Q J 9         ┌───────────┐      ♠ 7 5 4 2
    ♡ K J 8 4 3       │     N     │      ♡ 10 9
    ◇ K Q 4 3        W│           │E     ◇ 10 9 7
    ♣ —               │     S     │      ♣ 7 4 3 2
                      └───────────┘
                    ♠ A 8
                    ♡ 6 5
                    ◇ J 2
                    ♣ A K Q 10 9 6 5
```

Contract: 7 no trump by South, doubled by West.
Opening lead: King of spades.

Who can blame West for doubling this fantastic contract? But because the contract is fantastic and West holds the cards he does you have an opportunity to solve a fascinating problem. If and when you give up or want to check your solution, turn to page 359.

Two Problems by R. Gray

Problem No. 1

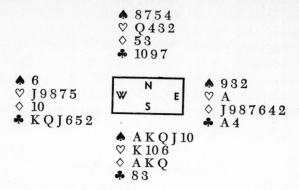

♠ 8 7 5 4
♡ Q 4 3 2
◇ 5 3
♣ 10 9 7

♠ 6
♡ J 9 8 7 5
◇ 10
♣ K Q J 6 5 2

♠ 9 3 2
♡ A
◇ J 9 8 7 6 4 2
♣ A 4

♠ A K Q J 10
♡ K 10 6
◇ A K Q
♣ 8 3

"South played the hand in four spades, and got the king of clubs, led. East played the ace and returned a small club to let West lead a third round. South ruffed and took three rounds of trumps. South was worried about the hearts but before tackling them he cashed his ace-king-queen of diamonds to pave the way for a possible strip. The position now was this:

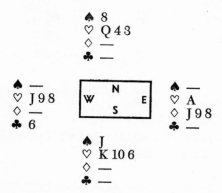

♠ 8
♡ Q 4 3
◇ —
♣ —

♠ —
♡ J 9 8
◇ —
♣ 6

♠ —
♡ A
◇ J 9 8
♣ —

♠ J
♡ K 10 6
◇ —
♣ —

"South led the six of hearts and played the queen from dummy. East won with the ace but his return lead of a diamond gave declarer a ruff-and-discard, and enabled him to make the contract. The other players congratulated South on his fine play, but as a matter of fact he went wrong. Where?" (And where did East go wrong?)

Solution is on page 359.

Problem No. 2

♠ 5432
♡ 6
♢ 5432
♣ 5432

"I was sitting East and held that hand. South opened with two hearts, North bid two spades, South three hearts, North three spades, then after some cue bids. . . . South played in six hearts. *And I made a trick!*"

Can you figure out three other hands and a situation that would permit this to happen without anyone making a mistake in the play?

Solution is on page 360.

Discard All Four Aces

Contract: 7 no trump by South.

Opening Lead: Queen of hearts.

Can you make your grand-slam contract without using *any* of the four aces to win a trick? It takes some doing.

Solution is on page 361.

Made or Down?

Number I

Study the following deal. Then decide which way you can make points on it — by being South as the declarer at a contract of three no trump, or East as a defender against that contract.

In other words, do you think such a contract can be made by the South player against the lead of the seven of spades, or do you believe it can be defeated by East against any play by declarer? Which hand will you take?

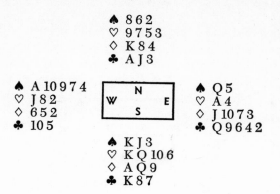

♠ 8 6 2
♡ 9 7 5 3
◇ K 8 4
♣ A J 3

♠ A 10 9 7 4
♡ J 8 2
◇ 6 5 2
♣ 10 5

♠ Q 5
♡ A 4
◇ J 10 7 3
♣ Q 9 6 4 2

♠ K J 3
♡ K Q 10 6
◇ A Q 9
♣ K 8 7

Contract: 3 no trump by South.
Opening Lead: 7 of spades by West.

When you've made up your mind, turn to page 361 for the solution.

Number 2

Can South fulfill a contract of four spades on the hand below or can his opponents defeat him? That is the question. Which side will you bet on, assuming an opening lead of the jack of hearts from West?

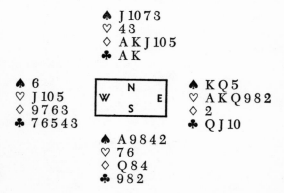

♠ J 10 7 3
♡ 4 3
◇ A K J 10 5
♣ A K

♠ 6
♡ J 10 5
◇ 9 7 6 3
♣ 7 6 5 4 3

♠ K Q 5
♡ A K Q 9 8 2
◇ 2
♣ Q J 10

♠ A 9 8 4 2
♡ 7 6
◇ Q 8 4
♣ 9 8 2

Work on it until you've come to some conclusion. Then turn to page 362 for solution.

Number 3

This has been called an "All-American" hand. The problem is: You are South at a contract of six spades with no competitive bidding. The lead is the queen of clubs. Can you make the hand?

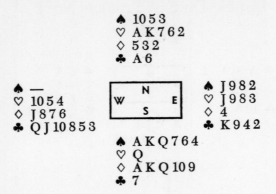

```
              ♠ 10 5 3
              ♡ A K 7 6 2
              ◇ 5 3 2
              ♣ A 6
♠ —                              ♠ J 9 8 2
♡ 10 5 4       N                 ♡ J 9 8 3
◇ J 8 7 6    W   E               ◇ 4
♣ Q J 10 8 5 3   S               ♣ K 9 4 2
              ♠ A K Q 7 6 4
              ♡ Q
              ◇ A K Q 10 9
              ♣ 7
```

When and if you do give up turn to page 362 for solution.

The Whitfield Six

One of the most famous of double-dummy problems is the six-card poser named after Professor William H. Whitfield who taught at Cambridge University in the 1880's. It is said that the problem was so difficult for the crack card analysts of that day that it took them weeks to solve.

Here is the set-up:

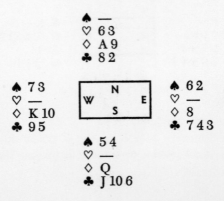

```
              ♠ —
              ♡ 6 3
              ◇ A 9
              ♣ 8 2
♠ 7 3                            ♠ 6 2
♡ —            N                 ♡ —
◇ K 10       W   E               ◇ 8
♣ 9 5            S               ♣ 7 4 3
              ♠ 5 4
              ♡ —
              ◇ Q
              ♣ J 10 6
```

The trumps are hearts. South is in the lead and must win all the tricks against the best defense.

Solution is on page 362.

Here are 30 double-dummy problems. Solutions begin on page 363.

Double-Dummy Problem No. 1

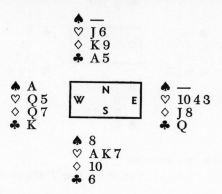

```
              ♠ —
              ♡ J 6
              ◇ K 9
              ♣ A 5

   ♠ A                          ♠ —
   ♡ Q 5      N                 ♡ 10 4 3
   ◇ Q 7    W   E               ◇ J 8
   ♣ K        S                 ♣ Q

              ♠ 8
              ♡ A K 7
              ◇ 10
              ♣ 6
```

Problem — No trump contract.

North-South to win all the tricks against the best defense. South leads.

Double-Dummy Problem No. 2

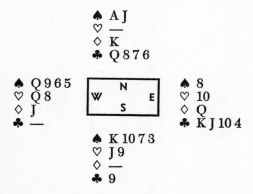

```
              ♠ A J
              ♡ —
              ◇ K
              ♣ Q 8 7 6

   ♠ Q 9 6 5                    ♠ 8
   ♡ Q 8       N                ♡ 10
   ◇ J       W   E              ◇ Q
   ♣ —         S                ♣ K J 10 4

              ♠ K 10 7 3
              ♡ J 9
              ◇ —
              ♣ 9
```

Problem — Spades are trumps.

North-South to win 6 of the 7 tricks against the best defense. South leads.

Double-Dummy Problem No. 3

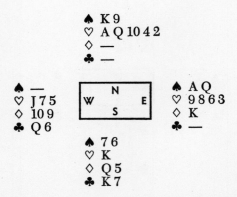

♠ A
♡ A Q 7
◊ —
♣ K 10 6

♠ —   **♠ K**
♡ J 6 5   **♡ 10**
◊ 10   **◊ A J**
♣ 9 8 7   **♣ J 5 4**

♠ J
♡ 9
◊ 9 8 6 5
♣ Q

Problem — Spades are trumps.
    North-South to win 6 of the 7 tricks against the best defense.
    South leads.

Double-Dummy Problem No. 4

♠ K 9
♡ A Q 10 4 2
◊ —
♣ —

♠ —   **♠ A Q**
♡ J 7 5   **♡ 9 8 6 3**
◊ 10 9   **◊ K**
♣ Q 6   **♣ —**

♠ 7 6
♡ K
◊ Q 5
♣ K 7

Problem — Contract is in no trump.
    North-South to win 5 tricks against the best defense.
    South leads.

Double-Dummy Problem No. 5

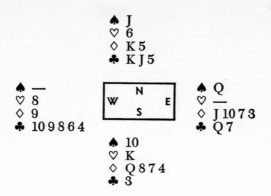

Problem — Hearts are trumps.

North-South to win 6 of the 7 tricks against the best defense.

South leads.

Double-Dummy Problem No. 6

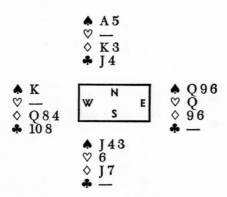

Problem — Spades are trumps.

North-South to win 5 tricks against the best defense.

South leads.

Double-Dummy Problem No. 7

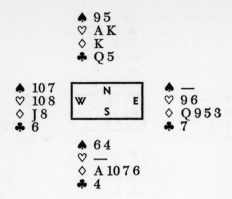

```
                    ♠ 95
                    ♡ A K
                    ◇ K
                    ♣ Q 5
    ♠ 10 7                        ♠ —
    ♡ 10 8         N              ♡ 9 6
    ◇ J 8        W   E            ◇ Q 9 5 3
    ♣ 6            S              ♣ 7
                    ♠ 6 4
                    ♡ —
                    ◇ A 10 7 6
                    ♣ 4
```

Problem — Clubs are trumps.

North-South to win 6 of the 7 tricks against the best defense.

South leads.

Double-Dummy Problem No. 8

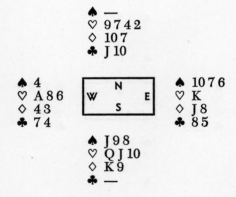

```
                    ♠ —
                    ♡ 9 7 4 2
                    ◇ 10 7
                    ♣ J 10
    ♠ 4                          ♠ 10 7 6
    ♡ A 8 6        N             ♡ K
    ◇ 4 3        W   E           ◇ J 8
    ♣ 7 4          S             ♣ 8 5
                    ♠ J 9 8
                    ♡ Q J 10
                    ◇ K 9
                    ♣ —
```

Problem — Diamonds are trumps.

North-South to win 7 tricks against the best defense.

South leads.

Double-Dummy Problem No. 9

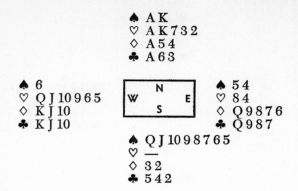

```
            ♠ A K
            ♡ A K 7 3 2
            ◇ A 5 4
            ♣ A 6 3

♠ 6                          ♠ 5 4
♡ Q J 10 9 6 5               ♡ 8 4
◇ K J 10                     ◇ Q 9 8 7 6
♣ K J 10                     ♣ Q 9 8 7

            ♠ Q J 10 9 8 7 6 5
            ♡ —
            ◇ 3 2
            ♣ 5 4 2
```

Problem — South is declarer.
          Spades are trumps.
          Make all the tricks against the best defense.
          Opening lead is queen of hearts by West.

Double-Dummy Problem No. 10

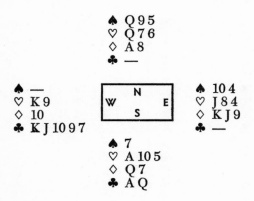

```
            ♠ Q 9 5
            ♡ Q 7 6
            ◇ A 8
            ♣ —

♠ —                          ♠ 10 4
♡ K 9                        ♡ J 8 4
◇ 10                         ◇ K J 9
♣ K J 10 9 7                 ♣ —

            ♠ 7
            ♡ A 10 5
            ◇ Q 7
            ♣ A Q
```

Problem — Contract is in no trump.
          North-South to win 7 of the 8 tricks against the best
          defense.
          South leads.

Double-Dummy Problem No. 11

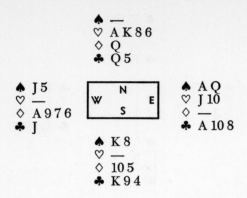

Problem — Hearts are trumps.

North-South to win 6 of the 7 tricks against the best defense.

South leads.

Double-Dummy Problem No. 12

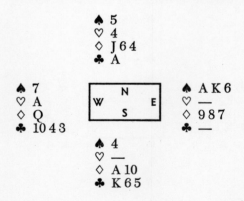

Problem — Contract is in no trump.

North-South to win 5 of the 6 tricks against the best defense.

South leads.

Double-Dummy Problem No. 13

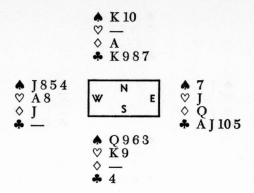

♠ K 10
♡ —
◊ A
♣ K 9 8 7

♠ J 8 5 4
♡ A 8
◊ J
♣ —

N
W   E
S

♠ 7
♡ J
◊ Q
♣ A J 10 5

♠ Q 9 6 3
♡ K 9
◊ —
♣ 4

Problem — Spades are trumps.

North-South to win 6 of the 7 tricks against the best defense.

South leads.

Double-Dummy Problem No. 14

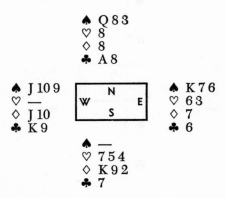

♠ Q 8 3
♡ 8
◊ 8
♣ A 8

♠ J 10 9
♡ —
◊ J 10
♣ K 9

N
W   E
S

♠ K 7 6
♡ 6 3
◊ 7
♣ 6

♠ —
♡ 7 5 4
◊ K 9 2
♣ 7

Problem — Hearts are trumps.

North-South to win all the tricks against the best defense.
South leads.

Double-Dummy Problem No. 15

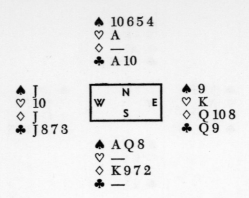

♠ 10 6 5 4
♥ A
♦ —
♣ A 10

♠ J   ♠ 9
♥ 10   ♥ K
♦ J   ♦ Q 10 8
♣ J 8 7 3   ♣ Q 9

♠ A Q 8
♥ —
♦ K 9 7 2
♣ —

Problem — Hearts are trumps.

North-South to make 6 of the 7 tricks against the best defense.

South leads.

Double-Dummy Problem No. 16

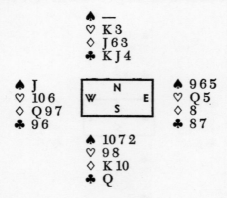

♠ —
♥ K 3
♦ J 6 3
♣ K J 4

♠ J   ♠ 9 6 5
♥ 10 6   ♥ Q 5
♦ Q 9 7   ♦ 8
♣ 9 6   ♣ 8 7

♠ 10 7 2
♥ 9 8
♦ K 10
♣ Q

Problem — Hearts are trumps.

North-South to win 7 of the 8 tricks against the best defense.

South leads.

Double-Dummy Problem No. 17

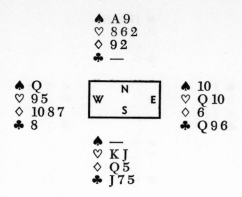

```
              ♠ A 9
              ♡ 8 6 2
              ◊ 9 2
              ♣ —
♠ Q           ┌─────────┐        ♠ 10
♡ 9 5         │    N    │        ♡ Q 10
◊ 10 8 7      │ W     E │        ◊ 6
♣ 8           │    S    │        ♣ Q 9 6
              └─────────┘
              ♠ —
              ♡ K J
              ◊ Q 5
              ♣ J 7 5
```

Problem — Spades are trumps.

North-South to win 6 of the 7 tricks against the best defense.

South leads.

Double-Dummy Problem No. 18

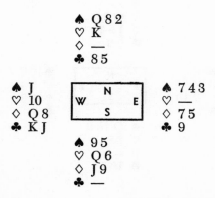

```
              ♠ Q 8 2
              ♡ K
              ◊ —
              ♣ 8 5
♠ J           ┌─────────┐        ♠ 7 4 3
♡ 10          │    N    │        ♡ —
◊ Q 8         │ W     E │        ◊ 7 5
♣ K J         │    S    │        ♣ 9
              └─────────┘
              ♠ 9 5
              ♡ Q 6
              ◊ J 9
              ♣ —
```

Problem — Spades are trumps.

North-South to win all the tricks against the best defense.

South leads.

Double-Dummy Problem No. 19

```
                    ♠ Q 10 9 5
                    ♡ A K
                    ◇ —
                    ♣ 6
        ♠ J                        ♠ 8 7 6 4
        ♡ Q 6        N             ♡ —
        ◇ 9 8 7 6   W   E          ◇ A J
        ♣ —             S          ♣ J
                    ♠ A K 3
                    ♡ —
                    ◇ Q 10 4
                    ♣ Q
```

Problem — Hearts are trumps.

North-South to win all the tricks against the best defense.
South leads.

Double-Dummy Problem No. 20

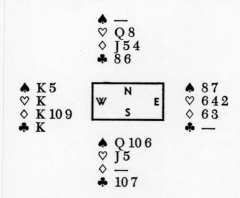

```
                    ♠ —
                    ♡ Q 8
                    ◇ J 5 4
                    ♣ 8 6
        ♠ K 5                      ♠ 8 7
        ♡ K          N             ♡ 6 4 2
        ◇ K 10 9    W   E          ◇ 6 3
        ♣ K             S          ♣ —
                    ♠ Q 10 6
                    ♡ J 5
                    ◇ —
                    ♣ 10 7
```

Problem — Clubs are trumps.

North-South to win 6 of the 7 tricks against the best
defense.
South leads.

Double-Dummy Problem No. 21

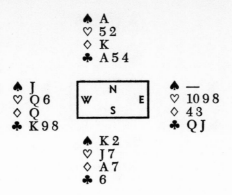

      ♠ A
      ♡ 5 2
      ◇ K
      ♣ A 5 4

♠ J   ♠ —
♡ Q 6   ♡ 10 9 8
◇ Q   ◇ 4 3
♣ K 9 8   ♣ Q J

      ♠ K 2
      ♡ J 7
      ◇ A 7
      ♣ 6

Problem — Diamonds are trumps.

North-South to win 6 of the 7 tricks against the best defense.

South leads.

Double-Dummy Problem No. 22

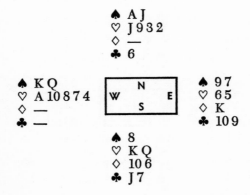

      ♠ A J
      ♡ J 9 3 2
      ◇ —
      ♣ 6

♠ K Q   ♠ 9 7
♡ A 10 8 7 4   ♡ 6 5
◇ —   ◇ K
♣ —   ♣ 10 9

      ♠ 8
      ♡ K Q
      ◇ 10 6
      ♣ J 7

Problem — Spades are trumps.

North-South to win 5 of the 7 tricks against the best defense.

South leads.

Double-Dummy Problem No. 23

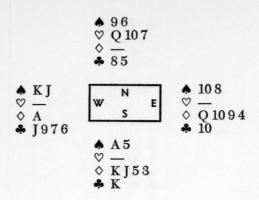

```
              ♠ 9 6
              ♡ Q 10 7
              ◇ —
              ♣ 8 5

  ♠ K J        ┌─────────┐      ♠ 10 8
  ♡ —          │    N    │      ♡ —
  ◇ A          │ W     E │      ◇ Q 10 9 4
  ♣ J 9 7 6    │    S    │      ♣ 10
               └─────────┘
              ♠ A 5
              ♡ —
              ◇ K J 5 3
              ♣ K
```

Problem — Hearts are trumps.
North-South to win all the tricks against the best defense.
South leads.

Double-Dummy Problem No. 24

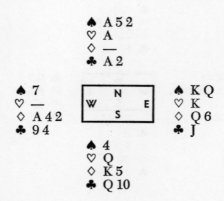

```
              ♠ A 5 2
              ♡ A
              ◇ —
              ♣ A 2

  ♠ 7          ┌─────────┐      ♠ K Q
  ♡ —          │    N    │      ♡ K
  ◇ A 4 2      │ W     E │      ◇ Q 6
  ♣ 9 4        │    S    │      ♣ J
               └─────────┘
              ♠ 4
              ♡ Q
              ◇ K 5
              ♣ Q 10
```

Problem — Clubs are trumps.
North-South to win all the tricks against the best defense.
South leads.

Double-Dummy Problem No. 25

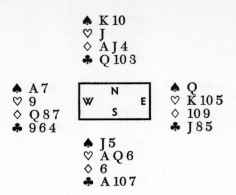

        ♠ K 10
        ♡ J
        ◇ A J 4
        ♣ Q 10 3

♠ A 7   ♠ Q
♡ 9   ♡ K 10 5
◇ Q 8 7   ◇ 10 9
♣ 9 6 4   ♣ J 8 5

        ♠ J 5
        ♡ A Q 6
        ◇ 6
        ♣ A 10 7

Problem — Clubs are trumps.

      North-South to win all the tricks against the best defense.
South leads.

Double-Dummy Problem No. 26

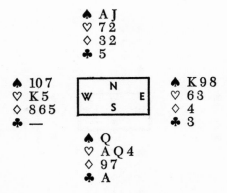

        ♠ A J
        ♡ 7 2
        ◇ 3 2
        ♣ 5

♠ 10 7   ♠ K 9 8
♡ K 5   ♡ 6 3
◇ 8 6 5   ◇ 4
♣ —   ♣ 3

        ♠ Q
        ♡ A Q 4
        ◇ 9 7
        ♣ A

Problem — Clubs are trumps.

      North-South to win 6 of the 7 tricks against the best
defense.
South leads.

Double-Dummy Problem No. 27

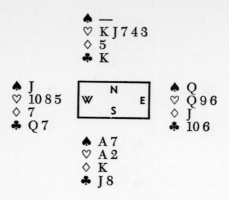

♠ —
♡ K J 7 4 3
◇ 5
♣ K

♠ J   N   ♠ Q
♡ 10 8 5   W   E   ♡ Q 9 6
◇ 7   S   ◇ J
♣ Q 7   ♣ 10 6

♠ A 7
♡ A 2
◇ K
♣ J 8

Problem — Diamonds are trumps.

       North-South to win all the tricks against the best defense.
South leads.

Double-Dummy Problem No. 28

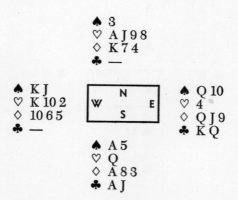

♠ 3
♡ A J 9 8
◇ K 7 4
♣ —

♠ K J   N   ♠ Q 10
♡ K 10 2   W   E   ♡ 4
◇ 10 6 5   S   ◇ Q J 9
♣ —   ♣ K Q

♠ A 5
♡ Q
◇ A 8 3
♣ A J

Problem — Hearts are trumps.

       North-South to win all the tricks against the best defense.
South leads.

Double-Dummy Problem No. 29

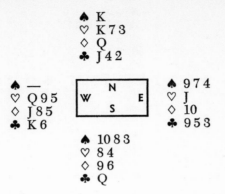

♠ K
♡ K 7 3
◊ Q
♣ J 4 2

♠ —   ♠ 9 7 4
♡ Q 9 5   ♡ J
◊ J 8 5   ◊ 10
♣ K 6   ♣ 9 5 3

♠ 10 8 3
♡ 8 4
◊ 9 6
♣ Q

Problem — Clubs are trumps.

North-South to win 6 of the 8 tricks against the best defense.

South leads

Double-Dummy Problem No. 30

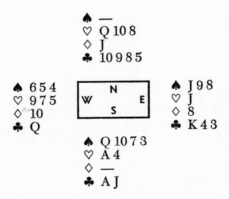

♠ —
♡ Q 10 8
◊ J
♣ 10 9 8 5

♠ 6 5 4   ♠ J 9 8
♡ 9 7 5   ♡ J
◊ 10   ◊ 8
♣ Q   ♣ K 4 3

♠ Q 10 7 3
♡ A 4
◊ —
♣ A J

Problem — Diamonds are trumps.

North-South to win 7 of the 8 tricks against the best defense.

South leads.

Solution to the Mississippi Heart Hand

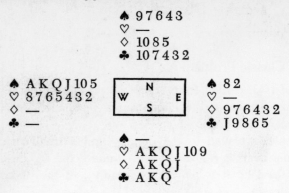

♠ 97643
♡ —
◇ 1085
♣ 107432

♠ AKQJ105   ♠ 82
♡ 8765432   ♡ —
◇ —   ◇ 976432
♣ —   ♣ J9865

♠ —
♡ AKQJ109
◇ AKQJ
♣ AKQ

West leads a high spade. With that trump-reducing play, South is helpless and can win only his six high trumps no matter how he maneuvers.

Solution to the Duke of Cumberland Hand

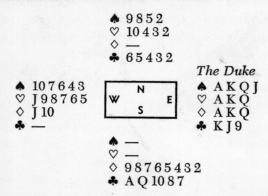

♠ 9852
♡ 10432
◇ —
♣ 65432

The Duke

♠ 107643   ♠ AKQJ
♡ J98765   ♡ AKQ
◇ J10   ◇ AKQ
♣ —   ♣ KJ9

♠ —
♡ —
◇ 98765432
♣ AQ1087

The story has the Duke, at whist, leading the nine of trumps to protect his holdings in the other suits. But whether that is done or, as in contract bridge, West leads a spade or heart the end result is the same.

The diamonds are set up with three ruffs in dummy, and two trump leads are made through East.

Solution to Making a Slam with Only
Four Trumps

Cash the three high spades, discarding a heart from dummy on the third round.

Play the king and ace of hearts.

Next cash the three high diamonds, discarding a heart from South.

Now cross-ruff diamonds and spades, using up the high trumps separately. Opponents get one trick in the end.

Solution to Classic Problem No. 1

A diamond is discarded from North on the opening lead. This is the key play, for without it, the hand cannot be made. Most players are likely to discard the deuce of spades.

Now a heart is played to the dummy and a small spade ruffed in South. Another heart is returned to the dummy and the queen of spades is ruffed. A third heart is played to dummy and the remainder of the trumps are drawn.

On the long trump, the ace of diamonds is discarded. The king of diamonds goes on the ace of spades. The unblocked diamonds are now run.

Solution to Classic Problem No. 2

Overtake the king of spades with the ace in South. Discard the ace and king of hearts on the queen and jack of spades. Discard the ace, king and queen of diamonds on South's hearts.

Now the diamonds are unblocked and can be run without interruption.

Solution to The Four Deuces Hand

West's opening lead was won by dummy's ace, declarer dropping the six. The three of spades was played next, East following with the seven and declarer winning with the queen.

Declarer now trumped the three of diamonds with dummy's four of spades, East's king falling. A second spade finesse was taken. Now the six of hearts was led and the queen finessed. The ace of hearts was played, declarer following with the four.

Back comes the ten of spades from dummy, the ace topping the king. The eight and six of spades were next led. This pressured both opponents.

The squeeze was completed on trick 10 when South played the deuce of spades. On this West played the heart king (giving up on the heart suit), North the nine and East the jack of hearts (to protect the clubs).

The second deuce, the heart, was now led and West discarded the jack of diamonds (to protect the clubs). Dummy played the ten of clubs and East the six.

The third deuce, the diamond, was led next for trick 12. And the fourth deuce, the club, was led to the ace for the last trick.

Solution to an "Impossible" Contract

The queen is played from dummy. The two high trumps cashed as well as the two high clubs and the ace of diamonds.

Now a heart is led to the ace. West's best defense is to discard. You then stick West in with the queen of trumps.

The position now is:

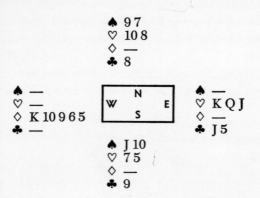

```
                ♠ 9 7
                ♡ 10 8
                ◇ —
                ♣ 8

    ♠ —          N          ♠ —
    ♡ —       W     E       ♡ K Q J
    ◇ K 10 9 6 5   S        ◇ —
    ♣ —                     ♣ J 5

                ♠ J 10
                ♡ 7 5
                ◇ —
                ♣ 9
```

West leads a diamond and you don't ruff and sluff. Instead you *discard a heart from one hand and a club from the other*.

West must lead still another diamond and now you ruff and sluff. The rest of the hand plays itself on cross-ruffs.

Solution to Bath Coups Galore

The Bath Coup is a hold-up with the ace-jack and one or more small ones when a king is led from your left. It gets its name from the famous resort in England for no particular reason.

In this hand West is allowed to win with all three of his kings — a triple Bath Coup — because only five club tricks can be won. The ninth trick must come from West being forced to lead to one of the other suits twice.

Solution to The Great Vienna Coup

The Vienna Coup has become a generic name for squeeze plays in which a card (or cards) is deliberately set up in an opponent's hand.

Note the operation in this hand. The high clubs are run from North. The fourth club, the three, squeezes East.

If East discards a diamond the entire diamond suit can be run after a finesse.

If East discards a spade, declarer cashes three spade tricks, four hearts and takes two diamonds with a finesse — which with four clubs gives him all the tricks.

Suppose East discards a heart. The ace of spades is cashed (setting up the Vienna Coup) and five rounds of hearts taken. The queen of spades and three small diamonds are discarded from North.

On the last heart East is in the painful position of giving up either the promoted king of spades or a diamond.

Solution to A Progressive Squeeze and Vienna Coup

South wins the lead with the ace of spades.

The ace of diamonds is next cashed (The Vienna Coup). West's king and queen of that suit are established.

Now the clubs are run. When the last club is played on the ninth trick, West is left with a high diamond, a high spade and three hearts.

South has two hearts, the jack of diamonds and the eight of spades. North has four hearts to the ace, queen and a spade.

West must discard. If he throws the diamond or the spade, South's card in that suit is good. The play of that card then squeezes West again.

Should West discard a heart the hearts in North can be run after a finesse.

Solution to Gray's Problem No. I

First East. He should have played his heart ace at trick two, then returned the club for West to give him a ruff in hearts.

Now South. He went wrong at the tenth trick, at the end position shown.

"At that point he knew that West had started with six clubs (for East had shown out on the third round), with one diamond and one spade (for West had shown out on the second round of both these suits). Therefore West had started with five hearts and East with one.

"At trick 10, South should have led the heart king. If East's singleton heart was the ace (as it was) he would be thrown in and would have to give declarer a ruff-and-discard. If East's singleton heart was a small one, then West would be thrown in. West would have to win with the ace and return a heart which South, knowing East had no more, could confidently let run to his ten. No defense by West, such as letting the king of hearts hold, could defeat the contract.

"The lead of the heart king wins against the distribution consistent with the data, and is therefore the correct play. The lead of the heart six loses if West holds ace, jack, nine, for instance, because North's queen will be allowed to win and then West's ace-jack will be two tricks."

Solution to Gray's Problem No. 2

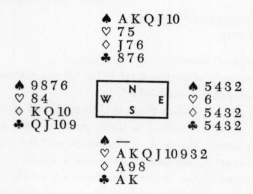

```
              ♠ A K Q J 10
              ♡ 7 5
              ◇ J 7 6
              ♣ 8 7 6

♠ 9 8 7 6          N          ♠ 5 4 3 2
♡ 8 4        W         E      ♡ 6
◇ K Q 10          S          ◇ 5 4 3 2
♣ Q J 10 9                    ♣ 5 4 3 2

              ♠ —
              ♡ A K Q J 10 9 3 2
              ◇ A 9 8
              ♣ A K
```

"Against the six-heart contract, West led the club queen which South took with the king. Now South had to get into dummy to get rid of the two losing diamonds and he saw two ways of doing that. He might drop the heart eight on the first round and then the seven would be an entry, or he could lead a low heart to the seven, hoping West had the eight. Since the chances of success were respectively twenty-six percent and fifty percent, he adopted the second method and led a low heart.

"Now West had been wondering at South's hesitation. He had been expecting South to claim about seven or eight heart tricks, five spade tricks, and a few more aces. Then it dawned on him that South had no entry into dummy. Consequently when South led the low heart, West thought rapidly and played the four. If South was willing to concede the heart eight, West didn't want it.

"South hesitated. The play of dummy's seven would win if West had the eight, but the play of dummy's five would win if West had the six —

both fifty percent chances. Since a great many Wests would have played the eight if they had had it, South decided to finesse the five — and lost.

"That was how East won a trick."

Solution to Discard All Four Aces

North wins the opening lead with the king of hearts and leads the king of diamonds; South plays the three and West discards the four of hearts. North leads the four of diamonds through East's jack winning in South with the ten, West discarding the six of hearts. South plays the queen of diamonds and West discards the ten of hearts. South continues play with the nine and seven of diamonds and throws off the *ace of hearts* and *ace of clubs* in North, West discarding two spades.

The position now is this:

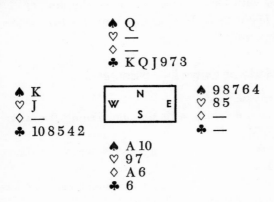

South leads the six of diamonds and West discards the jack of hearts, holding club length against dummy's clubs.

South leads the nine of hearts and West reluctantly releases a club.

South leads the six of clubs, finesses dummy's nine and cashes remaining clubs. On these he discards *the aces of spades and diamonds*.

Solution to Made or Down? — Number I

Take the East hand and defend.

Declarer's best play is not to take the queen of spades. Otherwise when East gets in with the ace of hearts he will lead through declarer's jack of spades for down one automatically.

But even the hold-up doesn't help. West wins the spade return with his ace and plays a third round of spades.

On this East chucks his *ace of hearts*. Declarer is nailed. He must play hearts to establish the ninth trick. West wins the third round of hearts with his jack and cashes his established spades.

Solution to Made or Down? — Number 2

The hand can be made.

Let's assume the best defense. East overtakes his partner's jack of hearts and plays his singleton diamond. If declarer goes after trumps now (leading the jack from dummy) East gets in with the second trump honor. He underleads hearts to partner's ten and the latter gives him a diamond ruff. Down one.

But declarer can cinch the contract by playing the ace and king of clubs from the dummy before he leads the jack of trumps. He wins East's covering honor with his ace and lays down the *nine of clubs discarding dummy's last heart on it*. East cannot now get his partner in to return a diamond for a ruff.

Solution to Made or Down? — Number 3

The hand can be made.

Take the queen of clubs with the ace. Trump the six of clubs in the closed hand (a key play).

Now lay down the ace of trump and when West shows out shift to the queen of hearts.

Continue with the ace and king of diamonds. East can trump this latter trick but he has no good return.

If he plays a heart, South's small diamonds are discarded on dummy's ace and king of hearts.

If East returns a club, a diamond is discarded from South and dummy ruffs. The remaining diamond goes on a high heart and East's remaining trumps are drawn.

Finally, if East plays a trump, dummy gets in and two diamonds are discarded on the high hearts.

Solution to The Whitfield Six

South cashes a club honor and drops the eight on it from dummy (the pivotal play).

He next leads a spade and ruffs with the three of hearts. The six of hearts is then played and on this goes the queen of diamonds.

East discards a diamond on this play. And West must therefore hang on to his diamonds to protect the suit. He also retains the nine of clubs to prevent South from pushing a finesse through East. So West lets go a spade.

The ace of diamonds is then led from North and East is squeezed. Whichever he discards, a spade or a club, South sluffs the opposite suit and gets the last two tricks.

Solution to Double-Dummy Problem No. 1

South wins the ace of hearts, and the jack is played from North. The six of clubs is then played from South, North winning both clubs. South discards the ten of diamonds on the second club.

This puts a squeeze on West. If he throws his queen of hearts, South will make two tricks in the suit by finessing through East. If he throws a diamond, the nine of diamonds will win (East discarded a diamond to protect the ten of hearts). If he throws the ace of spades, South's eight will be good.

Solution to Double-Dummy Problem No. 2

South plays the jack of hearts. West covers with the queen and North trumps with the jack of spades. North then plays the ace of spades, and follows with the king of diamonds which he trumps in South with a low spade. South plays the nine of hearts and then the nine of clubs. West must get into the lead with his trump and he is then forced to play into South's king-ten of spades.

Solution to Double-Dummy Problem No. 3

South plays the club queen and North puts on the king. North leads the club ten which East covers and South trumps. South then plays the heart nine and North's queen wins. North leads the spade ace. West must throw off a diamond or an extra trick is established for North in hearts or clubs. North then plays the club six which West wins. West is forced to lead a heart from his jack-six into North's ace-seven, and North wins the last two tricks.

Solution to Double-Dummy Problem No. 4

South plays the king of clubs. North and East throw off hearts. South plays the five of diamonds, North discards a heart and East wins the trick. East plays the six of hearts which South wins.

South then wins the queen of diamonds, North throwing off the nine of spades. South plays the seven of clubs and West wins with the queen of clubs, North discarding the king of spades.

West is now forced to lead into North's ace-queen of hearts which are two good tricks.

If at trick 3, East decides to cash his ace of spades and play the queen of spades, North wins. If West throws a heart, North plays ace, queen, ten of hearts. However, if West has kept all his hearts, North plays the ten of hearts at trick 5, wins with the king in South, and the rest of the tricks are South's.

Solution to Double-Dummy Problem No. 5

South plays the three of clubs and North overtakes with the king, leading the club five. South trumps and plays a small diamond which North's king wins. North leads the six of trump which West is forced to win. West now must play a club into North's jack. East has previously thrown off a diamond when the heart was led. If he now throws off a spade, North's jack is a winning trick. If he throws off another diamond, South will win two diamond tricks.

Solution to Double-Dummy Problem No. 6

South plays the spade three to North's ace. North plays the jack of clubs and:

1. If East discards a diamond, South trumps and leads a heart for North to trump. North wins the diamond king and leads the last club. If East ruffs with the nine, he over-ruffs. If East ruffs with the queen, he discards his diamond jack. Either way, he must make his spade jack.

2. If East trumps with the nine of spades, South overtrumps, and plays the same as described above. When North leads the second club, South will have no trouble winning a trick with his last trump.

3. If East trumps with the queen of spades, South throws off a diamond. East must return a spade to stop North from ruffing a heart. South's jack wins and he plays the last trump. West must save a club or North's four will be a good trick. When West is forced to throw off a diamond, North throws off the club. East cannot save two diamonds and the heart queen.

Solution to Double-Dummy Problem No. 7

South plays the six of diamonds. North wins with the king and then plays the ace of hearts. South throws off a spade on this trick and North continues with the heart king which South trumps.

South plays another small diamond and North must trump it with the queen of clubs. North plays the five of clubs. East must win and is forced to lead into South's diamonds.

Solution to Double-Dummy Problem No. 8

South plays the eight of spades which North trumps with the ten of diamonds. North then plays the jack and ten of clubs and South throws off two losing hearts. North continues by playing the seven of diamonds and South draws the remaining trump. South plays the queen of hearts conceding only one trick.

Solution to Double-Dummy Problem No. 9

North tops the opening lead of the queen with the king of hearts and South throws off a club. North proceeds to draw trumps; he plays the ace, king of spades and then enters South by trumping a low heart. South draws two more rounds of trumps and North discards the four of diamonds and three of clubs.

South then plays another round of trumps and West has a problem. He is caught in a squeeze for if he discards hearts and leaves himself with two hearts, one of North's little hearts can be ruffed by South, and the other will be set up as the thirteenth trick. West has no choice but to throw off in either diamonds or clubs leaving one of his kings unguarded. North throws off the same suit that West has discarded, leaving himself with the ace alone.

South then plays up to that suit, and North wins the ace of hearts; South throwing off in the other minor suit. A heart is led which South trumps. South now leads the last trump causing a double squeeze.

West must hold his heart or North's seven will be good, so he un-guards his remaining king. North then throws off the heart and East is in trouble. He cannot discard and at the same time protect both clubs and diamonds.

Solution to Double-Dummy Problem No. 10

South plays the ace of hearts. If West follows with the nine, South next plays a low diamond to the ace. Another heart lead puts West in.

He has to play clubs and South makes two club tricks. North keeps all three spades and East is caught in a succession of squeezes.

If West discards his king of hearts under the lead of the ace of hearts, South plays a spade to the queen and North plays a second spade. South throws off the queen of clubs. In this way North-South makes six tricks and when East makes his return, the seventh trick is assured.

Solution to Double-Dummy Problem No. 11

South plays a spade which North trumps. North leads the queen of clubs. If East wins it with the ace, South will be assured of making two club tricks, and North will have a chance to throw off the queen of diamonds. East's best play is not to cover.

South then overtakes the queen of clubs with the king and plays the king of spades. North trumps, plays his ace and king of hearts and throws off two clubs in South. North plays the queen of diamonds, and West must give South a diamond trick.

Solution to Double-Dummy Problem No. 12

South plays a club to North's ace, and East's best throw-off is the king of spades. North plays a low diamond to South's ace. South then wins the club king and North discards a spade. If East throws off a diamond, South plays his ten of diamonds, goes over it with the jack in North, and North will have two good diamond tricks.

If East throws a low spade, South will win his ten of diamonds and play a spade forcing East in the lead. East will then have to lead to the diamond jack. East therefore throws off his ace of spades.

South plays his ten of diamonds and now West has a problem. If he throws his heart, South can enter North with the jack of diamonds and cash his heart. If West throws a spade, the ten of diamonds will win the trick and a spade lead from South will force East in to play to the diamond jack. If West discards a club, South can make his extra trick in clubs.

Solution to Double-Dummy Problem No. 13

South plays the king of hearts and West tops it with the ace, and North trumps. North wins the king of spades and plays the ace of diamonds which South trumps. South makes the nine of hearts and then leads the four of clubs. West must trump and return a trump into South's queen and nine of trumps. South now makes the last two tricks.

Solution to Double-Dummy Problem No. 14

South plays a heart to the eight in North, North plays the queen of spades which East covers and South ruffs. South then plays the last trump on which North throws off the three of spades.

If West discards a diamond, all the cards in the South hand are winners. If West throws off anything else, South plays a club to the ace of clubs and cashes the trick that West's discard has established. This play squeezes West again.

If East doesn't cover the queen of spades at trick 2, South leads another spade and when the last trump is played, West is squeezed in the minor suits.

Solution to Double-Dummy Problem No. 15

South plays the king of diamonds and throws off the ten of clubs in North. South then plays the eight of spades which West wins. West must now lead a heart or a club, putting North in the lead. North wins both of these tricks, discarding the ace and queen of spades in South. North's remaining spades are the final winning tricks.

Solution to Double-Dummy Problem No. 16

South trumps the two of spades with the three of hearts and then plays the king of hearts. If East doesn't drop the queen, North wins the king and jack of clubs discarding the diamond ten in South on the second club lead. He then leads to South winning the king of diamonds. A trump is played to put East in the lead. East must now lead into South's spades giving him a finesse.

If East drops the queen of hearts under the king, North plays the low club to South's queen. South then forces West in the lead by playing a trump and West must give declarer entry to North's clubs.

If both East and West drop high trumps on the king of hearts, South takes his needed tricks without a problem.

Solution to Double-Dummy Problem No. 17

South plays a low club which North trumps with the nine of spades. North plays the ace of spades, and South throws off the queen of diamonds. North plays a heart through East and South wins both the jack and king of hearts.

South then plays the five of diamonds. West is forced to put North in with the nine of diamonds, and North's third heart gives him the sixth trick for his contract.

Solution to Double-Dummy Problem No. 18

South plays the jack of diamonds. If West puts on the queen, North trumps and plays a club which South trumps. South cashes his good diamond and North throws off the king of hearts. South plays a heart which North trumps and North leads a second club which is trumped by South. North's queen of spades takes the last trick.

If West doesn't put on the queen on the first diamond play, North throws off the heart king immediately, and South plays a second diamond which North trumps. After that the cross-ruff of clubs and hearts gives declarer the rest of the tricks.

Solution to Double-Dummy Problem No. 19

South plays the three of spades which North wins. North cashes his king of hearts and South throws off the king of spades, East discarding the diamond jack. North then plays the ace of hearts. If East throws off the ace of diamonds, South throws off the four of diamonds. The South hand is then good.

If East throws off a spade on the lead of the ace of hearts, South discards the ace of spades.

If East discards the jack of clubs, South throws his queen of clubs and North plays the six of clubs. This squeezes East in diamonds and spades.

Solution to Double-Dummy Problem No. 20

South plays the queen of spades. West tops it with the king and North trumps. North then leads a diamond which South trumps. South wins his ten of spades and North gets a heart throw-off. South continues with the six of spades, and if West trumps, North throws off his last heart. Now if West returns a heart, North trumps and South wins the rest with his trump and jack of hearts.

If West returns a diamond, North-South make their trump cards individually, in addition to North's jack of diamonds.

If West throws off a diamond when the third round of spades is played by South, North discards the last heart. Then North trumps a heart lead by South, and South trumps another diamond lead by North.

If West throws off a heart on the play of the third round of spades, North also throws off a heart, and South then plays the jack of hearts.

Solution to Double-Dummy Problem No. 21

South plays the ace and seven of diamonds. West and North throw off spades on the second round of diamonds played. South then plays the king of spades; West and North discard clubs, and East a heart on this trick. South plays the two of spades. If West throws the six of hearts, North throws off a club and South plays the seven of hearts.

If West discards a club, North throws off a heart and East is in a squeeze. If East drops a heart, South plays the six of clubs to North's ace, and returns to South with the jack of hearts. If East throws a club, North's clubs are winning tricks.

Solution to Double-Dummy Problem No. 22

South plays the king of hearts. If West covers with the ace and returns a trump, North takes it with the ace of trump. He plays the jack of spades and South gets a throw-off of the queen of hearts. Then North wins two heart tricks, the second of which puts East in a squeeze.

If West doesn't cover ace on the opening play of the king of hearts, South plays the eight of spades to the ace of spades, and North continues with the jack of spades. South throws off the seven of clubs. West is in and must return a small heart. South then plays a diamond which East wins, and South must make the last two tricks.

Solution to Double-Dummy Problem No. 23

South plays a small diamond which North trumps. North leads the five of clubs. South takes it with the king and wins his king of diamonds throwing off a spade in the North hand. South leads another diamond which North trumps. North plays the last trump. East must throw off a spade, otherwise South will win a spade and a diamond. South then discards his diamond. Now if West throws off his last club, North's eight of clubs is a winner. If West discards a spade, South will win two spade tricks.

Solution to Double-Dummy Problem No. 24

South plays the king of diamonds. If West doesn't play his ace, North throws off a spade. Now the five of diamonds is led and trumped with the ace. North plays the two of clubs and South makes both trumps, North throwing off the last low spade. North then cashes his aces to win all the tricks.

If West decides to cover the opening play of the king of diamonds with his ace, North trumps with the ace of clubs. The two of clubs is played and South makes both clubs. North throws off the ace of hearts on the second club lead.

If East throws off a spade, North's hand is set up to win the remaining tricks. If East throws off a diamond or heart, he gives South a winning trick. This card is then played to squeeze the East hand again.

Solution to Double-Dummy Problem No. 25

South plays a club which North takes with the queen of clubs. North leads the jack of hearts and South wins with the queen (or ace if East plays the king). South leads the six of hearts and North ruffs it with the ten of clubs. North leads the three of clubs and South wins two club tricks, North throwing off the ten of spades.

South plays the last heart and West is in trouble. He cannot discard his ace of spades for North will discard a diamond and South will lead through West to make two diamonds and the king of spades. If West discards a diamond, South's diamond lead to North will give him three diamond tricks.

Solution to Double-Dummy Problem No. 26

South plays the queen of spades to the ace and trumps North's jack of spades. South then plays the queen of hearts. West must take with the king or South will have no trouble winning six tricks. If West now plays a heart, North's seven takes the trick and North will play the five of clubs giving South a diamond throw-off.

If West decides to return a diamond instead of a heart, South takes the trick and plays the four of hearts to the seven. North plays the five of trumps and South throws off the ace of hearts. South then takes the final trick with the high diamond.

Solution to Double-Dummy Problem No. 27

South leads the ace of spades, and North throws off the king of clubs. South plays the jack of clubs, West tops it with the queen and North trumps. North leads a small heart to South's ace.

South cashes the king of diamonds and the seven of spades. East is now squeezed. If he throws a heart, his queen will fall under North's king. If he throws a club, South's eight is a good trick.

If West doesn't play the queen of clubs on South's play of the jack, North discards and South plays the next club for North to trump.

Solution to Double-Dummy Problem No. 28

South plays the queen of hearts. If West goes up king, North wins with the ace. If West doesn't cover, North plays small. Either way, South next cashes the ace of spades.

He then leads the ace of clubs. If West throws off instead of trumping, North discards a diamond and South plays the five of spades which North trumps. The king and ace of diamonds are then played and any lead from South takes out West's trumps, North being in a position to over-trump.

If West ruffs the ace of clubs, North over-ruffs and plays the high trump. South throws off the eight of diamonds, and North plays the last trump. East must hold onto a club (or South's jack will be a good trick). East must also save two diamonds or South will win the ace and finesse through West's ten of diamonds. East, therefore, throws off a spade. South now throws off his jack of clubs and West is in a squeeze.

If West throws off a diamond, North can establish his third diamond for a winning trick; if West throws a spade, South's five of spades will be a winning trick.

Solution to Double-Dummy Problem No. 29

South plays the queen of clubs. If West doesn't cover, North plays the four. South continues with a spade. West throws off and North takes. North plays the jack of clubs. West wins the trick and is forced to lead a diamond or a heart. North takes and then wins the top card in the other suit. He continues by playing the two of clubs. East must take the trick and lead a spade into South's hand to give him two spade tricks.

If West covers the first club trick with his king, he must return a suit which North will win. North plays the top cards in all four suits, and then puts East in by playing the two of clubs. The situation is the same if West doesn't cover the first club lead, and trumps the spade play on the second trick.

Solution to Double-Dummy Problem No. 30

South wins the ace of clubs and plays the four of hearts to North's queen. North plays the jack of diamonds and South throws off the ace of hearts. North wins the ten of hearts and then plays the eight of hearts throwing West in with the nine. On this trick, East must throw off the king of clubs or a spade while South discards the opposite suit. West is compelled to lead a spade into South's ten-ace.

If at trick 4, West throws his nine of hearts under the ten of hearts, East is put in with the king of clubs and is forced to lead from his jack-nine of spades into South's queen-ten.

Section 11

Bridge
for Two and Three Hands
and Variations for Four

BRIDGE FOR TWO

Straight Double Dummy

This form of two-handed bridge provides good practice in the techniques and problems of play. It is recommended for learning card placement and sharpening card memory.

The dealer, decided by cut, deals out four hands. Each player picks up the hand in front of him, leaving the other two face down on the table to be used later as dummy partners.

Looking only at their own hands, and not at face-down partner-hands, players bid competitively as in regular bridge. When the bidding is over, declarer's opponent takes the seat to the left of the declarer and leads. Declarer's partner-hand is then turned face-up opposite him and arranged into suits. Declarer makes a play from this hand.

Opponent then turns up his partner-hand and arranges it into suits. He plays from this hand. The last card of the trick is played by declarer.

After this, the play then proceeds as in regular bridge, each hand playing in regular order. Since, in effect, all hands are known plays are possible that would ordinarily be missed in a game with three concealed hands.

Scoring is as in regular bridge.

Variation: One of the dummy hands is dealt open. The bidding proceeds as in regular bridge. When it is over the successful bidder has a choice of dummy hands. He can select the visible one or take his chances with the face-down hand. After the choice has been made each player puts his dummy hand opposite him and the lead is made from declarer's left.

Double Dummy with a Widow

Try this one for a touch of excitement.

Deal four hands of twelve cards each. Place the remaining four cards face down in the center of the table, as a widow.

Bid, beginning with dealer. During the bidding contest each player may consult his face-down partner-hand as often as he likes.

The bidding over, declarer picks up the four cards of the widow and deals them face down, two to opponent and two to himself.

Each player looks at these two cards and places one in the dummy hand and one into his own. He may not, however, use any other cards in his hand for the purpose of adding to dummy.

Declarer now specifies which of opponent's hands, dummy or closed, makes the opening lead. His hand or his dummy must be the last to play to the trick.

Procedure in play and scoring is as in the regular game.

Partially Concealed Dummy

This is a game of surprises where the turn of a card can change the course of play completely.

Each of the players gets his hand dealt face down. But his dummy-partner is dealt to as follows: The first seven cards come face down in a row. The next six come face up. The face-up cards cover the face-down ones. The seventh face-down card is uncovered.

Each player bids on his own hand, basing the bids, of course, on the six visible cards in the dummy.

When the bidding is over, the lead is made from the hand to the declarer's left so that he is the last to play to the trick.

Each time a face-down card is uncovered it is turned face up and may be played. No card may be played while it is still face down.

Play and scoring is as in regular bridge.

Build-Up Bridge

Here is a thoughtful game.

Dealer gives player thirteen cards. Dummy-partners only get nine cards each, dealt face up. The remaining eight cards will be dealt to these hands later according to the rules of the game.

The bidding goes in two parts. In part one, the dealer has the first turn to bid. If he and opponent both pass, there is a new deal.

If dealer passes and opponent bids, the bidding is over. Dealer may not bid or double. (The game continues as explained later.)

If both players bid the bidding continues until there is a pass. Doubles are not permitted.

Either of the two bidding situations described constitute *Part one* of the bidding.

Next, two of the remaining eight cards are given to each player, leaving four still to be dealt. Both players reduce their hands back to thirteen by placing two of the cards in the dummy, face up. They do so at the same time.

Part two of the bidding starts with the player who last passed. If he had made no bid at all in *part one,* he may not now start with any bid less than game. Otherwise, he may bid normally or pass. If he passes, opponent is allowed one more bid.

The bidding over, the players each get half of the remaining four cards. They reduce their hands as before, but the two cards now played into the dummy go there *face down.* Either of these cards may be faced up any time it is dummy's turn to play to a trick and the faced card may be used, if playable. This adds an element of the unexpected.

There are restrictions concerning the placing of the last two cards into dummy. Declarer's opponent may not place trumps. Declarer may do so, provided he tells how many he is placing.

Play is as in regular bridge with the lead coming up to declarer on the first trick. Scoring differs from standard only in this respect: A player gets a double score if his contract is fulfilled in a declaration he made in *part one* of the bidding. He does not lose double, however, for going down.

Memory Bridge

A good game for training card memory.

Each player gets thirteen cards and the remaining twenty-six are put aside until later. There is no bidding now, only playing to tricks.

Dealer's opponent makes the first lead and the play is at no trump. Whoever wins a majority of tricks scores for one no trump plus a premium of 100 points.

The rest of the deck is now dealt out. A bidding contest follows with doubles and redoubles allowed. The opening lead is made by the declarer's opponent. It helps to remember the important cards played in the first deal. Score the result as in regulation bridge.

Gin Bridge

Each player gets thirteen cards. The remaining twenty-six go face down as a stock from which cards will be drawn as play proceeds. There is no bidding until later.

Dealer's opponent leads to the first trick and the play is at no trump. Optional rules for play: 1. Players *must* follow suit, if able to; or 2. Players need not follow suit. Agree on either rule.

Winner of the trick draws the top card of the stock, opponent the card beneath. When the stock is exhausted, each player has a hand of thirteen cards. Tricks are not counted during this phase of the game.

Now there is bidding and play as in the regulation game. Tricks are counted. Scoring is standard.

Variation 1. Turn the stock *face up* instead of face down. All cards to be drawn are thus visible. Memory becomes a factor.

Variation 2. No cards are dealt. Instead, players draw in turn from the face-down stock. If a player decides not to keep the card he drew, he tosses it into a discard pile, face down, and *must* take the next card from the stock.

Players draw in this fashion until each has a hand of thirteen cards. After which there is bidding and play.

Duel

Each player gets thirteen cards. The twenty-seventh card is placed, sideways and face up, under the stock which is also face up. This determines the trump. During the draw part of the game when hands are being built up for the kill stage, tricks do not count. If the under-stock card is a picture or an ace, the play is at no trump.

Dealer's opponent leads to the first trick and play goes according to regulation rules. Winner takes the top card of the stock, loser the card beneath. Player who draws the last (27th) card becomes the "offender." He will make the first lead in the play-out or "kill" stage of the game when the stock is gone.

After the kill stage is over players count tricks won during this part of the game. If offender has won more than six tricks he scores 20 points per odd trick, whether the play was at trump or no trump. If defender wins more than six tricks, he scores only 10 points per odd trick.

Scoring 100 points, whether in one deal or more, is "game" and earns an extra bonus of 100 points. First to score two games wins rubber. The bonus for rubber is the same as in standard bridge.

Variations. Bidding may be used before the kill stage.

Practice Games

Good practice for standard bridge can be gotten with the use of card-holders. The card-holder may be any small cardboard box of the size of a shoe-box. It rests on the table upside down with lid on. Cards can be stood up between the edge of the lid and the side of the box.

Each player has a card-holder placed opposite him on the table at such an angle that opponent cannot see the cards. The hands are dealt. Each player takes his dummy hand and arranges it in the card-holder. Bidding starts with the dealer and goes around the table as in regulation bridge. Each player bids for himself and his dummy hand in turn.

When the bidding is over the lead comes from the hand to the left of the declarer. His dummy hand then goes face up on the table as in a regulation game. The defender's partner-hand remains in the card-holder so that it cannot be seen by declarer and is played from in proper turn.

If a card-holder hand becomes declarer, its owner changes seats so that he holds that hand and his original hand becomes the dummy.

All other rules are as in regulation bridge.

Bridge for Three

◇ ♣ ♡ ♠ ◇ ♣ ♡ ♠ ◇ ♣ ♡ ♠ ◇ ♣ ♡ ♠ ◇ ♣ ♡ ♠ ◇ ♣ ♡ ♠ ◇ ♣ ♡ ♠ ◇ ♣ ♡ ♠

Cutthroat Bridge

Four hands are dealt, each player receiving one. The fourth hand is left face down. There are no set partnerships.

The players then bid in turn as in regular bridge. The bidding ends when two passes follow a bid, double or redouble.

Player at declarer's left leads to the first trick. Declarer then takes the dummy hand and arranges it face up between his opponents. Opponents of the declarer play as a team against him.

Play proceeds as in regular bridge with the winner of a trick leading to the next.

Scoring is regulation. Individual scores are kept for each player. Declarer records his score and any bonuses he earns. If he goes down, each opponent gets the full amount of the set.

Each player scores his own rubber. A 700-point rubber is scored only if both opponents have no game toward rubber. If either opponent has game, only a 500-point premium is scored.

Rules are as in the four-handed game.

Variations: 1. The first round of bidding may be only in suits; a no-trump bid is not allowed. And in the first round no bid may be higher than one.

2. The dummy hand is exposed from the beginning.

3. Players get twelve cards only. The other four are dealt as a widow, face down. The dummy is then exposed and the bidding begins. Declarer takes the widow cards and deals one to each hand. Play then proceeds.

4. Seven cards of the dummy hand are turned up at random, and

then there is bidding. After a lead has been made, the concealed cards in the dummy are turned up. Or play proceeds until the exposed cards are exhausted, after which the concealed cards are turned up.

Optional Partners

Each player receives a hand of thirteen cards. The fourth hand is left face down as a blind hand.

Dealer may open the bidding or pass. Next player may open the bidding if there has been a pass, overcall, support of dealer's bid, or pass. Third player may open the bidding if there were two previous passes, overcall, or support of a call made by either of the other players. Doubles and redoubles may be made.

When the final contract has been reached, declarer may choose either of the other players' hands or the blind hand as dummy.

1. If declarer chooses a hand that supported the suit (or no trump) of the final declaration, that hand goes down as his dummy. Its owner takes no part in the play but will share in the scoring. The third man gets the blind hand as his dummy. Before either dummy hand is exposed an opening lead is made from the hand to declarer's left. After that play goes double-dummy style.

2. If declarer chooses a hand that did not support the suit (or no trump) of the final declaration, that hand goes down as his dummy. The player whose hand he chooses picks up the blind hand and plays as partner of the third man. If the blind hand is at the left of declarer the opening lead is made by the player at declarer's right.

3. If declarer chooses the blind hand, the other two players combine as partners against him. The blind hand goes between them as dummy. The opening lead comes from declarer's left.

The scoring depends on which hand declarer took as dummy. In situation (1) he and the holder of that hand each get full credit for a fulfilled contract, but split any premiums. Defender collects a full penalty for setting declarer.

In (2) declarer receives full credit for a fulfilled contract, but only half credit for premiums.

In (3) declarer receives full credit for all scores. Opponents each collect full value for any penalties.

Each player keeps a separate score and there is no playing for rubber. Every hand is considered not vulnerable. Game bids earn a premium of 300 points added to the trick score. Partials add a premium of 50 points.

The rules are as in the regular four-handed game with these exceptions: Declarer may not take a doubler's hand as his dummy. If a third hand bids a suit already named by the other two players, he becomes the declarer with no further bidding.

Towie

Four hands are dealt, one to each player and one separately as a dummy. When the deal is finished, the dealer turns up six cards of the dummy.

Players then bid for the dummy, beginning with dealer and going in regular turn to the left. When the bidding is over, the player to the left of the declarer makes the opening lead, and declarer turns up the remaining cards of the dummy and arranges the hand. Opponents play against him as partners, the play going as in regular bridge.

Hands bid at less than game are not played. Instead they are redealt as a "goulash." Dealer sorts the dummy's hand into suits. The hands are picked up, beginning with dealer's and going to the left, and stacked into a pile. The pile is cut once (or not at all, if so agreed).

Dealer gives out five cards at a time to each player, five more and then finally three. He shuffles the dummy and turns up six cards. The bidding proceeds and if no game is bid another goulash is dealt. And so on.

No trump counts 35 points per trick. For the first game he wins, a player receives a premium of 500 points in addition to his trick score. First to win rubber receives a premium of 1,000 points. A new rubber then follows.

Undoubled overtricks score 50 points each regardless of suit. There are premiums of 50 points for making doubled contracts, not vulnerable, and 100 points for doubled contracts, vulnerable.

Undertricks, not vulnerable and undoubled, are 50 points each. Doubled and not vulnerable, they count 100 points each for the first and second tricks, 200 points each for the third and fourth tricks, 400 points each after that.

Undertricks, vulnerable and undoubled, are 100 points for the first trick and 200 for each additional. Vulnerable and doubled they are 200 and 400.

Other scoring is as in regular bridge.

Trio Bridge (George S. Coffin's rules)

1. The three players are designated as North and South, who call as

well as play against East and his open-dummy partner. There is no West player, no second dummy.

2. To begin a game, the three players draw cards; and the two players who draw the highest cards play as partners as North and South against East who has the dummy for the entire rubber.

3. For the first deal only, South shuffles either pack. Then East cuts and South deals while North shuffles the still pack. For the next hand, East cuts and North deals while South shuffles the still pack. Thereafter, North and South continue to deal alternately.

4. East never deals or shuffles, but he always cuts. He may and should pick up his own cards as they are dealt to him in order to have time to arrange his own cards and the dummy cards opposite him.

5. Dummy is opened before there is any bidding.

6. South always calls first regardless of who dealt. North calls second and dummy never bids since East calls on his combined 26 cards.

7. The opening lead is made by the hand to the left of declarer.

8. East cannot be penalized for a revoke unless either opponent calls attention to East's failure to follow suit on the revoke trick.

9. Regular contract scoring is used. After the net amount of a finished rubber has been computed, East wins or loses *twice* this net amount because he collects dummy's gain or suffers dummy's loss.

10. At the end of a rubber, North shifts into the vacant chair on his right; and becomes redesignated in his new position as South with his new partner redesignated North and his former partner as East.

Variations for Four Hands

◇ ♣ ♡ ♠ ◇ ♣ ♡ ♠ ◇ ♣ ♡ ♠ ◇ ♣ ♡ ♠ ◇ ♣ ♡ ♠ ◇ ♣ ♡ ♠ ◇ ♣ ♡ ♠ ◇ ♣ ♡ ♠ ◇ ♣ ♡ ♠

Dummy-less Bridge

This version of bridge furnishes an interesting change-off. Its best feature is that *everyone* gets to play on *every* hand. There are those who argue that it requires more playing skill and keener observation than the regulation game because no cards are seen except the ones played to tricks.

Four hands are dealt and the bidding goes on as in the standard game. The opening lead comes from the hand to the left of the declarer.

But no dummy hand is faced. The player who ordinarily would put down the dummy holds his hand and participates in the play with the others. Scoring and rules of play are regulation.

Deuces Wild

When a dash of spice is desired make all the deuces wild.

Bid and play as in the standard game. Or combine the no-dummy feature described above. An added rule is that when a deuce and the card it is said to represent are played to the same trick, the deuce beats the natural card.

There is an added premium of 250 points for winning the last trick with a deuce.

Contract with a Joker

Play with a fifty-three-card deck which includes one joker. Deal as usual and turn the fifty-third card face up. This is an exchange card and can be figured in with one's own hand when considering what and how high to bid.

After the opening lead has been made and dummy goes down, declarer may trade any unwanted card for the extra turned-up card. The unwanted card is placed face down and out of play in a corner of the table. The exchange can make a big difference in declarer's hand, creating a void, singleton, greater trump length or protection for a high card.

The joker is the top card of the suit with which it is identified when played, outranking the ace. The joker may not be identified with a suit which its owner has previously discarded to or trumped.

Goulash Hands

If hands are running on the dull side a few goulash deals will definitely put some life into them.

The method for forming goulashes is to pile one hand on top of the other with suits assorted. There is no shuffle of the pack and one cut is made or none. Cards are then dealt three at a time on the first round and then five at a time for the next two.

A passing-goulash feature may also be introduced to really build up freaks. Before the bidding, partners exchange three cards face down across the table. It may also be permitted to further exchange one card after a look at the line-up of cards and then two.

Four-Deal Rounds

When a fifth player is waiting to cut in or when it is desired to change partnerships as often as possible this procedure is recommended:

Only four deals are to be played with the same partnership. The first deal will be played and scored as though neither side is vulnerable. The second and third deals will be played and scored as though the dealer's side is vulnerable. The fourth deal will be played and scored as though both side are vulnerable.

For bidding and making a non-vulnerable game add a bonus of 300 points to the score for tricks. Credit to the fulfilling side as a single score, e.g. North–South bid 4 spades, non vulnerable, and make 11 tricks. They get 150 points plus 300, or 450 points total.

For a fulfilled vulnerable game add 500 bonus to score for tricks. For a part score add 50 points bonus, e.g. East–West bid 1 no trump and make 8 tricks. They get 70 plus 50, or 120 points total.

After four deals, scores are totalled and credited to the individual players. There is a change of partnerships.

Variation: Many prefer that scoring go as follows: A part score made on any one of the first three hands does not receive a bonus of 50 points. Instead the part score counts toward game and can be completed as in rubber bridge. A part score on the last hand is given a bonus of 100 points.

Five-Player Pivot

Five players may play a revolving four-handed game. Originally, all cut and two high cards are partners against two low, middle man out. Number the players from 1 through 5. Highest card is first dealer.

A rubber or a four-deal round is played (as described above). The new player then comes in and one goes out according to this plan, which is followed for five changes of partnerships.

<table>
<tr><td colspan="2" align="center">First Round</td><td colspan="2" align="center">Third Round</td></tr>
</table>

	First Round				*Third Round*	
	2				4	
3		4		5		2
	1				1	
	5 out				3 out	

	Second Round				*Fourth Round*	
	5				3	
2		3		4		5
	1				1	
	4 out				2 out	

	Fifth Round	
	4	
3		5
	2	
	1 out	

Each player gets to play with each other player once as partner and twice as opponent. Each player sits out one round in turn.

At the end of each round or rubber, scores for both sides are entered on an individual tally. Final winner is the one with the highest score, others ranking in descending order according to their scores.

Index

A

Abbot, Jane, 142
Ace, Goodman, 269
Aldrich, C. W., 11
American Auction Bridge League, 11
American Contract Bridge League, 11,
    16, 17, 18, 19, 20, 134, 169, 205,
    306
American Whist League, 11
Anderson, Clinton P., 71
Anecdotes, bridge, 75, 97, 98, 99, 100,
    167, 212, 216
    classic, 196
Approach-forcing, 9, 11, 66
Artificial bids, 304
    (see also CONVENTIONS, PSYCHICS,
    BLUFF BIDS)
Auction Bridge, 3, 5

B

Barclay, Shepard, 12, 51, 52
Barret, Wm. 14
Bath Groups Galore, 335
    solution to: 358
Becker, B. Jay, 36
Beinecke, Walter, 37
Bent, Silas, 66
Beynon, George W., 153
Bidding, 303
    approach-forcing, 9, 11
    artificial bids, 304
    Blackwood convention, 306, 307
    bluff bids, 179–183, 294–297
    conventions, 303
    cue bidding to slam, 309
    cue bids, 107, 209
    Culbertson 4-5 no trump, 73
    Fishbein Convention, 311
    Five-card majors, 314
    Four Aces system, 16, 18
    Gerber convention, 308
    Goren point count, 18
    grand slam bids (Sims), 13
    Lightner slam double, 316
    one-over-one, 15, 305

Bidding (Cont.):
    one-under-one, 305
    opening bid of two, 312
    overcall in clubs, 314
    overcalls, 110, 314
    point count, 16, 18, 85
    pre-emptive bids, 290, 311, 312
    psychics, 13, 43, 67, 172, 294
    psychology in bidding, 289
    Stayman convention, 85, 309
    take-out doubles, 31, 107
    two-club force, 313
    unusual no trump overcall, 314
    various systems, 305
    weak no trump, 314
    weak two-bid, 85
Bigelow, S. Tupper, 233
Blackwood convention, 306, 307
Bluff bids, 179–183, 294–297
Blum, Robert N., 184
Boners, 171
Bowers, Spotswood, 37
Brandt, Lee, 155
Bridge
    Auction, 3, 5, 6
    Build-Up, 376
    Commuter, 123
        (see also GHOULASH, GHOULIES,
        MAYONNAISE)
    Contract, 6
    Contract Story, 3
    Contract with a joker, 383
    Cutthroat bridge, 379
    Deuces wild, 383
    Double dummy, 375
    Double dummy with a widow, 376
    Duel bridge, 378
    Dummy-less bridge, 383
    Five-player pivot, 384
    Four-deal rounds, 384
    Gin bridge, 378
    Goulash bridge, 383
        (see also COMMUTER)
    Memory bridge, 377
    Optional partners, 380
    Practice games, 379

387

Bridge (*Cont.*):
  Quiz, 269, 298
  Tips on how to be a good player, 273
  Three-handed game, 379, 382
  Towie, 381
  Trio bridge, 382
  Two-handed game, 375
Bridge Battle of the Century, 15, 22
Bridge Clubs, 80
Bridge ethics, 213, 214, 316
Bridge hands,
  Double dummy, classics, curios,
    329–355
  Solutions to: 356–377
Bridge luck, 87, 281
Bridge Mathematics, 86, 90, 91, 92, 93,
    217
Bridge Memory, 217, 274, 277
Bridge Olympics, 10
Bridge Proprieties, 316
  (*see also* ETHICS)
Bridge Psychology, 275, 289
  (*see also* PSYCHOLOGY)
Bridge Quiz, 269, 298
Bridge Superstitions, 89, 284
Bridge World Magazine, 10, 22, 51,
    85, 210
Bruce, David, 12
  (*see also* DAVID BURNSTINE)
Brunner, Robt. K., 89
Bryan, Maurie C., 193
Build-Up Bridge, 376
Burnstine, David, 12, 13, 15, 16, 167

C

Card Battle of the Century, 9
Card instinct, 285
Card memory, 277
Card sense, 217, 274, 277
Carpenter, Jimmy, 12
Cartoons-H. T. Webster, 48, 56, 102,
    122, 132, 166, 195, 266, 302, 315,
    328
Cavendish Club, 81, 82, 83, 103
Cavendish Club Trophy, 12
Cayenne, 3
Clark, Mark Gen., 229
Classic hands, 329
  solutions to: 356
Classic Problems No. 1 & 2, 332
  solutions to: 357
Coffee-Housing, 316, 318, 322
Coffin, George S., 382
  (rules for Trio Bridge)
Collyer, Barbara, 35
Commuters Bridge, 72, 123, 124, 125
Contract with a Joker, 383
Contract Bridge (*see* BRIDGE)

Conventions, 303
  (*see also* BIDDING)
  Blackwood, 306, 307
  Culbertson 4-5 no trump, 73
  Fishbein, 311
  five-card majors, 314
  Gerber, 308
  Lightner Slam double, 316
  Opening bid of two, 312
  Stayman, 85, 309
  Two-club force, 313
  unusual no trump overcall, 314
  Weak no trump, 314
Cotton, Charles, 3
Crawford, John, 19
Crockford Club, 10
Cross-ruff, 40
Cue bidding to slam, 309
Cue bids (*see also* BIDDING), 107, 209
Culbertson 4-5 no trump bids, 73
Culbertson, Ely, 9, 10, 12, 14, 16, 17,
    19, 21, 34, 38, 51, 53, 99, 105,
    133, 139, 167, 212
Culbertson vs. Goren, 19
Culbertson vs. Lenz, 9, 21, 281
  hands from match, 27
Culbertson vs. Sims, 14, 34, 38
  hands from match, 39
Culbertson, Josephine, 10, 14, 22, 27,
    34, 38, 133, 139, 215
Cutthroat Bridge, 379

D

Davis, Elmer, 49
Deuces Wild Bridge, 383
Discard all four aces hand, 338
  solution to: 361
Dorbitzers, 100
Double Dummy Bridge for two, 375
Double Dummy Problems, 329–355
  solutions to: 356–371
Double Dummy with a Widow, 376
Duel Bridge, 378
Duke of Cumberland hand, 329
  solution to: 356
Dummy-less bridge, 383
Dunne, J. Patrick, 8
Duplicate boards, 11, 205
Duplicates, 11, 12, 85
  (*see also* TOURNAMENTS)

E

Eisenhower, Dwight D., 229
Eliot, Wm. Talley, 190
Ethics, bridge, 213, 214, 316
  (*see also* COFFEEHOUSING,
    PROPRIETIES)
Experts, bridge, 206, 211, 216, 228

F

False-carding, 292
Faro, 100
Finesses, 92, 93, 94, 168
Fishbein Convention, 311
Fishbein, Harry, 84, 285
Five-card majors, 314
Five-card pivot, 384
Foster, R. F., 3, 52
Four Aces, The, 13, 15, 16, 17, 69
 bidding system, 16
 point count, 18
Four-deal rounds, 384
Four Deuces hand, 333
 solution to: 357
Four Horsemen, The, 12, 15, 23
Frey, Richard L., 133
Fry, Samuel Jr., 36, 106, 216, 289

G

Games (see BRIDGE)
Gerber Convention, 308
Ghoulash, 124, 383
Ghoulies, 124, 125, 383
 rules for: 127
Gin Bridge, 378
Goddard, E. M., 35
Goodman, Jack, 318
Goren, Chas. H., 18, 19, 60, 83, 87, 99,
 151, 169, 206, 230
 point count, 18
Gotthelf, A. L., 35
Goulash hands, 383
 (see also GHOULASH, GHOULIES,
 MAYONNAISE)
Gould, Bruce, 246
Grand slam bids, 13
Grand slam hands, 42, 43
Gray, R.
 Problem No. 1, 337
 Problem No. 2, 338
 Solutions to: 359, 360
Gruenther, Alfred M. Gen., 23, 37, 84
 229

H

Halpin, Robert W., 11
Hands, classic, curios, double dummy,
 329–355
 solutions to: 356–371
Hays, Harold Dr., 57
Hazen, Lee, 96, 167, 228
Heilbroner, Robt. L., 80
Hoyle, Edmond, 100, 278
Husband & wife bridge,
 (see MAN & WIFE BRIDGE)
Huske, Wm. J., 4, 5
Hymes, Eddie, 103, 216

I

"Impossible" contract, An, 334
 solution to: 358
International Code, 17

J

Jacoby, Oswald, 10, 12, 13, 15, 16, 23,
 27, 84, 104, 151, 167, 207, 278
Jaeger, Henry P., 11

K

Kahn, E. J. Jr., 173
Kaplan, Fred, 231
Karn, Willard S., 12, 16
Kaufman, George S., 103, 170, 304
Kibitzer, 69, 94, 96, 103, 123, 130, 172,
 217
Kibitzing, 83, 94, 96
Knickerbocker Whist Club, 12, 13, 104

L

Lenz, Sidney S., 9, 10, 14, 16, 19, 21,
 22, 23, 241
Lenz vs. Culbertson, 9, 21
 hands from match: 27
Liggett, Winfield, Jr., 9, 10, 25, 278
Lightner, Theodore A., 10, 14, 22, 28,
 31, 36, 167
Lightner Slam double, 316
Link, Henry C., 64, 138
Lochridge, Chas., 171
Luck in bridge, 87, 281
 (see also CARD SENSE, CARD INSTINCT,
 BRIDGE MATHEMATICS, BRIDGE
 MEMORY, BRIDGE PSYCHOLOGY)

M

Made or Down Hands
 No. 1 & 2, 339
 Solutions to: 362
Making a slam with only four trumps,
 331
 solution to: 356
Malowan, Walter, 281, 294
Man & wife bridge, 54, 57, 71, 75, 133,
 137, 146, 153, 155, 158,
 anecdotes, 161
 tips for playing together, 159
 (see also WOMEN BRIDGE PLAYERS,
 MEN BRIDGE PLAYERS)
Marks, Jeanne S., 192
Master points, 11, 17, 18, 19, 205
 (see also DUPLICATES, TOURNAMENTS)
Masters, 11, 18
 classifications of, 206

Mathematics, bridge, 86, 90, 91, 92, 93, 217
Maugham, W. Somerset, 60, 84
Mayfair Club, 81, 82, 100
Mayonnaise, 124
    (*see also* GHOULIES, GOULASH HANDS)
Memory, bridge, 217, 274, 277
    (*see also* BRIDGE MATHEMATICS,
    BRIDGE MEMORY, CARD SENSE,
    BRIDGE PSYCHOLOGY)
Memory Bridge game, 377
Men bridge players, 73
    (*see also* MAN & WIFE BRIDGE)
Mississippi Heart Hand, 329, 330
    solution to: 356
Mixed-pair system, 133
Morehead, Albert H., 36, 137, 211, 267, 277
Mott-Smith, Geoffrey, 278
Moyse, A. Jr., 84, 146, 219
McKenney, Wm. E., 11, 278

N

New York Bridge-Whist Club, 82, 96, 172
New York Whist Club, 14
Nibitzer, 130
No trump overcall, unusual, 315

O

One-over-One bidding, 15, 305
Opening Bid of Two, 312
Optional Partners Bridge, 380
Ostrow, Albert A., 8
Overbidder, 107, 108, 109, 110
Overcalls, 110
    Overcall in clubs, 314
    Unusual no trump overcall, 314
    (*see also* BIDDING)

P

Pacific Bridge League, 17
Partners, 106, 112, 188
Perkins, Frank K., 114
Plafond, 8
Play of the hand, 116, 117, 118, 119, 120, 124, 127, 180, 181, 244, 245, 282, 286, 287, 288
Poe, Edgar Allan, 67
Point Count, 18, 85
    Four-Aces, 18
    Goren, 18
Poker, 67, 73, 75
Post-Mortem, 62, 129, 172, 233
Potter, Stephen, 24
Practice games, 379
Pre-emptive bids, 290, 311, 312

Progressive Squeeze & Vienna Coup, 336
    solution to: 359
Proprieties, bridge, 316
Psychic bids, 13, 33, 39, 43, 67, 172, 294
Psychic double, 43
Psychology and bridge, 54, 58, 64, 212
Psychology in bridge, 275, 289

R

Rosen, William, 207
Rathbone, Josephine Prof., 68
Rau, John, 14, 36
Regency Club, 81
Reith, George, 9, 15
Rice, Albert, 318
Rice, Grantland, 36
Richards, Ralph R., 11, 273
Roth, Alvin, 208
Roth, Chas. G., 304
Royals, 6

S

Schenken, Howard, 10, 13, 15, 84, 99, 172
Schwab, Charles M., 14
Schwed, Fred. Jr., 216
Seymour, Harry, 112
Shaw, Chas. Gray Prof., 54, 55
Sheinwold, Alfred, 159, 196, 303
Sims, Dorothy Rice, 13, 14, 34, 38, 139, 294
    on psychics, 13
Sims, P. Hal, 12, 14, 16, 19, 34, 38, 83, 139, 212, 306
    on grand slam bids, 13
Sims vs. Culberston, 14, 34, 38
    hands from match, 39
Six Bids in One Suit, 333
Smith, H. Allen, 9, 21
Sobel, Helen, 84, 134, 139, 151, 215
Solomon, Chas., 19
Stayman Convention, 85, 309
Straight Double Dummy Bridge, 375
Superstitions in bridge, 89, 284
Swenson, Harold Prof., 54, 55

T

Take-Out doubles, 31, 107
Tobin, E. J. (Ned), 11
Tournaments, 11, 12, 17, 85, 133, 135, 167, 205, 213, 228
    (*see also* DUPLICATES, MASTERS &
    MASTER POINTS)
Three-handed bridge, 379, 382
Towies, 381
Trio Bridge, 382
Tsitsers, 100
Two-club force, 313

U

Underbidder, 107, 11
United States Bridge Ass'n, 10, 17
Unger, George, 35
Unusual No trump overcall, 315

V

Vanderbilt Cup, 11, 16, 99
   match, 85
Vanderbilt, Harold S., 8, 16
Vienna Coup, the great, 335
   solution to: 358
Vienna Coup & Progressive Squeeze, 336
   solution to: 359
Von Zedwitz, Waldemar, 10, 12, 22, 36, 206
   Gold cup, 12

W

Watson, Louis H., 15, 216
Weak No trump, 314

Weak Two-bid, 85
Webster, H. T., 125, 137
   cartoons, 48, 56, 102, 122, 132, 166, 195, 266, 302, 315, 328
Wernher, Sir Derrick, 10, 25, 35, 36
Wertheimer, Phillip M., 124
Westrate, Edwin Victor, 188
Whist, 3, 5, 51, 329
Whist, bridge, 5
   Russian, 3
Whist Club of New York, 9
Whitehead, Wilbur C., 9, 22, 136
Whitfield Six, The, 340
   solution to: 362
Women Bridge Players, 133, 137, 142, 215
   (see also MAN & WIFE BRIDGE)
Woolfe, Irving Capt., 98
Work, Milton C., 9, 18, 22

Y

Young, Sally, 19